Early and Middle Childhood: Growth, Abuse and Delinquency

And Its Effect On
The Individual, Family, and Community

Edited by
Richard S. Greene, M.A.
Thomas D. Yawkey, Ph.D.

TECHNOMIC
PUBLISHING CO., INC.
LANCASTER · BASEL

Published in the Western Hemisphere by
Technomic Publishing Company, Inc.
851 New Holland Avenue
Box 3535
Lancaster, Pennsylvania 17604 U.S.A.

Distributed in the Rest of the World by
Technomic Publishing AG

Printed in the United States of America

10 9 8 7 6 5 4 3 2

Main entry under title:
   Early and Middle Childhood: Growth, Abuse and Delinquency

A Technomic Publishing Company book
Bibliography: p.

Library of Congress Card No. 82-50769
ISBN No. 87762-313-9

Contents

Section III — The Community

Section I

The Individual

Development of Memory in the Preschool Years

Marion Perlmutter
Institute of Child Development
University of Minnesota

Considerable work recently has been carried out to investigate the development of memory. At least three factors seem to contribute to this interest. First, memory is a relatively specific cognitive function, and studying its development may enhance our understanding of more general aspects of cognitive development. Second, memory significantly influences performance on a variety of more complex intellectual tasks, and the study of memory development is thus, in its own right, essential for a more complete understanding of intellectual development. And third, a developmental perspective should enrich our understanding of adult memory, complementing the substantial amounts of fairly sophisticated work presently addressing questions of adult memory.

The pervasive theoretical orientations presently guiding research on memory development are information processing and Piagetian points of view. While these conceptualizations contain some important differences, for the most part they may be viewed as complementary to one another.

3

Very briefly, the information processing perspective conceptualizes memory as the transfer of information within a cognitive system. This involves acquisition, storage, and retrieval of information. A data base evolves as a result of acquisition and storage, and may be remembered through recall and recognition.

The Piagetian perspective is quite different. Piaget posits that memory should not be regarded as a separate cognitive function, but rather, that it should be conceived as integrally bound to intelligence; memory, like all cognitive functions (i.e., perception, imagery, and memory) is assumed to depend upon intelligence.

While most information processoring theorists would agree that memory is, in some sense, inseparable from other cognitive functions, the emphasis is not comparable to that of Piagetians'. Information processing theorists generally analyze component processes of memory, and investigate age differences in memory performance hypothesized to be related to children's increasing repertoire and proficiency at memory skills. Piagetians, on the other hand, focus on the development of intelligence, and this has led them to examine the ways in which changing cognitive structures affect children's remembrances. While researchers with an information processing orientation generally study the mechanisms of memory, Piagetians usually concentrate on developmental changes in the contents of memory.

The conceptualization of memory used throughout this paper is certainly rooted within both of these perspectives, however, the work that is reviewed predominantly addresses questions concerning the growth of mechanisms involved in effective and efficient retention of previous experiences. That is, it examines developmental change in the way in which information is acquired and stored, and then activated or retrieved, so that it may be recalled or recognized.

Research on the development of memory generally has investigated grade school children, five years of age and older, and several recent interviews of this research are available (e.g. Brown, 1975; Flavell, 1977; Hagen, Jongeward, and Kail, 1975; Ross and Furth, 1976). Fairly consistent age-related improvement in memory has been documented, and in general, this has been attributed to age-related increases in strategy utilization. That is, as grade school children get older they tend to show increased effective use of a variety of mnemonic skills that facilitate memory performance. This may be the result of increasing competence in using memory processes, and is also surely the result of an increasing

4

propensity to engage in appropriate mnemonic activities.

With the exception of a considerable amount of work on infant memory (see Cohen & Gelber, 1975; Werner & Perlmutter, 1979), there has been a severe paucity of work on the development of memory in children under five years of age. This is quite astounding, especially since the preschool years generally are considered to be a time of important cognitive growth. For example, according to Piaget it is the time of transition from sensorimotor to operational thought, and the period in which symbolic and representational skills develop. Furthermore, it is a rare time when cognitive development is not hopelessly confounded with education (see Brown, 1977).

In order to begin to fill this gap we have, over the past several years, studied memory in preschool children between two and five years of age (Blair, Perlmutter, & Myers, 1978; Cohen, Perlmutter, & Myers, 1977; Goldberg, Perlmutter, & Myers, 1974; Perlmutter & Myers, 1974, 1975, 1976 a, b, 1979). Using a variety of memory tasks we have consistently observed age-related improvement in performance. Yet, unlike memory development during the grade school years, memory development during the preschool years can apparently not be attributed to increased effective strategy utilization (see Myers & Perlmutter, 1978).

In the next section research on memory development in preschool children will be reviewed, with particular emphasis given to our own work. Following that, a more theoretical, processing oriented analysis of early memory development will be outlined.

Review of Research on Memory in Preschool Children

The demonstrations of earliest memory have been carried out by Friedman and his colleagues (Friedman, 1972; Friedman, Bruno & Vietz, 1974; Friedman & Carpenter, 1971; Friedman, Nagy, & Carpenter, 1970). They have found that many infants as young as a day old show decreased visual fixation to repeated trials of checkerboard patterns, and furthermore, that they show recovery of attention to novel stimuli. This indicates that soon after birth some infants have the ability to store, retain, and recognize visual information.

Indeed, there is now a substantial literature on infant visual memory (see Cohen & Gelber, 1975). This work is predicated on the assumption that unequal response distributions to novel and familiar stimuli indicate the existence of a memory representation for the familiar stimulus. For example, while there is no obvious reason to expect more responding to old versus new stimuli, infants tend to show greater attention to novel stimuli.

Two general procedures have been developed to study infant recognition. Each involves a familiarization period, in which a stimulus repeatedly is shown to the child, and then a retention phase, in which memory of the stimulus is assessed. With a habituation-dishabituation technique, when familiarization involves habituation (i.e. a response decrement), memory may be assessed with a dishabituation procedure. This involves presenting a new stimulus, and determining whether it produces increased responding. This dishabituation procedure is needed to insure that the observed decrement in responding to the familiar stimulus is attributable to memory, rather than to fatigue or sensory adaption. With a paired-comparison technique, on the other hand, the familiarization period is followed by a retention test in which the old and new stimuli are presented simultaneously. A direct test of memory is made by comparing responding to the two stimuli.

Both methodologies permit examination of the effects of a number of variables on infant memory. For example, although the scope of this review does not permit a detailed presentation of all the manipulations that have been carried out, systematic variations in the simularity between familiar and novel stimuli make it possible to evaluate what information is actually encoded by the infant. Also, variations in time between the familiarization and retention period provide a means for evaluating length of retention, and incorporation of additional novel stimuli prior to the retention test is used to assess interference effects. Finally, subject variables, such as age and sex, can also be included, and thus individual differences investigated.

Although the habituation-dishabituation and paired-comparison techniques have been used primarily to study infants under one year of age, each has also been used with somewhat older children. Faulkender, Wright, & Waldron (1974) used a habituation-dishabituation procedure to show that 29 to 44 month olds can remember a number of stimuli, and further, that the stimuli are probably remembered in terms of their categories. They gave the toddlers six presentations of each of six stimuli from the same conceptual category (i.e. animals) and then tested them on a series of 18 stimuli, 6 identical to the familiarization stimuli, 6 new but from the same category, and 6 new and from a different category (i.e. fruits). They found that looking times were shortest for familiar stimuli, longer for categorically similar stimuli, and longest for categorically novel stimuli. Apparently the children remembered the familiar items, and also generalized this familiarity to new items in the same category.

Daehler and Bukatko (1977) used a paired-comparison procedure to show that 17 to 40 month olds remember large numbers of stimuli, even when they are only presented once, and that the number of intervening stimuli between presentation and test has relatively little effect on retention. Their subjects received 40 familiarization trials in which two pictures of the same stimulus were presented simultaneously, and 40 test trials in which the previously presented stimulus was paired with a novel stimulus. The children attended to the novel pictures more than to the familiar pictures, regardless of whether 0, 5, 10, 15, 25 or 50 trials intervened between the first (familiarization) and second (test) presentations of the stimulus. This surely reflects considerable retention skills in very young children.

While these visual attention measures of recognition memory attest to the fact that very young children remember information, they in no way assess the child's cognizance of that memory. That is, in both the habituation-dishabituation and paired-comparison situations there is still a question of whether the child "knows" that a familiar stimulus has been experienced previously. Of course, methodological problems probably limit addressing this question in preverbal children, however, Brown and Campione (1972), Brown and Scott (1971), Corsini, Jacobus, and Leonard (1969), Hall and Halperin (1972), and Perlmutter and Myers (1975) have investigated this with four year olds, and Perlmutter and Myers (1974, 1976a) with children under three.

In our first recognition study (Perlmutter & Myers, 1974) two age groups of children were tested. Their mean ages were 2 years 11 months and 4 years respectively. We presented them 18 stimuli, which were small attractive objects familiar to 2 year olds, and then used a yes-no testing procedure to examine recognition on a 36 item test list which contained 18 old items, identical to those originally presented, and 18 new items, not previously seen. We found that even the youngest children performed well; their average level of performance (on all items) was slightly over 80% correct. A significant developmental improvement was also oberved, however; the older children's average level of performance (on all items) was over 90% correct. Thus, while work with infants

7

and toddlers, using visual attention procedures, has demonstrated very young childrens' ability to encode, retain, and recognize information, this work demonstrates considerably more extensive memory skills in two to four year olds. These youngsters could accurately remember a series of stimuli presented only once, and perhaps more importantly, we demonstrated that they could purposefully distinguish remembered material from novel material. That is, they apparently were able to reflect upon their memories, and appropriately respond to our memory task. Of course, a further question that has not been addressed concerns how children's subjective assessments of recognition relates to more objective, experimentally assessed visual attentions measures of recognition.

The developmental improvement in recognition performance is also of interest. For example, it would be important to determine whether it is attributable to age-related changes in children's ability to encode and retain information, or their ability to monitor the memory status of items. One piece of evidence suggests that, at least for the two to four year old age range, it may be the first, rather the second, hypothesis that explains age-related increases in recognition performance. While a significant age difference was observed on old items, all children responded comparably well (around 90% correct) on new items. Of course, this age difference could merely reflect response biases that is, younger children may have been less willing to say that an item was old. However, a signal detection analysis, which separates response from retention components of recognition performance (see Banks, 1970; Lockhart & Murdock, 1970), failed to detect age differences in response criterion, although it did indicate age differences in retention components of recognition. Surely this age difference in recognition needs further research attention.

Recognition procedures also have been useful in assessing how stimuli are encoded and retained by very young children. For example, although we have demonstrated that even children under three are very good at recognizing highly discriminable stimuli (Perlmutter & Myers, 1974), confusion errors occur when distractor items are similar to original stimuli. Moreover, it may be inferred that if particular distractors produce incorrect recognition judgments, they contain information that matches that utilized in making recognition decisions. Examination of recognition errors as a function of distractors can thus be useful in characterizing the nature of memory representations used in making recognition decisions.

We have found (Perlmutter & Myers, 1975, 1976a) that even when only visual or verbal information is presented, three and four year olds have both visual and verbal information avaiable for making recognition judgments. This seems to indicate that very young children elaborate their representations. Yet, adding appropriate verbal labels to visual material, or producing visual images of words, are certainly not the only ways in which stimuli may be elaborated. Hall and Halperin's (1972) found that children as young as three make recognition confusion errors to high associates of presentation times, and that four and five year olds make such errors to acoustically similar distractors. This thus suggests additional dimensions of encoding.

In another series of studies (Perlmutter & Myers 1976b) we assessed whether preschool children engage in deep levels of semantic processing (see Craik & Lockhart, 1972), embellishing memory representations with pre-experimentally acquired world knowledge. After assessing that preschool children have color specificity knowledge, that is, that they know that certain items have a single color highly associated with them (i.e. banana) and other items do not (i.e. car), we used a forced choice recognition task to evaluate whether this knowledge affects their recognition of the colors in which picture objects are presented. The subjects were presented 48 pictures of objects, 24 color-specific and 24 non-color-specific. One half of the stimuli of each item type were presented in black and white and the other half in color, and testing always involved a color and black and white choice of the item. We found clear evidence of semantic effects on these young children's recognition. Color-specific chromatically presented items were responded to more accurately than color-specific achromatically presented items, color-specific items were responded to with color choices more often than non-color-specific items, and reaction times for color-specific achromatically presented items were significantly longer than color-specific chromatically presented items, although no such difference was observed for non-color-specific items. This demonstration of semantically based memory processing in preschool-aged children suggests deep level mnemonic processing in children younger than those generally showing deliberate deployment of mnemonic strategies. Of course, much more work will be required to more clearly characterize all of the ways in which young children interpret, encode, and retain stimulus materials, as well as to isolate the mechanisms responsible for these semantic effects.

Another procedure that has been used to assess memory in very

9

young children utilizes delayed response procedures. In these tasks children observe as an object is hidden in one of several possible locations, and, after a distraction period, they are required to find the hidden object.

Many investigators (see Gratch, 1977) have used these procedures to investigate the development of object concept in children between 9 and 18 months of age. In general, the rules of the task are not verbally communicated to the young children, and their performance probably is guided by the goal of finding the nonpresent hidden stimulus. Thus, only after object permanence has developed is proficient performance observed. However, consistent though incorrect search tendencies have been detected. Rather than searching the location where an object was most recently hidden, these children tend to return to the location in which an object was correctly found on a preceding trial.

These procedures also have been used with older children to whom the rules of the task have been verbally communicated. In this case, the task might be regarded as a recognition task; the locations are before the child, and he merely has to distinguish in which the object was hidden. Still, if performance is guided by the goal of finding a hidden object, then it may go beyond recognition. That is, it may involve recall skills, and demonstrate the child's ability to represent a nonpresent stimulus (i.e. the hidden object). Thus far these separate components of the task have not been adequately assessed, however, the paradigm has been valuable in elucidating what information very young children encode and utilize in memory tasks.

Hunter (1913, 1917) used a delay response task with 2½ to 8 year olds to determine how long a child could remember the correct location of hidden objects, even with extended delays, and even when body orientation was disrupted. Apparently kinesthetic cues are not essential for proficient performance.

Babska (1965), and Loughlin and Daehler (1973), used delayed response procedures to determine what information 18 to 60 month olds encode and utilize in localization. They compared performance on four choice trials in which only spatial information was available, with that in which spatial cues were augmented with discriminative picture cues. The conclusions drawn by the authors of both studies were that only children over three are likely to encode and use discriminative cues to find a hidden object.

In light of the considerable object knowledge and recognition skills of even much younger children these findings are somewhat surprising; it is unclear why children under three did not use appropriate picture cues. Daehler, Bukatko, Benson, and Myers (1976) hypothesized that while the young children apparently failed to link arbitrary picture cues between locations and hidden objects, they might make use of discriminative cues which are inherent components of location, such as the size and color of boxes. Indeed, all of their subjects, who ranged in age from 18 to 36 months, benefited from these added visual cues, with size cues being particularly facilitating.

We (Blair, Perlmutter & Myers, 1978) further hypothesized that verbal discriminative cues may be needed for children to profit from picture cues. Since two and three year olds may differ in their probability of producing verbal labels, this could explain the earlier failures to find picture cues facilitating in children under three. That is, if labeled pictures are required to enhance retention of the location of a hidden object, and if two year olds are less likely than three year olds to spontaneously produce labels, then labeling should differentially benefit younger children. In order to assess this hypothesis we tested 27, 33, and 45 month olds in a nine-choice delayed response task in which either only spatial cues were available, picture cues were added, or labeled pictures were provided. We found that each age group showed comparable gains in performance with the addition of extra cues. Even children under three apparently can make use of discriminative cues to facilitate memory and search for the location of a hidden object. In Daehler, Bukatko, Benson, and Myers' (1976) study both size and color cues facilitated performance of children as young as 18 months, and in our study (Blair, Perlmutter, & Myers, 1978) picture cues were facilitating to children as young as 27 months. Additionally, verbal labels apparently enhance the effect of picture cues, and even children almost four are probably not consistently effective in spontaneous verbal label production; they too profited from added labels. However, since our hypothesis that experiment provided labels might be more helpful to younger than older children was not confirmed, the developmental improvement in performance can probably not be attributed to an age-related increase in spontaneous verbal label production. This is consistent with the findings of an earlier recognition study (Perlmutter & Myers, 1976a), in which we found parallel effects of labeling, and no age changes in spontaneous labeling, over the preschool years.

In an additional study (Cohen, Perlmutter, & Myers, 1977) we have examined 2½ and 3½ year olds' memory for the locations of several items at once. We included two conditions which differed in terms of the array of locations that were used. In one we used a plain wooden box which had two rows of four equal sized compartments, and in the other we used a doll house which had eight locations. In both conditions a trial started with different small toy objects in each of the eight locations. We removed the toys with the child, and then had the child relocate the objects in their original locations. This task might be categorized as reconstruction; the stimulus components were before the child, and his task was to remember and reconstruct their original organization. In general, we found that the children did very well in this task. Both age groups performed comparably when plain spatial arrays were used (75% correct). When the more discriminative doll houses were used, however, the older children did somewhat better (88%), and the younger children somewhat worse (68%). We believe that the younger children's poorer performance in the doll house condition reflects the interference we observed as these children became distracted by the interesting aspects of the doll house, and that the older children's better performance relflects the facilitating effect that discriminative locations have on performance, as has already been demonstrated in other localization tasks (e.g. Blair, Perlmutter, & Myers, 1978). Of course, additional work will be needed to verify whether the younger children could have profited from the discriminative cues if they had been prevented from getting involved with them.

A final memory paradigm to be discussed is that of recall. With this type of task stimuli are presented to the child, then removed from view, and the child asked to demonstrate retention. In a true recall task, since external mnemonic support is not available, considerable additional cognitive processing is required for evidence of retention. Additionally, recall generally involves verbal report, although this may not be necessary; an important task for future investigators will be to develop nonverbal recall procedures. At any rate, because recall usually has been considered to involve verbalization, the youngest children to be tested with recall procedures have been over 2 years of age. Moely and Shapiro (1971), Rossi and Rossi (1965) and Rossi and Witrock (1971) all carried out investigations of recall with children under four, however, none of their papers reported actual levels of recall, nor other details of performance, such as serial position effects.

We (Perlmutter & Myers, 1979) therefore carried out a series of three studies to more extensively examine the development of recall in preschool children. We were interested in assessing how these young children retrieve and produce information about previously seen but no longer present stimuli, and how the semantic category knowledge these young children possess affects their memory. In each experiment we tested two age groups. The younger children were between approxiamtely 2 years 9 months and 3 years of age, and the older children between 4 years and 4 years 9 months of age. We used 9 item lists of small attractive objects familiar to young children. Half of the lists were made up of nine items from each of nine different conceptual categories, and half contained three items from each of three conceptual categories. Each item was individually shown to the child, labeled for him, and then hidden. After all items were thus presented the child was asked to remember as many as he could. Neither age group performed very well. In the first experiment the younger children's average level of recall was just over 2 items correct, and the older children's 3.4 items correct. Furthermore, the subsequent experiments replicated these low levels of recall, as well as the significant developmental improvement.

These results thus portray a sharply contrasting picture of memory proficiency in the preschool years; the rather poor recall performance points to memory skills that are not well developed by even 4½. Since the findings of many previously discussed studies, utilizing other paradigms, suggest that these children do acquire and retain substantial amounts of information, the results of these studies, using a recall paradigm, seem to point to deficiencies in memory components required for proficient performance in recall tasks, but not essential for performance of other memory tasks. For example, our data point to deficiencies in certain endocing operations, such as rehearsal, which may be differentially beneficial for recall performance (e.g. Naus, Ornstein, & Kreshtool, 1977). Also, we find a very strong report tendency, an echobox effect, in which the last item presented is reported first, which may be a recall strategy that actually inhibits proficient performance.

In spite of any apparent immaturity in these young children's recall skills, it is apparent that their memories are conceptually organized, and that they encode stimuli in terms of category dimensions. In all three recall studies using 9 item related and unrelated lists (Perlmutter & Myers, 1979), as well as in an earlier recall study using 2 item related and unrelated lists (Goldberg, Perlmutter, & Myers, 1974), we have found that even children under three remember related lists more completely than

unrelated lists. Furthermore, we have found shorter inter-response latencies between related than unrelated adjacently recalled items, above
chance level conceptual clustering in the children's limited recall pro-
tocols, and substantial benefits of categorical cuing.

Although the nature of the age-related improvement in recall is not
entirely clear, the data suggest that it may be related to categorical or
world knowledge effects. We have obtained age by list type interactions
which indicate that older children are somewhat more facilitated by list
relationship than younger children. This suggests that as children develop
they become increasingly sensitive to, or capable of utilizing, conceptual
information which undoubtedly facilitates memory.

Several other aspects of our data failed to reveal development. For
example, primacy effects in series position curves may be indicative of
rehearsal processing, but both age groups evidenced similar serial position curves, with neither age group showing a primacy effect. Additionally, clustering may be indicative of active organizational processing, but
there was little evidence of increased clustering with age. In sum, the improvement in recall performance that is observed over the preschool
years does not appear to be related to increased strategy use, as is the
case with recall improvement during the grade school years. But of
course, this is largely arguing from negative evidence, and additional
work will be needed to determine whether the lack of strategy use is due
to an inability (i.e. mediation deficiency) or merely a lack of use (i.e. production deficiency).

Summary of Research on Memory in Preschool Children

We know that shortly after birth infants have the ability to acquire,
retain, and recognize some stimulus information. Furthermore, although
it is beyond the scope of the present work, a substantial literature is now
accumulating on infant memory. On the other hand, almost no research
has examined the 1 to 2½ year olds' memory. The very few memory
studies that have been carried out with this age group indicate considerable ability to acquire, retain and recognize information in recognition tasks where the previously experienced stimuli are again before the
child, and nonintentional response measures are used. However, we do
not know about this age child's possible recall skills. Some work, including our own, has begun to allow us to describe the 2½ to 4½ year

old's memory skills; they are substantial. These older preschool age children can acquire and retain large amounts of stimulus information, and if it is again before them they are able to accurately reflect upon that fact. Additionally, they can recall nonpresent stimuli. However, in this situation, where the stimuli are not externally before the children, their lack of proficiency at deliberately re-presenting nonpresent information is apparent. Finally, improved performance is observed over the 2½ to 4½ year old range on virtually all memory tasks that have been investigated. However, this development does not seem to take place on the dimensions that are characteristic of memory development in the grade school years. That is, there is little evidence of increased strategy utilization.

The general problems for future research on early memory development seem clear: 1) to develop new techniques to study memory in 1 to 2½ year olds, an important age range that has until now been almost totally ignored, 2) to determine the nature of recognition development over the preschool years, and 3) to determine the basis of the preschool child's general incompetence in recall tasks, as well as to determine the nature of recall development over this age span. In the following section a more processing oriented analysis of preschool children's memory competencies and deficiencies will be outlined. This should lead to more precise questions for experimental testing.

Outline of Early Memory Growth

Recognition

Recognition apparently is a relatively primitive memory function (see Perlmutter & Lange, 1978; Piaget & Inhelder, 1973). It is evident very early in development, as well as in lower vertebrates. It appears to be largely genetically determined (at a species level), and is probably well canalized, that is, tied to a history of evolutionary development (see Scarr-Salapatek, 1976). The development of recognition does not appear to depend upon environmental stimulants; it seems to be a relatively automatic function that is not regulated by societal demands. For example, cross-cultural research suggests that recognition may not be greatly affected by cultural factors (e.g. Cole & Scribner, 1977).

While even very young children appear reasonably proficient at recognition, age related improvement is sometimes observed. Furthermore, although age-related improvement in recognition performance generally is not considered to be as great as in recall performance, clarification of the nature of recognition development will be important.

Since recognition performance generally depends upon information being acquired, retained, recognized, and then responded to (see Anderson & Bower, 1974; Crowder, 1976; Kintsch, 1970; Klatzky, 1975; Myers & Perlmutter, in 1978; Perlmutter & Lange, 1978), its development may be related to development in any or all of these components. For example, if there are age differences in acquisition, then, regardless of whether there is development in retention, recognitory, or response components, there would be age differences in recognition performance. Several investigators who work with older children have found greater age-related differences in recognition performance when complex stimuli, or very similar foils, are employed (e.g. Dirks & Neisser, 1977; Mandler & Stein, 1974). While this discrepancy may be related to an experimental artifact, whereby very high, sometimes ceiling level performance is obtained when very different stimuli and foils are used, it could also be related to acquisitional factors. That is, younger children may be less efficient at scanning, encoding, and discriminating more complex stimuli. If these information pickup factors, rather than retention or recognitory factors, are the source of age differences in recognition performance, then age differences would be evident on matching as well as recognition tasks. Matching studies will thus be useful for separating acquisition from retention, recognitory, and response components of recognition performance.

Another factor that may be related to any of these stages of processing concerns children's world knowledge. Much of the experimental materials used in laboratory tasks may be more familiar and meaningful to older than younger subjects, and recognition is probably better for meaningful than meaningless materials. Nelson and Kosslyn's (1976) finding that adults recognized labeled abstract pictures better than five year olds, but that there was no such age difference in recognition of labeled realistic pictures, would seem to support this view. Mandler and Day's (1975) findings of comparable recognition performance from second grade through adulthood, for left-right orientation of single familiar but not unfamiliar objects, also suggest that age differences in recognition performance may be related to familiarity factors. Additional studies which manipulate stimulus materials will help tease out this knowledge of familiarity factor. Furthermore, by carrying out these manipulations with both matching and recognition procedures, the stage at which an interaction between stimulus materials and subjects' own knowledge becomes critical should be made clearer.

In addition to information pick-up or acquisition and knowledge factors, it is possible that age-differences in recognition performance are related to retentional factors. That is, if younger children are less able to retain veridical memory traces over extended periods of time, their recognition performance would suffer. Yet, several studies suggest this is probably not the case. Hunter (1913, 1917) used a delayed response task with children betwen 2½ and 8 and failed to find age interactions with time intervals. Likewise, in studies in which Fagen (1973) used visual attention measures with infants, Daehler and Bukatko (1977) visual attention measures with young preschool children, and Brown and Scott (1971) yes-no recognition procedures with older preschool children, no age differences related to lag were detected.

The recognitory process, that is, matching process involving a memory representation, involved in recognition performance may also be a source of development. While research has not been carried out to isolate this factor, visual attention would seem to be an appropriate index of recognition, uncontaminated by response factors. Although overall looking time systematically increases with age, the percentage of looking to old versus new items can be used to evaluate age differences in recognition. Neither the infant literature (see Werner & Perlmutter, 1979), nor the one visual attention study with older children that included an age variable (Daehler & Bukatko, 1977), indicate consistent age differences in recognition. Obviously additional studies of visual attention measures of recognition should be carried out.

Finally, it is possible that age differences in recognition performance are related to age changes in response factors. For example, regardless of the efficiency of their memories, younger children may be more or less conservative in responding, that is, in indicating that an old item was previously seen. Perlmutter and Myers (1974, 1976b) used signal detection analyses to assess this possiblity but found no significant age differences in response biases between two and four years of age. Berch and Evans (1973), on the other hand, found that third graders were less conservative, and better than kindergarteners at gauging the accuracy of their recognition responses. It may be that response criterion changes are more evident in grade school than preschool children, however, it may also be that more sensitive measures of response criteria are required with preschool children. One possible way of addressing this problem involves comparing children's subjective assessments of recognition (i.e. verbal yes-no or pointing forced choice tests) with more objective experimental assessments (i.e. visual attention). If as the preschool child grows older he becomes more accurate at evaluating his memory, correlations between these types of measures would be expected to increase.

Recall

Recall is perhaps the most complex memory function (see Perlmutter & Lange, in press; Piaget & Inhelder, 1973). It seems to develop some time well after birth, and is probably specific to higher primates or man. Furthermore, the growth of recall skills seems to depend upon societal demands to direct their utilization (e.g. Kvale, 1975; Meacham, 1977 a, b; Reese, 1976; Smirnov, 1973; Smirnov & Zinchenko, 1969; Yendovitskaya, 1971). In general, it has been suggested that recall competence develops in several stages. First, there is learning of potential mnemonic operations (i.e. labeling or classifying) for their own sake, that is, as their own goal, unrelated to memory. Then, these operations are subordinated to further goals, such as remembering. Finally, the new goal (i.e. remembering) may be used to achieve a still more complex goal (i.e. problem solving). Development of mnemonic operations required for proficient recall thus appears to rely upon the exercise of these activities in situations that are not directed toward mnemonic goals. Yet, recall itself is goal directed, and its development appears to be stimulated by environmental factors that pose mnemonic demands. This view is similar to the position Cole and Scribner (1977) take in their review of cross-cultural research. They suggest that "the distribution of situations posing different demand characteristics vis-a-vis memory may itself be the source of differences in memory performance in different groups" (Cole & Scribner, 1977, p. 31).

Since recall performance depends upon information being acquired, retained, and recognized (see Anderson & Bower, 1974; Crowder, 1976; Kintsch, 1970; Klatzky, 1975; Myers & Perlmutter, 1978; Perlmutter & Lange, 1978), its development may be related to development of the factors already discussed in terms of recognition performance. However, since recall performance also involves additional processing (see again Anderson & Bower, 1974; Crowder, 1976; Kintsch, 1970; Klatzky, 1975;

Myers & Perlmutter, 1978; Perlmutter & Lange, 1978), its development undoubtedly also involves growth in other skills. For example, recall may require special encoding, search, generative, and verbalization skills (see Myers & Perlmutter, 1978), and deficiencies in these skills probably contribute to the discrepancy in preschool children's recognition and recall competence.

For example, several sorts of special encoding may be required for proficient recall. Naus, Ornstein, and Kreshtool (1977) have suggested that recall, but not recognition, may require linking stimulus items through cumulative rehearsal, and of course, we know that young children do not appear to engage in even the most primitive rehearsal processing (e.g. Flavell, 1970). Other manipulations, like simultaneous versus successive presentations of items may, however, be useful in assessing very young children's ability to link stimulus items. Perhaps too, recall may demand memory codes that are semantically elaborated or interpreted to a greater extent than required for recognition, and young children typically may not engage in such deep levels of processing (e.g. Geis, 1975). Incidental recall tasks, in which encoding processes are controlled, will be helpful for evaluating the extent to which a lack of deep level processing limits very young children's recall.

Proficient recall also involves search skills that very young children may not possess. For example, in delayed response tasks (e.g. Blair, Perlmutter, & Myers, 1978; Wellman, Ritter, & Flavell, 1975) very young children often appear to engage in impulsive, rather than systematic and exhaustive search. This task, in which search is overt, may thus be useful for further examining very young children's search processing. Additionally, covert search processing may be assessed by examining the effects of providing cues for recall (e.g. Perlmutter & Myers, 1979; Ritter, Kaprove, Fitch, & Flavell, 1973). Finally, it is possible that very young children's recall performance is actually limited by inappropriate search tendencies, for example, consistently reporting the last item first (Goldberg, Perlmutter, & Myers, 1974; Perlmutter & Myers, 1979) might interfere with more complete recall. This may be assessed by controlling the serial position at which recall is initiated.

The generative component of recall surely is also a skill that very young children may not be proficient at, and probably captures Piaget's (1968) concern with the involvement of semiotic mechanisms for recall. In a recall task stimulus information is not externally before the child, and he must internally or cognitively generate or construct the information.

19

Tasks that are intermediary on the dimension of generative demands will be useful in evaluating the development of these skills (e.g. Cohen, Perlmutter, & Myers, 1977). For example, in some tasks all the stimulus components could be placed before the child, and manipulations for requirements of reorganization carried out. On the other hand, in other tasks the actual amount of stimulus support provided could be manipulated.

Finally, the verbal response requirement that has been associated with nearly all recall studies cannot be ruled out as a factor that limits very young children's recall. Although familiar objects have been used and named for the children, their limited verbal facility may limit recall production. That is, even if the information is available, a general reticence to talk in the presence of a near-stranger (i.e. the experimenter) probably contributes to very young children's minimal verbal output, and a lack of response in recall is difficult to interpret unambiguously. Other kinds of tasks, such as recall of nonverbal gestures, which has been used with older children (Follenger & Trabasso, 1977), or drawing tasks, might be useful for better evaluating very young children's recall. Additionally, assessing the effects of manipulations that may change the probability of verbal assessibility for the child should help clarify the importance of this factor. Finally, new nonverbal techniques will have to be developed, particularly for studying recall of children even younger than those previously examined for recall. Field observations of very young children's naturalistic use of memory may be helpful.

General Summary and Conclusions

Memory is widely accepted to be an important cognitive function, and understanding it surely will be essential to gaining a better understanding of other higher mental functions as well. Furthermore, while our understanding of memory in adults has reached a relatively sophisticated stage, and even the study of memory development in grade school children five yers of age and older is now beginning to thrive, work on memory in preschool children is minimal. Yet, the preschool years span a time of substantial cognitive development. It marks the beginning of symbolic and linguistic functions, and, according to Piaget, the transition from sensorimotor to preoperational intelligence. The little work that is available suggests it may be a rather remarkable time for memory growth as well. While young infants have the rudiments of some acquisition, retention, and recognition skills, older preschool children's memory skills are considerably more substantial. For example, they begin to demonstrate the ability to re-present information in the absence of external support, and to deliberately remember as an end in itself, rather than as a means to achieving a meaningful goal.

The memory skills of one to three years olds only have been investigated in a very few studies. This is understandable; these age children are not easily assessable in nursery schools, and cannot be tested with usual verbal procedures. Yet, this neglect can no longer be justified; these age children are probably passing through a particularly interesting phase of development, when many memory skills may just be beginning to emerge.

Some recognition skills are evident in early infancy, and by the time children are verbal they demonstrate quite substantial recognition skills. For example, the two and a half year old can acquire and retain large amounts of stimulus information, and when it is again before him he accurately recognizes the information, as well as the fact that it was previously seen. Yet, some improvement in recognition performance is observed between two and a half and five years of age. It has been suggested that this improvement in performance may be related to artifactual factors, or to age differences in acquisition, knowledge, retention, recognitory, or response factors.

Recall skills have not been documented in preverbal children, and even older preschool age children's recall skills are quite inefficient. Thus, while some improvement in recall performance is observed between two and a half and five years of ago, this age span seems best characterized as a period of relative incompetence with respect to recall. While growth in the skills hypothesized to underlie recognition development also undoubtedly contribute to recall development, poor recall also may be related to several other processing requirements. Specifically, it has been suggested that very young children's recall inefficiency may be related to a lack of proficiency at special encoding, search, reconstructive or generative, and verbal skills.

The task of future research is threefold. First, to develop techniques that are both more adequate for studying the full gamut of memory skills available to one or three year olds, an important age group with which it is difficult to use usual verbal testing procedures, and sensitive to an ecological view of cognition. Second, to delineate the basis of improved recognition performance over the preschool years. And third, to determine the source of the preschool child's apparent incompetence in recall tasks, as well as the basis of the age-related recall improvement that is observed.

It seems likely that the increased understanding of preschool children's memory that future research will produce will have considerable practical application. As formal schooling extends downward there will be increasing pressures for a solid base of facts about very young children's cognitive skills in general, and memory skills in particular. Our present knowledge about very young children's cognitive capacities and limitations is not adequate for answering the increasingly important policy questions we are faced with.

References

Anderson, J.R., & BOwer, G.H. *Human Associate Memory.* New York: John Wiley and Sons, 1973.

Babska, Z. The formation of the conception of identity of visual characteristics of objects seen successively. *Society for Research in Child Development Monographs,* 1965, *30,* 112-129.

Berch, D.B., & Evans, R.C. Decision processes in children's recognition memory. *Journal of Experimental Child Psychology,* 1973, *16,* 148-164.

Blair, R., Perlmutter, M., & Myers, N.A. The effects of unlabeled and labeled picture cues on very young children's memory for location. *Bulletin of the Psychonomics Society,* 1978, *11,* 46-48.

Brown, A.L. The development of memory: Knowing, knowing about knowing, and knowing how to know. In H.W. Reese (Ed.), *Advances in Child Development and Behavior, Volume 10.* New York: Academic Press, 1975.

Brown, A.L. Development, Schooling, and the acquisition of knowledge about knowledge. In R.C. Anderson, R.J. Spiro, & W.E. Montague, *Schooling and the acquisition of knowledge.* Hillsdale, New Jersey: Lawrence Erlbaum Associates, 1977.

Brown, A.L., & Campione, J.C. Recognition memory for perceptually similar pictures in preschool children. *Journal of Experimental Psychology,* 1972, *95,* 55-62.

Brown, A.L., & Scott, M.S. Recognition memory for pictures in preschool children. *Journal of Experimental Child Psychology,* 1971, *11,* 401-412.

Cohen, E., Perlmutter, M., & Myers, N.A. Memory for location of multiple stimuli by 2 to 4 year olds. Unpublished manuscript, 1977.

Cohen, L.B., & Gelber, E.R. Infant visual memory. In L.B. Cohen & P. Salapatek (Eds.), *Infant Perception: From Sensation to Cognition, Volume 1. Basic Visual Processes.* New York: Academic Press, 1975.

Cole, M. & Scribner, S. Cross-cultural studies of memory and cognition. In Kail & Hagen (Eds.) *Perspectives on the Development of Memory and Cognition.* Hillsdale, New Jersey: Erlbaum Associates, 1976.

Corsini, D.A., Jacobus, K.A., & Leonard, D. Recognition memory of preschool children for pictures and words. *Psychonomic Science,* 1969, *16,* 192-193.

Craik, F.I., & Lockhart, R.S. Levels of processing: A framework for memory research. *Journal of Verbal Learning and Verbal Behavior,* 1972, *11,* 671-684.

Daehler, M.W., & Bukatko, D. Recognition memory for pictures in very young children: Evidence from attentional preferences using a continuous presentation procedure. *Child Development,* 1977.

Daehler, M.W., Bukatko, D., Benson, K., & Myers, N.A. The effects of size and color cues on the delayed response of very young children. *Bulletin of the Psychonomic Society,* 1976, *7,* 65-68.

Dirks, J., & Neisser, U. Memory for objects in real scenes: The development of recognition and recall. *Journal of Experimental Child Psychology,* 1977, *23,* 315-328.

Fagan, J.F., III. Infants' delayed recognition memory and forgetting. *Journal of Experimental Child Psychology,* 1973, *16,* 424-450.

Faulkender, P.J., Wright, J.C., & Waldron, A. Generalized habituation of conceptual stimuli in toddlers. *Child Development,* 1974, *45,* 351-356.

Flavell, J.H. Developmental studies of mediated memory. In H.W. Reese & L.P. Lipsett (Eds.) *Advances in Child Development and Behavior* (Vol. 5). New York: Academic Press, 1970.

Flavell, J.H. *Cognitive Development.* Englewood Cliffs, New Jersey: Prentice-Hall, 1977.

Foellinger, D.B., & Trabasso, T. Seeing, Hearing, and Doing: A development study of memory for actions. *Child Development,* 1977.

Friedman, S. Habituation and recovery of visual response in the alert human newborn. *Journal of Experimental Child Psychology,* 1972, *13,* 339-349.

Friedman, S., Bruno, L.A., & Vietze, P. Newborn habituation to visual stimuli: A sex difference in novelty detection. *Journal of Experimental Child Psychology,* 1974, *18,* 242-251.

Friedman, S. & Carpenter, G.C. Visual response decrement as a function of age of human newborn. *Child Development,* 1971, *42,* 1967-1973.

Friedman, S., Nagy, A.N., & Carpenter, G.C. Newborn attention: Differential response decrement to visual stimuli. *Journal of Experimental Child Psychology,* 1970, *10,* 44-51.

Goldberg, S., Perlmutter, M., & Myers, N. Recall of related and unrelated lists by 2-year-olds. *Journal of Experimental Child Psychology,* 1974, *18,* 1-8.

Gratch, G. Review of Piagetian infancy research: Objects concept development. In W.F. Overton & J. McCarthy Gallagher (Eds.), *Knowledge and Development.* New York: Plenum Press, 1977.

Hagen, J.W., Jongeward, R.H., & Kail, R.V. Cognitive perspectives on the development of memory. In H.W. Reese (Ed.), *Advances in Child Development and Behavior* (Vol. 10). New York: Academic Press, 1975.

Hall, J.W. & Halperin, M.S. The development of memory encoding processes in young children. *Developmental Psychology,* 1972, *6,* 181.

Hunter, W.S. The delayed reaction in animals and children. *Behavior Monographs,* 1913, *2.*

Hunter, W.S. The delayed response in a child. *Psychological Review,* 1917, *24,* 74-87.

Kintsch, W. *Learning, Memory and Conceptual Processes.* New York: John Wiley and Sons, 1970.

Klatzky, R.L. *Human Memory: Structures and Processes.* San Francisco: Freeman and Company, 1975.

Kvale, S. Memory and dialectics: Some reflections on Ebbinghaus and Mao Tse-tung. *Human Development,* 1975, *18,* 205-222.

Loughlin, K.A. & Daehler, M.W. The effects of distraction and added perceptual cues on the delayed reaction of very young children. *Child Development,* 1973, *44,* 384-384.

Mandler, J.M. & Day, J. Memory for orientation of forms as a function of their meaningfulness and complexity. *Journal of Experimental Child Psychology,* 1975, *20,* 430-443.

Mandler, J.H. & Stein, N.L. Recall and recognition of pictures by children as a function of organization in distractor similarity. *Journal of Experimental Psychology,* 1974, *102,* 657-669.

Meacham, J.A. Society investigations of memory development. In Kail & Hagen (Eds.), *Perspectives on the Development of Memory and Cognition.* Hillsdale, New Jersey: Elbraum Associates, 1977(a).

Meacham, J.A. A transactional model of remembering. In N. Datan & H.W. Reese (Eds.), *Life-Span Developmental Psychology: Dialectical Perspectives on Experimental Research.* New York: Academic Press, 1977(b).

Moely, B.E., & Shapiro, S.I. Free recall and clustering at four age level: Effects of learning to learn and presentation method. *Developmental Psychology,* 1971, *4,* 490.

Myers, N.A., & Perlmutter, M. Memory in the years from two to five. In P.A. Ornstein (Eds.), *Memory Development in Children.* Hillsdale, New Jersey: Lawrence Erlbaum Publishers, 1978.

Naus, M.J., Ornstein, P.A., & Krshtool, K. Developmental differences in recall and recognition: the relationship between rehearsal and memory as test expectation changes. *Journal of Experimental Child Psychology,* 1977, *23,* 252-265.

Nelson, K.E., & Kosslyn, S.M. Recognition of previously labeled or unlabeled pictures by 5-year-olds and adults. *Journal of Experimental Child Psychology,* 1976, *21,* 40-45.

Perlmutter, M. & Lange, G. A developmental analysis of recall-recognition distinctions. In P.A. Ornstein (Ed.), *Memory Development in Children.* Hillsdale, New Jersey: Lawrence Erlbaum Associates, 1978.

Perlmutter, M. & Myers, N.A. Recognition memory development in two- to four-year olds. *Developmental Psychology,* 1974, *3,* 447-450.

Perlmutter, M. & Myers, N.A. Young Children's coding and storage of visual and verbal material. *Child Develo9pment,* 1975, *46,* 215-219.

Perlmutter, M. & Myers, N.A. A developmental study of semantic effects on recognition memory. *Journal of Experimental Child Psychology,* 1976a, *22,* 438-453.

Perlmutter, M. & Myers, N.A. Recognition memory in preschool children. *Developmental Psychology,* 1976b, *12,* 271.

Perlmutter, M. & Myers, N.A. Development of recall in 2- to 4-year olds. *Developmental Psychology,* 1979, *15,* 73-83.

Piaget, J. *On the Development of Memory and Identity.* Barre, Massachusetts: Clark University Press, 1968.

Piaget, J., & Inhelder, B. *Memory and Intelligence.* New York: Basic Books, 1973.

Reese, H.W. The development of memory: Life-span perspectives. In H.W. Reese (Eds.), *Advances in Child Development and Behavior* (Vol. 11). New York: Academic Press, 1976.

Ritter, K., Kaprove, B.H., Fitch, J.P. & Flavell, J.H. The development of retrieval strategies in young children. *Cognitive Psychology,* 1973, *5,* 310-321.

Ross, B.M. & Furth, H.G. Children's Memory: Research and Theory. In J. Piaget, P. Mounoud & J.P. Bronckhart (Eds.), *Psychologie of the Encyclopedie de la Pleiade.* Paris: Editions Gallimard, 1976.

Rossi, E.L. & Rossi, S.I. Concept utilization, serial order and recall in nursery school children. *Child Development,* 1965, *36,* 771-779.

Rossi, S. & Wittrock, M.C. Developmental shifts in verbal recall between mental ages two and five. *Child Development,* 1971, *42,* 333-338.

Scarr-Salapatek, S. An evolutionary perspective on infant intelligence: Species patterns and individual variations. In M. Lewis (Ed.), *Origins of Intelligence: Infancy and Early Childhood.* New York: Plenum Press, 1976.

Smirnov, A.A. *Problems of the Psychology of Memory.* New York: Plenum Press, 1973.

Smirnov, A.A. & Zinchenko, P.I. Problems in the psychology of memory. In M. Cole & I. Matzman (Eds.), *A Handbook of Contemporary Soviet Psychology.* New York: Basic Books, 1969.

Wellman, H.M., Ritter, K. & Flavell, J.H. Deliberate memory behavior in the delayed reactions of very young children. *Developmental Psychology,* 1975, *11,* 780-787.

Werner, J.S., & Perlmutter, M. Development of visual memory in infants. In H.W. Reese & L.P. Lipsitt (Eds.) *Advances in Child Development and Behavior, Vol. 14.* New York: Academic Press, 1979.

Yendovitskaya, T.V. Development of memory. In A.V. Zaporozhets & D.B. Eklonin (Eds.), *The Psychology of Preschool Children.* Cambridge, Massachusetts: MIT Press, 1971.

Is Early Reading Independent of Mental Age?

Kamal Baig Ph.D.
Assistant Professor, Dept., of Child Study
Mount Saint Vincent University
Halifax, Nova Scotia, Canada

A healthy deaf child two years or older gets along famously despite his total inability to communicate verbally . . . There is no indication that congenital peripheral deafness causes significant adjustment problems within the family during the preschool years. This observation has an important bearing on the problem of motivation for language acquisition. Language is extremely complex behavior, the acquisition of which, we might have thought, requires considerable attention and endeavor. Why do hearing children bother to learn this system if it is possible for a child to get along without it? Probably because the acquisition of language is not, in fact, hard labor − it comes naturally − and also because the child does not strive toward a state of perfect verbal inter-course, normally attained only two years after the first beginnings. (Lenneberg, p. 140)

The first intellectual task which confronts an infant is the acquirement of spoken language. What an appalling task, the correlation of meanings with sounds! It requires an analysis of ideas and an analysis of sounds. We all know that the infant does it, and that the miracle of his achievement is explicable. But so are all miracles, and yet to the wise they remain miracles. All I ask is that with this example staring us in the face we should cease talking nonsense about postponing the harder subjects (Whitehead, p. 25).

Recent developments in educational psychology and related disciplines, largely through the work of Bloom (1964) and Hunt (1961), have placed increasing emphasis on preschool education. It is important that the first four years of life which account for the greater proportion of adult variance on I.Q. measures, also mark the point at which language is acquired (Lenneberg, 1967). The relationship between language and intellectual capacity (I.Q.) is well documented in the literature; hence the emphasis on language development in the preschool (Bereiter & Engelmann, 1966; Broadway, 1945; Bayley, 1966; Templin, 1958). When one considers the intimate connection between language and the reading process (to be discussed in a later paragraph) implications arise for initiating reading instruction at the preschool level.

Blanton (1972) in providing a rationale for early reading instruction cites the work of a) Hunt (1961) who emphasized that one could not wait for intellectual development to take place (contrary to 'readiness' theorists), b) Bloom (1964) who suggested that the period before four was possibly the period for acquisition of specific abilities which are extremely important for intelligent behavior, c) Hess and Shipman (1968) who demonstrated the effects of parental practices on the development of cognitive abilities in the preschool child, d) O.K. Moore (1964) who, having taught various levels of exceptional children to read using the "talking typewriter", suggested the ages between 2 and six to be the most creative and active, and 3) Montessori (1964) who suggested that the years between 3 and 6 are most crucial for the development of intellectual skills. Blanton's position on early reading is by no means common today however. Cegelka and Cegelka (1970) in reviewing research on reading and the Educable Mentally Handicapped state: "Though a mentally handicapped child may enter school at a chronological age of 6, his mental age is such that he may not be ready to read for three or four years". Implicit in their statement is a conception of reading as an intellectual act which requires a certain level of intellectual functioning (I.Q. or M.A.) before it can be learned (as distinct from the acquisition of spoken language which is learned at a much earlier mental age).

The view that a certain mental age is essential for success in learning to read is not an uncommon one today. The fact that reading instruction begins at grade one for most children in public schools, largely reflects this. A perusal of the early literature on reading brings to light the developments which gave rise to and sustained this, until recently, firmly entrenched position on reading.

In the early 1900's children started first grade at the age of six. And first grade and first steps in reading went together (Durkin, 1966). When school surveys became popular in the early years of the century, a number of reports were consistent in pointing to the large numbers of children who were failing first grade, generally because of inadequate achievement in reading.

In an effort to uncover the reasons for lack of success in reading, the role of intelligence in the reading process was implicated. The educational literature of the 1920's is filled with research reports citing the correlation between intelligence (or mental age) and the reading achievement of first grade children (Dickson, 1923; Holmes, 1927, Reed, 1927). A survey of this literature prompts the suggestion that all of these reports were preparing fertile ground for the quick and uncritical acceptance of the study of Morphett and Washburne (1931) in which the recommendation was made that a mental age of 6:6 is a prerequisite for success in beginning to read (Durkin, 1966, p. 7). Morphett and Washburne's conclusion was based on the finding that few children with a mental age less than six years six months successfully reached criteria set for reading ability. Although many questions should have been raised about the quality and especially about the general applicability of the Morphett-Washburne research, its findings, implying the need to postpone and to wait, were a "natural" for the early 1930's (Durkin, 1966, p. 7). With the support of professional educators and many psychologists, the Morphett-

Washburne thesis found itself in many professional texts written for reading methods courses where the claim was made that school instruction in reading should be postponed until a mental age level of 6:6 was reached (Cole, 1938, Harrison, 1936, Lamoreaux, 1943).

Gates (1937), on the basis of his studies which focused on the relationship between varied methods of instruction and first-grade reading achievement, objected to a mental age of 6:6 as essential for beginning reading. Commenting on his findings Gates writes: "Reading is begun by very different materials, methods and general procedures, some of which a pupil can master at the mental age of five with reasonable ease, others of which would give him difficulty at the mental age of seven." Gates, then, de-emphasizes the importance of mental age in favour of instructional mode. It is noteworthy nevertheless that five seems to be the minimum age at which reading instruction would be effective for the average student. This, it would seem can be accounted for by the fact that reading was not taught prior to the child's attainment of the age of five.

Engelmann (1967) supports the position of Gates. In describing his method of teaching reading to preschoolers, he states: "We tried to determine what kind of behavior is demanded for the children, asking ourselves: What must they be able to do? Next we try to develop tasks to teach them the appropriate behavior. And finally we tried to remain sensitive to the children's reaction to the presentation. If they stalled and failed to learn a skill, we tried to make the rule for that skill more obvious". If it is the case that reading success largely depends on the instructional mode utilized, then differential instruction should produce differing results. Cegelka and Cegelka (1970) addressed themselves to this point. Their conclusion was that "the results of the comparative investigations into the efficacy of various reading methodologies indicate that there is no one best method for teaching reading to classes of mentally handicapped children". This finding is in concurrence with Boyle's (1959) study in which he found no difference in the reading achievement of three groups of retarded adolescents exposed to traditional, experience or semiexperience instructional approaches. Each group did make significant gains in achievement leading Boyle to conclude that emphasis on reading irrespective of teaching methodology was the key to increased reading achievement.

To this point, two divergent positions on reading have been considered, positions which are as important today as they were in the past.

Although Morphett and Washburne's thesis may not have the support to-day that it enjoyed in the past, success at reading is still closely linked with the concept of mental age (Cegelka and Cegelka, 1970). The only difference lies in the fact that today, in light of the number of children who learn to read before grade one, a mental age lower than 6:6 is postulated. Engelmann (1967) suggests a mental age as low as four. What is left unconsidered in relating beginning reading to mental age is the effect of learning to read at one mental age as opposed to another. In other words if pupils can read at a mental age of four or a mental age of 6:6, what grounds are there for choosing one age in favor of the other? Also, if beginning reading is facilitated by mental age, it would then follow that the greater the mental age, the easier it is for the pupil to learn to read. A reductio ad absurdum argument of this sort would postulate 18 as the age most appropriate for instruction in reading! As regards the role of instruction on reading performance, the brief review of literature demonstrated that differential methodologies are not that efficacious. It would seem thus that of the two main trends which underlie instructional theory in reading, the "when" is of more importance than the "how". As regards the "when" or the time most appropriate for beginning reading instruction, a further question remains to be asked, namely the "why", or the justification for choosing a particular age level as opposed to any other. Before attempting this question which is the key concern of this paper a brief review will be made of preschool reading achievement.

One of the earliest documented cases of preschool reading achievement is that reported by Terman (1918) of a child whose father encouraged early reading by presenting her with letters and their sounds when she was only 14 months old. At 20 months the child knew letter names, at 21 months she could read words and at 23 months she discovered that should could connect the words into meaningful sentences. If one holds the view that mental age or general intelligence is responsible for reading capabilities, then surely this girl's I.Q. was in excess of 200 even if one uses the modest mental age for beginning reading of four quoted by Engelmann, (1967).

Davidson (1931) reported the extent to which children from four to six, with an M.A. of four years could learn to read. She placed 13 children into groups labelled as dull, average or bright, depending on the ratio of M.A. to C.A., and taught sessions of kindergarten games, play, and individual reading to each group for approximately one hour daily over a period of four and one half months. The Stanford Binet was used as a screening device at the beginning of the study. It was readministered at the end of the study. Test of vocabulary and reading were administered throughout the experimental period, and revealed steady progress for all children with the bright group out-scoring the average and dull groups. Analysis of data by age also indicated that bright younger children often outscored average and dull children. All groups gained on I.Q. measures.

Davidson's study is fraught with many problems. In the first place, the sample was too small. Also, the bright children were from rich economic and educational environments as was not the case for the subjects of the two remaining groups. No controls were used to determine whether increases in I.Q. could be attributable to the reading program. The study did however point out that children with a mental age of four could learn to read, and this at a time when 6:6 was the commonly accepted age for beginning reading. Fowler (1962) reports the case of his 2 year old daughter whom he taught to read within 9 months. The child was given daily stimulation in 20-30 minute time periods, and using a variety of methods. She was tested before, during and after the project. Fowler concluded that: 1) a two-year old could be taught to read and to acquire a fairly extensive meaning vocabulary, 2) that a variety of methods could be used successfully and a multi method approach might be best.

Dolores Durkin (1966) conducted 2 longitudinal studies of children who had learned to read prior to entering first grade. Results of her research led Durkin to conclude that:

1) preschool children are able to learn to read prior to entering first grade.

2) I.Q. is not a significant factor in preschool children's early acquisition of reading skills.

3) Children who learn to read early continue to read and achieve at a higher level than their counterparts who do not learn to read early.

4) that early reading is a pronounced advantage for children with low I.Q.

The review of literature on early-reading has pointed out that children with C.A.'s of under five can and do learn to read, that instructional mode is not an important variable and that learning to read at this age may not be dependent on I.Q. There is also the suggestion that low I.Q. children may profit from early reading. Engelmann (1967) found that culturally disadvantaged preschoolers after 48 hours of classroom instruction, read at the 1:25 grade level (WRAT). Another group of disadvantaged preschoolers who received instruction for two school years read at the 2:6 grade level at the end of their kindergarten year. Not one child read below the 1:6 grade level, although some of these children would not have been expected to read by the second or third grade if they had received traditional instruction (cumulative deficit hypothesis).

The fact that children under 5 can and do learn to read and that neither IQ nor instructional mode may be an important variable in beginning reading brings us to the focal issue of this paper. The point simply stated is that reading although an intellectual act is not necessarily an 'intelligent' act in that, like language, it is a species-specific capacity. Considering that a central argument of this paper centers around the species-specific nature of language, it is important that some discussion be devoted to this issue, for it is by no means the only theory of language acquisition.

Wardhaugh (1971) distinguishes 3 main theories of language acquisition: a) Behavioristic Theories, b) Cognitive Theories, c) Nativist Theories.

Behavioristic Theories

Perhaps the most distinguished proponent of this point of view is Skinner (1957). In his book *Verbal Behavior* he proposes a comprehensive theory of language acquisition and language behavior in which specific linguistic behaviors are acquired through operant conditioning and then extended through response generalization. One of the most ardent critics of Skinner's thesis is Chomsky (1959) who attacked the adequacy of reinforcement theory and the notion of generalization in explaining either language acquisition or language behavior. Chomsky is particularly critical of Skinner's failure to recognize the contribution that the child makes to language acquisition. He states that,

". . . a refusal to study the contribution of the child to language learning permits only a superficial account of language acquisition, with a vast and unanalyzed contribution attributed to a step called "generalization" which in fact includes just about everything of interest in this process. If the study of language is limited in these ways, it seems inevitable that major aspects of verbal behavior will remain a mystery" (p. 58).

Despite Chomsky's criticisms of the inadequacy of behavioristic theories, Staats and Staats (1962, 1963, 1968) use such terms as operant learning, reinforcing stimuli, time and scheduling of reinforcement, successive approximation, chaining extinction, and discrimination and generalization to explain how language is acquired. In Wardaugh's (1971) view, "such concepts can only weakly explain why all children exhibit much the same pattern of development how they construct novel utterances even in the earliest days of language use, and in what ways they master the abstract relationships that are not readily apparent in the utterances they hear (p. 173)".

Cognitive Theories

Slobin (1966a, 1966b) regards language acquisition as an active process in which certain abilities of the child develop. One is the cognitive ability to deal with the world; a second is the mental ability to retain items in short-term memory, and to process information increasingly with age.

Piaget's (1970) is also a developmental position on language acquisition. The child's activity brings him into situations which set up a tension. Through the complementary processes of assimilation and accomodation, the tension is resolved, and the child moves to a new level of equilibrium. However the developmental status of the child determines the kind of stimuli which will evoke a state of tension at any given time. During the sensori-motor period, for example, the child is learning about the environment by interacting with people and objects. His primary task is to discover permanence and regularity in the objective phenomena around him. Toward the end of this period, he can hold these objects in memory by means of images and labels.

With regard to the relationship of his theory to linguistics, Piaget (1970) states that,

> the contemporary work of Chomsky and his group on transformational grammars is not very far from our own operational perspectives and psychogenetic constructivism. But chomsky believes in the hereditary basis of his linguistic, whereas it will probably be possible to show that the necessary and sufficient conditions for the construction of the basic units on which are funded the linguistic structures are satisfied by the development of sensori-motor schemes. (1970, p. 729).

In commenting on the cognitive theories of language acqusition, Athey (1971) states:

> Perhaps the greatest criticism of cognitive models is that they fail to account specifically for the facts of language development. It is not so much that linguistic facts are incompatible with the models as they seem irrelevant to them. Yet the cognitive and language functions are interdependent, and their developmental paths are intertwined. It is difficult to see how a theory in either area can be considered adequate if it fails to take account of existing theories and facts in the other" (p. 44).

Callaway (1974) criticizes both behavioristic and cognitive theories on grounds that they are both equipotential theories of learning. He puts it this way,

> The equipotentiality assumption, which is an integral part of all established learning theory whether it be behavioristic or cognitive, holds that all learning is carried out by the same kind of mental processes. This assumption quite obviously makes any act of learning essentially like any other act of learning" (p. 12).

For Callaway, all acts of learning are not alike. The acquisition of language is an exceedingly complex task, a task which experts in the field cannot fully analyze today. Yet the child of three knows how to use the language effectively. This type of learning is unlike other types of learning in that it is facilitated by the biological matrix of the species.

Nativist Theories

Proponents of this point of view include Chomsky (1957, 1965), Callaway (1970, 1974), Mason (1970), McNeill (1966, 1970) and most important Lenneberg (1967).

Lenneberg (1967) proposes a theory of language acquisition heavily supported by biological evidence from studies of normal language development in children, and of abnormal language development brought about congenitally as in anencephalic dwarfism, or environmentally, as in brain damage or aphasia. He claims that language acquisition is a natural activity much as learning to walk is a natural activity. Both activities occur universally unless a pathological condition exists. Learning, as this term is traditionally defined, (equipotential theory of Callaway) based on general intelligence, is not involved.

In support of this thesis, Lenneberg makes the following sorts of statements: "There is, in fact, no evidence whatever that any conscious and systematic teaching of language takes place just as there is no special training of stance or gait" (p. 125).

> "Speech, which requires infinitely precise and swift movements of tongue and lips, as well-coordinated with laryngeal and respiratory motor systems, is all but fully developed when most other mechanical skills are far below their levels of future accomplishment. The evolvement of various motor skills and motor co-ordinations also has specific maturational histories, but the specific history for speech control stands apart dramatically from histories of finger and hand control. (p. 131).

This statement is a definite blow to adherents of the cognitive viewpoint who see the emergence of language as having its antecedents in the sensori-motor operations of the child. As Lenneberg illustrates elsewhere in his book, intact linguistic functions are independent of motor-skeletal maturation.

Although Lenneberg's thesis concerns the biological foundations of language, he does not negate the role of the environment on the quality of the child's language. He cites the study of Moley (1957) who found that the language habits which emerged at a common time soon showed signs of impoverishment in the underpriviledged, and unintelligibility occurred more commonly in second and subsequent children than in first. Lenneberg concludes that the influence of the environment upon speech habits is undeniable, even though the onset of speech habits is relatively unaffected (p. 136).

Athey (1971) in summarizing nativistic theories of language acquisition states, "we may say that nativistic models, especially Lenneberg's have made a profound impact on the study of language". (p. 36).

This paper takes the nativist position of language acquisition, namely that language is a species specific characteristic, the acquisition of which is facilitated by the biological matrix during a critical period which extends from roughly around two to the time lateralization of hemispheric functions sets in. Although the acquisition of language is recognized as an exceedingly complex intellectual event, it is not seen as a difficult task. This is so because it involves a learning process which is independent of general intelligence. As such, it is not the sort of process for which mental discriptives such as "smart," "stupid," "clever," are apt.* One is not amazed by the fact that a three year old can talk or walk, but one is amazed if the three year old uses language at a level expected of a much older child!

A central argument of this paper focuses on this nativistic position of language acquisition. The importance of the argument is emphasized in an analysis of the concepts of 'Speech', and 'Reading' as they relate to language. Reed (1971) makes the point that language is categorically distinct from 'speech' or 'writing'. This is in distinction to the view held by certain linguists that there is a primacy of speech over writing, and that speech *is* the language whereas writing is only a secondary form. (Furth's work, *Thinking Without Language* is definitely representative of this position). Although he concedes that in many respects, speech is primary over writing, Reed maintains that,

> the observed relationships between speech and writing will not justify our saying that speech *is* the language or that writing is merely a secondary representation of speech. If speech *were* the language, then deaf mutes would be people who have never learned a language — in spite of the fact that some of them read and write English, others German, others French, and so forth. (p. 221).

For Reed, "speech" and "reading" are linguistic forms of a language. A "linguistic form" is defined as a "linking of a unit of meaning to a physical representation in terms of a conventional system such as speech or writing". (p. 225). Braille and sign language are examples of other linguistic forms.

The importance of Reed's analysis to this paper is now fairly apparent. Considering that language is independent of the linguistic representational form, one cannot argue the supremacy of one linguistic form over the other. This is not to say that one form may not be more advantageous given certain conditions, only that one is not more of an "intellectual" or "intelligent" or "complex" form than the other. Any primacy of linguistic form is seen as largely the result of socializing and educational experiences. Perhaps the central argument for primacy of speech rests with the fact that the child acquires speech before he learns to read. This has been taken to mean that speech is a necessary prerequisite for reading. The deaf mutes cited by Reed contradicts this inference

---

*argument derived from Gilbert Ryle's *Concept of Mind*.

however. The fact that speech is seen as primary can be explained from point of view of socialization experiences. Speech is a linguistic form which utilizes a *public* representational system of sounds. The sounds, although arbitrary (Reed, 1971), are meaningful in that there is a regular correspondence between sound and referent. Through such correspondences the child acquires a grasp of the vocabulary of a language. The child first acquires a speech vocabulary rather than a sight vocabulary because speech is a public activity whereas reading is essentially a private one. As a result the child first learns that which is publicly accessible. It is a fact that the child of four has experienced at least a thousand fold the 'sound' vocabulary than she has the 'sight' or 'graphic' vocabulary. The primacy of speech can therefore perhaps be explained on ground that the child has had more experience in this linguistic representational medium. As regards the sensory mechanisms involved in the different linguistic forms of speech and reading, (auditory and visual), Schaffer (1971) in a review of the pertinent literature has pointed out that both auditory and visual discrimination are present to an extraordinary degree of sophistication even in the infant of less than 10 months of age. Thus one cannot cite the superiority of a particular modality to establish a case for the biological primacy of a particular linguistic form.

The above paragraph has treated 'speech' and 'reading' as linguistic forms of language. Any primacy of speech has been attributed to the fact that speech is essentially a public activity. A person usually speaks to others. If he speaks to himself, the habit seems 'odd', for it is not customary for people to go around speaking to themselves. Reading on the other hand is a private activity. A person sits with a book and one infers that he is reading without knowing in fact that he is. Thus the observer, who cannot read, has no way of knowing the content of what is being read even though the print may be confronting him. Correspondence between the arbitrary print and its referent needs to be set up in order for meaning to be derived from the print. This calls for direct instruction. Mere exposure to print is not sufficient, for, as has already been mentioned, recognition of print is a private activity. One does not read aloud every sign that one confronts. Thus the child, without some form of instruction, has no way of deciphering the graphic code. Apart from the fact that reading is a private linguistic form utilizing visual modalities whereas speech is a public linguistic form involving largely auditory modalities, there is little reason to suppose that reading is essentially different from speech. Also, as has been pointed out, the inference that speech is prerequisite for reading does not stand ground. If speech is not considered an *'intelligent' act, then it seems to follow that reading, another linguistic form, is not in itself, an intelligent act.

An earlier section of this paper dealt with the correlation between reading and I.Q. measures. It was shown that traditional theory required a certain standing in mental age before reading instruction could be profitable for the pupil. Implicit in this theory is the belief that reading is an intelligent act. This section of the paper broaches the question: "Is reading an intelligent act?"

The common sensical answer to the quetion posed above is in the negative. The fact that a grade one pupil reads at a grade one level is not the sort of information that throws anyone into ecstasy. One does not consider such a pupil an 'intelligent' reader or a 'weak' reader. He is just a reader. If the same pupil read at a grade two level, he would be considered an above average reader; if he read at the grade four level, he would be considered an exceptional reader. Adjectives such as "intelligent", "weak", "exceptional" etc. are used to describe the comparative reading ability of children, not the fact that they can read. In many instances such adjectives go beyond a mere description of reading capabilities in usggesting a state of mind or general intelligence. Either way, the descriptions used compare and classify pupils on their reading ability. Similar classifications could be made on the basis of speaking (or running) ability without the implication that speaking per se, is an intelligent act. These points will be elaborated in the succeeding paragraph through reference to the question: "What is reading?"

The nature of the reading process is a highly controversial issue and thousands of pages have been devoted to it. In dealing with this issue, two positions on reading will be considered, that of Goodman (1971) and Reed (1971). Goodman (1971) describes reading as a psycholinguistic guessing game.

> It involves partial use of available minimal language cues selected from perceptual input on the basis of the reader's expectation. As this partial information is processed, tentative decisions are made to be confirmed, rejected, or refined as reading progresses". (p. 260).

Reed (1971) on the other hand describes reading as the

---

*intelligent from a normative point of view, in the sense that it is not commonplace.

identification of linguistic forms from strings of written configurations that represent them, as evidenced by producing the conventional signs for the *same* linguistic forms in some other system of representation. (p. 223).

For Reed, reading and understanding do not have to go hand in hand. Anyone who has learned to read can read many sentences whose meanings are almost completely unknown to him. Although in polarity with each other, both Reed's and Goodman's analysis of reading contribute to our understanding of the reading process. It would seem that basic reading is the identification of the graphic linguistic form by producing the conventional sign for it in speech. Oral reading, it would thus appear, is little more than the translation of graphic linguistic forms into speech forms. Such a translation can be performed well or poorly, depending on a number of variables — practice effects, speaking ability, general intelligence or skill at psycholinguistic guessing games. The child who is more knowledgable of language, who is more intellectually able, will perform at a level higher than the duller child on a relatively difficult passage. But comprehension in terms of the hypothesizing of possible outcomes, and interpretive reading, although relying on basic reading skills, is more a function of general intelligence. The intelligent person can do such hypothesizing in situations where reading is not called for, eg. in conversation, debate etc. This would suggest that reading and general intelligence are two different things. General intelligence can nevertheless be reflected in reading as it can in speech or a number of other activities.

Further support for this view comes from Popper's (1972) position of language. Popper recognizes two lower functions of language which human language share with animal languages, namely 1) self-expression, 2) signalling or communication. The two most important higher functions of human language are, 3) the descriptive function and 4) the argumentative function. These latter functions of language serve to describe states of affairs, to present critical arguments, hypotheses etc. Broadly stated then, one can recognize two essential attributes of human language, namely 1) a means of communication at the concrete level, which resembles the language of animals e.g. "I want food", 2) a means of description and of abstraction. It seems fair to state that all human beings, in the absence of gross pathology, should perform linguistically at level 1). If reading is a linguistic form, as this paper argues, then reading at the level 1) should not be beyond the capabilities of such humans. Also, with increasing intelligence (general ability) language use should move to a descriptive, and then an abstract level, whether in speech or reading. The point is again made that general intelligence will affect the 'quality' of the speech or reading, not the presence of speech or reading.

This paper has so far considered that early reading does take place, and that early reading is not dependent on I.Q. The acquisition of language was emphasized as an event not dependent on general intellectual ability, but largely the result of a biological facilitation. Reading was analyzed, like speech, as a linguistic form of language. General intelligence was not seen as an important factor in the acquisition of reading, although its role in the quality of reading was emphasized. The above issues were considered as they relate to the central argument that early reading, like language acquisition, is not as dependent on the general intellectual functioning of the individual as it is on the species specific biological facilitation at the time of language acquisition.

Callaway (1970) presents strong arguments from a biological standpoint to support the above thesis. He states

> Innate mechanisms predispose organisms to respond to certain stimuli and ignore others, and the stimuli to which they are prediscposed grow and mature. (p. 18).

To paraphrase, he is stating that mechanisms within the individual are innately attuned to certain types of stimuli, exposure to which serves to *develop* such mechanisms. Mason (1970) expresses the point this way: "From a structural point of view schemes are inherent, species typical tendencies toward organizing experience in certain ways, (p. 37). . . . . One of the properties of open schemas is that they develop cumulatively and can be built up or elaborated as development proceeds, (p. 42)". It is important to recognize the hierarchical nature of this development. Without exposure to appropriate stimuli, the developmental hierarchy is disturbed. Disturbance of the hierarchy can result in inappropriate, disturbed or arrested behavior at a future time. Mason (1970) cites several instances of emotional disturbances in sensory deprived animals. Facilitation of the hierarchy, on the other hand will result in the "translation of potential abilities into concrete achievement", (Mason, 1970, p. 45).

Specific to reading are notions dealing with language acquisition and form perception. Language acquisition as an inborn, species-specific disposition has been considered in a previous section. As regards form perception a number of investigators (Berlyne, 1958; Spears, 1964) have demonstrated that infants tend to be most attracted to complex rather than simple stimuli. Fantz (1966) found that infants can resolve, discriminate and differentially attend to visual patterns, preferring these to such stimulus characteristics as color, brightness and size. He implicated form perception as an innate ability. This remarkable ability to distinguish between forms at an early age, regresses if not exercised (Gregory and Wallace 1963, von Senden 1960), leading Callaway (1970) to postulate a sensitive period for form perception. The fact that children have this remarkable ability to differentiate between forms at a period when language is acquired effortlessly seems to spell a period when beginning reading instruction may be most profitably initiated.

The argument has sometimes been made that were reading a species-specific ability, facilitated by a sensitive period in the child's ontogeny, then there should be no reason why today's child, bombarded with print that he is at an early age, should have problems with reading. Two answers suggest themselves: 1) genes do not carry capacities but rather potentialities:

> A genotypic potentiality for an organism's developmental response to its environment, given a certain genotype and a certain sequence of environmental situations, the development follows a certain path . . . The carriers of the other genetic endowments in the same environmental sequence might well develop differently, but also, a given genotype might well develop phototypically along different paths in different environments (Dobzhansky, 1969).

2) A 'certain sequence of environmental situations' is required before the child learns to read. The fact that a child is exposed to print is not sufficient grounds for him to learn reading. There has to be some meaningful sequence, for as has been stressed previously, reading,unlike speech, is a private activity and the child has to be directly instructed if he is to find meaning in the graphic forms.

This paper has attempted to provide grounds for refuting the position that a mental age of roughly, 6, is necessary for beginning reading. To this purpose an attempt was made to distinguish the reading process from general intelligence. While fully aware of the interaction between intelligence and reading, the purpose was to remove general intelligence as the casual factor in learning to read. Also, by highlighting the nativistic position on language acquisition and the predisposition of infants to differentiate between complex forms, a rationale was provided for introducing children under five, including low I.Q children, to reading.

References

Athey, I.J., Language models and reading, *Reading Research Quarterly*, Vol. VII, no1, International Reading Association, Newark, Delaware, 1971, p. 44.

Bayley, N., Learning in adulthood: the role of intelligence. In H. Klausmeier & C. Harris, (eds.), *Analyses of Concept Learning*, New York: Academic Press, 1966.

Bereiter, C. and Engelmann, S., *Teaching Disadvantaged Children in the Preschool*, Englewood Cliffs, New Jersey: Prentice-Hall Inc. 1966.

Berlyne, D.E. "The influence of the Albedo and Complexity of Stimuli on visual fixation in the human infant", *Brit. J. of Psychology*, Vol. 49, pp. 315-18.

Blanton, W.E., Preschool Reading Instruction: A Literature Search, *Evaluation and Interpretation: Final Report.* Indiana Un. ED069345 (1972).

Bloom, B.S. – *Stability and Change in Human Characteristics.* New York: John Wiley and Sons, 1964.

Boyle, R.C., How Can Reading be Taught to Educable Retardates who have not learned to Read? Project No. 162. Washington: U.S. Office of Education, 1959. Cited by N.R. Ellis (Ed.), *Handbook of Mental Deficiency*, New York: McGraw-Hill, 1963, p. 682.

Broadway, K.P., Predictive Value of Stanford-Binet preschool items. *Journal of Educational Psychology*, 1945, 36, 1-16.

Callaway, W.R. Jr., Early Reading From a Biological Perspective. Proceedings from the 1974, Transmountain Far West Regional Reading Conference, Edited by Lloyd O.Ollila, Edward G. Summers, J. Downing, P.J. Viel, 1974, p. 12.

Cegelka, P.A. and Cegelka, W.J., a Review of Research: Reading and the Educable Mentally Handicapped. *Exceptional Children*, Vol. 37, Nov. 1970, pp. 187-200.

Chomsky, N.A. *Synthetic structures.* The Hague: Mouton, 1957.

Chomsky, N.A. *Aspects of a theory of syntax.* Cambridge, Mass.: M.I.T. Press, 1965.

Chomsky, N.A., "Review of B.F. Skinner, *Verbal Behavior".* Language, 1959, 35, pp. 26-58.

Cole, L., *The Improvement of Reading*, New York: Farrar & Rinehart. 1938.

Davidson, H.P. "An Experimental Study of Bright, Average and Dull Children at the Four-Year Mental Level", *Genetic Psychology Monographs*, 9. 1931, pp. 125-289.

Dickson, V.E. *Mental Tests and the Classroom Teacher.* New York: World Book Company. 1923.

Dobzhansky, T., Introduction. In *Science and the Concept of Race.* (M. Mead, T. Dobzhansky, E. Tobach, and R.E. Light. eds.), pp. 77-79, Columbia University Press, New York, 1969.

Durkin, Dolores, *Children Who Read Early,* Teachers College Press, Columbia University, 1966.

Engelmann, S., "Classroom Techniques: Teaching Reading to Children with Low Mental Age", *Education and Training of the Mentally Retarded,* 2, (1967), pp. 193-201.

Fantz, R.L., "Pattern discrimination and selective attention as determinants of perceptual development from birth", in A 41. Kidd and J.L. Rivoire (des.), *Perceptual Development in Children;* International Universities Press, 1966.

Fowler, W., "Teaching a Two-Year-Old to Read: An Experiment in Early Childhood Learning", Genetic Psychology Monographs, (66), 1962, pp. 181-283.

Gates, A.I., "The Necessary Mental Age for Beginning Reading", *Elementary School Journal,* 37 (March, 1937), pp. 497-508.

Gregory, R.L. and Wallace, J.G. Recovery from Early Blindness. *Experimental Psychological Society Monographs,* No. 2, 1963.

Harrison, M.L. *Reading Readiness,* Boston:Houghton Mifflin Company, 1936.

Hess, R. & Shipman, V. Maternal Influences upon early learning: The cognitive environments of urban pre-school children. In R. Hess and R. Bear (Eds.), *Early Education.* Chicago: Aldine Publishing Company. 1968.

Holmes, M.C., "Investigation of Reading Readiness of First Grade Entrants". *Childhood Education,* 3 (Jan. 1927), pp. 215-221.

Hunt, J. McV., *Intelligence & Experience,* New York: The Ronald Press Company, 1961.

Lamoreaux, L.A. & Lee, D.M., *Learning to Read Through Experience.* New York: Appleton-Century-Crofts, 1943.

Lenneberg, E.H., *Biological Foundations of Language* John Wiley & Sons, Inc., New York, 1967.

Mason, W.A., Early Deprivation in Biological Perspective, In *Education of the Infant and Young Child,* Ed. by V.H. Denenberg. New York: Academic Press Inc., 1970.

McNeill, D., The Creation of Language by Children. In J. Lyons & R. Wales (Eds.) *Psycholinguistics Papers.* Edinburgh:University of Edinburgh Press, 1966.

McNeill, D., The Development of Language. In P.H. Mussen (Ed.), Carmichael's manual of child psychology. Vol. 1 (3rd ed.) New York: Wiley, 1970. pp. 1061-1161.

Montessori, M. *The Montessori Method,* Cambridge: Robert Bentley, 1964-65.

Moore, O.K., "Autotelic Responsive Environments and Exceptional Children". In *The Special Child in Century 21,* Ed. by J. Hellmuth, pp. 87-138., Seattle, Washington: Special Child Publications, 1964.

Morley, M., *The Development and Disorders of Speech in Childhood,* Livingstone, London, 1957.

Morphett, M.V. & Washburne, C., "When Should Children Begin to Read?" *Elementary School Journal,* 31 (March, 1931), pp. 496-503.

Piaget, J., Piaget's theory. In P.H. Mussen (Ed.), *Carmichael's manual of child psychology.* Vol. 1 (3rd ed.) New York: Wiley, 1970. Pp. 703-732.

Popper, K.R., *Objective Knowledge,* An Evoluntary Approach, London: Oxford University Press, 1972.

Reed, M.M., *An Investigation of Practices in First Grade Admission and Promotion.* New York: Bureau of Publications, Teachers' College, Columbia Univ., 1927.

Reed, D.W., A Theory of Language, Speech and Writing. In *Theoretical Models and Processes of Reading* (Eds.) H. Singer & R.B. Ruddell. International Reading Association, Newark, Delaware, 1970.

Ryle, G., *The Concept of Mind,* Penguin Books Ltd., England, 1968.

Schaffer, H.R., *The Growth of Sociability.* Middlesex, England: Penguin Books Ltd., 1971.

Skinner, B.F., *Verbal Behavior,* New York: Appleton-Century-Crafts, 1957.

Slobin, D.I., Comments on developmental linguistics: A discussion of McNeill's presentation. In F. Smith & G.A. Miller (Eds.), *The genesis of language.* Cambridge, Mass.: M.I.T. Press, 1966 (b).

Slobin, D.I., The acquisition of Russian as a native language. In F. Smith & G.A. Miller (Eds.) *The genssis of language.* Cambridge, Mass.: M.I.T. Press, 1966 (a).

Spears, W.C., "Assessment of Visual Preference and Discrimination in the four-month-old infant," *J. Comp. Physiol. Phsychol.,* Vol. 57, pp. 351-6.

Staats, A.W. & Staats, C.K. A Comparison of the Development of Speech and Reading Behaviors with Implications for Research. *Child Development,* 1962, (33), pp. 831-846.

Staats, A.W. & Staats, C.K., *Complex Human Behavior,* New York: Holt, Rinehart & Winston, 1963.

Staats, A.W., *Language, Learning and Cognition.* New York: Holt, Rinehart & Winston, 1968.

Templin, N.C., Relation of speech and language development to intelligence and socio-economic status. *Volta Review,* 1958, (60), pp. 331-334.

Von Senden, M., *Space and Sight.* Translated by P. Heath. New York: Glencoe Free Press, 1960.

Wardhaugh, R., "Theories of Language Acquisition in Relation to Beginning Reading Instruction", In *Reading Research Quarterly,* Vol. VII, No. 1, Fall, 1971.

Whitehead, A.N. *The Aims of Education,* The MacMillan Company, New York, 1929, 3rd printing, 1966.

Role-Playing and Imaginative Behaviors: Their Effects on the Child's Learning and Development

Thomas Daniels Yawkey and Wendy L. Gebert
Early Childhood Faculty
The Pennsylvania State University
Division of Curriculum and Instruction
159 Chambers Building
University Park, Pennsylvania 16802

Introduction

The relationship of play to children's learning and development has been characterized by conflicting theoretical positions and overlapping definitions. Although the value of play has been acknowledged, it is only within the past fifteen years that play has gained respectability as a legitimate and worthwhile activity within the realm of educational curricula (Sutton-Smith, 1971). Prior to the 60's the influence of the Puritan ethic "work before play" had been overwhelming, and play was not an acceptable "work" activity (Sutton-Smith, 1971). Even during the 60's and early 1970's recognition of the value and importance of play was greatly effected by the response to America's desperate call for instant education. The abandonment of traditional objectives for the more academically oriented programs caused many educators to forget the importance of play. During this period educators were concerned that children would not be able to survive the "testing threat" unless exposed to constant drill of the subject matter which was assumed to be essential for later school achievement.

The problem was further confounded by the lack of unitary definition. Although the potentialities of play had been understood and appreciated, it had not been established exactly what was learned through play or what role the teacher assumed in teaching through play. Both a defined purpose and methodology were necessary if play was to assume a position within the educational curriculum.

Although ambiguity existed, this was not meant to imply that play had not been defined. On the contrary, play had been defined and redefined at some point in time by individuals within almost every discipline related to childhood development and learning. Accordingly, Gilmore (1966) had labeled play as a "waste-basket" category of behavior into which unclassifiable and uncertain behavors of children were thrust. Feitelson and Ross have stated that "play has absolutely defied definition, classification, and measurement" (1973, p. 202), Yawkey and Silvern (1979) have attributed the lack of systematic examination, analyzation, and investigation to the (a) sheer quality of writings on play; (b) lack of clear definitions; and (c) numerous psychological perspectives.

At this point in time it appears that the period of intuitive hypothesizing of play and its relationship to learning and development is near the end of its reign (Weber, 1970; Hartley et al., 1952; Isaacs, 1935). Perhaps the impetus for change occurred with the findings of Piaget (1962) in terms of the child's symbolic play, which spurred interest in the relationship between play and intellectual development. Piaget (1962) described symbolic play as representational thought or imaging projected upon objects such as self, people, situations, and objects. Furthermore, Piaget hypothesized that play schemes were a necessary condition for intellectual development. Imaging — was seen as the connective between representational thought and symbolic play. Play effectively bridged the gap between knowledge and understanding, or in Piagetian terms, between accommodation and assimilation. In opposition, the programmed curriculum approach often superimposed a learning event without regard for individual variations in interest, readiness, and ability.

Marbach and Yawkey (1979) have identified three empirical mainstreams of research that have investigated Piaget's (1962) link between symbolic play and cognitive processes. These included: (a) the relationship of qualitative levels of play to cognition (i.e. Wolfgang, 1974; Pulaski, 1973; Pederson & Wender, 1968; Lieberman, 1965); (b) the improvement of cognitive performance relative to various types of play training (i.e., Lovinger, 1974; Feitelson & Ross, 1973; Sutton-Smith, 1971); and (c) the effects of particular imaginative play actions on behavior or cognitive processes. (i.e., Yawkey & Silvern, 1979; Marbach & Yawkey, 1979; Smilansky 1968).

Definition of Role-Play

Play and its various forms have the potential for meaningful learning and development within the school curriculum. By reducing the heavy emphasis upon fact and rote memory as Featherstone (1967), Deardon (1968), Kohlberg (1968), Weber (1971), and critics of school curriculum suggested, more time could be allotted to exploring, discovering, and problem-solving using direct and indirect guidance in and through play. Imaginative play appeared to contribute to the cognitive functioning of the child in many ways.

The focus of this chapter was a form of imaginative play which appears to be key to intellectual growth. This area of play, labeled as role-playing, had perhaps the greatest potential for use within modern educational programs since it was dependent upon the immediate concerns, interests, daily experiences, and age of the child. In the "age of individualized instruction" there was little more that could be requested or expected in terms of meeting the individual needs of the children. The challenge was in accepting role-play as an instructional tool and developing programs to implement it into the daily curriculum. Yawkey (1978) presented two reasons why play has been pointedly neglected within early and middle childhood classrooms. First, the definition of role-playing as a "curricular frill" has been abundant among educators; and secondly, its contribution to the language arts, which comprise the bulk of elementary curriculum, was not as easily understood as its position in reference to dramatics.

Role-taking involved putting oneself in the place of another and cognizing the role attributes, thoughts, and feelings (Mead, 1934).

According to Volpe (1979) the cognitive activity produced by role-playing was the basis of prosocial behaviors such as cooperation; helping; altruism (i.e., the unselfish concern for the welfare of others); and higher levels of moral reasoning. Role playing had been defined as Curry and Arnaud as

> . . .when the child transforms himself in pretend play to
> be a person or object rather than himself, as indicated by
> his verbal and/or motoric enactment of his perception of
> that role (1974, p. 27).

Specifically the role playing may be analyzed along several overlapping but developmental sequences. Curry and Arnaud (1974) viewed these sequences of role play in make-believe as:

1. symbolic elaboration of the role
2. thematic content
3. integration of affect and intellect
4. distinction between reality and fantasy
5. modes of interpersonal transaction

Symbolic elaboration of the role referred to the manner or style that children chose in showing their conception of the role being enacted (Curry & Arnaud, 1974). Basic imitation of actions acquired through the child's day to day living experiences was the foundation of symbolic elaboration. Basic and concrete imitation facilitated and developed mental representation and abstract thinking. The process indicated children's current levels of intellectual growth through three key aspects of role taking. These were: (a) the child's perception of the role; (b) modes of enacting the role; and (c) medium of expression. The child's perception of the role referred to the growth of thinking from concrete to abstract levels. At the higher level, abstract thinking required the ability to cognize in general terms. The second factor was the mode of enacting the role. This referred to the "hows" of expressing and enacting the role. Both quality and quantity of expression were directly related to the child's perception of the role. The final factor, medium of expression, referred to objects used to show and demonstrate expressions in play situations. Initially self-action was the primary medium which later developed into toy action.

The second sequence, called thematic content, was described by Curry and Arnaud (1974) as:

> . . . the basic thrust or nature of the behaviors portrayed
> in association with the specific role, and in socio-dramatic
> play, the nature of the interactions among the role
> players (p. 275).

Basically, the thematic content was related to the social and emotional concerns of the children. They tended to be immediate in nature and initially surrounded the family.

The third developmental aspect basic to role play was labeled integration of affect and intellect. This integration, developmentally speaking, proceeded from a direct channelling and displacement of emotional-social behaviors to the increasing use of mediational processes shown through the use of words and symbolic representation.

Distinguishing between reality and fantasy, the fourth sequence, referred to the recognition of differences between what was imagined and what was real. Children progressed from actually becoming the objects themselves to the use of terms which maintained distance between the imagined and real events through "pretend" or "make-believe."

The fifth developmental sequence was the mode of interpersonal transaction. These developmental aspects referred to the growth of egocentric and highly personalized play that focused only on the child, toward an increased awareness of relationships and empathy for others.

Prior to age six the child's play was basically symbolic in nature. Piaget (1962) postulated that symbolic play was the representation of images projected upon environmental objects, and viewed play as a vehicle for inducing the organism to image. Between the ages of six and eleven children manifested a transitional change. Egocentrism, the predominance of their own point of view, transformed to perspectivism. It became coordinated in their perspective with the perspective of others. Transitions involved a change from perceptual to conceptual thought, a change from prelogical to logical thinking (Piaget, 1950). Central to development was the concept of conservation (i.e., the realization that properties like substance, weight, and volume remained the same in spite of transformation. Piaget (1950) maintained that conservations were necessary prerequisites for all rational activity. Since the ability to decenter or shift perspective was central to role-play, children below six could generally not rôle take because their cognitive structures would not allow the information to be processed in such a manner.

Although total understanding of role-playing may not be established, the child is involved in role-taking through sociodramatic play prior to the onset of logical thinking. According to Piaget (1950), sociodramatic play provided a "pivot" for the separation of self from others, and the shift from an egocentric to sociocentric perspective. Children were able to view relationships as reciprocal rather than undimensional.

They began to see themselves and the environment around them from other points of view.

> In fact, it is precisely by a constant interchange of thought with others that we are able to decentralize ourselves in the way, to coordinate internal relationships deriving from different viewpoints . . . (Piaget, 1967, p. 164).

Smilansky studied dramatic play, or sociodramatic play and defined the following process:

> In dramatic play the child takes on a role: he pretends to be somebody else. While doing this he draws from his first-or secondhand experience with other persons in different situations. He imitates the person, in action and in speech with the aid of real or imagined objects (1968, p. 7).

When the theme became elaborated in cooperation with at least one other person and the interaction included verbal exchange the play was labeled sociodramatic. Smilansky (1968, p. 9) defined six components as essential to dramatic and sociodramatic play.

1. *Imaginative role play* where the child undertakes a make-believe role and expresses it in imitative action and/or verbalization.

2. *Make-believe in regard to objects* in which movements or verbal declarations are substituted for real objects.

3. *Make-believe in regard to actions and situations* in which verbal descriptions are substituted for actions and situations.

4. *Persistence* where the child persists in a play episode for a minimum of ten minutes.

5. *Interaction* involving at least two players in the framework of the play episode.

6. *Verbal communication* of some type related to the play episode.

Smilansky contended as its major contribution that it

> affords them the opportunity at playing at life and gives them a greater understanding of it . . . children who are exposed to it are better prepared and more readily integrated into real life patterns of their immediate environment at an earlier age than children who do not engage in sociodramatic play at all or play very little (p. 61).

Smilansky (1968, pp. 12-15) summarized generalizations which concerned mental representation and social collaboration within the context of dramatic role-play in the following:

1. In socio-dramatic play children learn to gather scattered experiences and create out of them new combinations.

2. Children learn to concentrate around a given theme.

3. Children learn to discipline their own actions in relation to a new context.

4. Children develop from predominantly egocentric beings into those capable of cooperation and social interaction.

5. Children learn to develop toward advanced stages of abstract thought.

6. Children learn vicariously from the experience and knowledge of their children.

The Relationship Between Play and Cognition

During the past ten years extensive empirical research has been completed which supported Smilansky's findings (e.g. Yawkey & Silvern, 1977; Lovinger, 1974; Sutton-Smith, 1971) and further established the importance of the relationship between children's play and their cognitive abilities. In addition, the absence of play among particular populations of children has also been a primary focus of research, and results of Freyburg (1973) and Rosen (1974) further substantiated the relationship between cognition. The fact that enhancement and facilitation of play could have a direct effect on the development and learning of children provided implications for the implementation of play within educational curriculums.

According to Volpe (1979), a number of studies have found that restrictions arising from social class, ethnicity, regionality, emotional disturbance, delinquency, orthopedic disability, anxiety, child-rearing, and role-taking model differences adversely affected general cognitive and role-taking development. (Chandler, 1973; Hollos and Cowan, 1973; Sullivan & Hunt, 1967; and Volpe, 1975; 1976). If experiential deprivations could have such an influence, it appeared feasible that environmental enrichment through play training should have implications for remediation, and even possible acceleration.

Gulick (1920) also described an absence of play among lower-class children in crowded metropolitan areas. Hetzer (1929) proposed a lack of play among urban children due to the lack of space. They both supported the belief that the idylic conditions of rural life caused play to naturally emerge (Feitelson & Ross, 1973).

More recent research among rural communities (LeVine & LeVine, 1963; Ammar, 1954; Feitelson, 1954) disputed the advantages of rural environment as a result of findings which showed a paucity of play among village children in Egypt and Kenya. Thus, contrary to Gulick's (1920) opinion, the mere fact that more space and privacy was perhaps available to the rural child did not appear to ensure the presence of play. Research had also investigated other factors which contributed to the occurrence of play such as the availability of play materials (Van Alstyne, 1932) and the richness of the environment (Valentine, 1938).

Studies by Feitelson and Ross (1974), Rosen (1974), and Murphy (1962) suggested that children from economically advantaged homes were more likely to engage in sociodramatic play than those from socially disadvantaged homes. Lovinger (1974) suggested that the lower-class children did not receive the maturational learning provided by assistance in fantasy that middle-class children received from their mothers. Lovinger noted that a life that was consumed with the constant struggle to maintain its existence did not encourage these communications.

Smilansky (1968) focused upon disadvantaged Israeli children. Her results indicated that disadvantaged children were unable to reorder the fragmentation of play to lead to problem-solving or alternate modes of functioning. The results stated explicitly that these children lacked the flexibility necessary to alter and resequence their play.

> Instead they tend either to stick to one repetitious activity without elaborating it or jump from one activity to another disconnected one . . . It seems that the lack of flexibility characterized of these children, their inability to develop a theme, a thought, or game, points to some discontinuity in their chain of concepts (Smilansky, 1968, p. 2).

Since every bit of information appeared to remain separate and unrelated, the children were prevented from molding existing concepts into new ones and unable to see things from differing points of view.

Other research with disadvantaged children (John & Goldstein, 1967) indicated differences in expressive language. Lovinger (1974) hypothesized that make-believe would increase verbal interaction between children which would necessarily enable them to use whatever concepts and language they had developed internally in an overt manner. Lovinger additionally proposed that the sharing of thoughts and ideas central to sociodramatic play would allow children to conceptually join disparate ideas and experiences. In the end, this produced the flexibility which Smilansky (1968) had determined was crucial to intellectual functioning and problem-solving.

The Value of Role-Play

The preceding was indicative of the efforts of research to ascertain the paucity of play within disadvantaged populations in order to establish the potential of play as a means of overcoming academic deficits.

Although Smilansky (1968) recognized the need to provide children with additional knowledge, skills, and experiences not received within the home; greater importance was attached to developing a means of helping children integrate already existing experiences and isolated concepts. By finding ways for children to integrate and converge into new conceptual schemes, additional information and experiences could be more meaningfully utilized toward learning. Based upon the lack of flexibility evidenced in these children, Smilansky advocated the use of role-play, which was somewhat predetermined by a script, in contrast to make-believe play which required the alteration of the role to fit the need at any point in time.

In direct opposition to Smilansky's (1968) viewpoint, researchers such as Bereiter and Englemann (1966) advocated educational programming which supported the notion that the only effective method of overcoming academic deficits in disadvantaged children was to increase the quantity of information presented to them. The question arose that if children did not already possess the skills to effectively organize the data into meaningful concepts which could be used flexibly to further conceptual development and problem-solving, then what benefit would a deluge of information present to children?

The authors proposed that play was inherent in its ability to produce the flexibility necessary for the alteration and development of ideas. This viewpoint was consistent with Lovinger's (1974) findings which suggested the value of play in increasing the language skills necessary to promote cognitive functioning. Similarly, Smilansky (1968, p. 148) concluded that, "improvement in sociodramatic play resulted in improvement of verbalization during play" are hypothesized this would further facilitate cognitive growth. In sum, to learn the necessary skills and material was not enough for intellectual functioning. A method to accept, integrate, and process information in an effective and productive manner was necessary. The use of play, in particular role-play, was a viable means of providing this methodology to children.

An important point to mention was that there may be other factors which contribute to the lack of play within certain children other than socioeconomic or environmental disadvantage. Although play was often suggested as being expressive of anxiety and aggression, Erixkson (1950) found that play was often disrupted when anxiety became too great; or when conditions frustrated the child (Barker, Dembo & Lewin, 1941). Consideration of this approach would include the possible expansion upon the "disadvantaged population" and serious questioning as to what factors were actually play preventive. To restate in simplified terms, was it the actual economic disadvantage or other environmental factors which were play preventive.?

The results of a study by Rosen (1974) provided evidence which supported the importance Smilansky's environmental factors and their relationship to play to see if Smilansky's findings would be applicable to the United States since there were extreme differences in familial structure between the two studies. The disadvantaged families studied by Smilansky were male-dominated and intact, in contrast to those in the United States which were characterized by a single parent and primarily female-dominated. Rosen's findings supported Smilansky's results indicated that play differences were not related to the emotional atmosphere of the home environment or the quantity of toys. Rather, the play of the disadvantaged was attributable to a failure of the home to equip these children sufficiently with the required verbal, cognitive, and social skills necessary for social achievement. Although the results of this study were also based upon a disadvantaged population, the findings were certainly generalizable to populations which are not characterized as disadvantaged. Failure of the home environment to provide the essential elements of an optimal environment for learning and development was not necessarily dependent upon economic conditions.

Based upon the research it appeared that play training could produce significant changes within children's learning and development. Various research studies have provided substantial evidence that training studies were based upon the assumptions that imaginative play was: (a) trainable; (b) important for the development of intellectual and social abilities; and (c) often undeveloped in young children.

Play is children's business; it is the area most easily understood. It is only logical that an area of considerable understanding to children be used advantageously toward the acquisition of skills that are difficult for them to acquire. Of particular interest should be children plagued by academic failure who often have so much difficulty within structured academic curriculums. Certainly children from disadvantaged socioeconomic backgrounds could benefit from teaching methods other than traditional academic curricula which were often so remotely distant from their repertoire of experiences and personal understandings. Play is adaptable. The basic elements of play as described by Newmann (1971, p. 8) were its dependence upon "internal reality, intrinsic motivation, and internal locus of control" (p. 8). Certainly these elements would be recognized as transferable toward the promotion of academic achievement and success in life's endeavors. According to Smilansky (1968) it was not the content of play which deserved recognition, but rather, the elaboration in itself would exert the changes necessary for improvement. Meaning that the mere attention to play itself resulted in academic improvement.

Considerable research resulted from the establishment of the importance of play. Marbach and Yawkey (1979) identified four areas of research which have been the primary focus. Play has been researched as (a) an integral aspect of cognitive development; (b) a facilitator for language growth; (c) a facilitator for language learning; and (d) as a facilitator or problem-solving. A great deal of research has been upon language growth and the learning relationship to cognitive development. Weikart, Rogers, Adcock, and McClelland (1970) advocated the use of sociodramatic play within preschool programs to increase cognitive functioning as a direct result of the relationship with language. Based upon research and evaluation within these areas, Yawkey (1979) proposed five major contributions of role-playing to children within the area of language arts:

1) By changing himself into a person or object other than himself the child uses and extends speaking, listening, and practices other language skills which contribute to memory, attention, and concentration.

2) Requiring children to fill gaps between planning for roles and actually carrying them out. Role-play requires the child to bridge the gaps through the use of language.

3) Language also bridges the gap between their life experiences to play people and situations. Language enables the child to perform even if their is no experiential background.

4) It creates an opportunity at playing at life. Role-play assists the child in resolving conflicts, enriching attitudes, and establishing beliefs.

5) Role playing facilities listening, which when combined with increasing powers of attention and concentration has a direct impact in promoting an increase in reading comprehension.

Lunzer (1959) saw play as an active form of representation before language was sufficiently advanced to fulfill the functions unaided. He proposed that play was the natural medium to increase and develop facility in language among children who were academically deficient.

Lovinger (1974) investigated the possibility of sociodramatic play increasing the use of language and whether the use of lanuage in play would be transferable to cognitive tasks. Treatment consisted of nonstructured interaction as to: (a) following, adding to, and enriching the natural play of children; (b) using experiences the children played out; and (c) creating a play situation and encouraging the children to become involved. The results indicated that the development of sociodramatic play in preschool disadvantaged children resulted in an increased use of language and greater ability to deal with cognitive tasks. Lovinger proposed that the mere chance to become involved in sociodramatic play would enhance the development of the flexibility. This agreed with Smilansky's (1968) position which had established flexibility as crucial to cognitive functioning and extremely lacking in disadvantaged children.

Also from a language learning perspective, Yawkey (1978) in a year long study of imaginative play found that imaginative play components built into reading readiness activities significantly facilitated the young child's initial language performance relative to non-imaginative play and reading and to reading only conditions using group referenced assessments. Yawkey and Blohm proposed that the addition of imaginative play to reading could result in a more effective teaching methodology to begin reading instruction (1977).

An instructional model which utilized imaginative play would provide early childhood specialists with procedures to capitalize on children's spontaneous imaginative play episodes to establish meaningful direct experiences (Yawkey & Blohm, 1978). Direct experiences would provide the framework for the developing communicative language processes of listening, spelling, writing, and reading.

Wolfgang (1974) found that imaginative play in its various forms of random activity, simple symbolic, complex symbolic, and diagnostic symbolic facilitated reading ability, and that "advanced" readers employed higher levels of imaginative play than those readers classified as disabled. Wolfgang (1974) drew a distinct parallel between the components of play and initial reading:

> In the microsphere of toys and playing the child gives a schematic of sensorimotor elaboration to symbols (toys) that conveys to the observer a signified meaning that reflects the child's internal ideas. In reading the symbol or "toy" gives way to the social "sign" in terms of words, and instead of an outward elaboration the reader brings forward an internalized schematic of thought that gives meaning to the "sign" (p. 338).

Thus, in both reading and play there was the signifier and the signified. The parallel implied that those children who had developed the capacity to use high levels of integrated symbolic play later displayed success in using signifiers as signs in reading. Contrastingly, those who did not play symbolically reflected delays in the ability to utilize signs in reading. Wolfgang's study, designed to compare the relationship between the cognitive aspects of reading and certain aspects of play in first grade boys, the presence of such a relationship. The advanced readers achieved high levels of play, yet were below the delayed readers in their ability to sustain play at the dramatic play level and the number of toys selected. Wolfgang suggested that the advanced readers had attained an equilibrium between assimilation (play) and accommodation which enabled their advanced reading. Contrastingly, the delayed readers were still assimilating freely in imaginative play. This suggested the presence of an interference in their accommodation to reading "signs" or using signifiers.

Fein (1948, p. 30) also referred to play as "serving to separate meaning from action and object, helping children to acquire a system of signifiers to represent meaning." Fein also suggested that play provided an opportunity to use signifiers to organize higher levels of meaning.

Levin (1973, p. 19) based research upon "the premise that reading comprehension involved complex organizational strategies on the part of the reader." The organizational strategies allowed the reader to deduct meaning and interrelationships from the reading material. Levin made a distinction between two types of poor readers, those who exhibited deficits due to a lack of prerequisite skills and those who showed problems due to differences in reading habits rather than a lack of skills. Levin proposed that the addition of imagery strategies to reading would facilitate comprehension. The findings positively supported that attention to visual imagery and thematic content produced dramatic improvements in the comprehension of poor readers. However, one finding particularly noteworthy was that the addition of visual imagery only produced an increase in those children with "differences" in comprehension, not "deficits." It could be implied that children without the adequate prerequisite reading skills would not benefit from the additional strategies supplied by role-playing.

In contrast to Levin's (1973) findings was a report by Saltz and Johnson (1974) which indicated that children who receive training in sociodramatic play were improved in skills such as sequencing, reconstructing events, identifying casual relations, and making inferences. In a second study, Saltz, Dixon, and Johnson (1977) reported an increase in intellectual performance as measured by standardized I.Q. tests and an increased ability to distinguish reality from fantasy.

In conclusion, research supported the position that play serves a definite role in the acquisition and development of language. If language facility is a necessary prerequisite to successful cognitive functions, then the value of play should certainly be considered a substantial segment of every curriculum, regardless of the philosophy and goals upon which the program has been established.

Use of Props in Role-playing Activities

The importance of materials in role-play has not yet been thoroughly explored. However, Vygotsky (1967) discussed the importance of the role of objects, which he called "pivots", as impelements to promote the transition from the world of reality to the world of play.

Research evidence (e.g., Fein, 1975; Lowe, 1974; Overton and Jackson, 1973; Piaget, 1962) has supported the value of play objects. Pulaski (1971) found that five-year old children with a high disposition for fantasy preferred minimally structured toys, whereas children with low fantasy preferred highly structured toys. Pulaski (1973) also reported that children between the ages of five and eight produced a greater variety of pretend stories when toys were minimally structured. Additionally, Smilansky (1968) found a similar difference between the play of middle and lower class disadvantaged children. Disadvantaged children used more highly representational play objects than middle class children.

Piaget (1962) also recognized a relationship between the use of props and the development of children's intellectual capacities. Piaget defined transformations as the intellectual ability of children to change themselves into some other person, object or being. Piaget's (1962) theory had recognized distinctions between self-transformations and transformations of objects, people, and situations.

Self-transformations involved the use of the children's own bodies as imagined beings and things, whereas objects and people transformations required the use of concrete things. Situational transformations were the most difficult and required the entire event to be conceptualized by children as a whole.

In role-play all types of transformations occured, differing both quantitatively and qualitatively according to age. Young children were extremely restricted to reality and required objects which were more concretely representational of the "real" thing in order for transformations to occur. Older children were less conceptually restricted to reality. Conceptually they were able to make transformations regardless of the present reality; however, the difference being that unlike the young children, their transformations often imitated reality more than fantasy. Thus, the transformations have increased quanitatively and decreased qualitatively.

The Role of the Teacher in Role-Playing

According to Smilansky (1968) the natural processes of children's growth, a passive environment, and an encouraging atmosphere were not sufficient factors to accomplish the developmental success of disadvantaged children. Smilansky discovered that teacher intervention was absolutely necessary. Smilansky identified autonomy, self-motivation, social interaction, exploration and experience, flexibility, and the acquisition of skills as necessary components of any program.

Research conducted in the Soviet Union (e.g. El Konin, 1966; Chauncey, 1969), as well as, by Feitelson (1972), supported Smilansky's findings which stressed and supported the notion that modeling was an essential precondition for the development of role-play. This viewpoint was based on the premise that unless children saw others engaged in similar experiences, the "as-if" perspective would not occur on its own (Feitelson & Ross, 1974).

According to Fein (1978, p. 41) criticisms of play-oriented programs had consistently addressed specific concerns throughout recent years regarding:

(a) the stress on an unobtrusive teacher role which may amount to detached (though benign) neglect in the hands of the unskilled or untalented;

(b) individual differences either in the ability of some children to use play effectively or in the needs of others for well-structured activities; and

(c) the pervasive lack of clarity regarding the function of play in development.

The results of recent research represented the beginnings of response to the criticisms by establishing adult behaviors and strategies for the enhancement of play, and evaluating and documenting the benefits of play in terms of learning and development. Fein (1978, p. 41) stated:

> In a sense, symbol acquisition is a structural issue and play is a motivational issue. Although the two can be separated for analytical purposes, theories should be addressed to a synthesizing framework that enables structural and motivational issues to be joined.

Play Training

Having examined: (a) definitions of play; (b) relationships between play and cognition; (c) values of role-play; and, (d) uses of play tangibles in role-play episodes within the previous sections of this chapter, play was found to significantly enhance language and cognitive actions of young children. More specifically, numerous investigations (e.g., Lovinger, 1974; Strom, 1974) have utilized children's play as a training vehicle to facilitate language and cognitive learning and growth. These play training studies have a number of similarities in their foci and procedures. The great majority of the studies have employed low-income children perceived to lack make-believe or imaginative capacities relative to their nondisadvantaged counter-parts. Secondly, the play of the children in the experimental and/or control groups was guided by an adult. Accordingly, training studies have attempted to increase the quantity as well as the quality of play which, in turn, was thought to contribute to cognitive and language growth and learning. These two similarities and research outcomes have characterized the area of play training research. Examples of research investigations that have explored play as a vehicle for language growth and learning include: (a) Yawkey (1980); (b) Marbach and Yawkey (1980); (c) Yawkey and Silvern (1979); (d) Lovinger (1974); (e) Strom (1974); (f) Freyburg (1973); (g) Wolfgang (1973); and, (h) Smilansky (1968). Those who have examined play for cognitive development and learning have included: (a) Guthrie and Hudson (1979); (b) Smith and Sydall (1978); (c) Golumb and Cornelius (1977); (d) Saltz, Dixon, and Johnson (1977); (e) Zammarelli and Bolton (1977); (f) Fink (1976); (g) Rosen (1974); (h) Saltz and Johnson (1974); and (i) Feitelson and Ross (1973).

Play for Language Growth and Learning

Yawkey (1980), in a year long investigation employing 96 children five years of age, investigated the effects of play on reading performance and imaginative behaviors. Training in the experimental groups involved rehearsing story content through play. Guided by an adult, children role-played story passages.

In the control groups, the children, in lieu of role-playing selected stories after hearing them, were invited to perform arts and craft activities under the guidance of an adult. Accordingly, the children performing the arts and crafts activities had no opportunity to use role-play to rehearse the story they had heard. The results indicated that children in the experimental yielded significantly higher mean scores than the control group on reading readiness and imaginative behaviors. Similarly, Marbach and Yawkey (1980) investigated differences between self and puppet action play (as two forms of play) and control conditions, as well as comparing boy versus girls on aural comprehension measures (i.e., a modified cloze technique for the total number of correct words the participants remembered). Twenty children using puppets and 20 employing self action forms of play rehearsed story content after hearing the entire passage of 250 words. Twenty other participants colored in line drawings and cut and pasted them together after listening to the passage. Although there were no initial differences between treatment groups and boys and girls on scores from the Peabody Picture Vocabulary and Harris-Goodenough Draw-A-Man Tests, the analyses of results (after treatment conditions were completed) indicated a number of interesting results. First, children using body action play yielded significantly higher mean scores than either puppet or control groups. Secondly, girls remembered significantly more correct words than boys.

In a third study, Yawkey and Silvern (1979) with 240 children — 80 participants per each of three age levels, five, six, and seven — investigated the effects of imaginative play an aural language comprehension as measured by a modified cloze technique. Accordingly, 120 children, 60 using puppet and 60 employing body action play, rehearsed a story selection. Within both forms (i.e., conditions) of play, 30 children rehearsed the story during the episode (i.e., at the conclusion of each set of 50 words in the passage) and 30 practiced it after the entire narrative was heard. Regardless of whether the children practiced the story during or after hearing the passage, the total amount of time spent on rehearsal across both conditions was the same. Further, 120 children in the control condition heard the story and at the end of the passage were asked selected questions over the content. There were a number of results.

First, the children in the play group (collapsing across both forms and timing of play) remembered significantly more correct words from the story than those in control. Secondly, each age group differed significantly from one another on the total number of correct words that were remembered from the story. In analyzing the data in the play treatment groups, the results indicated that: (1) six and seven year old children remembered significantly more correct words than the five year olds; (2) five year olds – using puppet-action during and body-action play after – significantly outperformed other five year olds – using puppet-action after and body-action during – on the number of correct words remembered from the story; and, (3) the forms of play (i.e., puppet versus vody) and timing (i.e., play during versus play after) across the three age groups did not significantly differ on the dependent measure.

In the fourth study, Lovinger (1977), with preschool children from low-income populations, investigated the use of sociodramatic play to increase language actions and its transfer potential from play to cognitive tasks. Twenty participants in the experimental group acted out various experiences such as going to the zoo through spontaneous group-play episodes (with and without adult direction and guidance). Seventeen children in the control treatment received no involvement with sociodramatic play routines. Using a pre- and post-test design, children in the experimental group yielded significantly higher number of words emitted and displayed greater facility with language on cognitive tasks (i.e., transfer of play quality) given differences between pre- and post-test measures. The children in the control troup did not significantly differ either on quantity of words emitted in sessions or on facility of words in transfer (based on differences between pre and post assessments). The results indicated that when children in the experimental group used sociodramatic play their language increased, as well as its transferability from play to cognitive tasks in pre-post assessment.

Strom (1974), in a fifth investigation, examined the effects of play on language learning (i.e., language fluency) with preschool children enrolled in the Toy Talk Curricula. Mothers, acting as tutors of their children in the Toy Talk Curricula, trained them to use new vocabulary words through their play episodes. The words chosen for training were taken from a vocabulary list used as pre- and post-assessment measures. Significant differences between pre and post measures were observed with these children using Toy Talk Curricula on word recognition, language definitions (i.e., conceptual understandings), and elaboration.

Freyburg (1973) trained 40 low-income children five years of age in imaginative play. The experimental children were told a series of stories using a set of toys as props. The control group of children received neither training in imaginative play or used props. Comparing the children's performance between pre and post measures within experimental and control groups, Freyburg noted that those given imaginative play training exhibited greater communication and labeling, greater discriminative use of language, more complex sentences, and increased attending behaviors than before training. Within the control group no such differences were noted for the participants on pre and post measures. Wolfgang (1973) investigated the effects of play on reading ability with 30 boys, age seven, from low-income populations. Using reading scores from the Stanford Achievement Test, Wolfgang identified 15 participants who were "advanced readers' and 15 who were "disabled readers." In spontaneous play sessions, imaginative play levels (i.e., random, simple symbolic, complex symbolic, and, dramatic involvement activities); length of time; and the number of toys used in the play sessions for all 30 children were recorded. The results showed that children categorized as "disabled readers" played for a significantly longer period of time than those classified as "advanced readers." It was hypothesized that advanced readers were developmentally beyond the sociodramatic level of play and became fatigued with the activity. Differences between the two groups on imaginative play levels and number of toys used in the play session were not observed.

Noting differential performance between children from low and high socioeconomic status (S.E.S.) groups on play and verbal abilities, Smilansky (1968), in a classic study, trained low S.E.S. participants on play behaviors reflective of high S.E.S. ones. With various control and experimental treatments, the results indicated that low S.E.S. children in the adult guided play group who received training on play behaviors reflective of the high

S.E.S. ones, and those who received additional life experiences to extend the training, changed their play behaviors relative to the high S.E.S. subjects. In addition, children who improved on play behaviors also significantly improved on mean frequencies of: (1) words used in a sentence; (2) contextual words; and, (3) nonrepeated words compared to baseline language samples recorded prior to the treatment conditions.

Play for Cognitive Learning and Growth

Guthrie and Hudson (1979), with 15 girls and boys who four years of age and from middle-class populations, replicated and extended the research on training dramatic play to facilitate conservation abilities reported by Golumb and Cornelius (1977). After children were individually pretested for conservation of mass and liquids, they were assigned to experimental and control treatments, systematically counterbalancing for age range, sex, school location, and number between conditions. The experimental participants individually participated in imaginative play training where they engaged in make-believe situations (e.g., making "food" items from Play-Doh for a pretend picnic) under the guidance of adults who subsequently challenged their beliefs in the pretend experiences. In challenging the children, the adults initially performed conservation transformations and children in turn were asked to perform the transformations. Participants in the control groups attended individual constructive play sessions where they: (a) assembled puzzles; (b) made Play-Doh animals; and, (c) drew pictures with paper and pencil. After the termination of the sessions, all the children were tested for conservation in the order of mass, liquid, number, and length. The results from the initial analyses between children in experimental and control groups indicated that training in imaginative play had little effect on facilitating conservation behaviors. Differences between the results of Guthrie and Hudson and those of Golumb and Cornelius were attributed to: (a) socioeconomic populations; (b) experimental procedures; and, (c) use of several experimenters.

Smith and Sydall (1978), questioning the validity of general research procedures in play training, hypothesized that differential gains on performance measures were attributable to contact with the adult in the experimental groups, rather than through increased play repertoires of the children. Fourteen participants, three and four years of age from low-income populations, were randomly assigned to play and skill's tutoring groups. The experimental design permitted Smith and Syddall to investigate the contributions of the quantity and quality of adult contact within the groups as well as examine the contributors of imaginative play to general congitive (and language) abilities. The results indicated that regardless of group, imaginative play significantly facilitated general cognitive (and language) abilities. Further, children in the play-tutoring group vis-a-vis those in the play skills-tutoring group showed a significant gain on role-taking abilities given imaginative play treatments. Finally, the results indicated that contact with adults in the experimental treatment groups could be a plausible explanation for the facilitative effects of imaginative play on children's competencies relative to their performance in control groups.

In the third investigation, Golumb and Cornelius (1977) explored the effect of play training on conservation abilities of 30 nonconserving preschool children from low-income populations. After assignment to treatment conditions, 15 children in the experimental group were individually trained by an adult to demonstrate imaginative play routines. Within the control treatment, 15 participants played individually with mosaic forms and puzzles and drew pictures — all of which were conducted in the presence of an adult. The results of the analyses indicated that children in the experimental treatment demonstrated a significantly greater number of conservation behaviors than those in the control groups. The results suggested that training in imaginative play facilitated the learning and development of reversible thought structures which were basic prerequisites to conservation abilities.

Saltz, Dixon, and Johnson (1977) worked with preschool children from low-income populations and trained them in one form of group imaginative play consisting of either (a) thematic play; (b) sociodramatic play; or, (c) fantasy discussion. The participants in the control treatment performed paste and cut and other kinds of arts and craft activities. The children in the experimental and control groups both received contact with adults in the classroom while they participated in the treatment conditions. The results indicated that children in the fantasy and sociodramatic play groups yielded significantly higher scores on standardized tests of intelligence and interpretation of sequential events. The results in addition showed that participants in the thematic-fantasy play group yielded significantly higher scores than those in the realistic-sociodramatic group on several selected measures. Accordingly, training in thematic-fantasy and sociodramatic play had the potential to facilitate cognitive growth as measured by selected indices.

Zammarelli and Bolton (1977) with older children, ages 10 and 12, from middle-class populations were randomly divided into three groups of eight participants and matched on the classroom teacher's rating of mathematics ability. Within the two experimental groups, they permitted the children to observe play and play materials. The play tangibles used by the children in the other experimental group permitted them to gain practice in decision-making skills in a controlled setting. Participants in the experimental group that actually became involved with the play tangibles yielded significantly higher scores on mathematics tasks than those in either of the other two groups. The results indicated that play involvement with a specially designed toy had the potential to develop problem solving rules embodied in mathematic problems.

Fink (1976), with 36 nonconserving five year old children from middle-income populations, investigated the effects of play training on conservation abilities and imaginative capacities. In the experimental treatment groups, children received structured group training in imaginative play. In another treatment condition, children participated in spontaneous play in the presence of an adult. In the control groups, the children received no training and were permitted to perform routine activities not related to play. Using a pre and post design, the children in the experimental group (who received structured group training in imaginative play) yielded significantly higher mean scores (than those in the other two groups) on social role perspective taking, and imaginativeness. However, the results also indicated significant differences between children in the treatment groups on the conser-

69

vation of number; acquisition of the continuous quantities and judgment of left to right progression. Fink noted that imaginative play training had the potential to facilitate cognitive learning and growth under specific conditions that employed role taking, role enhancement and integration, and dramatic and sociodramatic activities.

In an eighth study, Saltz and Johnson (1974) trained low-income preschool children in thematic-fantasy play. The participants, receiving the thematic-fantasy play treatments, were trained to dramatize folk tales; imagine; and, in turn, performed roles of imaginary characters in these folk episodes. The children in the control treatments received ordinary paste and cut activities by adults who employed nondirect supervision. With a pre- and post-design, the results of analyses indicated that children who were trained in thematic-fantasy play received significantly higher mean scores from subtests on the Wechsler Preschool and Primary Scale of Intelligence and on assessments of story sequence and memory, as well as, indices of story verbalization skills (as measured by subtests of the Illinois Test of Psychologistic Abilities). The results showed that training in imaginative play facilitated preschool children's cognitive abilities on selected measures relative to procedures in the control groups.

Feitelson and Ross (1973), with 24 low-income children five years of age, examined the effect of imaginative play training on growth of creative behaviors. Children in the experimental groups were trained to demonstrate imaginative play routines while those in the control treatments received no such play training. Using a pre- and post-test design, the results of the analyses showed that participants in the imaginative play group yielded significantly higher scores on creativity as measured by selected subbatteries taken from the Dorrance Tests of Creativity. The results showed that imaginative play and subsequent training had the potential to facilitate selected creative abilities.

In sum, the majority of investigations surveyed in the above section trained the participants to demonstrate dramatic and/or sociodramatic play through experimental treatments and compared their performance with others in control conditions. The results from the majority of studies surveyed have suggested the potential of imaginative play to facilitate language and cognitive repertories of young and older children. From a more learning (rather than developmental) perspective, and in support of the findings concerning the merits of playful activities on language and cognitive repertories, Glickman (1979, p. 454) hypothesized that, "achievement scores have declined over the past generations because children have less time and fewer opportunities to play." The Glickman thesis coupled with the selected empirical research results most assuredly required additional substantive exploration and research. With growing evidence that a child's language and cognitive learning and development were based on play experiences, additional opportunities for children in imaginative play must be provided for them in preschools, more formal school settings, homes and communities.

In the following section, implications for facilitating imaginative play based on selected research studies were presented and discussed.

Imaginative Play: Some Implications for Adults Working With Children in Home and School Settings

Young children have played with objects and at situations. Playing with objects has meant the use of tangibles such as dolls, hammers, peg sets, tricycles and toy phones. Playing at situations has largely meant the use of the pretend in episode fashion — i.e., dramatic and sociodramatic play. The materials environment has been classified by the types and functions that the play objects served. By understanding the types of play materials, adults have better understood the "what" and "how" of providing for children in play situations. The categorizations of play objects were: (a) instructional; (b) constructional; (c) toys; and (d) real play objects (Yawkey & Dank, in press).

Constructional Materials

Constructional play objects have been extremely functional. They have been used in many versatile ways by young children. Since constructional materials have served many purposes, they had global rather than specific functions. Researchers (e.g.,

Freyburg, 1973), in the area of play, have considered them multipurposeful — given that they fit any and all play episodes. Building blocks and constructional sets were the two largest subcategories in the constructional group of objects. Building blocks have been manufactured in many many sizes and shapes. Some building blocks were large and had hollow interiors. Large building blocks with hollow interiors were ideal for young children for they can be carried from one play setting to another. The ones manufactured from cardboard were also sturdy for they had reinforced multiple layers. Manufacturers have reported that building blocks with reinforced multiple layers have the potential to support 200 or more pounds. Building blocks have also come in small sizes. 'For example, the table blocks have also been grouped within the category of building blocks. They were easily picked up and carried-about by young children and have been used on tables and floors. These smaller blocks had solid rather than hollow interiors and were usually manufactured from wood. Building sets, the second large subcategory of constructional materials, have been very popular with young children and adult caregivers. having a large number of individual pieces. They have been extremely flexible in function and use. They have also been used in many play situations. The building sets usually have been recognized by their manufacturer's names. Examples of building blocks included: (a) "Make-It-Toys"; (b) Tinkertoys; (c) Lincoln or Canadienne Logs; (d) ABC blocks; (e) Parquetry sets; and, (f) Design cubes.

Instructional Materials

Another very large category of play materials was the instructional materials. They were constructed with specific rather than broad goals and "taught" concepts and skills taken largely from the three 'R's of reading, 'riting, and 'rithmetic. Instructional materials, as a subcategory of play tangibles, have been found in homes and schools in large quantities. Like constructional materials, instructional tangibles have been subdivided into various kinds depending on the type of skill or concept "taught." Included within the subtypes of instructional materials were: (a) puzzles; (b) stacking toys; (c) string sets; (d) nesting toys; and, (e) pegboard sets.

Having been designed by the manufacturer to "teach" part to whole relationships and sequencing skills, puzzles came in numerous varieties. Formboards and jigsaws were the two varieties of puzzles. Formboards having removable pieces with insert were the most common type of puzzle for the very young child. The knobs on each puzzle piece helped the young child grasp and hold or carry them from place to place. Depending on the age of the child, formboards have been manufactured with two or more pieces. Like formboards, jigsaws have also been manufactured with removable pieces. Given that older children at the preschool level usually played with jigsaws, the knobs on each piece have been eliminated. Older children usually have developed some degree of fine motor control and were able to use them quite easily. There were numerous types and kinds of scenes painted on jigsaws. Some jigsaws have shown very simple scenes — e.g., pictures of objects or people including fruits, animals, or Olympic heroes. The more complicated scenes on some have whole illustrated episodes such as farm life; animals at the zoo; pictures of the city; and, people at work. The number of pieces in the jigsaws have ranged from two or more pieces.

Stacking toys have created much enjoyment and had much learning potential. They were manufactured from wood or plastic. They consisted of a base or platform with a dowel inserted in the middle of a wood or plastic base. The centers of the individual pieces have been drilled-out and the pieces have been varied in size and shape. In turn, each of the pieces are inserted over and through the dowel. Youngsters have learned skills such as sizes, colors, and shapes. In addition, teaching skills associated with stacking materials have provided practice with learning small muscle movements and eye-hand coordinations.

A third type of instructional material was called stringing sets. They have usually been manufactured from waxed shoelaces, string, or cord and various shaped wooden or plastic pieces. In turn, the centers have been drilled or bored out and the children have inserted the waxed cord or string through the holes. String sets have been used over and over again because they were versatile and have been used in numerous ways. A fourth kind of instructional tangible was the nesting toy. The nesting toys have been manufactured from wood or plastic and were varied by size and shape. Ranging from small to large in size and including treasure chests, fish, dolls and others for shape, the nesting toys were multipurposeful. The curriculum skill usually associated with nesting toys was taking apart the pieces from large to small and putting them back together again from small to large.

The fifth type of material was pegboards and pegs. The pegboards have usually been manufactured from wood (and its variations such as plywood) or plastic. Usually found on pegboard sets were designs of animals, people, or various types of scenes. The youngster was required to complete the design or outline of the figure or scene by inserting pegs into the board. With simple designs, rubber bands have been placed around the pegs for purposes of outlining the figure or object. Pegboards and pegs were ideal for "teaching" skills such as; part to whole relations; sequencing; and, body coordinations.

Real Objects

The category of real objects has always been intriguing to young children. The category included materials used by children as play tangibles such as: (a) sand and water; (b) wood; (c) clay; and, (d) adult clothing. Usually real materials were initially manufactured for adults for use in their world and have, in turn, been used by children in their imaginative play environments.

Sand and water were two sound examples of materials that had specific uses in the adult world. They were largely inexpensive to purchase or found in nature. Sand and water were ideal as play tangibles because they lacked definite shape or form. Instead, these materials have taken the shape of containers in which they were used. Wood was a second large subcategory of real objects. They also were plentiful and have been purchased from lumber yards or found in natural states. For use as a play tangible, soft woods have been recommended and were most pleasurable and enjoyable to use. They have been readily used with hammers, sandpaper, glue, pliers, and long nails. Clay, a third example of real materials, has been used as a play object for centuries. Like sand, water, and wood, clay has been found in nature or was purchased in learning shops, department stores, and teacher supply houses.

Adult clothing as a real object was very useful in assisting the growth of imaginative play episodes. Clothing such as men's and women's work and sporting outfits, as well as big sister's and brother's garments, were ideal as play objects. Other examples of adult clothing have been found in every home and school.

Toy Objects

The toy object as the fourth category of play tangible has been most useful to young children. Like constructional items, they were versatile and have been used in play and in many many ways. Toy tangibles have been described as miniature versions of real people, objects, and animals (Yawkey & Dank, in press). Since the objects were scaled-down versions of real items, they were easily used by young children in play settings. Like the other large categories of play tangibles, toy objects were numerous and have been subdivided into classes which included: (a) housekeeping toys; (b) transportation items; and, (c) animal objects. The toy object can be further subdivided into other classes depending on the function they served or the item they represented.

Housekeeping materials have depicted items associated with daily and practical living. Some of these items have included objects related to thhe skills of working, eating, sleeping, washing or caring for objects or people. Examples of housekeeping objects associated with practical living have included cots, tables, chairs, electric ranges, doll clothing, ironing boards, pots, pans, and numerous others. Another very large subcategory of toy objects was transportation toys. Also scaled down versions of real objects, transportation toys have included those items that children can easily manipulate with their hand, fingers, and arms and others on which they ride. The former subset of transportation toys included items such as toy trucks, cars, airplanes, space vehicles, and ships. The type on which children ride or drive themselves from place to place have included objects such as scooters, wagons, tricycles, and "Big Wheels."

Animal toys as miniature objects from the real world included crocodiles, elephants, tigers, cats, dogs, and others from circus, zoo, farm or jungle. Another subdivision of animal toys has included those that depict people in various occupational roles or situations. These included soldiers, "daddies," "mommies," monsters, indians and numerous others.

The four differing subcategories of play tangibles have been useful in providing the children with variety of materials in their home and school environment. Variety has meant that children have the opportunity to choose and decide which of the objects they wish to use. In addition to understanding the various categories of play tangibles that have existed and were used by children in individual and group pretend sessions, a second implication for adults working with young children in play sessions was associated with adult-child-physical object interaction. The quality and quantity of adult-child-physical object interaction that occurred in the play setting had the potential to facilitate cognitive and language development and learning of young children. The adult-child-physical object interaction was also a necessary factor that was characteristic of facilitative play environments (Seaver & Cartwright, 1977).

In order to encourage adult-child-physical object interaction in imaginative play, several caregiver strategies have been found useful. Essentially the strategies were: (a) developing complexity; (b) giving cues; (c) developing novelty; and, (d) adding unrelated objects. Each of the four strategies for facilitating adult-child-physical object interaction were described in the following sections.

Developing Complexity

The strategy of developing complexity in imaginative play enriched the adult-child-physical object interaction which was basic to cognitive and language learning and development. Developing complexity meant the modification of selected characteristics of children's play objects. For example, some of the physical characteristics of toy cars were: (a) texture; (b) color; (c) shape and others. To use the strategy of developing complexity, adults simply modified one or several of the physical properties of the toy car. The characteristic of color was modifiable by simply changing the color of the car from "blue" to "red." The texture of the car was also changeable from "smooth" to "rough" by pasting strips of sandpaper on its roof and hood. By altering one or several of the characteristics, the play tangible became more complex than the original object with its previous characteristics. In turn, the children have regarded changes in physical characterstics of objects as new and novel play tangibles which were explored and used in their play situations. With modifications of physical properties of play tangibles the interaction between child and object and the functions it served in play situations increased.

Giving Cues

Another type of strategy that has been used to increase child-adult-physical object interaction was "giving cues." Giving cues has meant that the adult volunteered relevant verbal statements concerning the use of object in the play episode. Examples of statements which suggested additional functions that objects could serve in the play situation were: (a) "Show the object (e.g., toy bear) how you think it felt when . . .?"; and, (b) "How else might you use the object (e.g., toy house) in hunting for the monster?" The strategy of verbal cues has provided additional suggestions to children in using objects in their play sessions. At the same time, verbal cues have increased the depth of the imaginative play as the youngsters incorporated the statements and suggestions into their episode. Verbal cueing increased language and cognitive development and learning.

Developing novelty

The third effective strategy, developing novelty, has been employed two ways. The first way was to add other play objects to the setting in addition to the ones the children were using. The new objects added to the play setting, however, had to be related to the ongoing theme of the episode. For example, children engaged in playing "house" were using common household utensils. The adult in observing the types of materials used by the children provided them with: (a) two large spoons; and, (b) plastic quart container. When the children incorporated these new and unfamiliar items into their play, the play theme became enriched by their addition and the children had to develop methods of using them in their imaginative theme. A second method of employing the strategy of developing novelty was to totally remove play tangibles from the center or home for a short period of time. Over a period of time, interest in play objects decreased. Having employed the objects in numerous ways, the functional use and exploration potential that children demonstrated with play tangibles decreased. Removing the play objects from the setting for a short time period tended to increase their novelty value for the youngsters. When the play objects were re-introduced into the play environment, children employed them again in their pretend transportations. Regardless of the method used in the strategy of "developing novelty," it resulted in increasing the children's play and had the potential to further develop language and cognitive learning and growth.

Adding Unrelated Objects

The final strategy used to challenge the youngsters in their pretend play was called "adding unrelated objects." Similar to the strategy of "developing novelty," "adding unrelated objects" meant that the adult provided play tangibles to children that were not associated with their present pretend episode. For example, the adult in observing the youngsters in a pretend episode entitled "going shopping" has noted that they have been using tangibles such as (a) plastic shopping bags; and, (b) empty soup cans. In using the strategy of "adding unrelated objects," with the episode entitled "going shopping," the adult asked the children to incorporate a play tangible with the other materials and employed it effectively in the pretend episode. Similar to the other strategies, the children expanded their imaginative play episode after they incorporated the unrelated objects within the plot. As the integration of the objects occurred in the play episode, it enriched and expanded and increased opportunities for cognitive and language learning and development occurred.

The four strategies were extremely useful for adults working with children in play sessions. They were useable with children in home, schools and communities.

Conclusion

Having examined the background research studies; the importance of make-believe; the various definitions of play; relationships of play to cognitive and language development and learning; and, implications for caregivers in working with children in play settings, the significance and function of play was established. The world of imaginative play has the potential to contribute to the growth and learning of young children in home, school and community settings.

References

Ammar, H. *Growing up in an Egyptian village.* London: Rutledge and Kegan, 1954.

Barker, R.G., Dembo, L., and Lewin, K. Frustration and regression: An experiment with young children. *University of Iowa Studies in Child Welfare,* 1941, *18* (386).

Bereiter, C. and Engleman, S. *Teaching disadvantaged in the preschool.* Englewood Cliffs, N.J.: Prentice-Hall, 1966.

Blohm, P.J. and Yawkey, T.D. Language and imaginative play experience approach (LIPEA) to reading: Fact or fantasy? Unpublished manuscript, The Pennsylvania State University, University Park, Pennsylvania, 1977, p. 1-30.

Chandler, M.J. Egocentrism and antisocial behavior. The assessment and training of social perspective. *Developmental Psychology,* 1973, *9*(3), 326-332.

Chauncey, H. (ed.) *Social preschool education,* Vol. 2, New York: Holt, Rinehart, and Winston, 1969.

Curry, N.E., and Arnaud, S.H. Cognitive implications in children's spontaneous role play. *Theory Into Practice,* 1974, 13(4), 273-277.

Deardon, R.F. *The philosophy of our primary education.* London: Rutledge and Kagan Paul, 1968.

El'Konin, D. Symbolics and its function in the play of children. *Soviet Education,* 1966, *8,* 35-41.

Erickson, E.H. *Childhood and society.* London: Imago, 1950.

Featherstone, J. The new primary school revolution in Britain. *The New Republic,* 1967, (71), 66-84.

Fein, G., and Rabertson, A. Cognitive and social diversions of pretending in two-year olds. New Haven, Connecticut: Yale University, 1974. (ERIC Document Reproduction Service Number ED 119-806).

Fein, G. A transformational analysis of pretending. *Developmental Psychology,* 1975, *11*(3), 291-296.

Fein, G. *Play and the acquisition of symbols,* Unpublished manuscript, The Merrill-Palmer Institute, 1978.

Feitelson, D. Patterns of early education in the Kurdish community. *Megainot, 5,* 1954, 95-109.

Feitelson, D. Developing imaginative play in preschool children as a possible approach to fostering creativity. *Early Child Development Care, 1,* 1972, 181-195.

Feitelson, D., and Ross, G.S. The neglected factor − play. *Human Development,* 1973, *16,* 202-223.

Fink, R.S. Role of imaginative play in cognitive development. *Psychological Reports,* 1976, *39*(14), 895-906.

Freyburg, J.T. Increasing the imaginative play of urban disadvantaged kindergarten children through systematic training. In Singer, J.L. (ed.) *The Child's World of Make Believe,* New York: Academic Press, 1973.

Gilmore, J.T. Play a special behavior. In Haber, R.N. (Ed.), *Current research in motivation.* New York: Holt, Rinehart, and Winston, Inc. 1966.

Glickman, C.D. Problem-declining achievement scorles: Solution − let them play. *Phi Delta Kappan,* 1979, *60*(6), 454-455.

Golumb, C. and Cornelius, G.G. Symbolic play and its cognitive significance. *Developmental Psychology,* 1977, *13*(3), 246-252.

Gulick, Z. *A philosophy of play,* New York: Scribner, 1920.

Guthrie, K. and Hudson, L.M. Training conservation through symbolic play: A second look. *Child Development,* 1979, *50*(16), 1269-1271.

Hartley, R.E., Frank L.K., and Goldenson, R.M. *Understanding children's play.* New York: Columbia University Press, 1952.

Hetzer, H. *Kindheit and Armut.* Hirzel, Leipzig, 1929.

Hollow, M. and Covan, P. Social isolation and cognitive development. Logical operations and role taking abilities in three Norwegian social settings. *Child Development.* 1973, 44, 630-641.

Hnrcir, E. *Symbolic vehicles in transformations and operative/figurative framework for understanding the emergence of symbols.* Unpublished manuscript, The Pennsylvania State University, 1980.

Isaacs, S. *Intellectual growth in children.* New York: Harcourt Brace, 1935.

John V.P., and Goldstein, L.S. The social context of language acquisition. In M. Deutsch (Ed.), *The disadvantaged child.* New York: Basic Books, 1967.

Kohlberg, L. Early education − A cognitive-developmental view. *Child Development,* 1968, *39*(4), 1013-1062.

Leiberman, J.N. Playfulness and divergent thinking: An investigation of their relationship at the kindergarten level. *Journal of Genetic Psychology,* 1965, 107, 219-224.

Levin, J.P. Inducing comprehension in poor readers. A test of a recent model. *Journal of Educational Psychology,* 1973, 65, 19-24.

LeVine, R.A. and LeVine, B. Hyansogo. A Gusii community of Kenya. In Whiting. *Six cultures.* New York: Wiley, 1963, 15-202.

Lovinger, S.L. Sociodramatic play and language development in pre-school children. Psychology in the Schools, 1974, 11, 313-320.

Lowe, M. Trends in the development of representational play in infants from one to three years — an observational study. *Journal of Child Psychology and Psychiatry,* 1975, 16-33-47.

Lunzer, E.H. Intellectual development in the play of young children. *Education Review,* 11, 1959, 205-217.

Marbach, E.S. and Yawkey, T.D. The effect of imaginative play actions on language development — five-year-old children. *Psychology in the Schools,* 1980, in press.

Mead, G.H. *Mine, self, and society.* Chicago: University of Chicago, 1934.

Murphy, L. Infant's play and cognitive development. In H. Puis (Ed.), *Play and development.* New York: Norton, 1962.

Newmann, E. *Elements of play,* New York: MSS Information Corporation, 1971.

Nicholich, L. A longitudinal study of representational play in relation to spontaneous imitation and development of multiworld utterances. Government Report, N.I.E. No. NE-G-11-3-0027, 1975.

Overton, W.F., and Jackson, J.P. The representation of imagined objects in action sequences. A developmental study. *Child Development,* 1973, 44, 309-314.

Pederson, F.A. and Wendee, P.H. Early Social correlates of cognitive functioning in six-year-old boys. *Child Development.* 1968, 39, 185-193.

Piaget, J. *The psychology of intelligence.* New York: Harcourt Brace, 1950.

Piaget, J. *Play, dreams, and imitation in childhood.* New York: Norton, 1962.

Pulaski, M.A. *Understanding Piaget.* New York: Harper Row, 1971.

Pulaski, M.A. Toys and imaginative play. In Singer, J.L. (Ed.) *The Child's world of make-believe.* New York: Academic Press. 1973, 74-103.

Rosen, C.E. The effects of sociodramatic play on problem-solving behavior among culturally disadvantaged preschool children. *Child Development,* 1974, 45, 920-927.

Saltz, E., Dixon, D., and Johnson, J. Training disadvantaged preschoolers on various fantasy activities on cognitive functioning and impulse control. *Child Development,* 1977, *48,* 367-380.

Saltz, E., and Johnson, J. Training for thematic-fantasy play in culturally disadvantaged children: Preliminary results. *Journal of Educational Psychology,* 1974, *6,*(4), 623-630.

Seaver, S. and Cartwright, C.A. A pluralistic foundation for training early childhood professionals. *Curriculum Inquiry,* 1977, *1*(4), 305-329.

Singer, J.L. *The child's world of make believe.* New York: Academic Press, 1973.

Similansky, S. *The effects of sociodramatic play on disadvantaged preschool children.* New York: Wiley, 1968.

Smith, P.K. and Syddall, S. Play and nonplay tutoring in preschool children. Is it play or tutoring which matters? *British Journal of Educational Psychology,* 1978, *48*(18), 315-325.

Strom, R.D. Play and family development. *The Elementary School Journal,* 1974, *74*(14), 359-368.

Sullivan, E., and Hunt, D. Interpersonal and objective decentering as a function of age and social class. *Journal of Genetic Psychology,* 1967, *110,* 199-210.

Sutton-Smith, B. The role of play in cognitive development. In Herron, R.E. and Sutton-Smith, B. (Eds.), *Child's Play.* New York: Wiley, 1971, 252-260.

Valentine, C.W. A study of the beginnings and significance of play in infancy. *British Journal of Educational Psychology,* 8, 1938, 188-200, 285-306.

VanAlstyne, D. *Play behavior and choice of play materials of preschool children.* Chicago: University of Chicago Press, 1932.

Volpe, R. Social experience and the cognitive and social development of orthopedically disabled and non disabled children in Maggery, J. etal. (Eds.) *Applied Piagetian Theory and The helping professions.* 1975, 204-218.

Volpe, R. Orthopedia disability, restriction, and role taking activity. *Journal of Special Education, 10,* 1976, 311-381.

Volpe, R. Developing role taking activity. *Child Study Journal,* 9(1), 1979. 61-68.

Vygotsky, L.S. Play and its role in the mental development of the child. *Soviet Psychology,* 1967, *5,* 6-18.

Weber, E. *Early childhood education: Perspectives on change.* Ohio: Charles A. Jones, 1970.

Weber, L. *The English infant school and informal education.* Englewood Cliffs: Prentice-Hall, Inc., 1971.

Weikart, D., Rogers, L., Adcock, C., and McClelland, D. *The cognitively-oriented curriculum: A framework for preschool teachers.* Urbana: Illinois, University of Illinois, 1970.

Wolffgang, C. An exploration of the relationship between the cognitive area of reading and selected developmental aspects of children's play. *Psychology in the Schools,* 1974, *11,* 338-343.

Yawkey, T.D. Role playing, language learning and development. Some effective strategies for educators in working with children. Research paper read at the Fifth Annual Reading Institute, Pennsylvania, 1978, 1-5.

Yawkey, T.D. An investigation of the fourth R — "relationships" — and sex on reading and imaginativeness in young children. Research paper read at the Annual Meeting of the American Educatioal Research Association, San Francisco, 1979.

Yawkey, T.D. The effects of social relationships curricula and sex differences on reading and imaginativeness in young children. *Alberta Journal of Educational Research,* in press.

Yawkey, T.D. and Dank, H. *Playing inside and ... out: For teachers and parents of young children.* Menlo Park, California: Addison-Wesley in press.

Yawkey, T.D. and Blohm, P.J. Imaginative play: Language and imaginative play experience approach. In Weizemann, R. Brown, R., Levinson, P.S., and Taylor, P.A. (eds.) *Piagetian Theory and its implications for the helping professions.* Los Angeles: The University of Southern California Press, 1978, 315-319.

Yawkey, T.D. and Silvern, S.B. Investigation of types of play and aural language growth in young children. Research Paper Presented at the American Educational Research Associatin, San Francisco, April 1979.

Social Learning, Violence, and Reform

Gary G. Brannigan, Ph.D.
*State University of New York
College at Plattsburgh*
and
David F. King, M.A.
Dover Children's Home

Abstract

This paper examines violence and reform from Rotter's
(1954) social learning perspective. There are two major sections. The first deals with cultural and social organizational
determinants of violence. The second section deals with intervention strategies. In addition to describing several techniques for individual psychotherapy, the specialized encounter
group is discussed from the social learning viewpoint. The
specialized encounter method provides a mini-social structure
offering opportunities for individuals to learn and practice new
behavior. Receiving positive reinforcement and help from the
group enables the individual to define his self worth in a proper
perspective, leads to increased self-esteem, and reduces the
need for verbal and physical aggression in interpersonal relations.

Introduction

Violence, as Etzioni (1971, p. 711) states, "has been rampant throughout American history." In recent years, a surge of interest in violence has been kindled by the war in Vietnam, assassinations of public figures, and radical political groups who preach violent methods of social change. This focus on violence has been responsible for the appointment of three national commissions to study the causes, manifestations, and prevalence of violence in the United States.

But what is violence? Gelles and Straus (1978), in a detailed comparison of the concepts aggression and physical violence, define the latter term as an act "carried out with the intention of or perceived as having the intention of physically hurting another person." Aggression — frequently confused with violence — is a broader concept that encompasses acts of violence as well as other malevolent acts (e.g. psychological suffering and material deprivation) carried out with the intention or perceived intention of injuring another.

This chapter will be restricted to the relationship between social learning and physical violence. The significance of this relationship is highlighted by several major research findings.

(1) The family is the primary mechanism for teaching norms, values, and techniques of violence (Gelles, 1974).

(2) Violence among family members is extensive (Gelles, 1974, and Straus, 1977).

(3) There is a significant correlation between observation of violence as a child and subsequent approval of violence (Owens & Straus, 1975).

(4) Those individuals who abuse their children were abused as children themselves (Gelles, 1973, Gil, 1971, and Steele & Pollack, 1968).

It is also evident from these research related findings that cultural and social organizational variables are important determinants of violent behavior. Since cultural norms are generally shared by the sector of society inhabited by an individual or group, they therefore help to explain different levels of violence between societies or between different subgroups within a society. Similarly, social organizational variables have an affect on the type of family, subculture, and culture that will arise as well as how these collectives will function. Cloward and Ohlin (1972), for example, pointed out that violent gang subcultures arise when

86

adolescents who are oriented toward achieving higher positions are cut off from institutional channels (criminal as well as legitimate). Relying upon their own resources to solve this adjustment problem, these lower class youth learn that they can achieve high levels of self-esteem by demonstrating "guts" and acquiring a "rep" for violent acts. The use of violence, therefore, is functional for increasing self-esteem since physical cruelty is abhored by society, and the commission of violent acts allows one to gain attention and rise from anonymity to notoriety relatively quickly. This has been demonstrated in Columbian bandits (Leon, 1969) and cases of civil disorder in the United States (Usdin, 1969). Violence can also be a method of attacking an individual or social structure which blocks access to highly valued goals or reinforcers. Violently attacking these individuals or social structures, then, gives the individual a sense of power and increases self-esteem. Cloward and Ohlin (1972, p. 156) in addition state, "As long as conventional and criminal opportunity structures remain closed, violence continues unchecked . . . if new opportunity structures are opened, however, violence tends to be relinquished." These "opportunity structures," as Palmer and Linsky (1972) explain, consist of two separate parts: a learning structure and a performance structure. First, a person must find access to situations and environments within which he can acquire skills, values, and knowledge requisite for success within a particular role. Secondly, he must have access to situations within which he can perform the role once it is learned. A person's family can be considered an opportunity structure. The class, size, race, and religion of the family can have an effect on the development of personality traits and interpersonal skills that are related to success in both academic and occupational situations. Other factors such as age, sex, geographical location, and degree of deprivation also influence access to opportunity structures.

Access to both deviant (violent) and conformity (nonviolent) roles is not equally open to all. Hence, the underlying social structure has a causal influence on violent interpersonal behavior within families, subcultures, or cultures. Owens and Straus (1975) pointed out that experience with violence as a child leads to approval of interpersonal and political violence as an adult. They concluded that the reduction of childhood experience with violence could reduce the high level of violence that characterizes American society. It is important to note that although one learns certain cultural prescriptions for conduct, learning does not explain how and why such a culture came about. The underlying assumption is that, "for any set of characteristic behaviors of a population, there will develop a normative counterpart that rationalizes and justifies that behavior." (Owens & Straus, 1974, p. 210). "Therefore, . . . one might state that cultural norms (in American society) concerning violence primarily reflect an adaptation to certain aspects of American social structure" (Owens & Straus, 1974; p. 194).

Social Learning Theory

Social learning theory (Rotter, 1954) combines the major aspects of Hull's S-R theory and Tolman's cognitive theory (i.e. reinforcement and expectancy) into a unitary explanation for the complex social behavior of humans. The expectancy-reinforcement viewpoint revolves around three basic constructs: behavior potential, reinforcement value, and expectancy.

Behavior potential is defined as "the potentiality of any behavior's occurring in any given situation or situations as calculated in relation to any single reinforcement or set of reinforcements." (Rotter, 1954; p. 105). The concept of behavior used in the definition is a broad one, including any action of the organism in response to a meaningful stimulus. Included within the definition are both explicit and implicit forms of behavior, as well as complex behavior patterns emphasized by the dynamic psychologists (e.g. repression, projection, and withdrawal).

Reinforcement value is defined as "the degree of preference for any reinforcement to occur if the possibilities of their occurring were all equal." (Rotter, 1954, p. 107). In this definition of reinforcement, Rotter departs from the Hullian tradition involving drive reduction, in favor of a more empirical interpretation (i.e. reinforcement is any observable event which changes the probability of occurrence of a given behavior pattern). Since a reinforcement is something that changes behavior in some observable way by increasing or decreasing the probability of its occurrence, the effect of reinforcement can be measured and predictions made about its effect on behavior.

Expectancy is defined as
> "the probability held by the individual that a particular reinforcement will occur as a function of a specific behavior in a specific situation. Expectancy is independent of the value or importance of the reinforcement."

(Rotter, 1954, p. 107). Expectancy is the central concept in Rotter's system. It is also used to describe the degree to which the individual believes that he is the agent controlling his behavior (Internality) and therefore that reinforcement is contingent upon his own behavior rather than forces outside of himself (Externality) such as fate, chance, or luck.

Although Phares (1957) was the first to attempt the measurement of individual differences in generalized expectancy for reinforcement, more recently the Internal-External scale (Rotter, 1966) and the Locus of Control Scale for Adults (Nowicki and Duke, 1974) have been used to measure this dimension.

Based on the assumption that expectancy is: (a) a function of probability, based on past history of reinforcement; and (b) a generalization of expectancies from related behavior-reinforcement patterns, research has centered on the socialization process as the primary factor in the shaping of an individual's expectancy. There is considerable empirical support for this assumption in that individuals from varying social environments, and presumably having different social learning experiences, show differences in this dimension. For example, locus of control differences have been reported for individuals varying in ethnic background (e.g. Battle and Rotter, 1963, and Lefcourt and Ladwig, 1965), socioeconomic status (e.g. Battle and Rotter, 1963), birth order (e.g. MacDonald, 1971a) and sex (e.g. Brannigan and Tolor, 1971a).

Still other investigators (Brannigan and Tolor, 1971b, Chance, 1972, Cromwell, 1963, Davis and Phares, 1969, Katkovsky, Crandall, and Good, 1967, MacDonald, 1971b, Solomon, Houlihan, Busse, and Parelius, 1971, Tolor, 1967, and Tolor and Jalowiec, 1968) have concentrated on the key figures in an individual's life (i.e. parents) in trying to determine the etiology for the development of an internal versus an external expectancy. On the whole, these studies reported positive parent-child relationships (e.g. warmth, supportiveness) to be related to internality and negative parent-child relationships (e.g. authoritarianism, rejection) to be related to externality.

The formula below represents a summary of the interaction of the above concepts for a specific situation and a specific reinforcement:

$$B.P.x, ra = f(E.ra + R.V.a)$$

The formula states that the potential for a specific behavior (x) to occur in relation to a specific reinforcement (a) is a function of the expectancy of the occurrence of reinforcement a following behavior x and the value of reinforcement a.

Intervention Strategies

Singer (1970, p. 16) states that the fundamental proposition of psychotherapy is "that man is capable of change and capable of bringing this change about himself." Therefore, the principal goal of all forms of psychotherapy is the belief in personal control, ". . . with health being defined by the degree to which a person is free to perceive himself as an independently acting and reacting unit, experiencing consciously the choices at his disposal, and making choices with a conscious sense of responsibility for them." (Singer, 1970, p. 18). Similarly, Rotter (1954) has suggested that since learning and psychotherapy involve the same basic process – changing behavior, psychotherapy is a learning process. Rotter (1954, p. 397) also states that changing expectancy is a prime function of therapy;

> "with the emphasis being on a quite active role of inter-
> pretation on the part of the therapist. Interpretation
> serves the purpose of changing expectancies for specific
> behaviors or groups of behaviors and of changing the
> values of reinforcements or needs by changing the expec-
> tancies for subsequent reinforcements. Such interpreta-
> tion should be made in common sense terms, based on
> maximum use of the individual's own experience."

Therefore, the purpose of therapy is not to solve all of the individual's problems, but rather to increase his ability to solve his own problems (e.g. through reinforcing the expectancy that problems are solvable by looking for alternative solutions).

Psychotherapy, in the social learning framework, is primarily concerned with changing expectancies. In the case of interpersonal violence, the therapist has the choice of either weakening violent responses, strengthening nonviolent responses, or doing both. Optimally, however, the therapist would concentrate on lowering the expectancy that violent behavior leads to gratification, and increase the expectancy that alternative or new behaviors lead to greater gratification in the future.

Rotter (1954) suggests five methods of increasing the expectancy for gratification for new behaviors.

(1) The most direct way of increasing behavior potential or probability is through direct reinforcement. In his contacts with the individual, the therapist has the opportuni-
ty to respond, either positively or negatively, to the be-

havior of the individual. However, the relative effectiveness of reinforcement is related to the degree to which an individual feels that what happens to him will be contingent on his own behavior or is independent of his own behavior. Individuals having a belief in "external" control, being less susceptible to the influence of positive reinforcement, may require an analysis of this attitude before change can take place.

(2) The therapist can place the individual in, or help him to find and enter, situations where he may observe in others alternative behaviors and their consequences, or where by discussion and interpretation he can try to understand the behavior of others retrospectively.

(3) The therapist may deal with the individual's history of alternative behaviors, reducing his expectancy that they will now result in negative reinforcements as they did in the past, and verbally increasing his expectancy that these alternative behaviors will now lead to gratification.

(4) The therapist may discuss possible alternatives, showing how the behaviors are carried out and creating an expectancy that they may lead to gratification.

(5) The therapist can create and reinforce an expectancy that the individual may solve his problems more effectively by looking for and trying out alternative solutions or behaviors.

Rotter (1954) also states that when an individual does not display behavior that the therapist might reinforce directly, alternative methods of behaving might be discussed with him. The individual may be made aware of how others use different behaviors and encouraged to try new behaviors. More recently, Bandura (1965) has emphasized the effectiveness of "modeling" procedures in transmitting new response patterns. Bandura and Walters (1963) have indicated three major effects of modeling:

(1) The observer may acquire new responses that did not exist in his behavior repertoire.

(2) Exposure to models may also strengthen or weaken (depending on the desired outcome) inhibitory responses in the observer.

(3) The behavior of models may elicit previously learned responses that match precisely or bear some resemblance to those exhibited by the model.

Bandura (1965) further suggests that the acquisition of matching responses takes place through contiguity, whereas reinforcements administered to a model exact their major influence on the performance of imitatively learned responses. Research relevant to these points has been clearly illustrated in several investigations (e.g., Bandura, Ross, and Ross; 1961, and 1963) designed to explore the social transmission of novel aggressive responses. In these studies, nursery school children were exposed to either aggressive adult models or to models who displayed inhibited and nonaggressive behavior. For the aggressive-model group the model exhibited unusual forms of physical and verbal aggression toward a large inflated plastic doll. After exposure to their respective models, all children were mildly frustrated and then tested for the amount of imitative and nonmatching aggressive behavior they would exhibit in the situation. The results of these experiments show that children who observed the aggressive model displayed a number of precisely imitative aggressive responses, whereas such responses rarely occurred in the nonaggressive-model group. Furthermore, children in the nonaggressive-model group displayed the inhibited behavior characteristic of their model to a greater extent than did the control children.

Bandura (1965) also stressed the use of modeling in a hierarchical progression. Such a procedure would be similar to Wolpe's (1958) use of the behavioral hierarchy in systematic desensitization. Both methods involve taking an individual through a series of progressively more difficult behaviors. In modeling, a person views an adequate handling of these situations, while in desensitization he associates a more adjustive response to the stimulus situations.

The research of Bandura and his associates on modeling behavior offers an important step in applying the principles of social learning theory. Bandura (1969, p. 163) states that

> "Behavioral enactment methods are frequently utilized for a wide variety of purposes in which people who want to develop new competencies are provided with actual or symbolic models of desired behavior. They are given opportunities to perform these patterns initially under nonthreatening conditions before they are encouraged to apply them in their everyday lives. Since, in modeling approaches, a person observes and practices alternate ways of behaving under lifelike conditions, transfer of learning to naturalistic situations is greatly facilitated."

Therefore, the modeling approach appears to be an effective means of bringing about expectancy change. This expectancy change may be further enhanced by the individual's observation of the reinforcing consequences of both the model's behavior and his own attempts.

Encounter Groups: Alternatives to Violence

Specialized encounter groups can be utilized to effect change in behavioral expectancies by:

(1) Placing the individual in a situation where both the therapist and other group members may directly reward adjustive behavior.

(2) Allowing the individual to enter a social situation where he may observe and discuss alternative behaviors and their consequences.

(3) Providing an opportunity structure for alternative behavior to be carried out within the group and using the group to create expectancies that such alternatives can be more effective than present response patterns.

(4) Strengthening the use of alternative behaviors through group structure and support.

Presently, however, many so-called encounter groups focus on "leveling" or cathartic techniques which stress confrontation and give free rein to verbal aggression between group members (Straus, 1974). Advocates of catharsis, such as Bach and Wyden (1968), state that holding back aggression leads to an increase in anger and hostility which will eventually trigger a more violent outburst and cloud the issues. In fact, Bach and Wyden, in their book "The Intimate Enemy" (1968, p. 1), described an encounter group technique based on verbal aggression between marital partners. The technique was based upon the assumption that "verbal conflict between intimates is not only acceptable, especially between husbands and wives; it is constructive and highly desirable."

On the other hand, Steinmetz and Straus (1974) found that the cathartic technique, relying on verbal aggression as a means of avoiding violence, actually increases the probability that physical violence will occur. College students were asked to complete a questionnaire that asked for information about what the respondents considered the three major conflicts or disagreements between their parents during their senior year in high school. The information sought in the questionnaire was the frequency of the different conflict resolution techniques used during arguments or fights between the respondents' parents. Conflict resolution techniques ranged from discussing issues in a calm manner to actual physical hitting. Data on 385 families were reported, and Steinmetz and Straus (1974, p. 18) concluded that "as the level of verbal aggression increases, the level of physical aggression increases dramatically . . . That is, as verbal aggression increases, the level of physical aggression does not merely keep up — it increases even more rapidly."

The encounters described by Bach and Wyden (1968) involved certain limits, such as the "belt line", below which certain verbal blows are unfair, or the "Achilles heel", which is a weak spot or psychologically sensitive area. Bach and Wyden (1968) state that limits need to be set by partners before encounters begin. Goodwill on the part of the combatants is expected. However, the encounter process described by Bach and Wyden "scores points" for or rewards catharsis; specific attacks and counterattacks are limited to each partner's observable behavior — aggression focuses on the here and now. The ultimate objective of an intimate fight or encounter is, for Bach and Wyden, a joint win or loss for the two engaged in the encounter, not a win or loss for one participant or the other. Reduction of tension and anger, increased communication, and sharing of information between intimates are considered positive gains for the encounter participants.

The proponents of catharsis are partially correct in that getting issues "out on the table" and expressing feelings lead to better understanding and resolution of conflicts. However, the long term effects of verbal aggression may be devastating to the individual. Verbal aggression usually reduces the emotional state preceeding the aggression. This reduction in tension is rewarding and therefore strengthens the expectancy that aggressive activity reduces tension.

Finally, Rotter (1954) points out that catharsis was originally a therapeutic technique that allowed an individual to discuss his past history and experiences, problems, wishes, and fears. There is no dramatic recall of long repressed experiences or vivid reliving of previous emotional reactions. Catharsis is helpful to the degree to which an individual acquires new insights into his own behavior, and thereby reduces the behavior potential of present maladaptive behaviors.

Denson-Gerber (1973) described a residential program for drug abusing adolescents and adults which utilizes special encounter groups

94

to solve problems between residents. However, these encounter groups are structured in a much different manner than leveling encounter groups in that ventilation is only a method to allow issues to surface. As King (1978) notes, the major emphasis of these specialized encounter groups is to provide insight into the individual's present behavior and thereby reduce the behavior potential for present maladaptive behaviors and facilitate the learning of alternative nonviolent behaviors. The therapy group is well structured to prevent the encounters from becoming verbal aggression matches. Rotter (1954) suggests that structuring is of the utmost importance in therapy involving rational techniques, verbal communication, and insight. Structuring involves a discussion between the group members and the therapist about: 1) the purposes and goals of the group, and 2) the respective roles and responsibilities of the group members.

When an individual group member becomes disturbed or upset with the behaviors or attitudes of one or more of the group members, that individual requests the therapist to run an encounter between himself and another group member. The individual requesting the encounter is the sender, and the other is the receiver. The sender faces the receiver and explains which behavior or attitude of the receiver disturbed him. The sender, if very upset, is allowed verbal aggression in order to get issues out into the open. This feature helps those with problems of self expression present their issues and, after a period of time, weakens inhibitions to self expression. While the sender is presenting his problem, the group and the receiver must remain silent. When the sender completes his statement, the receiver must indicate whether the encounter is or is not valid. If the receiver agrees with the sender, the receiver will state that the encounter is valid (i.e. the receiver has really done something to cause the sender to be upset), and help the sender to resolve his feelings. Resolution of feelings can involve a simple apology and/or a plan of action on the part of the receiver which will correct such transgressions in the future. The receiver is not allowed to respond with verbal aggression. Without such a restriction, the encounter may lead to heightened aggression which is likely to produce retaliatory aggression rather than conflict resolution. He must be concerned with helping the sender resolve his feelings. The resolution of the sender's feelings by the receiver, therefore:

> (1) Positively reinforces the sender for presenting the issues troubling him and expressing his feelings.

(2) Provides a model of non-violent problem solving behavior (that is rewarded) to other group members.

(3) Provides the receiver with insight into his behavior and its effects on others.

(4) Strengthens inhibitions to verbal and physical violence and weakens inhibitions to self expression and discussing issues.

In instances where the encounter is invalid, the receiver does not agree that he has done anything to cause the sender to be upset. The therapist and group help the receiver provide the sender with insights into his behavior by stating the reasons why the encounter is invalid. The therapist can aid reticent members to participate by encouraging them to help senders and receivers with alternatives to the behavior being encountered.

The Roles of the Therapist and Group Members

In order to learn the norms, rules, and culture of any social group, the group members must learn to take the role of others or to put oneself in the place of those who are significant to oneself (Mead, 1934). The term "significant other" involves the relationship between the therapist and the group members. Rotter (1954) discusses these relationships in terms of "acceptance", "reassurance", and "transference". The terms acceptance and reassurance refer to the therapist's and group's attitude toward one another's problems. In other words, the therapist and group members need to accept an individual by indicating their interest and their desire to understand his problems as well as reassuring him that his problems are genuine and his attempts to do something about them are justified. Transference refers to the degree of involvement each individual feels towards the therapist and group and is a direct function of the amount of reinforcement that he either has received or has expectations of receiving from the therapist and group.

As acceptance, reassurance, and transference increase, the group members become significant others. Consequently, as members take on the role of others, they can make judgments about how others will respond to their behavior. This creates an expectancy of reinforcement for the individual's behavior. This process, which is a transaction between the individual and the group, is called socialization. It is through this process of socialization that group members learn the rules and norms of the encounter method.

Correlative to increasing involvement in the encounter process is increasing interpretation. Interpretation refers to what the therapist and group members do to help the individual see new relationships or to clarify relationships. Interpretation is usually minimal during the early stages of the group, but as the relationship between the group members and therapist strengthens, then the therapist more actively helps members see new relationships for their behavior. These relationships might deal with goals, motivations, or reinforcements, following behavior; with the effects of previous experiences on present behavior; or with present behaviors and future outcomes. Resistance to interpretation should be expected. An individual may be encountered many times for a certain behavior or attitude by group members and helpful interpretation will consequently have to be repeated and supported by these different encountering experiences before it is accepted.

In sum, the specialized encounter method described above presents a mini social structure offering an opportunity for decreasing the expectancy that positive reinforcement will follow violent behaviors and increasing the expectancy for positive reinforcement for self expression and rational methods of problem solving. By using social learning techniques within a setting that allows the individual to learn and practice these new behaviors, he becomes better able to obtain success in his new nonviolent role. Receiving positive reinforcement and help from others, obtaining success in a new role, and providing the individual with insights to enable him to define his self worth in a proper perspective; lead to increased individual self-esteem and thus reduce the need for verbal and physical aggression in interpersonal relations.

References

Bach, G.R., and Wyden, P. *The intimate enemy.* New York: Avon Books, William Morrow and Co., 1968.

Bandura, A. Behavioral modifications through modeling procedures. In L. Krasner and L.P. Ullman (Eds.), *Research in behavior modification.* New York: Holt, Rinehart and Winston, 1965, pp. 310-340.

Bandura, A. *Principles of behavior modification.* New York: Holt, Rinehart and Winston, 1969.

Bandura, A. Ross, D., and Ross, S.A. Transmission of aggression through imitation of aggressive models. *Journal of Abnormal and Social Psychology*, 1961, 63, 575-582.

Bandura, A., Ross, D., and Ross, S.A. Imitation of film-mediated aggressive models. *Journal of Abnormal and Social Psychology*, 1963, 66, 3-11.

Bandura, A., and Walters, R.H. *Social learning and personality development.* New York: Holt, Rinehart and Winston, 1963.

Battle, E.S., and Rotter, J.B. Children's feelings of personal control as related to social class and ethnic group. *Journal of Personality*, 1963, 31, 482-490.

Brannigan, G.G., and Tolor, A. Sex differences in adaptive styles. *Journal of Genetic Psychology*, 1971, 119, 143-149. (a)

Brannigan, G.G., and Tolor, A. Self-parental distance, control of reinforcement, and personal future time perspective. *Journal of Genetic Psychology*, 1971, 119, 151-157. (b)

Chance, J. Academic correlates and maternal antecedents of children's belief in external or internal control of reinforcements. In J.B. Rotter, J.E. Chance, and D.J. Phares (Eds.), *Applications of a social learning theory of personality.* New York: Holt, Rinehart and Winston, 1972, pp. 168-179.

Cloward, R.A., and Ohlin, L.E. The conflict subculture. In S. Palmer and A. Linsky (Eds.) *Rebellion and retreat: readings in the forms and processes of deviance.* Columbus, Ohio: Merrill Inc., 1972, pp. 153-158.

Cromwell, R.L. A social learning approach to mental retardation. In N.L. Ellis (Ed.), *Handbook of mental deficiency.* New York: McGraw-Hill, 1963, 41-91.

Davis, W.L., and Phares, E.J. Parental antecedents of internal-external control of reinforcement. *Psychological Reports*, 1969, 24, 427-436.

Densen-Gerber, J. *We mainline dreams.* New York: Doubleday, 1973.

Etzioni, A. Violence. In R.K. Merton and R. Nisbet (Eds.) *Contemporary social problems.* New York: Harcourt, Brace, Jovanovich, Inc., 1971, pp. 709-741.

Gelles, R.J. Child abuse as psychopathology, a sociological critique and reformulation. *American Journal of Orthopsychiatry*, 1973, 43, 611-621.

Gelles, R.J. *The violent home: a study of physical aggression between husbands and wives.* Beverly Hills, California: Sage Publications, 1974.

Gelles, R.J., and Straus, M.A. Determinants of violence in the family: toward a theoretical integration. In W.R. Burr, R. Hill, F.I. Nye and I.C. Reiss (Eds.) *Contemporary theories about the family.* New York: Free Press, 1978. press.

Gil, D.O. *Violence against children: physical child abuse in the United States.* Cambridge, Mass.: Harvard University Press, 1970.

Katkovsky, W., Crandall, V.C., and Good, S. Parental antecedents of children's beliefs in internal-external control of reinforcement in intellectual achievement situations. *Child Development*, 1967, 38, 765-776.

King, D.F. The control of violence: the Odyssey House method. Unpublished Master's Thesis. University of New Hampshire, Durham, New Hampshire, 1978.

Lefcourt, H.M., and Ladwig, G.W. The american negro: A problem of expectancies. *Journal of Personality and Social Psychology*, 1965, *1*, 377-380.

Leon, C.A. Unusual patterns of crime during LaViolencia in Columbia. *American Journal of Psychiatry*, 1969, *125*, 1564-1575.

MacDonald, A.P. Birth order and personality. *Journal of Consulting and Clinical Psychology*, 1971a, *36*, 171-176.

MacDonald, A.P. Internal-external locus of control: Parental antecedents. *Journal of Consulting and Clinical Psychology*, 1971b, *37*, 141-147.

Mead, G.H. *Mind, self, and society.* Chicago, Free Press, 1934.

Nowicki, S., and Duke, M.P. A locus of control scale for noncollege as well as college adults. *Journal of Personality Assessment*, 1974, *38*, 136-137.

Owens, D.M., and Straus, M. The social structure of violence in childhood and approval of violence as an adult. *Aggressive Behavior*, 1975, *1*, 193-211.

Palmer, R.D. Parental perception and perceived locus of control in psychopathology. *Journal of Personality*, 1971, *39*, 420-431.

Palmer, S., and Linsky, A. *Rebellion and retreat: readings in the forms and processes of deviance.* Columbus Ohio: Merrill Inc., 1972.

Phares, E.J. Expectancy changes in skill and chance situations. *Journal of Abnormal and Social Psychology*, 1957, *54*, 339-342.

Rotter, J. *Social learning and clinical psychology.* Englewood Cliffs, New Jersey: Prentice-Hall, 1954.

Rotter, J.B. Generalized expectancies for internal versus external control of reinforcement. *Psychological Monographs*, 1966, *80*, (1, Whole No. 609).

Singer, E. *Key concepts in psychotherapy.* New York: Random House, 1970.

Solomon, D. Houlihan, K.A., Busse, T.V., and Parelius, R.J. Parent behavior and child academic achievement, achievement striving and related personality characteristics. *Genetic Psychology Monogrphs*, 1971, *83*, 173-273.

Steele, B.F., and Pollack, C.B. A psychiatric study of parents who abuse infants and small children. In R.E. Helfer and C.H. Kempe (Eds.). *The battered child.* Chicago: University of Chicago Press, 1968, pp. 103-147.

Steinmetz, S.K. and Straus, M. *Violence in the family.* New York: Harper and Row, 1974.

Straus, M. Leveling, civility, and violence in the family. *Journal of Marriage and the Family*, 1974, *36*, 13-29.

Straus, M. Normative and behavioral aspects of violence between spouses: preliminary data on a nationally representative USA sample. Paper presented at the Symposium on Violence in Canadian Society, Toronto, 1977.

Tolor, A. An evaluation of the Maryland Parent Attitude Survey. *Journal of Psychology*, 1967, *67*, 69-74.

Tolor, A., and Jalowiec, J.E. Body boundary, parental attitudes, and internal-external expectancy. *Journal of Consulting and Clinical Psychology*, 1968, *32*, 206-209.

Usdin, G.C. Civil disobedience and urban revolt. *American Journal of Psychiatry*, 1969, *125*, 91-97.

Developmental Correlates of Child Abuse and Neglect: Perspectives for Interpretation

Martin Millison
School of Social Administration
Temple University
and
Mary Ann Heverly and Howard Margolis
Developmental Disabilities Center
Temple University
and
Joseph Fiorelli
Director of Education
Moss Rehabilitation Hospital
Philadelphia, Pa.

Controversy exists concerning the exact number of children who are abused and neglected each year. Light (1973), for example, has cited Kempe et al's estimate of 60,000 cases in 1972, Fontana's estimate of 1.5 million cases in 1973 and Gil's estimate of 3.5 to 4 million cases of physical abuse in 1965. Regardless of the exact number, it is clear, from both legal and moral standpoints, that abused and neglected children deserve the best treatment society is capable of providing. Precise knowledge of the short term and long term effects of abuse and neglect on the children involved is essential for accurately planning the services needed for reducing, eliminating or preventing problems which directly stem from abuse or neglect. This knowledge is also needed for dispelling possible misconceptions and stereotyped ideas about the nature of abused and neglected children; such misinterpretations may influence the treatment strategies proposed for helping these children, as well as the experiences to which the children are subjected.

Unfortunately, detailing the effects of abuse and neglect on the children involved is not as simple and straightforward as it may first appear. As with virtually every other issue concerning abuse and neglect, controversy, fueled by inconsistent and often contradictory research findings, characterizes the literature. Yet for systematic progress to occur, the research cannot summarily be dismissed as "inconclusive." Nor is it wise to depend solely upon impressionistic clinical judgments, no matter how astute the clinicians, or how broad their experiences may be. Progress, to a large extent, depends upon sophisticated, well controlled and accurately focused research. Thus, this chapter will have four major and equally important thrusts: (1) an examination and evaluation of the salient research concerned with the effects of abuse and neglect on children as they mature into adolescence and adulthood; (2) the identification of important research findings from other highly related areas (e.g., punishment) which may shed further light on the short term and long term effects of abuse and neglect; (3) a summary of the weaknesses in the existing literature; and, (4) recommendations for future research and programmatic strategies.

Before dealing directly with these topics, however, selected trends in the literature concerned with definition, incidence and precipitating factors will be summarized to provide a contextual perspective for viewing both the data on effects of abuse and neglect and the conclusions and implications drawn from the literature.

The Literature on Abuse and Neglect

Definition

Definitions of child abuse and neglect have been many and varied. Some definitions focus on intentional physical abuse, thus separating it from emotional abuse and neglect (cf. Gil, 1970; Parke & Collmer, 1975; Spinetta & Rigler, 1972; Steele, 1970). Also excluded from the usual definition are abuse and neglect occurring in the context of institutional settings (U.S. Dept. of HEW, 1977). Perhaps the most comprehensive definition is that of Kempe et al (cited in Light, 1973), which includes the following: non-accidental infliction of serious injury; suffering harm due to neglect, malnutrition or verbal abuse; lacking basic physical care; and, growing up under survival-threatening conditions. This definition includes both physical and emotional abuse and neglect. Gil's definition (1970), while referring specifically to *physical* abuse and neglect, stresses the intentional, non-accidental nature of abuse. Gil (1971) recognizes the problem of a definition based on intent, i.e., one must infer the motivation of the parent or caretaker at the time of the incident. In spite of the difficulties involved in evaluating intent, most definitions do use intention as a criterion. Parke and Collmer (1975) go a step beyond this basic criterion; they suggest varying the definition so that different community standards are taken into account. This implies that abuse and neglect must be defined in terms of deviations from the norms of a specific social class, subculture or ethnic group.

Incidence of Abuse and Neglect

As mentioned previously, controversy exists over the actual number of children abused and neglected annually. Light (1973) reported estimates ranging from 60,000 cases to 4 million cases. There are several reasons for such wide variation in the incidence estimates of child abuse and neglect. The first is the increasing number of state laws requiring designated professionals to report cases of suspected abuse and neglect. This, in combination with federally supported public awareness programs, may account for the marked increases in the number of cases reported each year. There is disagreement as to whether annual increments in reported cases reflect actual increases in abuse and neglect. Gil (1970) has argued that the increases are an artifact of recent legislation encouraging reporting and of heightened public awareness of the problem. A second factor is that states differ in their definitions of abuse and neglect, in whom they require to report cases of suspected abuse and neglect, and in the degree of compliance and enforcement achieved (U.S. Dept. of HEW, 1977).

In a nationwide survey of child abuse, Gil (1970, 1971) obtained and analyzed data on cases reported in 1967-68. He reported that abused and neglected preadolescent children were more likely to be male than female. Among teenagers, however, girls were more likely than boys to be abused and neglected. Although many authors have suggested that children under age 3 are the most likely targets of abuse, Gil stressed that almost half of his reported cases involved children over the age of 6 years. Many of the families of abused and neglected children were characterized by low socio-economic status. Roughly one-third of the families received public assistance, and in 29% of the reported cases, the natural father was absent from the home.

Gil's data (1970) has served to renew the controversy over socio-economic status and its relation to abuse and neglect. Gil's position has been that poverty and other environmental stresses attendant to low socio-economic status predispose poor families to child abuse and that abuse is actually more frequent among these families. Others have pointed out (e.g., Steele, 1970) that environmental stresses are experienced by middle income families as well, and therefore abuse may occur just as frequently among middle income families. The issue cannot be resolved at this time, since the rate of abuse among middle income families has not been documented.

Etiology – Environmental Factors

As might be expected, discrepancies also exist in the literature concerning the precursors and correlates of abuse and neglect. The approach with the broadest scope evaluates the etiology of abuse and neglect in terms of social factors affecting the family unit. As noted earlier, Gil (1970, 1971) has concluded that poverty-stricken environments precipitate child abuse and neglect. He has cited several aspects of family life in such environments which contribute to abuse and neglect: cultural approval of physical punishment, lack of inhibitions in expressing aggression, the presence of environmental stresses, and lack of opportunities to have occasional relief from the tasks of child-rearing. These precursors of abuse and neglect may characterize only a small proportion of lower income families. Erlanger (1974) has pointed out that it is not the lower income family in general, but rather the segment that is *severely* impoverished, in which corporal punishment and physical abuse are most predominant.

Light (1973), after re-analyzing Gil's data, found that unemployment, large families and social isolation were related to abuse and neglect. Garbarino (1976), using more recent data on the incidence of abuse and neglect, reported that lack of environmental support systems placed parents at risk for abuse. These findings are congruent with the notion that abuse and neglect will be more common among disadvantaged families. Yet the possibility remains that abuse and neglect occur among middle income families, but do not get reported through the established channels. Middle income parents are more likely to have access to private physicians, who may seek to deal with suspected cases of abuse through means other than the legal reporting system, e.g., by referring patients for therapeutic intervention. Abuse in middle income families may be more difficult to detect, partly because of the image abuse and neglect have achieved as lower income phenomena and also because abuse is more difficult to detect in neighborhoods where single family dwellings are the rule (Parke & Collmer, 1975).

There is no consensus that low socio-economic status is a correlate of child abuse and neglect. Galdston (1965), from his observations of incidents of child abuse and neglect occurring in middle income families, has concluded that social class is not the crucial variable. It has also been argued that child abuse and neglect are tied to the violent nature of our society in general and to our tendency to condone physical punishment. Indeed, cross-cultural data support the notion that level of societal violence is associated with the rate of child abuse (Parke & Collmer, 1975). The relation of social class to child abuse and neglect remains a clouded issue, its resolution awaiting valid data on the incidence of abuse and neglect within the population as a whole.

Etiology — Individual Differences

Abusing and Neglectful Parents – The precursors of child abuse and neglect can be conceptualized as individual difference variables, rather than as global socio-economic variables. The individual difference approach examines specific characteristics of children and parents, as well as the quality of interactions among abused and neglected children and their parents. This section will review the literature as it pertains to individual characteristics linked to abuse and neglect and to variables which affect the quality of interaction within the family unit.

The most frequently encountered individual characteristic cited in the literature concerns the history of abusive parents; they tend to have been abused themselves as children and/or have lacked maternal affection (Parke & Collmer, 1975). Viewed from the perspective of social learning theory and the data on children's tendencies to exhibit behaviors modeled by others (cf. Bandura & Walters, 1963), this would not appear to be a surprising finding. Unfortunately, data on the proportion of *non-*

abusive parents who have a history of abuse or maternal deprivation are lacking. Reports that abusive and neglecful parents were abused or deprived as children (e.g., Gil, 1970; Steele, 1970) are difficult to interpret without knowledge of the proportion of previously abused and deprived individuals among parents who do not abuse or neglect their children. As far as the intellectual capability of abusive parents is concerned, there is no clear relation between parental IQ and parental tendency toward abuse. Steele and Pollock (1968) reported a wide range of IQ levels among abusive parents, with the majority of these parents falling into the average range.

The search for personality characteristics that might distinguish abusive and neglectful parents has suggested that no single typology is associated with abuse and neglect (Steele, 1970). Individual characteristics that have been noted among abusive and neglectful parents include immaturity, dependence, low self-esteem, social isolation, lack of basic trust, and poor interpersonal relations. These parents generally condone physical punishment and are likely to report dissatisfaction with their family life (Melnick & Hurley, 1969; Steele, 1970). A recurrent finding has been the tendency of abusive parents to exhibit a reversal of roles in their relationships to their children. In the typical role-reversal situation, the parent expects his or her needs to be fulfilled by the child, i.e., the parent expects to be taken care of by the child and is emotionally dependent on the child. This phenomenon is reflected in the excessive maturity demands placed upon the child (Steele, 1970); for example, an eighteen-month-old child may be penalized for not speaking with the maturity of a five-year-old. As Spinetta and Rigler put it, child abusers "implement culturally accepted norms for raising children with an exaggerated intensity and at an inappropriately early age" (1972, p. 299).

Steele (1970) has reported that negative attitudes, such as expectations of trouble and dissatisfaction, are often expressed by abusive parents before the birth of a child. Lynch (1976) found a number of prenatal and perinatal variables to be related to later abuse: mothers of abused children experienced abnormal pregnancy, labor and delivery; they were frequently separated from their children during the neonatal state and during the first six months after childbirth; and, both mother and infant were likely to be ill during the year following childbirth. Martin (1976b) was unable to document that early mother-child separation was more frequent in cases of abuse; however, he reported that preliminary data show maternal responses to the neonate to predict the later quality of the mother-infant relationship.

Light (1973) has cited a study separating abuse from neglect which found that among families in which neglect has been reported, mothers tended to be quite young at the birth of their first child. These families tended to be large in size and the neglected children were characterized by low birth weights. Polansky, Borgman & De Saix (1972) have described the mothers of neglected children as emotionally immature; in fact, Polansky et al identified two emotionally immature groups: apathetic neglectful women, who projected an air of futility, and impulsive neglectful women, who periodically engaged in behavior destructive toward themselves and their children.

These findings suggest that the potential for child abuse and neglect can be generated at a number of points during the developmental process, from the parents' childhood through the prenatal and perinatal stages of a particular child's development to the specific circumstances triggering abuse or neglect. These triggering circumstances may be socio-economic, as described earlier (e.g., extreme and continuous financial inability to procure life's necessities) or may arise from specific characteristics of a particular child (e.g., bed wetting). As will be discussed in the following section, the characteristics of children which predispose parents to abuse and neglect are difficult to isolate, since they operate in a complex manner which is quite dependent upon the parents' perceptions and expectations.

Abused and Neglected Children – Some researchers have tried to determine why a particular child within a family is singled out as a target for abuse. Attributes that have been cited include: prematurity, retardation, physical handicaps, temperament, and parental perceptions that the child is different or "difficult" (Friedrich & Boriskin, 1976).

Dion (1974) conducted a controlled laboratory experiment in which adults of both sexes had the opportunity to punish task behaviors of children differing in sex and in degree of physical attractiveness. Women tended to be more lenient with attractive boys than with either attractive girls or unattractive boys. Among men sex and attractiveness of the child did not affect the degree of leniency. While Dion's study did not directly address the issue of child abuse and neglect, her report of an interaction effect suggests that parent-child relationships within abusive and neglectful families may be extremely complex.

Premature or low birth weight infants have been reported to be at risk for abuse even when socio-economic status is controlled (Klein & Stern, 1971). A number of explanations have been offered to account for this relationship. From an ethological point of view, the premature baby lacks the physical features thought to elicit and support maternal behavior. In addition, premature infants are more likely to have difficulty feeding, to suffer from developmental lags, to be irritable, and to be irregular or unpredictable in bodily functioning (Parke & Collmer, 1975). These problems increase the concern and stress experienced by the parents. Also contributing to the breakdown of the child-parent bond is the traditional practice of separating mothers from their prematurely born infants. Klaus and Kennell (1976) have argued that neonatal separation disrupts the process of emotional bonding between mother and infant, a process which they consider to be critical for the child's later development. Unfortunately, most research concerning early parental bonding has focused on mother-child bonding. An examination of father-child bonding and the effects on the father of numerous protracted experiences with his newborn may provide insight as to whether such experiences should be systematically encouraged by society.

It is not clear whether physical and psychological defects exhibited by the child contribute to abuse and neglect. According to Green, Gaines and Sandgrund (1974), a child with a defect may predispose a parent to abuse and neglect, but the trait in question may be perceived as a defect only by the parent. For example, a child of the "wrong" sex or with the "wrong" temperament is likely to be abused, according to Steele (1970). These are not defects in the sense that they are traits objectively identifiable as deviant. Martin (1976b) has come to a similar conclusion. He found that the obviously different baby does not have a higher risk of abuse, but a child who does not meet parental expectations is likely to elicit abuse or neglect. As noted previously, it is the potential abuser who is likely to have unrealistic expectations of the child. Moreover, unrealistic expectations may be generated at different stages in the child's development. For example, a mother who has established a warm and loving relationship with her infant may be threatened by the increasing autonomy and independence exhibited when the child becomes a toddler (Martin, 1976b).

Research on individual differences among infants has suggested that certain patterns of temperament may pose a threat to the parent-child relationship. For example, Thomas, Chess & Birch (1968) reported that "difficult" infants and young children (children who show irregularity in biological functioning, withdrawal from novel stimuli, slowness in adapting to new stimuli, predominantly negative moods and predominantly intense reactions) create more stress for most parents than do infants and children with "easy" temperaments (i.e., regularity in biological functioning, approach to new stimuli, quickness to adapt to new stimuli, predominantly positive moods and predominantly mild reactions.) Moreover, parents confronted with a difficult child may interpret the child's behavior as an unfavorable reflection on the parent's competence. The frustration resulting from this kind of parent-child interaction is thought to endanger the child's later development, since a disproportionately high incidence of behavior problems has been reported for "difficult" children (Thomas, Chess & Birch, 1968).

Thomas and Chess (1977) have argued that temperamental patterns are fairly stable over time. Yet a difficult temperament does not guarantee later problems for the child; professional guidance to aid parents in understanding temperament and in dealing with the "difficult" child can reduce parent-child conflicts and improve the quality of the parent-child relationship. A logical hypothesis evolving from this research is that difficult children may be at risk for abuse. A definitive study of this has yet to be conducted, but the degree of risk is likely to depend on parental perceptions of the child's temperament. Thomas and Chess (1977) have noted that difficult children whose parents approved their behavior (as in the case of a father who delighted in his difficult son's behavior), were less likely to develop behavioral disorders.

Consequences of Abuse and Neglect — Although there has been a great deal of speculation about the long term effects of abuse and neglect, few empirical studies have examined the status of abused and neglected children as they mature into adolescence and adulthood. The literature in this area tends to be retrospective and correlational; as a result, important information is available on the variables correlated with abuse and neglect, but except in cases of immediate and observable physical difficulties traceable to specific incidents of abuse and neglect (e.g., a child was was burned with scalding water), it has not been determined whether the characteristics displayed by these children developed before or after the onset of abuse or neglect. Prospective studies are extremely rare and the generalizability of their results is limited by nonexistent, inadequate or biased control groups. It is therefore advisable to view the following discussion as a summary of variables associated with abuse and neglect; their status as direct effects of abuse and neglect has not been demonstrated.

The most obvious consequence of abuse and neglect is bodily injury which, on occasion, can be serious enough to lead to death. The literature on maternal deprivation suggests that these results are not restricted to *physical* abuse and neglect. Extreme emotional neglect (i.e., lack of social and emotional interaction with caretakers) has been associated with illness and death, even when adequate physical care and nutrition have been provided (Rutter, 1972; Spitz, 1965). Children who have been abused or neglected have displayed developmental lags and/or abnormalities in virtually every area of functioning: physical, intellectual, emotional and social (Soeffing, 1975). Physiological deficits have included a variety of neurological deficits among abused children (Sarles, 1976) and neurological dysfunctioning among maternally deprived children (Martin, 1976a).

Deficits in cognitive abilities have been reported by a number of researchers. Martin and Rodeheffer (1976) reported that abused children as a group performed below average on IQ tests. Child neglect has also been linked to below average intellectual functioning (Polansky et al, 1972; Rutter, 1972). In addition, abused and neglected children have been reported to have a higher than average rate of learning disabilities and other educational handicaps (Martin, 1976a). Exceptions to this general trend were noted in the Martin and Rodeheffer (1976) study, where a small group of abused children with high I.Q.s was identified. Further analysis indicated that these children, although victims of physical abuse, had not suffered from parental neglect. The parents of these children tended to value "smartness," and the authors point to the children's ability to learn, in spite of physical abuse, as an indication of how abused children can adapt to demands specific to their environment.

Blager and Martin (1976) have reported delays in language development among abused preschoolers. They suggest that these delays could be due to lack of appropriate stimulation in the home or to a fear of speaking. The latter explanation would appear to be applicable to the small group of children in Blager and Martin's sample who understood language but failed to use speech to communicate with others.

Martin and Beezely (1976) were unable to identify a single typical personality profile of the abused and neglected child. A variety of psychiatric and behavioral symptoms were reported (e.g., compulsivity, pseudo-mature behavior, low self-esteem), but children differed in both the type and severity of symptoms. An interesting observation was made by Martin and Breezely — abused and neglected children who perceived their present residence as stable tended to have few symptoms of maladjustment.

Polansky, Borgman and De Saix (1972) in one of the few works that has focused specifically on child neglect, reported that children of apathetic, neglectful mothers tended to be withdrawn and unsociable. Children of impulsive neglectful mothers, however, tended to exhibit hostile and aggressive behavior. The similarities in behavior of mothers and their children is an important finding and points up the need for careful identification of different types of abuse and neglect.

The key articles on the consequences of child abuse and neglect are those which have undertaken to follow-up children who have been identified as abused and neglected. An early study which accomplished this was conducted by Elmer and Gregg (1967). Of 50 children initially identified as physically abused or neglected, 20 were located one to ten years later and were evaluated in terms of their physical, intellectual, and emotional functioning. Of the children who could not be located at follow-up, 13 either were deceased or had been institutionalized. Only 2 of 20 children evaluated at follow-up were functioning normally; half were mentally retarded and 8 were diagnosed as emotionally disturbed. The study lacked a control group and could not demonstrate that the developmental problems identified were directly linked to abuse; nevertheless, it is illustrative of the kinds of disabilities frequently reported to be correlates of abuse and neglect.

More recently, Elmer (1977) reported a longitudinal study employing control groups. A group of 17 infants who had been physically abused were followed-up one year and eight years after the reported abuse. Also studied longitudinally was a control group of infants who had been injured in accidents. A third, untraumatized group of infants was included to control for the effects of injury and hospitalization. The three groups were matched on age, race, sex and social class. Elmer hypothesized that the abused children would show deficits in height and weight, health, intelligence, language development and self-concept. She further hypothesized that the abused group would have a higher incidence of impulsivity and aggression and have a greater number of illnesses and accidents. At the one year follow-up, the abused children exhibited lags in physical development and had significantly more health problems. No other group differences were observed. At the time of the eight year follow-up, none of the hypothesized differences were present. However, Elmer pointed out that all of the children studied came from disadvantaged families, families in which the home environment was described as "chaotic and disorganized" (1977, p. 278). Many of the parents used

111

drugs and alcohol, and violent behavior was an everyday phenomenon. Furthermore, the proportion of children in *all* groups with language problems and poor school performance was extremely high. Elmer concluded that child abuse per se may be less critical as a determinant of maladjustment than socioeconomic status. Elmer also stated that since violence was a common feature in the lives of these children, it is possible that the control children had also been abused, but that the abuse had not been detected. Another explanation, not cited by Elmer, is that the abused children available for study at the eight year follow-up represented a select group of "survivors." This possibility gains plausibility from the previously cited Elmer and Gregg (1967) study, in which a quarter of the abused children were either deceased or institutionalized at the time of the follow-up. In spite of the varying interpretations permitted by Elmer's study, the design and procedures represent a vast improvement over earlier works focusing on child abuse and neglect.

Another study which used a longitudinal design was conducted by Morse, Sahler and Friedman (1970). Children who had been reported as abused or neglected were evaluated two to four and one half years after the reported incident. Of the children for whom height and weight information was available at follow-up, approximately half were in the lowest tenth percentile. Fewer than a third of the children were within the normal range of intellectual and emotional functioning. Social maladjustment was frequently observed and the children with the most adequate functioning in this area tended to be those who had been removed from their families.

Although Morse et al (1970) did not include a non-abused control group in their design, they did separate the abused children into two groups, based on the adequacy of social and emotional functioning at follow-up. These groups did not differ significantly in the number of reported abuse incidents, in developmental status at follow-up, in amount of agency involvement, nor in parental perceptions of the effectiveness of agency involvement, parental emotional adjustment, parents' marital status, or parental mental adjustment. Only one variable differentiated the two groups: abused and neglected children who were socially and emotionally well-adjusted at follow-up tended to have mothers who *perceived* the mother-child relationship as good. This finding is somewhat surprising, especially in view of Morse et al's report that their own evaluations of the mother-child relationships in these families were generally unfavorable.

112

Social learning theory, as well as the observation that many abusive parents were abused themselves as children, has led to speculation that aggressive and violent behavior may be a long term effect of abuse. Violent behavior has been observed to precipitate further violence and to be handed down from generation to generation (e.g., Oliver & Taylor, 1971; Silver, Dublin & Lourie, 1969).

Increased incidence of child abuse, however, may be only one concept of a general pattern of intra-familial violence. Silver, Dublin, and Lourie (1969) examined the records of a group of abusing families and reported that over half of the records indicated that abusive behavior was a pervasive part of familial interaction between parents, as well as between the parents and siblings of abused children. It has also been reported that both abusive and neglectful families, when compared with a control group of "normal" families, tend to have less communication among family members; furthermore, the interaction that does take place in abusive and neglectful families tends to be negative (U.S. Dept. of HEW, 1977).

Physical punishment has been criticized as an ineffective disciplinary technique; the behavior being punished may not be suppressed at all, or it may be diminished only temporarily (Gardner, 1974). Furthermore, physical punishment may lead to undesirable side effects such as feelings of anger and anxiety; heightened anxiety, in turn, has been linked to outbursts of aggressive behavior (Feshbach, 1973). A cycle of violence is thus created. This linkage of punishment to later aggressive behavior has prompted speculation concerning the relationship of child abuse to juvenile delinquency and adult criminality (Curtis, 1963). Empirical studies bearing on this issue have been surprisingly rare. In one study, juvenile delinquents recalled high levels of violence in their childhood (U.S. Dept. of HEW, 1977). Similarly, Welsh (1976) reported that severe corporal punishment was the only variable consistently present in the records of 1800 delinquents.

The use of control groups is infrequently encountered in this area of research. However, Button (1973) did look at both delinquent and nondelinquent males and found abuse to be more common in the delinquent group. Sendi and Blomgren (1975) studied a group of adolescents who had committed murder, a group of adolescents who had threatened or attempted to commit murder, and a group of hospitalized controls. Violence was reported to be a strong element in the environments of those who had murdered. Adolescents who had committed murder, as well as those who had threatened or attempted murder, were more likely than the controls to have been subjected to abuse and neglect. Brutal treatment has also been reported to be a recurrent phenomenon in the histories of adult criminals. For example, Duncan, Frazier, Militin, Johnson and Barron (1958) reported that parental violence had been a common experience among adults accused of first-degree murder.

In contrast to the evidence supporting a connection between abuse and later delinquency, violence and criminal behavior, are reports that abused children are passive and submissive. This childhood passivity may reflect anxiety and repressed hostility which erupts into violence only after puberty (U.S. Dept. of HEW, 1977). The conflicting pictures presented, vis-a-vis the aggressive behavioral patterns of adolescents and adults recalling a violent past and the passive behavioral patterns of recently abused children may be due to: (1) the retrospective nature of the investigations supporting the "aggressive" hypothesis; (2) failure of the researchers to distinguish abuse from neglect; or (3) the influence of variables yet to be identified and controlled.

As noted previously, Polansky et al (1972), who studied neglected children from rural Appalachia, reported different behaviors among neglected children, depending on whether the children's mothers exhibited apathetic or impulsive behavior. In general, the children displayed behavioral patterns similar to those of their mothers. While social learning theory would reasonably lead one to predict that as adults, the children would still be displaying behaviors modeled on those of their mothers, there is little empirical data on the *adult* behavior of neglected children. In short, it is not yet clear whether abuse and neglect produce violence or passivity in adulthood. It may be that abuse or neglect should be considered as part of the child's life experience, with different outcomes for different children. As Ross (1974) has suggested, one's life experiences may interact with genetic and constitutional attributes, physiological status, and environmental conditions to produce behavior, which is the result of the interaction of these factors. Expecting abuse or neglect to have the same effect on all children and expecting all victimized children to behave in a similar manner may be to underestimate the complexity of factors influencing behavior and development. It is reasonable to expect that different types of abuse of neglect, occurring for differing periods of time and at different points in a child's life, and interacting with a different set of genetic, constitutional, familial and cultural factors, would produce different behavior patterns.

Related Areas of Research

In the context of a specific research study it is often convenient to dichotomize children into abused and non-abused groups and then try to determine how those two groups differ. This approach facilitates our thinking of abuse and neglect as extreme aberrations of parental behavior and as a topic of little import for the "average" parent. This viewpoint, however, may be an invalid conceptualization of the importance of abuse and neglect literature. If abuse and neglect are re-evaluated as extreme points on a continuum representing the quality of the parent-child relationship, we can take the tentative, inconclusive data in this area and integrate it with larger, better-established bodies of literature.

Child abuse, for example, may be viewed as an extreme example of punishment. There is a large body of literature dealing with the effects of punishment, which indicates that severe punishment, as well as frequently occurring mild punishment, can adversely affect the child's emotional and social development (cf. Gardner, 1974). In reviewing the adverse effects of punishment, Blackham and Silberman concluded that punishment "may lead to: (a) generalized inhibition of behavior similar to the punished response; (b) avoidance of the punisher and others similar to the punishing agent; (c) undesirable behavior (secrecy, lying) to escape and avoid the punishment; (d) reduction of the punisher's ability to positively reinforce desirable behavior; and (e) modeling of the punisher's aggressive behavior, thereby increasing aggressive behavior in the punished" (1975, p. 83). An example of points (a) and (b) might take the following form: three-year-old Judy is yelled at by her mother anytime the child apears to be heading in the direction of a male adult; if Judy speaks to a male adolescent or adult, she is slapped for "bothering" him. Judy might well grow up as a social isolate, staying in her apartment as much as possible and avoiding social situations. Judy may continue to act in the same way years after her mother is no longer physically present. It should be noted that punishment need not refer to forceful, physical action. Judy's mother need not have slapped her for the same result to occur; continual and intense screaming could have a similar effect. Thus, punishment can be verbal or psychological, just as abuse may be verbal or psychological and need not take the form of corporal punishment to have a devastating effect on the child.

As noted previously, families headed by abusive and neglectful parents tend to have less communication than other families (U.S. Dept. of HEW, 1977). Reserach has indicated that parents who make greater use of verbal communications to direct, guide, explain, and teach tend to have children with higher levels of cognitive skills than do non-communicative parents (cf. Hess & Shipman, 1965). The similarities between the abuse and neglect literature and the literature of verbal interaction between parents and children thus lends credence to studies which have reported cognitive deficits among abused and neglected children.

Child neglect, on the other hand, can be viewed as an extreme form of maternal deprivation. While we lack a large body of literature on the effects of neglect, the work on maternal deprivation has consistently linked deprivation to delays and anomalies in physical, cognitive, emotional, and social development (cf. Rutter, 1972; Spitz, 1965). Supporting the correlational research on human infants is Harlow's extensive and well controlled research on maternal deprivation in infant monkeys. Harlow (1974) has observed childhood depression among deprived monkeys, as well as abusive and neglectful parental behavior among monkeys who had experienced maternal deprivation as infants. To the extent that maternal deprivation represents a form of neglect, the data on effects of child neglect receive support from the deprivation literature.

Although we have few adequately designed studies linking child abuse to aggressive, violent behavior in adolescence and adulthood, the data which do exist gain credibility from a large body of data on imitation and modeling. Researchers may not agree on the process involved, but it is clear that models serve as powerful influences on learning (Bandura and Walters, 1963). Furthermore, inconsistent discipline — whether it be inconsistency over time, inconsistency between parental words and deeds, or inconsistency between parents — has also been indicated as harmful to the child's development and to the parent-child relationship (Becker, 1964).

What emerges from a perusal of other areas of research is a set of data which complements and supports the data on child abuse and neglect. These other areas of research not only give us more confidence in the existing child abuse and neglect literature, but they also serve to remind us that child abuse and neglect are examples, however extreme, of shortcomings all parents exhibit at one time or another. Martin has gone so far as to argue that ". . . all adults have some potential to abuse their children" (1976b, p. 38). Viewed from this perspective, child abuse and neglect become issues of relevance to all parents and to all individuals who are concerned about the quality of parent-child relationships.

Weaknesses of the Literature

The body of research concerning child abuse and neglect tends to suffer from certain general weaknesses. The most serious of these are: inconsistency in definitions of child abuse and neglect, use of ex post facto and retrospective methods, selection of narrowly defined samples, lack of hypothesis-testing procedures, reliance on either case history data or group data with extremely small samples, and lack of control groups (Gelles, 1974; Spinetta and Rigler, 1972; U.S. Dept. of HEW, 1977).

Inconsistencies in the definition of child abuse and neglect make it difficult to compare studies. Some research (e.g., Green et al., 1974) focuses on children who have been physically abused, thereby distinguishing these children from children who have been neglected. On the other hand, most research which utilizes data extracted from state agency files aggregates abuse and neglect cases, since most state reporting laws do not distinguish abuse & neglect (U.S. Dept. of HEW, 1977). Although abused, non-neglected children may be difficult to locate, Martin and Rodeheffer (1976) found a small group of such children in their sample of abused children. Distinguishing this group from others is important, since Martin and Rodeheffer suggested that the effects of abuse may differ for this select group of abuse victims (see pages 102-114).

Most research on child abuse and neglect tends to be ex post facto (Gelles, 1974; Spinetta and Rigler, 1972); measures are obtained after the abuse or neglect has occurred and the researcher has no control over the variables being studied. Research of this nature cannot untangle causal relationships. For example, suppose that abused children are found to have a higher than average incidence of hyperactivity. Several explanations are possible: (1) abuse results in children becoming hyperactive, regardless of their initial levels of activity; (2) children who are hyperactive are more likely to become targets of abuse; or (3) a third factor may be responsible for the observed relationship between abuse and hyperactivity. One example of a third factor would be lack of space — perhaps children living in densely populated quarters are more likely to be diagnosed as hyperactive because their activity interferes with other family members; perhaps lack of space also increases parental stress to the point that abuse is likely to occur. The number of such third factor explanations is legion; experimental research, which controls for these extraneous variables, is required to evaluate such alternative explanations.

Ex post facto research can vary greatly in strength of design. One of the weaker designs in the child abuse and neglect literature involves the use of retrospective recall. Some researchers, for example, have asked juvenile delinquents to recall events from childhood. It has been reported that delinquents recalled high levels of violence during childhood (U.S. Dept. of HEW, 1977). Yet memory of past events is a notoriously poor basis for judging what actually occurred in the past, since memory tends to be selective. A more defensible retrospective procedure is to seek historical data for which records already exist. For example, if a researcher wished to study whether the population of abused and neglected children has a higher than average proportion of prematurely born individuals, birth records could be examined without the danger of the data having been changed or distorted over time.

In general, prospective studies in which the same children are followed up at various developmental stages, are preferred to retrospective investigations. However, this method can also present a difficulty which may affect the nature of the final data. Often a substantial proportion of children identified as abused and neglected cannot be located for the follow-up evaluations. Unless the researcher can demonstrate that the "lost" cases do not differ systematically from those children reached for follow-up, the results of the study cannot be generalized to the children represented by the "lost" group. Elmer and Gregg (1967), for example, began their study by identifying 50 abused children, but only 20 were available for follow-up. The researchers noted that those parents who refused to allow their children to participate in the follow-up represented a slightly higher socio-economic class than the parents whose children participated in the follow-up. The results of Elmer and Gregg's investigation may be limited to abused children from the socio-economic levels represented by children participating in the follow-up and cannot be generalized to those who were "lost." The problem of losing subjects over time is generally referred to as subject "mortality" (Campbell & Stanley, 1963). This term is a chilling reminder of another possible reason for not locating subjects at follow-up – the missing children may differ from the others in having suffered more severe physical abuse and neglect.

An additional problem of research design in the child abuse and neglect literature has to do with the characteristics of the sample studied

(Gelles, 1974; Spinetta & Rigler, 1972). Results of any study can be generalized only to persons similar to those sampled in the study. Most child abuse and neglect research has focused on persons of lower socio-economic background, perhaps because abuse and neglect are more often reported for this sector of the population. (As noted earlier, there is some controversy over whether abuse actually occurs more often among lower income families or is just reported more often among these families.) As a result, few data have been gathered on abused children from middle income families and our current base of knowledge may describe an unrepresentative sample of the population of abused children.

The literature focusing directly on child abuse and neglect has also been hampered by the failure to use specific hypothesis-testing pro-cedures (Gelles, 1974; Spinetta & Rigler, 1972). Most studies have been exploratory, proceeding on an ill-defined basis of intuitive ideas about what variables might be relevant. Exploratory research can be useful and appropriate, especially when an area of study is in its infancy (Kerlinger, 1973). However, the abuse and neglect literature has developed enough leads as to which variables appear to be promising, and how they seem to be related to abuse and neglect, to justify turning now to hypothesis-testing research. Elmer's (1977) study is one of the very few in which specific hypotheses to be tested were clearly outlined. Elmer has set a precedent which should be followed by other researchers.

There are several weaknesses in the design of child abuse research which lead to inadequate statistical analyses of the data or even to a complete lack of data which can be subjected to statistical analysis. All too often, authors base conclusions on case history reports. Case history data can be valuable for certain purposes; for example, by studying a single case a rich and detailed account of behavior can be obtained. However, information on a single case of abuse does not permit one to generalize to the population òf abused children. Recently, researchers have been shifting to the question of what distinguishes *most* abused children from non-abused children. Group data, rather than anecdotal case history reports, are required to answer such questions.

A limitation of those studies which do use group data is that the samples tend to be rather small. Small samples present serious problems as far as statistical power is concerned (Keppel, 1973). For example, if a researcher is comparing a group of ten abused children with a group of ten non-abused children, differences between the two groups on any given variable will be detected by statistical analysis only if the differences are relatively large. Larger samples (e.g., 100 abused children and 100 non-abused children), on the other hand, would enable the researcher to detect smaller differences between the two groups. This is an important consideration in interpreting the research on child abuse; it is possible that studies reporting no significant differences, such as Elmer's (1977) eight-year follow-up comparing abused and non-abused children, did not use samples large enough to detect small but statistically significant differences between the groups. Since Elmer reported that her non-abused children tended to come from environments similar to those of the abused children, it is highly likely that any differences between abused and non-abused children would be small and that the sample size of 17 children per group was not large enough to detect the differences.

A major weakness related to the design and analysis of many of the child abuse and neglect investigations is the lack of appropriate control groups (U.S. Dept. of HEW, 1977). Without such groups, one cannot interpret results with a high degree of confidence. For example, many studies of abused children report a higher than normal incidence of intellectual deficits; other investigations report that children who have been abused tend to come from families of relatively low socio-economic status. A substantial body of literature suggests that children from the lower socio-economic classes are at a significant disadvantage on tests of intellectual skills (cf. Ross, 1974). Without appropriate control groups, it cannot be determined whether the lower levels of cognitive ability are due to abuse or are merely a correlate of socio-economic status. When abused and non-abused groups of children are matched on all known relevant variables (e.g., age, race, family composition, and socio-economic status), the problem of uncontrolled variables is reduced considerably.

A relatively high proportion of abuse and neglect studies are flawed by one or more of the limitations cited in the preceding paragraphs. Even so, the current body of literature provides initial clues as to which avenues of investigation are apt to be most productive and revealing. The following section outlines some of the methodological approaches researchers might appropriately employ to evaluate the hypotheses developed in the "first generation" research previously discussed in this chapter.

Recommendations for Future Research

Given the weaknesses observed in the current literature, future research should: (1) aim to develop distinct definitions of abuse and neglect, so that abuse may be clearly distinguished from neglect and so that different patterns of abuse and neglect may be identified; (2) use of prospective research designs with larger sample sizes; (3) draw samples from a more representative and more clearly specified population of abused and neglected children; and (4) select comparison groups that will control for specified variables. Achieving these goals may require far more complex and comprehensive research designs than is currently the norm. The utilization of multiple comparison groups is one example of a complex research design that may be needed if contaminating variables are to be successfully controlled.

Another illustration of the need for more comprehensive research designs than are typically found in the literature has to do with the problem of unrepresentative samples of abused and neglected children. Such samples limit the generalizability of the data obtained. For example, reports of child abuse and neglect gathered from inner city hospitals or clinic populations are likely to provide unrepresentative samples of abused or neglected children. In the typical urban setting, the number and variety of sources of medical care make it difficult for researchers to obtain representative samples. The cost of sampling abuse and neglect cases in all or most urban facilities would be prohibitive, and abuse and neglect cases are usually more accessible in inner city clinics, which tend to serve a disproportionate number of lower class families. One possible means of circumventing this problem is to mount a study in a rural area where only one or two facilities are available for medical care.

Implementing more tightly controlled and more comprehensive studies is becoming more feasible than ever, since federal funding for research concerning child abuse and neglect is now becoming available through the National Center on Child Abuse and Neglect (U.S. Dept. of HEW, 1977). An additional factor that may aid researchers is the recent increased national effort to educate the public about child abuse and neglect. These national campaigns, in conjunction with state laws mandating specified professionals to report cases of suspected abuse, may change the social climate in such a way that both professionals and private citizens will be more comfortable about reporting suspected cases of abuse and neglect. As individuals become less hesitant to report child abuse and neglect, researchers may gain easier access to previously hidden segments of the population of abused and neglected childen. Although most research questions concerning abuse and neglect can be answered ethically only by some form of ex post facto research, approximations to experimental research design are not impossible. Garbarino (1976), for example, has suggested matching groups of counties on relevant socio-political variables and then introducing experimental treatment or prevention programs into one group of counties, while utilizing the remaining counties as a control group. This kind of design would certainly be superior to most of the current methods of evaluating programmatic strategies (Parke & Collmer, 1975).

As Gelles (1974) has noted, research in this area could also profit from multivariate techniques of data analysis. Garbarino (1976) has already set an example by using multiple regression analysis to identify demographic variables related to child abuse. The advantage of such analyses has been recognized by researchers in other areas of human studies. For example, the complex and intricate processes of human growth and development can be better understood through analyses which permit the researcher to consider how complex combinations of variables operate as independent or dependent variables (cf. Friedrich & Van Horn, 1976; Huck, Cormier & Bounds, 1974). Multivariate methods are far more powerful than the traditional approach of examining the relationship between a single independent variable and a single dependent variable.

Researchers in the area of child abuse might also borrow from the emerging field of developmental methodology. Studying development involves studying both qualitative and quantitative change. The area of developmental methodology is evolving methods which load on multiple variables in order to evaluate patterns of change, both qualitative and quantitative (Friedrich & Van Horn, 1976). A further methodological implication of studying developmental processes is that longitudinal designs are necessary. While traditional experimental design tends to be cross-sectional, examining how groups of individuals differ on a single variable at a given time, a multivariate longitudinal design permits the researcher to examine inter-individual differences in intra-individual change (Friedrich & Van Horn, 1976), i.e., how groups of individuals differ in patterns of change over time.

The recommendations listed above can be combined in a single design. For example, Baltes and Nesselroade (1973) have formulated ways of utilizing the multivariate technique of factor analysis in a longitudinal design in such a way that one can distinguish between qualitative change (which is evaluated by examining changes over time in factor (*loading* patterns) and quantitative change (which is evaluated by examining change in factor *scores* over time)). Incorporating these tools into the design and analysis of child abuse and neglect studies would enable researchers to pose more complex questions and to reach more definitive conclusions concerning child abuse and neglect.

Recommendations for Programmatic Strategies

The founding of the National Center on Child Abuse and Neglect in 1974 provided a source of financial support not only for research, but also for programmatic efforts directed toward the prevention of child abuse and neglect and the treatment of the families involved (U.S. Dept. of HEW, 1977). As a result of this support, a variety of programmatic strategies have been developed for prevention, detection, and/or treatment (cf. Parke & Collmer, 1975; U.S. Dept. of HEW, 1977). It is not our purpose to review and evaluate these programs; existing programs have been reviewed by Parke and Collmer (1975) and evaluation efforts are just beginning to yield data. However, we do wish to point out some programmatic implications suggested by the current child abuse and neglect literature.

One theme that seems to emerge from the literature is that the *perceptions* of family members are at least as important as the actual behavioral interactions occurring within the family. For example, several authors have suggested that abuse may be precipitated by parental perceptions that a child is different or defective, regardless of whether other individuals would judge the characteristic in question to be a defect (Friedrich & Boriskin, 1976; Green et al, 1974). Data supporting the importance of parental perceptions are provided by Morse et al (1970), who reported that the only variable which distinguished abused children with good social and emotional development from abused children with poor social and emotional development was maternal *perception* of the quality of the parent-child relationship. Martin & Breezely (1976) reported that abused children who perceived their residence as stable had a lower incidence of maladaptive behavior than abused children who did not share this perception. Professionals working in the area of child abuse may find that it is appropriate to focus not only on the actual behaviors of parents and children, but also on their perception of one another and of their environment.

There is some convergence of opinion concerning abusive and neglectful parents' lack of knowledge about what are realistic expectations of children at different stages of development (Martin, 1976; Steele, 1970). Another recurring finding is that abusive and neglectful parents tend to be socially isolated and to lack opportunities for relief from child care (Schneider, Helfer, and Pollack, 1968; Steele, 1970). These findings suggest that programmatic efforts should integrate educational and socialization components into their therapeutic intervention strategies.

Professionals working directly with children who have been victims of abuse should be aware of the broad range of areas in which these children may exhibit developmental delays or anomalies. Even though it is not clear that these problems are directly attributable to abuse, the issue of cause and effect is irrelevant to individuals working with children. What is crucial is that professionals be aware of the many areas in which abused and neglected children may require remediation.

Aside from the programmatic implications the literature holds for individuals working with abused and neglected children, persons with more peripheral concerns can also benefit from our current knowledge. For example, Lynch's (1976) findings concerning prenatal and perinatal factors contributing to abuse could be employed to sensitize physicians, parent educators and social service personnel to potentially dangerous situations. There is, however, a danger in educating professionals concerning the sketchy and tentative data on child abuse and neglect, namely, that professionals will take the data literally and interpret factors associated with abuse as definitive predictors of abuse. Professionals working with parents and children must realize that no single characteristic should be used to label a parent as abusive or neglectful. We can only note that the quality of parent-child interaction is in question and that child abuse or neglect is a potential adverse outcome – the most extreme adverse outcome – for which the parent-child dyad is at risk.

References

Baltes, P.B., and Nesselroade, J.R. The developmental analysis of individual differences on multiple measures. In J.R. Nesselroade and H.W. Reese (Eds.) *Life-span developmental psychology: Methodological issues.* N.Y.: Academic Press, 1973.

Bandura, A., and Walters, R.H. *Social learning and personality development.* New York: Holt, Rinehart, & Winston, 1963.

Becker, W.C. Consequences of different kinds of parental discipline. In M.L. Hoffman and L.W. Hoffman (Eds.), *Review of child development research.* Vol. 1. New York: Russell Sage Foundation, 1964.

Blackham, G.H., and Silberman, A. *Modification of child and adolescent behavior,* (2nd ed.). Belmont, California: Wadsworth Publishing Company, 1975.

Blager, F., and Martin, H.P. Speech and language of abused children. In H.P. Martin (Ed.), *The Abused Child: A multidisciplinary approach to developmental issues and treatment.* Cambridge, Mass.: Ballinger, 1976.

Button, A. Some antecedents of felonious and delinquent behavior. *Journal of Clinical Child Psychology,* 1973, *2* (3), 35-37.

Campbell, D.T., & Stanley, J.C. *Experimental and quasi-experimental designs for research.* Chicago: Rand McNally, 1963.

Curtis, G.C. Violence breeds violence — perhaps? *American Journal of Psychiatry,* 1963, *120,* 386-387.

Dion, K.K. Children's physical attractiveness and sex as determinants of adult punitiveness. *Developmental Psychology,* 1974, *10* (5), 772-778.

Duncan, G.M., Frazier, S.H., Militin, E., Johnson, A.M., and Barron, A.T. Etiological factors in first degree murder. *Journal of the American Medical Association,* 1958, *168,* 1755-1758.

Elmer, E. A follow-up study of traumatized children. *Pediatrics,* 1977, *59,* (2), 273-279.

Elmer, E., and Gregg, G.S. Developmental characteristics of abused children. *Pediatrics,* 1967, *40* (4), 596-602.

Erlanger, H.S. Social class differences in parents' use of physical punishment. In S.K. Steinmetz and M.A. Strauss (Eds.) *Violence in the family.* New York: Dodd, Mead, 1974.

Feshbach, N.D. The effects of violence in childhood. *Journal of Clinical Child Psychology,* 1973, *2* (3), 28-31.

Friedrich, W.N., and Boriskin, J.A. The role of the child in abuse: A review of the literature. *American Journal of Orthopsychiatry,* 1976, *46* (4), 580-590.

Galdston, R. Observations on children who have been physically abused and their parents. *American Journal of Psychiatry,* 1965, *122,* 440-443.

Garbarino, J. A preliminary study off some ecological correlates of child abuse: The impact of socioeconomic stress on mothers. *Child Development,* 1976, *47,* 178-185.

Gardner, W.I. *Children with learning and behavior problems: A behavior management approach.* Boston: Allyn & Bacon, 1974.

Gelles, R.H. Child abuse as psychopathology: A sociological critique and reformulation. In S.K. Steinmetz and M.A. Strauss (Eds.), *Violence in the family.* New York: Dodd, Mead, 1974.

Gil, D.C. *Violence against children: Physical child abuse in the U.S.* Cambridge, Mass.: Harvard University Press, 1970.

Gil, D.C. Violence against children. *Journal of Marriage and the Family,* 1971, *33* (4), 637-648.

Green, A.H., Gaines, R.W. and Sandgrund A. Child Abuse: Pathological syndrome of family interaction. *American Journal of Psychiatry,* 1974, *131,* (8), 882-886.

Harlow, H.F. Syndromes resulting from maternal deprivation: Maternal and peer affectional deprivation in primates. In J.H. Cullen (Ed.), *Experimental behavior: A basis for the study of mental disturbance.* New York: Wiley, 1974.

Hess, R.D., & Shipman, V. Early experience and the socialization of cognitive modes in children. *Child Development,* 1965, *36,* 869-886.

Huck, S.W., Cormier, W.H., & Bounds, W.G., Jr. *Reading statistics and research.* New York: Harper & Row, 1974.

Keppel, G. *Design and analysis: A researcher's handbook.* Englewood Cliffs, N.J.: Prentice Hall, 1973.

Kerlinger, F.N. *Foundations of behavioral research.* New York: Holt, Rinehart, & Winston, 1973.

Klaus, M.H. & Kennell, J.H. *Maternal-infant bonding.* St. Louis: C.V. Mosby, 1976.

Klein, M., & Stern, L. Low birth weight and the battered child syndrome. *American Journal of Diseases in Children,* 1971, *122,* 15-18.

Light, R. Abused and Neglected children in America: A study of alternative policies. *Harvard Educational Review,* 1973, *43* (4), 556-598.

Lynch, M. Risk factors in the child: A study of abused children and their siblings. In H.P. Martin (Ed.) *The abused child: A multidisciplinary approach to developmental issues and treatment.* Cambridge, Mass.: Ballinger, 1976.

Martin, H.P. Neurologic studies of abused children. In H.P. Martin (Ed.), *The abused child: A multidisciplinary approach to developmental issues and treatment.* Cambridge, Mass.: Ballinger, 1976 (a).

Martin, H.P. Which children get abused: High risk factors in the child. In H.P. Martin (Ed.), *The abused child: A multidisciplinary approach to developmental issues and treatment.* Cambridge, Mass.: Ballinger, 1976 (b).

Martin, H.P. & Beezely, P. Personality of abused children. In H.P. Martin (Ed.), *The abused child: A multidisciplinary approach to developmental issues and treatment.* Cambridge, Mass.: Ballinger, 1976.

Martin, H.P., & Rodeheffer, M. Learning and intelligence. In H.P. Martin (Ed.), *The abused child: A multidisciplinary approach to developmental issues and treatment.* Cambridge, Mass.: Ballinger, 1976.

Melnick, B. & Hurley, J.R. Distinctive personality attributes of child-abusing mothers. *Journal of Consulting and Clinical Psychology,* 1969, *33* (6), 746-749.

Morse, C.W., Sahler, J.Z., & Friedman, S.B. A three-year follow-up study of abused and neglected children. *American Journal of Diseases in Children,* 1970, *120,* 439-446.

Oliver, J.E., & Taylor, A. Five generations of ill-treated children in one family pedigree. *British Journal of Psychiatry,* 1971, *119,* 473-480.

Parke, R.D., & Collmer, C.W. Child abuse: An interdisciplinary analysis. In E.M. Hetherington (Ed.), *Review of child development research,* Vol. 5. Chicago: University of Chicago Press, 1975.

Polansky, N.A., Borgman, R.D., and DeSaix, C. *Roots of futility.* San Francisco: Jossey-Bass, 1972.

Ross, A.O. *Psychological disorders of children,* New York: McGraw-Hill, 1974.

Rutter, M. Maternal deprivation reconsidered. *Journal of Psychosomatic Research,* 1972, *16* (4), 241-250.

Sarles, R.M. Child Abuse. In D.J. Madden & J.R. Lion (Eds.), *Rage, hate, assault, and other forms of violence.* New York: Spectrum, 1976.

Schneider, C. Helfer, R.E., & Pollock, C. The predictive questionnaire: A preliminary report. In C.H. Kempe and R.E. Helfer (Eds.) *Helping the battered child and his family.* Philadelphia: Lippincott, 1972.

Sendi, I.B., & Blomgren, P.G. Comparative study of predictive criteria in the predisposition of homicidal adolescents. *American Journal of Psychiatry,* 1975, *132* (4), 423-427.

Silver, L.B., Dublin, C.C. & Lourie, R.S. Does violence breed violence? Contributions from a study of the child abuse syndrome. *American Journal of Psychiatry,* 1969, *126* (3), 152-155.

Soeffing, M. Abused children are exceptional children. *Exceptional Children,* 1975, *42* (3), 126-133.

Spinetta, J.J. & Rigler, D. The child-abusing parent: A psychological review. *Psychological Bulletin,* 1972, *77* (4), 296-304.

Spitz, R. *The first year of life.* New York: International Universities Press, 1965.

Steele, B.F. Parental abuse of infants and small children. In E.J. Anthony & T. Benedek (Eds.), *Parenthood: Its psychology and psychopathology.* Boston: Little, Brown & Co., 1970.

Steele, B.F., & Pollack, C.B. A psychiatric study of parents who abuse infants and small children. In R.E. Helfer & C.H. Kempe (Eds.), *The battered child.* Chicago: University of Chicago Press, 1968.

Thomas, A., & Chess, S. *Temperament and development.* New York: Brunner/Mazel, 1977.

Thomas, A., Chess, S., & Birch, H.G. *Temperament and behavior disorders in children.* New York: New York University Press, 1968.

U.S. Dept. of Health, Education & Welfare, Office of Human Development, Office of Child Development, National Center on Child Abuse and Neglect. *1977 Analysis of child abuse and neglect research.* Washington, D.C.: Dept. of HEW, January, 1977.

Welsh, R.S. Violence, permissiveness and the overpunished child. *Journal of Pediatric Psychology,* 1976, *1* (2), 68-71.

Juvenile Delinquency
A Dilemma of Theory and Practice

Azmy I. Ibrahim, Professor
Department of Sociology
San Jose State University

Abstract

In general, this article deals with the rising rate of juvenile delinquency and, in particular, the tendency for juvenile delinquents to resort to the commission of serious crime. The analysis includes three aspects: first, the meaning of the delinquent act; second, the status of social structure which permits such acts to occur; and, finally, the reasons delinquents resort to violent crimes. The article explains contradictions practiced by judician as well as correctional systems when dealing with juvenile delinquents, and shows how this contributes to the problem of juvenile delinquency. Furthermore, suggestions for a more radical approach for prevention of juvenile delinquency are introduced.

In the analysis of the normal and pathological, Durkheim stated that crime consists of an act which offends certain very strong collective sentiments. He further commented that in a society in which criminal acts, as we know them, are no longer committed, crime would not thereby disappear. The sentiments they offend would find other acts which previously may have offended the public sentiment lightly, and raise them to the level of crimes. (Durkheim 1950).

To understand, in modern society, the involvement of the juvenile in serious crimes, one can reverse Durkheim's analysis. As the public sentiment tends to tolerate certain acts by juveniles, which used to offend it in the past, the juveniles will resort to other acts which are more serious in the level of the offense. In other words, the permissiveness of the modern society, may contribute to the rising rate of violent crimes committed by juveniles.

In order to understand such a phenomenon, an examination is necessary of the meaning of the delinquent acts in general, the status of the society in which such acts are committed; and the resort to violent acts in particular.

The meaning of the delinquent act may be explained if one considers a short review of empirical studies and conceptual theories which are analyzing delinquency. Thrasher (1963) in his early work *"The Gang,"* found support for the general assumption that juvenile gangs were most prevalent in the ghetto or what he called interstitial, or crime producing areas. He collected information from 1,313 gangs in Chicago with approximately 25,000 members. To obtain this information he used personal observation and interviews with gang members, juvenile court records, and census data. He stated that gangs represented the spontaneous effort of boys to create a society for themselves, in an attempt to meet the needs which were otherwise non-existent in their daily lives. He also noted, that membership in a gang was a source of delinquent values for juveniles residing in high crime areas, where the breakdown of social control created a tradition of delinquency easily transmitted to others.

Shaw and McKay (1969), reached the same conclusions as Thrasher. During their work in the Institute for Juvenile Research, they traced the incidence of officially recorded delinquency in various city neighborhoods in Chicago. They used spot maps on which the addresses of 60,000 juveniles had been highlighted. These youths were delinquents who had been brought before the Cook County Juvenile Court, committed to correctional institutions by the court, or handled formally or informally by police probation officers. Shaw and McKay agreed that delinquency was transmitted by the culture or traditions prevalent in the community, and that it was highest in areas where social rewards and economic advantages were limited. They found that the communities with the highest rates of delinquents were occupied by those segments of the population whose position was at a disadvantage in relation to the distribution of economic, social, and cultural values. Such communities had the fewest facilities for acquiring the economic goods indicative of status and success in the conventional culture. They had fewer opportunities provided for securing and training, education, and contacts which facilitated advancement in the fields of business, industry, and the professions.

Tannenbaum (1938) emphasized the cultural transmission theory. He stated that criminal conduct is learned in response to a situation made by others. The individual's behavior is shaped by several elements i.e. the smile, the frown, approval and disapproval, praise and condemnation, companionship, affection, dislike, instruments, opportunities, denial of opportunities, – etc. Although it was not essential for the individual to have the approval of the whole world of his behavior, it was essential that the limited world to which the individual was attached give that approval.

In 1939, Edwin Sutherland introduced the theory of differential association. (Sutherland and Cressey, 1974). Differential association theory stated that criminal behavior is learned and not inherited. It is learned through communication that occurs in social interaction in primary groups. The learning of criminal behavior includes rationalization for actions, motives, skills, attitudes, and self definition. Delinquents are individuals who have been associated with societies, neighborhoods, families, or groups, which favor the violation of the law instead of conformity with it.

Whyte (1943) in *Street Corner Society* studied an Italian neighborhood in Boston. He focused on one corner group known as the Norton gang. He compared this group with the college boys who were members of the Italian Community Club. Whyte found that juvenile delinquents had no immediate access to power even though upward social mobility was their goal. He pointed out the difficulties involved when a community remains isolated from the larger city. Such a community fails to provide the young adults with options for conformity and recognition. The path to social success is seen as incompatible with the reality of the juveniles' environment.

Cohen (1955) emphasized the importance of the delinquent subculture surrounding the delinquent. He described a set of reactive attitudes that the youth obtains from the gang. Cohen characterized these as nonutilitarianism, maliciousness, and negativism. According to Cohen, on the surface the delinquent does not seem to want rewards or recognition from the middle class, but subconsciously he knows that they are beyond his reach. Hence, respectable middle class society becomes the enemy. The gang is formed when individuals, who feel alienated from the prevailing social norms, seek the support of one another. The members of the gang become involved in a collective problem-solving process. Cohen described this problem-solving process as a "conversation of gestures," which serves at least four important functions. First, it permits the gang members to explore the extent to which each is willing to go in accepting alternative rules for action. Second, it enables them to explore the extent to which they can rely on each other for support if they take a daring, rebellious, or delinquent path. Third, it gives each member an opportunity to test the degree to which his techniques for neutralizing the influences of law-abiding society are accepted by others. Fourth, it enables the gang to collectively try out various courses of delinquent action and to judge the commitment that each member of the gang is willing to make to each type of action.

In correspondence with Cohen's view, Cloward and Ohlin (1960) wrote *Delinquency and Opportunity*. They stressed the uniformity of conventional success goals, and the fact that the delinquent gang or subculture arises when one is prohibited from achieving these goals. According to Cloward and Ohlin, the individual who cannot achieve the goals he has set for himself will be frustrated, and may seek to obtain them through illegitimate, delinquent, or criminal alternatives. They discussed three delinquent subcultures which arise when opportunities are blocked. The criminal subculture which thrives on activities such as extortion and theft. Such a subculture flourishes in neighborhoods where illegitimate opportunity exists, and criminal elements are available. Second, the conflict subculture, which is characterized by violence in response to structures where legitimate and illegitimate opportunities are closed to the individual. Frustration is released through gang fights, personal attacks, and hostility toward others. And, third, the retreatist subculture in which drugs become a way of life. To avoid the inevitable failure, the individual retreats from the struggle. Furthermore, Cloward and Ohlin stated that gang behavior is motivated by failure, or the anticipation of failure, in achieving success goals by socially approved means. Lower class male adolescents find themselves at a competitive disadvantage in gaining access to legitimate routes to success. If they attribute their failure to injustice in the social system, rather than to their own inadequacies, they may bend their efforts to reform the social order, dissociate themselves from it, or rebel against it.

Merton (1957) designed a model of analysis of social and cultural sources of deviant behavior. He demonstrated that the social structure exerts pressure on some individuals and groups to engage in nonconforming behavior rather than conforming behavior. Consequently, the rates of deviant behavior in such groups will be higher than the rest of the society. Merton's analytical approach emphasized the discrepancy between culturally defined goals and institutionally accepted means, as the producer or anomie, or normlessness. He stated that there are three cultural axioms: first, that everyone should strive for the same lofty goals since these are open to all; second, that present seeming failure is but a way-station to ultimate success, and third, that genuine failure consists only in the lessening or withdrawal of ambition. The problem with the social structure, according to Merton, is that it ignores the fact that certain stratum in the society do not have equal access to opportunity. He formulated five types of adaptations as possible alternatives in dealing with the cultural goals and institutional means. The conformist type of adaptation in which the individual accepts the cultural goals and institutional means. The innovator type in which the individual accepts the cultural goals, but rejects the institutional means. The ritualist type, where the individual rejects the cultural goals, but accepts the institutional means. The retreatist type, when the individual rejects both cultural goals and institutional means. Finally, the rebellion type in which the individual rejects some of the cultural goals and some of the institutional means, with some aspiration for possible changes. According to Merton, with the exception of the first type of adaptation all others lead to deviance. In his further analysis, Merton concluded that the greatest pressures toward deviation are exerted upon the lower classes. The absence of realistic opportunities for advancement beyond their lower levels, result in a marked tendency toward deviant behavior. The involvement in deviance, organized vice, and crime are consequences of the inability of the low income groups to compete in terms of legitimate and socially established means. Using wealth as an established cultural goal, Merton stated that of those located in the lower reaches of the social structure, the culture makes incompatible demands. On one hand, they are asked to pursue the prospect of large wealth, on the other hand, they are denied the effective opportunities to do so institutionally.

The above mentioned models may be summarized as:

1. The delinquent act is a product of a sociological process.

2. The delinquent act is a negative reaction to certain conditions which exist in the immediate environment of the individual.

3. Finally, the delinquent act, whether it is committed by an individual or a group, is a form of *rebellion.*

Such conclusions paved the way for the second part of the analysis: that is the status of modern society. If delinquent acts are the products of sociological processes, they necessarily do not exist in a vacuum. They are part of the structure of the general society. Therefore, an examination of the society in which we live may throw some light on the magnitude of the problem of juvenile delinquency.

Sociologists have provided theories explaining the impact of the social structure on the behavior of the individual. Lately, some sociologists have tended to view the existing social structure as the cause of all our ills. Quinney, (1975), identified the structure of the American society as the source of delinquency. And, Merton (1957) stated that the social structure itself produces Anomie, a state of normlessness or a breaking down of the norms which in turn causes deviancy, delinquency, and crime.

Illustrations of such general theories of the influence of social structure are not hard to find in modern society. Bacon's (1976) article, "Ripoffs: New American Way of Life" covered a large spectrum. He claimed that government officials and taxpayers, businessmen and consumers are all cheating and stealing. He used the Watergate scandal as an example. The exposures of large scale corruption within some of the nations' biggest corporate institutions seem to have had a particularly unsettling effect on American complacency. Bribery, kickbacks, under-the-table campaign contributions and other serious charges have been leveled against more than eighty-five major U.S. companies. Bacon further stated that the average American today believes that the political system is dishonest and unresponsive to the needs of the people. He also gave evidence of the increase of embezzlement and white-collar crime. In answer to the question, "Are Americans becoming more corrupt?," Bacon used the response of sociologists and historians who have claimed that moral standards have degenerated over the years.

In an article entitled "Valiumania", Cant (1976) said that while the person with needle tracks in his arm is obviously a drug abuser, so too is the matronly housewife in her suburban home, gulping tranquilizers for her 'case of nerves'. Cant also stated that among physicians, psychologists, sociologist, and moralists, Valium is now generating as much anxiety as it was designed to allay. The television program "60 Minutes" showed how easy it is for anybody to enter one doctor's clinic after another and get various prescriptions for Valium.

Commenting on the new sexual morality, Francoeur and Francoeur (1976) stated that the low esteem in which sex has been held in the societies of Western civilization for several thousands of years is about to be supplanted by an ethic in which sex will be considered primarily for its pleasure giving value. They illustrated this point by citing the removal of taboos from sex, the alternatives to monogamy such as sexually open marriage, and the rising rate of homosexuality.

On the same subject of sex, Kuby (1974) noted many men, including police officers, and rapists, are convinced that rape is a legitimate form of sex, and that women ultimately "love it". However, women who have experienced rape, see it quite differently.

Discussing the institution of the family Novak (1976), wrote that the family, and all the old fashioned values that go with it, are currently held in disfavor in our society. But, according to Novak, a society with weak marriage and family institutions cannot long remain stable.

Turning to the schools, the picture is not any different. Reimer (1970) stated that schools have become the universal church of a technological society, but that today's education is a religion that can only save the few, while it dooms the many to ignorance, poverty, and powerlessness.

The problem of the inability of achieving real equality in the society has left many segments of it in misery. Addressing the National Conference on Social Welfare in Columbus, Ohio, 1966, Paul Jacobs commented that while the poor are accused of being withdrawn, uncommunicative, impulsive, incapable of deferring gratification and of living in the present only, there are valid reasons for such behavior. Principally, the poor are always short of money, a fact that makes them victims of the most appalling types of exploitation.

From the above mentioned statements one can only conclude that the standards of morality in our modern society are certainly weakened if not lowered. It is also evident that the basic elements of the social

135

structure, i.e., government, family, school, etc., have deviated from their functions, and may have created a state of normlessness.

Considering the first conclusion, that the delinquent act is a rebellious act; and the second finding, that the standard of morality in the general society is weakened; it is acceptable to add then a third observation, that the rate of delinquency will continue to rise and the delinquent act will rise in its level of seriousness.

From the Uniform Crime Reports for the United States, facts can be gathered which support the above mentioned observations. For example, the number of juveniles under age 18 arrested for all offenses increased 144 percent from 1960 through 1973, an increase which is greater than the natural increase of juveniles within the population. Again while the numbers of children between 10-17 years of age decreased between 1974 and 1977 (from 33,136,000 to 32,787,000), the rate of court delinquency cases increased from 3.7% to 4.3% (from 1,226,000 to 1,410,000). (Gemighani, 1972).

Within the recent years, the public has become tolerant of many acts of delinquency such as the use of foul language, smoking, truancy, running away from home, and the use of alcohol or drugs. As the public begins to tolerate some forms of delinquency, delinquents appear to resort to other more serious acts. When smoking cigarettes by the teenager became tolerated by the society, the young delinquent began to smoke marijuana. As states begin legalizing marijuana, the young delinquent may begin using other forms of drugs. When premarital intercourse is tolerated by the society, abortion may take the form of delinquency. When abortion is legalized, the continuation of pregnancy and having illegitimate babies may become an act of defiance. In fact, the number of pregnancies and illegitimate births among girls under 18 years old has been rising. The results of a study on teenage sex activity by Zelnick and Kant (1978) stated that teenage girls are having more premarital sex and many more babies out of wedlock than they did five years ago. Furthermore, more than three-quarters of all teenage pregnancies occur out of wedlock, and the percentage of teenagers who give their babies away for adoption has declined drastically from 7.6% in 1972 to 2.6% in 1976.

One can differentiate between two forms of delinquent acts, those which inflict personal injury on the delinquent; and those which inflict injury on the society and others. While society has tended to close its eyes in regard to the first type of crime, delinquents have resorted to those which injure the society and others. The data of the Uniform Crime Index Reports of the United States revealed that persons under 18 years old in 1973 accounted for 57% of all auto thefts, 54% of all burglaries, 48% of larceny-thefts, 34% of robberies, 20% of forcible rapes, 17% of aggravated assaults, and 10% of all murder and non-negligent manslaughter. The report also revealed that the number of arrests of persons under 18 has increased from 1960 to 1973 by 50% for auto theft, 104% for burglary, 124% for larceny-theft, 299% for robbery, 132% for forcible rape, 206% for aggravated assault, and 255% for murder and non-negligent manslaughter.

The *Times* (1977) stated that more girls are getting involved in violent crimes. In 1975, for example, 11% of all juveniles arrested for violent crimes were females. From 1970 to 1975, the arrest rate for girls under 18 for serious offenses climbed 40%, vs. a climb of 24% for boys.

Now that the meaning of the delinquent act and its increasing seriousness have been analyzed, it is time to examine the societal reaction to such phenomena. One approach sees punishment as the answer to crime while the other believes in rehabilitation. Adherents to each approach argue with each other and enumerate the other's failure to explain crime. The climbing rate of juvenile delinquency in our modern society today has escalated this debate further and further. However, the engagement in these arguments is useless since neither punishment nor rehabilitation in dealing with juvenile delinquents has been applied.

Ideally, a system which deals with juvenile delinquents in a manner which lessens the trauma of delinquency and which helps them to change their delinquent behavior and become useful citizens in the future should be established. Several ideas have been suggested. A brief summary of these approaches follows.

An ideal system would differentiate between juveniles who are charged with adult crimes such as murder, and those who commit non-adult crimes such as truancy. For the latter, a process known as diversion should be used. Diversion is the screening out of the justice system those juveniles who do not require the formal restraints and compulsory services of the juvenile court. Diversion places the burden on the citizens as well as the administrators of the organizations and agencies of the community. Phelps (1976) has suggested that such people should consider the following points:

1. Diversion is the most appropriate community response when juveniles misbehave.

2. The juvenile offender should be treated in the home community when resources are available and when the youth himself has agreed.

3. Juveniles should be confined within an institution as long as needed to protect the community – but no longer. Release from the institution should be predicated upon a professional prognosis that a resumption of delinquent activity is unlikely.

4. The forms of treatment appropriate for different types of delinquents can be distinguished and applied.

5. As the juvenile goes step by step through the justice system, each decision about him influences the selection of treatment strategies and the imposition of restraints. Therefore, thoughtful attention should be accorded this decision-making process.

According to Phelps, for those juveniles who commit adult crimes and whose presence in the community constitutes a real danger, confinement should be imposed in the hope of changing their behavior. However, certain required conditions are necessary for such practice. Edwards (1972) urges the following minimum services:

1. Police youth bureaus trained in methods of delinquency prevention and detection. Such a bureau should be headed by officers of high enough rank to be able to demand full use of commodity facilities for pre-delinquents and, where necessary, arrest and detention methods suited to juvenile cases.

2. Family social casework services capable of aiding both court and community by carrying needed help into the homes of delinquents and pre-delinquents.

3. Probation services for the juvenile court, with sufficient trained personnel to hold caseloads below 50 so that the probation officer can actually get to know and to help his charges.

4. Modern detention facilities where youngsters can be handled in small groups.

5. Shelter facilities to insure separation of delinquent juveniles from non-juveniles.

6. A specialized Juvenile or Family Court, headed by a judge (or judges) with adequate court time and concern for rehabilitation of their young charges.

7. Psychiatric and psychological services for the Juvenile Court, preferably in a court clinic, to guarantee accurate diagnosis at court hearings.

8. Foster home services. Many of our difficult delinquency cases can be handled well simply by providing decent homes.
9. Adoption services, which really seek to place the hard-to-place child. There is no room in the case record form of the good adoption services for the notation: "not suitable for adoption." The only children not suitable for adoption are those for whom institutionalization is mandatory.
10. Good, open-type boarding schools for both boys and girls available for Juvenile Court Placements.
11. State vocational schools for delinquent boys and girls for whom custody is required, manned not by ex-wardens of penitentiaries, but by teachers, counselors, and social workers who have had training in treatment work and are interested in and like youngsters.
12. State mental health clinics and hospitals for mentally and emotionally disturbed children, oriented not toward custody but toward cure.

However, the dreams of idealism do not correspond to the realities of pragmatism. John F. Kennedy and Lyndon B. Johnson endeavored to eliminate poverty and reduce delinquency through programs such as: Job Corps; the Neighborhood Youth Corps; Operation Headstart and Follow Through; VISTA; community action agencies; legal services for the poor; neighborhood health centers; and The Office of Economic Opportunity. Passing through the bureaucracy, the original conception of many of those programs was lost or altered which doomed them to inefficiency. Richard M. Nixon then dismantled these programs in the final years of his presidency. President Ford placed all federal juvenile justice and delinquency prevention programs under the guidance of the Law Enforcement Assistance Administration. However, he refused to allow any funds to be used to implement the act. Therefore, it can be seen that both administratively and financially, no sincere effort has been made to guarantee the success of positive steps in order to deal with the problem of delinquency.

Edwards, (1972) who has proposed the idea of minimum services for juveniles, stated that he is unaware of any state or community which claims that it possesses adequate facilities for delinquency prevention and control. Edwards further mentioned that half of the counties in America have no juvenile probation service and, where they do exist, 60% of all the probation officers have no professional training whatsoever. According to Edwards, the detention homes are understaffed and their programs enforce idleness. Since troublesome children must be handled in large groups, detention periods do more harm than good. Only a small minority of detention homes currently can afford modern facilities and a trained staff. In addition, for lack of juvenile detention facilities, 100,000 children each year are held in jails. Edwards also pointed out that to place a non-delinquent child, taken into custody because of parental neglect, into a detention home where he will be surrounded by delinquents, is as irrational as putting a patient suffering from malnutrition into a TB ward.

A closer look at the Juvenile Court today reveals the magnitude of the problems of dealing with delinquency. A summary of reports submitted by the President's Commission on Law Enforcement and Administration of Justice in 1967; and The National Advisory Commission on Criminal Justice Standards and Goals in 1973; may give some explanation of the situation. These reports concluded that the great hopes which were originally held for the juvenile court have not been fulfilled. The juvenile court has not succeeded significantly in rehabilitating delinquent youth, in reducing or even stemming the tide of juvenile criminality, or in bringing justice and compassion to the child offender. Juvenile courts have failed to achieve their goals just as criminal courts in the United States have failed to achieve theirs. Several reasons have been mentioned for the failure of the juvenile court. First, the community is unwilling to provide the resources, the people, the facilities, and the concern necessary for courts to realize their potential and prevent them from taking on some of the undesirable features typical of lower criminal courts. Second, juvenile court judges hold lower status in the eyes of the bar. Third, many juvenile court judges have not received undergraduate degrees, others have not received a college education, and some are not members of the bar. Fourth, the judicial hearings often are little more than attenuated interviews of 10 or 15 minutes duration. Fifth, psychologists and psychiatrists are scarce in the juvenile court. Where clinics do exist, their waiting lists usually are months long and frequently they provide no treatment only diagnosis. And treatment, even when prescribed, is often impossible to carry out because of the unavailability of adequate individual and family casework, foster home placement, and treatment in youth institutions. Sixth, the dispositional alternatives available to the court fell far short from meeting the individual needs of the delinquent. The only alternatives available are outright release, probation, and institutionalization.

Probation means little, if any, supervision, since some courts have no probation services, and those that do, have caseloads so high that counseling and supervision take the form of occasional phone calls and perfunctory visits instead of the careful, individualized service that was intended. Institutionalization too often means isolation from the outside world in an overcrowded, understaffed, high-security institution with little education, vocational training, counseling, job placement, or guidance upon release. Programs are subordinated to everyday control and maintenance, where children spend weeks in limbo-like detention, awaiting bed space. (Winslow, 1976).

Besides all the above mentioned criticism, there are those who believe the Supreme Court decisions in the last few years such as; Kent, v. United States, 1966; In re Gault, 1967; In re Wittington, 1968; In re Winship, 1970; and McKeiver v. Pennsylvania, 1971; have forced the juvenile court to deviate from its original structures and goals.

The juvenile delinquents themselves are aware of the inefficiency of the justice system. The *Times* (1977) describes the activities of 14 and 15 year old youth involved in drug pushing, mugging, robberies, and murders. According to the *Times*, these youngsters have no respect for the justice system. Once arrested and brought to court, they sit, not only bored with the procedure, but smiling and indifferent. The youngsters know that it is unlikely that the court will prosecute them; if they are prosecuted, they may not be sentenced; if sentenced, there may be no place to institutionalize them; if institutionalized, they may be paroled shortly; and if paroled there may be no supervision. The *Times* also stated that older youths employ younger confederates to push drugs, commit robberies, and sometimes even murder, because the younger delinquent tends to get off easily if caught.

It is apparent that although there are theories and methods of prevention and control of juvenile delinquency, they have not been adequately applied. This lack of application usually hinders any effort to give credit to the effectiveness of punishment or rehabilitation as means of reducing the rising rate of juvenile delinquency. This conclusion confirms the saying that there is nothing worse than a theory without a practice, except a practice without theory.

The following is a somewhat radical approach which may help in the prevention of juvenile delinquency.

Most of the methods of prevention and control of juvenile delinquency deal with the delinquent act after the fact. In other words, the authorities wait until the delinquent has committed a crime before they confront him. Relatively little attention has been given to the attempt to prevent the delinquent act before it actually takes place. In order to achieve this goal of prevention, several points should be considered.

First, an attemptt should be made to eliminate what is known today as "crime zones." Such zones are known and recognized as such by scientists, administrators and officials, as well as many citizens in the society. In such zones, crime is a form of life. Here crime is the norm rather than the exception. These communities breed juvenile delinquents. Many of the theories discussed in the first part of this chapter imply that the process of delinquency is highly influenced by where the child lives. Television documentaries such as those appearing on the program *60 Minutes* give a picture of the criminal lifestyle which the teenagers have to lead in order to survive in such places as Harlem and The Bronx. It is the responsibility of the general society to find ways and means to change the way of life in such zones, and to create a much safer and secure environment where crime will not be prevalent. A radical approach would employ the National Guard in order to maintain an element of security and control in these communities. In the general society, it is common to use the National Guard when crime is generated beyond the tolerable level, such as in the cases of riots and looting. However, an intolerable level of crime is the everyday situation in some locations in many cities. The presence of the National Guard in these localities would be a temporary stage to be followed by a force of police soldiers. These soldiers would be walking patrolmen who would be visible on every street corner. They would be placed in specific locations on a permanent basis. Police buses would take them to and from their locations. Theoretically, their presence would eliminate the chances for the commission of crimes. College degrees would not be necessary for such a force, which would make possible reasonable salaries. Many college students or other citizens might be willing to join the ranks of such a force on a part-time basis. Although such practices as police soldiers are alien to the people in the American society, they are common in many Western democracies such as England, France, and Germany.

Police soldiers could also be maintained in places where there is a high probability that a crime will be committed, such as downtown areas, large companies, banks, garages, grocery stores, department stores, schools, etc. The effect of a police soldier in his uniform at a department store is quite different from that of a plain clothes police officer. The plain clothes policeman plays the role of a detective. He waits until a crime is committed and then takes action. On the other hand, a police soldier in in his uniform would undoubtedly eliminate the commission of crimes before they happen. Knowing that the citizen pays a great portion of his taxes in order to deal with criminals, it may be cheaper in the long run if we can succeed in eliminating crimes before they take place.

Another approach which is gaining momentum is the concept of collective control. Collective control is the involvement of the citizens in the element of control. The simplest way of administering collective control is by offering a monetary reward to any citizen who gives information which leads to a conviction. Such a practice is already a common occurrence when a severe crime has been committed and the police cannot find the offender. A generalization of this practice may lead to the involvement of many citizens in the society in the element of control. The day may come when groups will be formed in order to protect their neighborhoods from crime and delinquency rather than to participate in criminal and delinquent acts. The need for a system in which the chances for the commission of crime and delinquency are reduced, is necessary.

In this chapter, three main points were discussed. First, the rising rate of delinquency and the resort to serious crimes may be related to the state of normlessness or anomie in a society. Second, the failure to adequately apply methods and theories in dealing with delinquency may contribute to the problem of juvenile delinquency. Third, sincere efforts should be given to the implementation of existing ways of dealing with the prevention and control of delinquency, and a new approach should be sought in order to eliminate the chances of committing delinquent acts.

References

Bacon, D.C. Ripoffs: New American Way of Life. *U.S. News and World Report,* May 31, 1976.

Cant, G. Valiumania. *The New York Times Magazine,* February 1, 1976, pp. 34-44.

Cloward, R.A. & Ohlin, L.E. *Delinquency and Opportunity: A Theory of Delinquent Gangs.* Glenco: Free Press, 1960.

Cohen, A.K. *Delinquent Boys: The Culture of the Gang.* Glenco: Free Press, 1955.

Durkheim, E. The Normal and The Pathological. In A.S. Sarab & J.H. Mueller (trans.), *Rules of Sociological Method.* Glenco: Free Press, 1950.

Edwards, G. In Defense of Juvenile Court. *Juvenile Justice,* 1972, 23 (No. 2).

Francoeur, R.T. & Francoeur, A.K. The Pleasure Bond: Reversing the Antisex Ethic. *The Futurist,* August 1976, pp. 176-180.

Gemignani, R. Youth Services Systems: Diverting Youth From the Juvenile Justice System. *Delinquency Prevention Reporter,* July-August, 1972.

Kuby, L. Man, Women — and Rape. *Cleveland Magazine,* August, 1974, pp. 70-74.

Merton, K. Social Structure and Anomie. *Social Theory and Social Structure.* Glencoe: Free Press, 1957.

Novak, M. The Family Out of Favor. *Harper's Magazine,* April 1976, pp. 37-46.

Phelps, T.R. *Juvenile Delinquency: A Contemporary View,* Pacific Palisades, California: Goodyear Publishing Company, 1976.

Reimer, E. *School is Dead: Alternatives in Education.* Doubleday & Company, 1970.

Shaw, C.R. & McKay, H.D. *Juvenile Delinquency and Urban Areas* (rev. ed). Chicago: The University of Chicago, 1969.

Sutherland, E. & Cressey, D. *Criminology* (9th ed.). Philadelphia: J.B. Lippincott, 1974.

Tannenbaum, F. *Crime and the Community.* New York: Columbia University Press, 1938.

The Youth Crime Plague. *Time,* July 11, 1977, pp. 18-28.

Thrasher, F.M. *The Gang: A Study of 1313 Gangs in Chicago* (Adr. Ed.). The University of Chicago, 1963.

Whyte, W.F. *Street Corner Society.* Chicago: University of Chicago Press, 1943.

Winslow, R.W. (ed.) *Juvenile Delinquency In A Free Society.* Encino, California: Dickenson Publishing Company, Inc., 1976.

Zelnick, M. & Kant, J.F. Teenage Girls Premarital Sex. *San Jose Mercury.* January 13, 1978.

Rurban Delinquency and Early Childood Development

Richard A. Ball
West Virginia University
and
J. Robert Lilly
Northern Kentucky University

The need for delinquency-related research on males and females in less urbanized areas stems from an over emphasis on males in urban areas. To counter this bias the research summarized here focused on males and females in a rurban setting. Attention was given to testing several hypotheses derived from containment theory, e.g. neutralization, anomia, and self concept. Norm violation for the working class sixth grade sample (N = 398 males and 407 females) was determined by the abridged Nye-Short inventory. The findings revealed a significant positive relationship between personal neutralization and norm violation. No significant difference was found between the attributed neutralization scores for the boys and girls; however, the attributed neutralization scores were significantly higher than personal neutralization scores. A significant positive relationship between a juvenile scale (a modified Srole

Anomia Scale) and basic norm violation was found. Family and school anomia scores were also found to be significantly related to basic norm violation. Significantly different self concept scores for boys and girls were found, with the boys' scores less "favorable" than the girls. For both sexes the hypothesis of a significant relationship between negative self concept and basic norm violation was confirmed. Implications for early childhood development are addressed.

Introduction

Delinquency research in the United States has focused primarily upon the serious offenses of adolescent males in large cities. In order to counteract this bias, the work reported here centered upon the study of early manifestations of delinquency among both boys and girls in less urbanized areas. A series of studies, which have been concerned with factors involved in the early emergence of delinquent behavior is now available for summary. The data provided an interesting picture of patterns of early childhood development and associated manifestations of delinquency.

Because of the conceptual problems with the terms "rural" and "urban", the ecological range is a rural-urban "concatentation", by which is meant only a unified series. The samples used here were drawn from one complex portion of the concatentation, a type of area which exists between the urban centers and the rural countryside. This context was designated by the term "rurban", a term sometimes used in ecological studies. For the research the rural-urban concatenation in terms of the complementary principles of gradience and differentiation. According to the gradient principle, the extent of urban influence varies directly with the proximity and size of the nearest city (Martin, 1957). The principle of differentiation states that urban influence also varies directly with the extent to which an area is ecologically differentiated by specialization and functional interdependency of the ecological components within the particular area (Martin, 1957). Thus, the "rurban" area combines certain characteristics associated with both the rural and urban extremes.

Rather than generalize about "delinquency", this work focused upon a particular phase of delinquency *emergence,* further defined in terms of "basic norm violation". *Basic norm violation* is behavior contrary to the *fundamental* normative restrictions placed on youth with respect to driving, drinking, theft, vandalism, truancy, parental defiance and sexual behavior. Although students of the delinquency problem have argued over the "seriousness" of these activities, they do represent violation of the *basic* normative restrictions which collectively define the status of youth. The Nye-Short Scale (Nye and Short, 1956) was used as an operational measure of basic norm violation.

While there are obviously important differences among various ecological areas which might be termed "rurban", this research has been concentrated upon Marion County, West Virginia. Marion County is located approximately two hours driving time from Pittsburgh and is composed of a small central city of 29,000 population surrounded by small towns (most of which have populations of less than 2,500) interspersed through a satellite fringe area of essentially nonfarm character. The county is an economically differentiated area producing coke, coal, tar, cement products, clay products, powder, lumber, pumps, chemicals, foundry products, aluminum products, glass, glassware, fluorescent lamps, chemical foundry products, corrugated boxes, machinery, electronic parts, novelties and other products (Lilly, 1969:58-66). The population is essentially working class, with only 34.6% of the work force in white collar occupations.

The area has a population density of 197.3 per square mile, with 54% of the 61,356 residents living in areas which the Census designates as "rural" and 46% residing in "urban" areas. For the research summarized here, data were gathered on 96.5 percent of the sixth graders enrolled in the 41 public elementary schools of Marion County with analysis confined to subsamples of 398 males and 407 females, all of whom were white, working class youth. Working class was defined by a socre of 70 or below on an interpolated North-Hatt Scale as described by Kahl (1957). Previously reported have been detailed findings for the boys (Ball and Lilly, 1971), the girls (Ball and Lilly, 1976), and a secondary analysis comparing the two samples (Ball, 1977).

Throughout this research, selection of independent variables has been guided by the "containment theory" developed by Reckless (1967:469-483). Containment theory argues that certain specified "self-factors" comprise an "inner containment" which, along with various environmental factors that together comprise an "outer containment", seriously affect the risk of delinquent or criminal behavior. The research discussed here has concentrated upon norm neutralization, anomia, and self concept as the potentially important social psychological or "self" factors.

147

There are several problems involved in any attempt to relate juvenile delinquency to patterns of early childhood development. If very young children are studied, research may have to be conducted on the prospective construction of the likelihood of children becoming juvenile delinquents. If researchers wait until the delinquency appears then they may have to engage in "retrospective reconstructions" of the offender's pasts. Short of a longitudinal study over a 15-20 year period, these problems are insurmountable. But what about a compromise approach? It is possible to examine children at the elementary school level, to get some indication of their pattern of offenses and their views of themselves, their schools, their families and the law.

The possible impact of early childhood development upon patterns of delinquent behavior is obvious, and a number of writers have tried to distinguish the effects upon boys and girls. Perhaps the major problem at this time is the confusion over the patterns which do exist. Novick (1962), for example, insists that the female engages in offenses by which she "hurts herself" while the males "tends to hurt others," Chesney-Lind (1973) denies this interpretation maintaining that the official data are misleading. To get beyond the official data, research must be turned to self reports of the youngsters themselves. That has been the general research policy guiding the work summaried here. Therefore, the youth directly involved were asked about their behavior in a way which would guarantee their anonymity.

One of the most interesting ideas which may be applied to an understanding of the place of early childhood development in later juvenile delinquency is the concept of *sex role*. Konopka (1966) has concluded that the female delinquent is characterized by an inability to develop the capacity for the usual female sex role, and that the problem can be traced to serious disturbances in family life which complicate the Oedipal problem of such girls and make it difficult for them to identify with their own mothers. Male delinquency has been said to be the result of the *successful* socialization of boys, who are taught a more "manly" role of aggressiveness and violence and it has been occasionally argued that the female delinquent is rebelling against her passive role and imitating a role denied her (Cowie, Cowie, and Slater, 1968).

Norm Neutralization

Sykes and Matza (1957) proposed that delinquency represents the

148

behavior of fairly conventional individuals who apply to their actions culturally available excuses which serve as "techniques" to "neutralize" the cultural norms in given situations. These "techniques of neutralization" are much like the familiar psychological defense mechanisms of rationalization. The difference was that the techniques of neutralization are said to be excuses learned *prior* to norm violation excuses which are learned along with the norms themselves. In this view, neutralization is a matter of normal subcultural learning rather than a psychological defense mechanism. Specifically, Sykes and Matza asserted that these techniques of neutralization include: (1) denial of responsibility, (2) denial of injury, (3) denial of the victim, (4) condemnation of the condemners, and (5) appeal to higher loyalties. Taken as a whole these techniques were thought to be associated with work which suggested that delinquency outside large cities involved "troublemaking" (Polk, 1967:346) and "norm erosion" (Reckless and Shoham, 1963) rather than a highly developed system of delinquent norms. Furthermore, earlier research indicated that norm neutralization was probably a factor in norm erosion (Ball, 1966). This resulted in directing attention toward neutralization as a likely factor in the norm violations of rurban youth.

One of the principle concerns was the possibility that delinquency may be less the result of personal neutralization than of the misperception of peer group attitudes (Matza, 1964). Such a possibility suggests that relatively few delinquents actually accept the norm neutralizing excuses, but that they *act* as if they do, each believing that his peers accept them. To explore this an applied *attributed neutralization* was used. Norm neutralization has been measured by an Abridged Neutralization Inventory with a corresponding Attributed Neutralization Inventory for measurement of the perception of friends' attitudes.[1] All the work has been guided by three distinct hypotheses: (1) *Rurban sixth graders will tend to attribute significantly more neutralization to their friends than they report for themselves;* (2) *The attributions will significantly overestimate the neutralization which actually exists among these friends;* (3) *Attributed neutralization among rurban sixth graders will be related to basic norm violation at a higher level of confidence than will personal neutralization.*

Anomia

Srole (1956) describes the "anomic" person as one who feels that

(1) social leaders are indifferent to his problems, (2) there is little chance for accomplishment in what is essentially an unpredictable society, (3) goals are receding from him, (4) no one can really be counted on to support him, and (5) life itself is meaningless and futile. Most of the previous research dealing with anomia has been based upon the Srole Scale (Clinard, 1964). Since the Srole Scale is aimed at adults, a Juvenile Anomia Index for use with the Srole Scale is another measure of generalized anomia was developed.[2]

The problem with studies of anomia among adolescents is that they have not yet become full participants in society. Their contact with the larger social system is mediated by such proximate social systems as family and school (Jarrett and Haller, 1964). Indeed these proximate systems may be assumed to exert a greater impact than the rather abstract "larger society". The research summarized here has followed an interest in the possibility that anomia will exist in specific as well as generalized form and that certain specific forms may be more clearly related to delinquency than is general anomia. This possibility has been pursued by use of a Family Anomia Index and a School Anomia Index.[3] Four distinct but related hypotheses have been stated as follows: *Basic norm violation among rurban sixth graders will be significantly and positively related to (1) Srole Scale scores, (2) juvenile anomia scores, (3) family anomia scores, and (4) school anomia scores.*

Family background has of course been emphasized for many years as a factor in juvenile delinquency (Lumpkin, 1931; Glueck, 1934, Epps, 1954; Morris, 1964; Stern, 1964; Schofield, 1965). The relationship of the youth to authority figures, a relation which comes to a head in the schools (Stinchcombe, 1964), is itself often traced back to early childhood experiences in the family.

Previous research (Reckless, Dinitz, & Murray, 1956, 1957; Reckless, Dinitz, & Kay, 1957; Dinitz, Reckless & Kay, 1958; Scarpitti, Murray, Dinitz & Reckless, 1960; Dinitz Scarpitti & Reckless, 1962; and Reckless & Dinitz, 1967) has suggested that the self concept provides "insulation" against delinquency. Since criticism of this research has centered upon the definition of self concept implied by the items in the Self Concept Inventory (Schwartz & Tangri, 1965; Tangri & Schwartz, 1967; Hirschi & Selvin, 1967; and Orcutt, 1970), some clarification has been necessary. We have shown that the Self Concept Inventory actually measures the *attribution* phase of self concept formation, a phase in which the individual is assessing others' judgments of him. Using this new interpretation of the Self

Concept Inventory, our basic hypothesis has been that a *significant, positive relationship will exist between "unfavorable" self concept scores and basic norm violation scores among rurban sixth graders.*

Recapitulation of Major Findings

The abridged Nye-Short Scale included 6 items specifying basic norm violations. With respect to the most common norm violation, "defying parents' authority to their face", no difference between the boys and girls was found. All of the other percentage differences have been statistically significant (P < .001), with boys reporting more basic norm violation in every case.[4] They steal more often, vandalize more often, and are more often truant. The greatest differences however, tended to appear for drinking violations and driving offenses, where more than twice as many boys had committed these offenses. The mean basic norm violation score have been significantly higher (P < .01) for the boys than for the girls. Mean scores for both the boys and girls turned out to be significantly lower (P < .01) than those obtained in our earlier studies of 125 white, 15 year-old males and those obtained in a study of 114, white, 15-18 year old males in an area institution for delinquents (Ball, 1966).

Somewhat surprisingly in view of the arguments set forth in the delinquency literature, there has been no significant difference between the mean norm neutralization scores of these rurban sixth graders and the mean obtained in our earlier study of institutional delinquents. On the other hand, these means have been significantly higher (P < .001) than that obtained for the earlier sample of boys from a high delinquency, urban area. The hypothesis of a significant positive relationship between personal neutralization and basic norm violation has been supported (τ = .09, P < .05) for the boys only.

As noted in an earlier discussion (Ball, 1977), there were certain patterns within the data which suggested the need for further analysis. The most likely possibility was that self concept might account for the relationship discovered between norm neutralization and basic norm violation among the boys. Containment theory indicates that self concept is the key factor which may either "insulate" one from the effects of deviant pressures or open the way for these pressures, and this proposition has been supported by previous research. The relationship between norm neutralization and basic norm violation declined to statistical insignificance when self concept was held constant. The correlation between personal neutralization and basic norm violation also declined to statistical insignificance when the effect of attributed neutralization was controlled for. None of the remaining variables has had an appreciable effect upon the zero order correlation.

These data showed no significant difference between the mean attributed neutralization scores of the boys and girls, but the means in both cases turned out to be significantly higher (P < .001) than those obtained for personal norm neutralization, supporting our hypothesis that rurban sixth graders will tend to attribute significantly more neutralization to their friends than they report for themselves. Since one of the research assumptions was that these friends are likely to be other local youth of about the same age, the data also tended to support the hypothesis that attributions of neutralization significantly overestimate the actual level of personal neutralization which exists among the friends of the respondents. However, the data showed that attributed neutralization was related to basic norm violation at a higher level of significance (T = .15, P < .001) than was personal neutralization, only among the boys. Neither personal norm neutralization nor attributed neutralization turned out to be significantly related to basic norm violation among the girls. Controlling for the other independent variables had little effect on the zero order correlation.

As for Srole Scale scores, the means have not been significantly different for the boys and girls, nor has either been significantly different from that obtained for our sample of 125 15-18 year-old boys from the high delinquency, urban area. On the other hand, both means have been significantly lower (P < .001) than the mean score obtained for the earlier sample of 115 institutionalized, delinquent boys. No significant relationship has been found between scores on the Srole Scale and basic norm violation among the boys. However, a modest but statistically significant relationship (T - .08, P < .05) between scores on the Srole Scale and basic norm violation has appeared. Among the girls it appeared only to decline to statistical insignificance when juvenile anomie was controlled, and to statistical insignificance when either family anomia or school anomia was controlled. The only other variable which has been able to account for the relationship is self concept; the correlation has declined to statistical insignificance when self concept has been controlled.

The mean juvenile anomia scores have not been significantly different for the boys and girls, but there has been a significant, positive relationship between juvenile anomia and basic norm violation for both boys (τ = .09, P < .05) and girls (τ = .11, P < .001), and none of the other independent variables, including the Srole Scale itself, could account for this relationship. The fact that Juvenile Anomia Index scores could account for the positive relationship discovered between Srole Scale scores and basic norm violation, but that Srole Scale scores could not account for the relationship between Juvenile Anomia Index and basic norm violation, has demonstrated the potential power of the age specific measure as a possible predictor of such norm violation.

This data has shown no significant difference between the mean family anomia scores for boys and girls, but these scores have been significantly related to basic norm violation for both boys (τ = .13, P < .001) and girls (τ = .15, P < .001). Controlling for the effect of self concept, the correlations declined appreciably, holding statistical significance for the boys, but falling to statistical insignificance for the girls. None of the other independent variables has shown appreciable effect upon the zero order correlations.

As to school anomia scores, the means have not been significantly different for the boys and girls. There has been significant, positive relationship between school anomia and basic norm violation has remained statistically significant among the girls, but has dropped to statistical insignificance for the boys.

The mean self concept scores have been significantly different for the boys and girls, with the mean for the boys significantly higher (P .05) or less "favorable" than that for the girls. The hypothesis of a significant relationship between unfavorable self concept scores and basic norm violation among rurban sixth graders has been supported for both boys (τ = .28, P < .001) and girls (τ = .28, P < .001). None of the other independent variables has had more than a negligible effect upon our zero order correlations.

Implications

In the context of youth attitudes and early childhood development, the fact that levels of norm neutralization and anomia are high or higher among these sixth graders than among older youth in a high delinquency area, and that the scores of the girls are essentially the same as those of boys, suggests the need for careful research to determine the source of such attitudes. It seems logical to assume that factors in early childhood development must play a major part here. If it is not the environment then perhaps early family and school relationships have something to do with it.

The initial research relating norm neutralization to male delinquency (Ball, 1966) showed neutralization to be significant in explaining the *emergence* of delinquency to the point of juvenile court appearances but found no consistently significant relationship which might explain either the persistence of delinquent behavior or the *severity* of offenses. The work reviewed has shown that *attributed* neutralization is the important form of neutraliation among rurban, sixth grade *males* and that a significant, positive relationship between personal norm neutralization and basic norm violation occurs *only if self concept scores are "unfavorable."* Up to this point it would appear that neither form of neutralization has much relevance to emergency delinquency among rurban, sixth grade *females,* but this is apparently not simply the result of the greater prevalence of social fictions among boys, for the girls have been found to attribute just as much norm neutralization to their friends as do the boys. It is suggested that the difference may lie in the likelihood that the boys tend to *act* on the basis of the mistaken attributions while the girls do not. This tendency may be connected with sex roles learned much earlier (Broverman *et al.,* 1972). According to these stereotypical roles, boys are expected to be more aggressive, to seek what they want more directly, and to engage in more adventurous activities. If the difference in behavior is more a matter of learned sex roles than of "bad attitudes," and if it is true that the sex role of females is taking on more of a traditionally "masculine" character, then we may expect an increase in basic norm violation among girls to accompany this "emancipation" from older stereotypes.

On the other hand, it is possible that the measure of neutralization has contained a sex bias, and that a different measure employing different excuses might disclose the same relationship among the girls which we have found for the boys. It is also possible, of course, that the offenses of the boys are such that neutralization will be a significant factor while the offenses of girls may not involve this set of attitudes at all. Aside from these and other possibilities, it remains to be seen whether our basic findings themselves will hold up with different age groups in different ecological settings.

Although the validity of the Srole Scale is somewhat questionable

with adolescents, particularly because of "ambiguous items" which expresses "cliches" in "unilateral positive wording" (Carr, 1971), the fact is
that corroborative data have been obtained through use of the Family
Anomia Index and the School Anomia Index, both of which include an
equal number of positively and negatively worded items with very
specific referents. The data have demonstrated the importance of
anomia at this age and suggest the need for further development of
measures of general anomia applicable to adolescents and to younger
children. The data here also demonstrated the advantages to be gained
by reconceptualizing anomia in terms of specific forms.

The greater importance of family anomia among boys and school
anomia among girls has been somewhat unexpected given the literature
which stresses the special significance of family life for girls and of the
pressures of school on boys (Stern, 1964; and Polk & Schafer, 1972). Stern
(1964) has argued that family climate should have a much greater impact
upon girls than upon boys, and Knopka (1966) has agreed, suggesting
that family difficulties produce more serious Oedipal problems for the
girls since they make it difficult for her to identify with her mother and to
internalize the female role. The data reported here give no real answers
to these questions, but the data do not support any notion that the family
is a more salient factor among girls. The rurban boys seem to have been
more affected by family anomia than were their female classmates.

Since the levels of norm neutralization and anomia among these
youth are comparable to the levels to be found among older youth from
high delinquency, urban areas, or among institutionalized delinquents, it
is concluded that some factor was indeed operating to minimize the
likelihood that such attitudes would be expressed in delinquent
behavior. While differential opportunity may be an important ecological
factor, these data indicated that self concept is a more significant factor in
basic norm violation than is either neutralization or anomia. What has
been found is that it accounts for the apparatus significance of personal
norm neutralization among the rurban boys and for certain forms of
anomia, including school anomia among boys and family anomia among
girls. Furthermore, self concept has been the only independent variable
which showed significantly different mean scores for boys and girls. The
argument that the Self Concept Inventory really seems to be measuring
attribution rather than internalization has led to the conclusion that the
boys are more likely to believe that others expect them to be involved in
trouble. This tends to support an earlier agreement with respect to early
learning of sex roles.

The data examined leads to one major conclusion. It seems highly likely that one link between delinquency and early childhood development is to be found in the process of learning one's sex role and developing one's own self concept. Sex role and self concept would seem to be two intimately related aspects of the same general process. One is more of a sociological formulation, the other more of a psychological formulation. Both may be conceptualized as elements of "containment". In the language of containment theory, sex role represents an aspect of "outer containment" imposed by society which self concept is an aspect of "inner containment" produced within the individual. The common bond is believed to be *attribution:* What does the child believe others to think of him? These attributions are made on the basis of environmental ones, mainly the behavior of significant others toward the child. As has been seen, an anomic environment in home or school is especially important here.

Sixth graders, of course, have not yet entered the years of highest delinquency risk, and it is possible that factors such as self concept might decline in significance under increased pressure. Still, the evidence from high delinquency areas, where the pressure toward delinquency *is* great, leads one to expect that this variable will retain its significance with advancing age, perhaps become even more important (Reckless, 197:475). More rigorous comparisons by age, sex, and ecological context, and an examination of differences by race is suggested. With respect to the self concept variable, Gould (1969) has argued that the label of troublemaker is so commonly applied to blacks as to have little personal relevance to self concept, and Jenson (1970:89) has produced some evidence in support of this contention. It may well be that self concept bears a different relationship to various forms of delinquency among blacks than it does among whites. The problem of sex role should be investigated in terms of early learning connected to self concept.

The focus reported here upon early emergence of basic norm violation has left us with several important technical problems. The narrow range of norm violation at this stage leaves open the possibility that greater variance will disclose different relationships than those described. Partly for this reason, this cohort will be followed to at least the ninth grade, where the range of delinquency should be broader. There is also the possibility that the extent of relationship among sets of variables may be influenced by factors such as the validity of the measures employed and the variance of different dimensions tapped, so that one relationship may only *appear* to be more "pronounced" than another.

Footnotes

1   *Note.* The Neutralization Inventory is comprised of four situational subscale of ten items each (Ball, 1966). In the research summarized here, norm neutralization was measured by a more efficient Abridged Neutralization Inventory consisting of the subscale on shoplifting, which has in previous research shown alpha coefficients of approximately .09 and correlations of .79 to .89 with scores for the entire Inventory. The Attributed Neutralization Inventory is identical except that respondents are instructed to answer as they feel their friends would respond.

2   *Note.* The Juvenile Anomia Index included four of the original Srole Scale items, the sole variation being that one item ("The older my friends and I get, the more disgusted we get with things,") was substituted for an original ("It's hardly fair for adults to bring children into the world the way things look for the future."). Previous work (Ball, 1969) has traced a major part of the measurement error involved in the use of the Srole Scale with adolescents to the single item which was replaced.

3   *Note.* The Family Anomia Index and the School Anomia Index consist of ten items each, with the same five Likert-type response categories used on the Srole Scale, according to a method by Edwards and Kirkpatrick (1948). The items parallel those of the Srole Scale except for specific references to parents and teachers. The Coefficients of Reproducibility for both indexes have exceeded .80. Beaver (1972) has provided an extensive analysis of the items.

4   *Note.* Although most of the argument over the use of parametic or non-parametic statistics has centered around the issue of measurement level, the basic norm violation scores post an additional problem in that the scores do not approximate a normal distributiion even with a large sample size. Because of the various measures can be considered as essentially ordinal, Kendall's tau ( ) was used to test for relationships between the independent and dependent variables. Here a problem was encountered. The previous research dealing with norm neutralization anomia and self concept had reported central tendencies in terms of mean scores, using the t-test to establish the significance of differences, and we wished to follow this tradition, so as to facilitate comparisons. For the sake of consistency, the significance of all t-tests was verified by a comparison of median scores. Although significance levels varied slightly, the findings showed no basic differences. This mixture of parametric and non parametric statistical tests is somewhat unconventional, but it does appear to provide the nearest approximation to a solution.

References

Ball, R.A. An empirical exploration of neutralization theory. *Criminologica*, 1966, 4(2):22-32.

A comparison of incipient alienation, anomia and MMPI scores, as indicators of delinquency. *Criminologica*, 1969, 6(4):13-24.

Ball, R.A. and Lilly, J.R. Juvenile Delinquency in a Rurban Area. *Criminology*, 1971, 9(1):69-85.

Female delinquency in a rurban county. *Criminology*, 1976, 14(2):279-281.

Emergent Delinquency in a Rurban Area. In T.N. Ferdinand (Ed.), *Juvenile Delinquency: Little Brother Grows Up.* Beverly Hills, Calif.: Sage, 1977.

Beaver, W. Anomia and the sixth graders of Marion County. Unpublished M.A. Thesis, West Virginia University, 1972.

Broverman, Inge K., Susan R. Vogel, Donald Broverman, Frank Clarkson and Paul Rosenkrantz. Sex-role sterotypes; A Current Appraisal. *Journal of Social Sciences*, 1972, 28(2):59-78.

Carr, L.C. The Srole items and acquiescience. *American Sociological Review*, 1971, 36(2):280-293.

Chesney-Lind, Meda. Jedicial Enforcement of the female sex role; the family court and the female delinquent. *Issues of Criminology*, 1973, 8(2):51-61.

Clark, J.P. and Wenninger, E.P. Socioeconomic class and areas as correlates of illegal behavior among juveniles. *American Sociological Review*, 1962, 27(6): 826-834.

Clinard, M. Anomie and deviant behavior. New York: Free Press, 1964.

Cowie, John, Valerine Cowie, and Eliot Slater. *Delinquency in Girls.* London: Heineman, 1968.

Dinitz, S.W., W.C. Reckless, and B. Kay. A self gradient among potential delinquents. *The Journal of Criminal Law, Criminology and Police Science*, 1958, 9(2):230-233.

Dinitz, S.F., F.R. Scarpitti, and W.C. Reckless. Delinquency vulnerability: a cross group and longitudinal analysis. *American Sociological Review.* 1962, 27(4):515-517.

Edwards, A.L. and Kirkpatrick, R.P. A technique for the construction of attitude scales. *Journal of Applied Psychology*, 1948, 16(1):125-128.

Epps, P. A Further Survey of Female Delinquents undergoing Borstal Training. *British Journal of Delinquency*, 1954, 4:265-271.

Gibbons, D.C. Crime in the hinterland. *Criminology*, 1972, 10(2):177-192.

Glueck, Sheldon and Eleanor Glueck. *Five Hundred Delinquent Women.* New York: Knopf, 1934.

Gould, L.C. Who defines delinquency: a comparison of self-reported and officially reported indices of delinquency for three racial groups. *Social Problems*, 1969, 18(1):152-163.

Hirschi, T. and H.C. Selvin. Delinquency research: an appraisal of analytic methods. New York: Free Press, 1967.

Jarrett, W.H. and A.O. Haler. Situational and personal antecedents of incipient alienation: an exploratory study. Genetic Psychology Monographs, 1964, 69:151-191.

Jensen, G.F. Delinquency and adolescent self-conceptions: a study of the personal relevance of infraction. Social Problems, 1970, 20(1):84-103.

Kahl, J. The American class structure. New York: Holt, Rinehart and Winston, 1957.

Konopka, Giseta. The Adolescent Girl in Conflict. Englewood Cliffs, N.J.: Prentice-Hall, 1966.

Lilly, J.R. Self factors and delinquency in a rural-urban county. Unpublished M.A. Thesis, West Virginia University, 1969.

Lumpkin, Katherine. Factors on the Commitment of Correctional Schoolgirls in Wisconsin. American Journal of Sociology, 1931, 37:222-230.

Martin, W. Ecological change in satellite rural area. American Sociological Review, 1957, 22(2):173-183.

Matza, D. Delinquency and drift. New York: Wiley, 1964.

Morris, Ruth R. Female Delinquency and Relational Problems. Social Forces, 1964, 43:82-89.

Novick, Abraha. The Female Institutionalized Delinquent. Institutional Rehabilitation of Delinquent Youth. Albany, N.Y.: Delmar, 1962.

Nye, F.I., and J. Short. Scaling delinquent behavior. American Sociological Review, 1956, 22(3):326-331.

Orcutt, J.D. Self concept and insulation against delinquency: some critical notes. Sociological Quarterly, 1970, 11(4):381-391.

Polk, K. Delinquency and community action in nonmetropolitan areas. President's Commission on Law Enforcement and Criminal Justice, task force report: juvenile delinquency and youth crime. Washington, D.C.: U.S. Government Printing Office, 1967.

and W.E. Schafer. Schools and delinquency. Englewood Cliffs, N.J.: Prentice-Hall, 1972.

Reckless, W.C. The crime problem. New York: Appleton-Century-Crofts, 1967.

Reckless, W.C. and S. Dinitz. Prineering with self-concept as a vulnerability factor in delinquency. The Journal of Criminal Law, Criminology and Police Science, 1967, 58(4):515-523.

Reckless, W.C., S. Dinitz, and B. Kay. The self component in potential delinquency and potential non-delinquency, American Sociological Review, 1957, 22(4):566-570.

Reckless, W.C., S. Dinitz, and E. Murray. Self concept as insulator against delinquency. American Sociological Review, 1956, 21(5):744-764.

The good boy in a high delinquency area. *The Journal of Criminal Law, Criminology and Police Science,* 1957, *48*(2):18-26.

Reckless, W.C. and S. Shoham. Norm containment theory as applied to delinquency and crime. *Excerpta Criminologica,* 1963, *3*(6):637-644.

Scarpitti, F.R., E. Murray, S. Dinitz, and W.C. Reckless. The good boys in a high delinquency area: four years later. *American Sociological Review,* 1960, *25*(6):922-926.

Schafeld, M. *The Sexual Behavior of Young People.* London: Langmans, 1965.

Schwartz, M. and S. Tangri. A note on self-concept as an insulator against delinquency. *American Sociological Review,* 1965, *30*(6):922-926.

Srole, L. Social integration and certain carallaries: an exploratory study. *American Sociological Review,* 1956, *21*(5):709-716.

Stephen, C. Attribution of intention and perception of attitude as functions of liking and similarity. *Sociometry, 36*(4):463-475.

Stern, R.S. *Delinquent conduct and broken homes.* New Haven: College and University Press, 1964.

Stinchcombe, A. *Rebellion in a high school.* Chicago: Quadrangle Books, 1964.

Sykes, G. and Matza, D. Techniques of neutralization: a theory of delinquency, *American Sociological Review,* 1957, *22*(6):664-673.

Tangri, S. and M. Schwartz. Delinquency research and the self concept variable. *The Journal of Criminal Law, Criminology and Police Science,* 1967, *58*(2); 182-190.

Triandis, H.C. and E.E. Davis. Race and belief as determinants of behavioral intentions. *Journal of Personality and Social Psychology,* 1965, *2*(5):715-725.

Section II

The Family

Forgotten Caregiving: Reciprocal Interactions in the Family Triadic Unit

Elizabeth J. Hrncir
The Pennsylvania State University
University Park, Pennsylvania 16802

Abstract

The chapter focused on social ecological changes as depicted by the research on mother-infant interactions, father-infant interactions, and interactions within the family triadic unit. The perspective of the chapter not only allowed delineation of changing research trends but also underlined how research interests can be used for viewing social ecological changes in the society. Results of current research provided the means for reaching conclusions regarding the future of the child within the family unit. The needed focus of future research was specified. Research that focuses on the family triadic unit has implications for all child care services.

Introduction

The father, though, in the main, an excellent man,
never gave the least intimation in a single instance, of any
plan for the future. He had a plan in his head, indeed, but
was never announced beforehand. It was his custom to
say, Go, and come, to his family or laborers, just as fast as
he wanted a certain thing done by them, but no faster
(Alcott, 1851, p. 131).

Society in the mid-1800's gave power to father; the father's role in caregiving was established and unquestionable. The roles of husband, wife
and children involved interaction defined by a history of psychogenetic
tradition (deMause, 1974). Reciprocal interactions or abandoned roles
were unused terms. Changing societal values and changing research
trends have established terms for describing the interactions between
parents and children. Reciprocal interactions have been defined as two-
way interactions in which both parent and child significantly influence the
other's behavior (Lewis & Rosemblum, 1974).

The scope of the paper recognized the importance of reciprocal interactions in the family triadic unit or the three way interactions between
parents and child. Recent observations and research on the father
caregiving role were a particular focus. Such focused attention allowed a
clearer perspective of social ecological change or ongoing changes in
society and the culture which affect and are affected by the family triadic
unit. Furthermore, the view allowed description of "supportive" caregiving characteristics not necessarily defined by sex or role. In particular the
issue of reciprocal interactions in the family triadic unit was analyzed with
regard to the indices: a) social ecological perspective; b) definition of
caregiving role; c) mother-child research; d) father-child research; and e)
research on triadic interactions.

The chapter has not attempted to extensively review the mother-
infant attachment literature. Rather, it has shown that with changes in
society, the field, too, has changed its focus from one that solely considers mother-child interactions to focus on the father's contributions to
child development. Finally, and due to the research on father-infant interactions, the approach has become centered on triadic as well as
reciprocal interactions. The forgotten caregiving roles are becoming
defined by new research perspectives that consider the interactional

influences among primary caregivers and the infant. No longer simplistically defined, the interactions delineated by researchers are, at the very least, triadic.

Bronfenbrenner (Note 2) has warned that present day society is experiencing the breakdown of the nuclear family with the role of parents increasingly abandoned. More recently he stated:

What these data reveal is progressive fragmentation and isolation for the family in its child rearing role. To begin with a familiar fact every year more and more mothers are going to work, now over half of those with school age children, over one third with children under six and one-third with infants under three; two-thirds of all those mothers are working full-time. A second change accompanies the first. As many more mothers go to work the number of adults left in the home who might care for the child has been decreasing in two ways. First what sociologists call extended families, those that contain other adult relatives besides the parents, have been gradually shrinking and disappearing. But shrinkage and disappearance have been even more pronounced in the so-called nuclear family consisting of mother, father, and children. Today more than one in every six children under eighteen is living in a single-parent family, with the one parent generally also being the head of the family and holding down a job, usually full time (Bronfenbrenner, Note 2, p. 6).

Bronfenbrenner (Note 2) defined the critical factors of family breakdown as resulting from the conditions under which the family lives. The current trend is not limited to the urban poor. All stratus of society have changed.

What are the implications of these trends? What does it mean for children that more and more others, especially mothers of preschoolers and infants, are going to work, the majority of them full-time? What does it mean that, as these mothers, leave for work, there are also fewer adults in the family who might look after the child, that in even more families there is only one parent who is usually also the breadwinner, and working full-time? (Bronfenbrenner, Note 2, p. 7).

Statistics on American families and children are cited because research and policy must take into account the major changes in roles patterns and expectations (Bronfenbrenner, Note 2). The need for vocational and career options for both men and women has facilitated the emergence of alternative mother-father role patterns (Rendina & Dickerschield, 1976). Yet, multivariate and longitudinal strategies are needed for conceptualizing and investigating determinants of parenting for understanding of the family (Sawin, Note 4). Many factors that have comprised the child's social ecology must be considered. Characteristics of all family members (including the child), family arrangements, relationships among members of the family unit, and effects on each person as mediated through another person are required (Sawin, Note 4).

Social Ecological Perspective

Changes within the society have been realized through focus on the breakdown of the family (Bronfenbrenner, Note 2) and through changing role perceptions and actualizations within the family (Sawin, Note 4). Studies of father involvement have provided one view for understanding the impact of alternative family arrangements on the child's development (Rendina & Dickerschield, 1976). Additionally knowledge of father-child interaction has provided information for parenting and substitute caregiving (Rendina & Dickerschield, 1976). Therefore, recent trends in research and application of father involvement strategies with children have revealed social ecological change within the culture.

Gordon (Note 3) described five parent involvement programs and criticized the lack of information resulting from focus on "father absence" studies.

> The studies of father absence from the psychological viewpoint still beg the question of family organization as it may exist in many of our centered cities. The studies use as the norm the regular husband-wife, self-contained unit. They do not describe extended family patterns or patterns in which there may be a consistent matriarchal form with the expectation of the husband playing a lesser role. It may be somewhat dangerous to infer from the above studies just what impact the father has on the behavior and development of his child in a disadvantaged home (Gordon, Note 3, p. 7).

Mother-child attachment has been the focus of the professional literature. Literature that did mention the father's role usually emphasized pathology or the effects of absent fathers. Therefore, views reflected by lacking as well as existing literature were: a) fathers were uninterested in and uninvolved with their own children; b) fathers were less nurturant than mothers; c) fathers preferred non-caretaking roles and left caretaking up to the mother; and d) fathers were less competent than mothers to care for children (Parke & Sawin, 1976). Changes in society, such as the rising divorce rate and the increase in single parent families, prompted the extensive research interest with father absence upon children (Gearing, 1978). The recognition of lacking information on fathering, growing concern over pathological father-child interactions, and demands from feminists to restructure sex roles led to research of paternal behavior in whole families (Gearing, 1978). However, the nature of the roles of father and their contributions to children's development still remains relatively uncharted and unknown (Clarke-Stewart, 1978). Only a few recent studies have examined paternal infant attachment and the impact of the father on child development (Greenberg & Morris, 1974, Lamb, 1975, 1976; Lynn, 1976).

The actual extent to which American fathers currently spend time with their children has not been revealed by research (Lewis, Freneau, & Roberts, 1979). Furthermore, research on the social ecological perspective of the family has suggested that little is actually known about behaviors within the "privacy of homes" (Clarke-Stewart, 1978). Data must be based on the actual behaviors that parents engage in with children and the nature and quality of the patterns of parenting (Sawin, Note 4). Furthermore, parents' own self conceptions for defining their role in relation to each other and to the child must be defined. Research and strategies for understanding fatherhood and the family requires distinctions among socioculturally given roles (Sawin, Note 4).

Caregiving Role — Definition

In order to research supportive roles of adults, investigators have attempted to define the term "caregiver." However, consistent use of the definition of caregiver has been difficult. Furthermore, the use of "father" or "mother" has often suggested sex role stereotypes (Sawin, Note 4). Research on individuals' self reports of their masculine and feminine characteristics indicated that "parent" characteristics should be viewed rather than role classification by "father" or "mother" (Sawin, Note 4). Designations of the caregiver as "father", "mother", "aunt", or "grandmother" as being necessary for understanding the child social ecology and patterns of parenting behavior are not required (Sawin, Note 4).

Primate literature (e.g., Devore, 1963; Harlow, 1958; Mitchell, 1969) as well, has been concerned with definition of role characteristics of nurturant caregivers. And, like the literature on human caregivers, discrepancies of a common name for the "nurturant caregiver" have persisted.

Devore (1963) found that baboons were not interested in the infants but played a protective role for the entire group of primates. Harlow (1958) found that females were four times as likely to express nurturant behavior to an infant than males. The males were ten times as hostile to the infants as the females. Primate fathers appeared to be less interested and involved in the care and nurturance of infants than the mothers (Parke & Sawin, 1976).

However, other animal evidence (e.g., Mitchell, 1969; Mitchell, Redican, & Gomber, 1974) has shown males assuming a parental role with infants. The male rhesus monkey has been found capable of nurturant caregiving in the laboratory when given the opportunity (Mitchell, Redican, & Gomber, 1974).

Primate newborns may have a strong impact upon males of many species. Greenberg and Morris (1974) noted male involvement with the care of newborns throughout the vertebrate animal world. The complexity of the infant monkey's environment seemed to influence whether or not the male adult became involved in nuturant caregiving.

Likewise research has concluded that human infants, like primate infants, benefit from the opportunity to interact regularly with a consistent variety of adults and children (Lamb, 1976; Schaffer & Emerson, 1964). Thereby, definition of the nurturant caregiver has relied on definition of various adults in the infant's environment.

Mother-Child Interactions

Ainsworth (1973) and Bowlby (1958) and Yarrow and Pederson (1972) have emphasized the mother-infant relationship as the most important in the infant's life. Harlow and Harlow's (1966) studies established the importance of "love" for the development of the primate infant. Bowlby's (1969) theory of attachment showed the primary importance of love for the development of *human* infants. Bowlby (1969) argued for the biological unity of mother and infant insisting that the mother infant dyad was derived from biological and evolutionary pressures and based on a very unique system of interactions.

Bowlby's (1969) beliefs aligned other researchers (e.g., Ainsworth,

1964; Schaffer & Emerson, 1964) who also became interested in the mother-child relationship. The resulting "attachment literature" helped establish the importance of recognizing the early caregiving relationship and the effects on the infant's later development (Lamb, 1975).

Not surprising, historically, the mother-child bond has been the focus of concern for those interested in the influence of early experience. Research on institutionalized children as well as psychoanalytic theory (e.g., Bear, 1954; Bowlby, 1951; Goldfarb, 1943; Spitz, 1945) has produced for the early experience proponents evidence that deprivation of mother impairs the development of strong maternal attachment. The belief has led to the conclusion that if daycare involves danger to the mother-child attachment, parents must be informed (Bronfenbrenner, Note 2).

Such fears, at last, have not been well supported by research. Schaffer and Emerson (1964) found that the amount of time the mother spent with the child was uncorrelated with intensity of the child's attachment to her. Furthermore, Fein and Clarke-Stewart (1973) suggested that duration of time of proximity between mother and child may be a poor index of the security of the infant's attachment.

Father-Child Interactions

Language has long abounded with terms that underline the importance of the mother's role (e.g., "maternal infant bonding"; "class mothers") (Resnick, Resnick, Packer & Wilson, 1978). Unusual and awkward sounding have been words such as "paternal infant bond" or "class fathers" (Resnick, et al., 1978). Perhaps one of the clearest indices to the changing social ecological perspective of the father role in caregiving is the beginning use of the term "engrossment" (Greenberg and Morris, 1974).

Greenberg and Morris (1974) defined engrossment as the newborn's ability in reflexive activity to elicit emotional responses from new fathers. Results of the study defined the father as feeling gripped and held by a particular feeling and desire to look at, hold, and touch the infant (Greenberg & Morris, 1974). Moreover the father felt bigger with increased self-esteem and worth when engrossed with the infant (Greenberg & Morris, 1974). Infant activity (i.e., grasp reflex) when occurring in the presence of the father was perceived by the father as a response to him (Greenberg & Morris, 1974).

Engrossment or fathers expressing strong interest in their infants and willingness to share caretaking activities has surprised many researchers (Gearing, 1978). Neglected, perhaps, has been the use of anthropological literature that has long supported the notion that fathers do experience fatherliness and that nurturing characteristics are human characteristics (Gollober, 1976). In environments (i.e., primate and human) where the feelings of fathers are allowed freedom of expression, fathers have shown warmth, affection and tenderness for their infants (Hines, 1971). However, males have often been surprised at their new found feelings for newborn infants resulting, in part, from lacking cultural supports. The expectant father lacks a clearly defined role and must accept pregnancy and subsequent parenthood without the physiological changes the woman undergoes to reinforce reality. Consequently, the father's ability to "engross" or attach to the infant has been difficult when physiological and cultural supports are lacking. Yet Greenberg and Morris (1974) asserted that engrossment was a basic innate potential among fathers and that there should be interaction between fathers' innate potentials and the cultural arena.

Research has attempted to show that fathers have been engrossed in their infants (Greenburg & Morris, 1974) and have been as nurturant, affectionate, responsive and active as mothers (Parke & O'Leary, 1976). Most of the research has distinguished the caregiving role along two basic lines: feeding and playing. Because of the physiological preparation of the mother for motherhood and the biological link between mother and infant many have suggested that the mother's role has involved physical caregiving while the father's role has involved fun and games and a link to the outside world (Lamb, 1975; Lewis & Weinraub, 1974). Based on parental interviews Kotelchuck (1976) supported the view of caretaking in mother-child interactions and playing in father-child interactions. Lamb (1976) also presented observational evidence for these differentiated interactional patterns. He determined that the fathers' play was more physical and unpredictable while the mothers' activity was more conventional and related to materials. Additionally the fathers' play involved physical tapping games; the mothers' play was verbal (Lamb, 1976).

Several other researchers (e.g., Rendina & Dickerscheid, 1976; Rebelsky & Hanks, 1971) suggested basic differences in interaction patterns between infant-father and infant-mother dyads. Rendina and Dickerscheid (1976) asserted that the fathers' greater social play involvement with infants rather than physical need caregiving demonstrated the cultural role expectation placed on the mother. Furthermore, they expressed concern with the results of divided role taking:

> If mothers are primarily involved in caring for physical needs and have little time to participate in social activities, children reared in homes without actively participating fathers may lack experiences necessary for their optimal development . . . duplicating mothers' involvement may diminish the unique experiences fathers offer to the infant. Mothers' roles in such instances may need expansion to include a portion of the social stimulation formerly provided by fathers (Rendina & Dickerscheid, 1976, p. 377).

Rebelsky and Hanks (1971) concluded that fathers talked infrequently and for shorter periods of time with their infants during the first three months of life. Clarke-Stewart (1978) suggested that many studies showed that fathers were as active as mothers or involved in differential caregiving, but did not establish how much fathers actually did care for infants in the privacy of their homes. In the attempt to address the issue of "privacy of the home", Clarke-Stewart (1978) conducted a longitudinal study of 14 children, 1 to 2½ years of age. Data were gathered in five different ways: a) unstructured "natural" observations; b) semistructured "probe" situations; c) records kept by mothers; d) attitude questionnaires completed by both parents; and e) standardized developmental tests (Clarke-Stewart, 1978).

Results of the Clarke-Stewart (1978) study showed children enjoying and cooperating more in play with their fathers than with their mothers. The study proposed that the play style the parent adopted was the style the parent enjoyed, and the style involved praise of the child and social-physical rather than intellectual activities with objects (Clarke-Stewart, 1978). Clarke-Stewart (1978) questioned why the "play" style was more common for fathers than mothers. They suggested the style must be a function of a) biological sex differences; b) cultural expectations; or c) the extent of experiences mothers and fathers have with their children.

Clarke-Stewart (1978) generalized that mothers and fathers were unalike in quantity of interaction with their children but alike in quality except for the variable, social play. The need to investigate whether the influence of the mother's presence on the fathers' behavior was identical to the influence of the father's presence on the mother's behavior was evidenced (Clark-Stewart, 1978). Hypothesized was the casual direction: mother influenced child; child influenced father; father influenced mother — over the time period assessed (Clarke-Stewart, 1978).

Triadic Interactions

While recognizing the contribution of the father to the child's development many of the investigations have ignored the concurrent contribution of the mother (Clarke-Stewart, 1978). Yet researchers with differentiated perspectives have concluded that both mothers and fathers play crucial and qualitatively different roles in the socialization of the child (Lamb, 1975). Lamb (1975) asserted that differentiated roles accounted for the socializing performance of the nuclear family.

My thesis is not that the father is the sole important member of that system; rather, it is that the recent trend toward a denigration of his role is misguided. Both parents contribute to the psychological development of their offspring, and it is unlikely that their contributions are independent, although I have implied this in the present essay. Dyadic models, while simpler to conceptualize seriously distort the psychological and sociological realities of the ecology in which children develop (Lamb, 1976, p. 30).

Researchers have begun to focus on conceptualization of the father's role within the family unit.

We have found it most useful to conceptualize the father's role in terms of a theoretical model of the family unit as a triadic system of reciprocal influences which contribute to the development of the infant (Sawin & Parke, 1979, p. 510).

The triadic model has been defined according to the additional important dimensions of: a) direct effects of father on infant through his behaviors with infants; b) indirect effects of the father that have been mediated through the mother's behavior with the infant and have moderated the father's involvement; and c) bidirectional influences on parent-infant interactive behaviors on which the infant has determined the parents' behaviors (Sawin & Parke, 1979).

Direct Effects of father on infant

Parke, O'Leary and West (1972) observed the behavior of fathers in the family triad of mother-infant and father-infant. The primary questions raised by the researchers concerned the extent of father's interest and involvement with newborn infants. The procedure in the hospital setting included bringing the child to the mother's room and asking the parents, "To whom should I give the baby?" Evaluation of who held the baby first and for how long was made and the observer recorded the occurrence of the following infant and parent behaviors. Recorded for the infant were the variables of: a) cry; b) vocalize; c) move; d) movements without or with object; e) look at mother; f) look at father; and g) look around. Recorded for the parents were the variables of: a) look; b) smile; c) vocalize; d) hold; e) touch; f) imitate; g) explore; h) feed; and i) hand over to other parent. Results indicated that fathers were just as involved as mothers and that mothers and fathers did not differ on the majority of measures. However, the investigators concluded that the results may have occurred because fathers were: a) in supporting presence of mother; b) middle income status; c) involved in Lamaze classes; and d) well educated (Parke-O'Leary & West, 1972).

Infant effects on parents

Furthermore and equally as important, success in caretaking has been determined to be dependent on the parents' ability to correctly interpret the infant's behavior (Sawin & Parke, 1979). The need to focus on the child's contribution in shaping the parents' behavior has been stressed (Bell, 1968; 1971; Harper, 1971; Kagan 1971; Rheingold, 1968). In fact, researchers have stated that the quality of interaction (Bell, 1971; Pedersen & Robsen, 1969; Schaffer & Emerson, 1964) and the adult's sensitivity to the infant's signals (Ainsworth & Bell, 1974; Schaffer & Emerson, 1964) are by far the most significant variables deserving study. The child is an active contributor to the interaction and the child's characteristics and behaviors modify the parents' behavior in initiating and terminating interaction. The child is capable of sophisticated modes of relating to others (Bell, 1968, 1971; Lewis & Rosenblum, 1974; Osofsky, 1972; Rheingold, 1968). The affective quality of the infant's interaction with each parent must be recognized; the opportunity for brief emotionally charged interaction with the father may offset longer hours spent with a dissatisfied mother (Yarrlow, Waxler, and Scott, 1971). Indices that influence caregiver behavior including sex differences developmental level (Kagan, 1971); and temperament (Bell, 1974; Chess and Thomas, 1973; Schaffer & Emerson, 1964) must be considered by researchers.

The newborn has been determined to have an impact on both parents. Both parents must differentially interact with and care for the newest member of the family system (Lamb, 1975).

In brief, in two-parent families at least, fathers and mothers have roles that contain substantial similarities, but are also distinct. They share in, but do not duplicate, each other's efforts. Though both may contribute to children's development, they do not contribute equally or in the same way. They do, quite clearly, create a concellation in the home, that is truly, one family, under God, indivisible with liberty and justice for all (Stewart, Note 6, p. 17).

Indirect effects of father on mother

The father's involvement has been shown to support the mothers' interest and affect toward the infant (Sawin & Parke, 1979). Sawin and Parke (1979) found that the father had additional influence on the infant as mediated by the enhanced attitudes and behaviors of the mother (Sawin & Parke, 1979).

Discussion

Research on the interaction of mother-father-infant in the family unit has suggested that the essence of caregiving is far more complex than previous investigators believed. Understandably, many investigations have been plagued by conceptual and methodological inadequacies. Major criticisms of these investigations have included the methodological problems: a) parents were not seen together in the laboratory but in two separate sessions; b) few measures were used to record only specific attachment behaviors; c) often either child or parent contribution was ignored; all three interactional patterns were often ignored (Lamb, 1975).

The focus must be upon the interaction, which means that we must examine the behavior of each person in the context of the contingent behaviors of the other. Secondly, we must pay greater attention to the ecological context in which observations are made (Lamb, 1975, p. 251).

Additionally, the newborn period should be viewed not only as a starting point for observation but as a potential intervention point (Parke & Sawin, 1976). Fathers, although shown to be interested and competent, need support just as mothers need support for reciprocal participation in caregiving routines. Paternal behavior might then be modified, both quantitatively and qualitatively early in life (Parke & Sawin, 1976).

Further research is demanded on the differentiation of maternal and paternal roles in caretaking and socialization practices. While there is evidence of qualitative differences in the interactions between infants and their mothers and fathers, additional research should concentrate on the developmental course of this trend, and the extent to which deviations from the normal pattern have an effect upon subsequent development (Lamb, 1975, p. 258).

The little research conducted on father-infant reciprocal interaction patterns as well as the total complex interaction patterns in the family triadic unit has allowed the chapter to draw only weak conclusions and implications. Knowledge is yet scarce as to the differential effects of behaviors on both infants and parents. However the chapter has fulfilled the purpose of delineation of the importance of reciprocal interactions in the family triadic unit. The chapter is not well substantiated by huge numbers of research studies and therefore lacks effective impact. Perhaps the chapter's basic premise can be actualized as a framework for the addition of future studies and for a guidepost for suggesting future directions in research.

Conclusion

Recognition of shifting parental roles and the general redefining of the appropriateness of early-father involvement has provided fathers with opportunities to both learn and practice caretaking skills during the newborn period. Redefinition of father involvement may allow the father to share these responsibilities and view the behaviors as role-consistent (Sawin & Parke, 1979). Society then becomes responsible for changing its perspective of the father role. No longer appropriate is:

A society which is hostile to the concept of active fathers who feed, bathe, and comfort their children rather than briefly roughhouse with a smiling powdered bundle" (Resnick, et al., 1978).

The self esteem of male caregivers should be supported for change in the social ecological perspective and definitions of "supportive" characteristics of caregivers:

> We believe that if the self-esteem of fathers was reinforced by the assurance that they, like their wives, have important roles to play in the socialization of their children from infancy onwards, this would significantly reduce the incidence of marital conflict engendered by a baby's birth. In addition to this, one might predict that an enthusiastic commitment to fatherhood would expand the amount and improve the quality of father-infant interaction (Lamb & Lamb, 1976, p. 383).

With changing social ecological perspectives and changing role patterns, programs must also change their definitions of caregiver involvement.

> Generally, current programs are designed to offer parental assistance to mothers with young children and infants. It would be worthwhile to consider including the fathers in this type of support program (Rendina & Dickerscheid, 1976, p. 377).

The definition of early supportive caregiving characteristics would also allow programs to meet the needs of parents and children.

> If we are able to determine the characteristics features of early father-child relationships, it will be easier to counsel families on the probable effects of separation, as well as easier to suggest arrangements for single parent families which might diminish the impact of the father's absence . . . consequently the demonstration that fathers are important in the eyes of their infants, and that they have an important role to play in the socialization of their children from infancy onwards, would not only enhance the self-esteem of fathers, but might in so doing strengthen their commitment to their marital and parental roles (Lamb & Lamb, 1976, p. 379-380).

Many options for the future are evolving which will continue to have direct effects on families and children: a) creation of new opportunities for caring for children; b) new life plans for women and for men; c) family centered childbirth; d) creation of dialogue about fatherhood; and e) revision of child rearing manuals (Levine, 1976).

Additionally, legislation or lack thereof will influence caregiving. Proponents for support of fathers through legislation have voiced their beliefs.

In considering the impact of legislation on the family, I would like to emphasize the importance of including the impact of such legislation on fathers. I am not here referring to the situation in which fathers desert, a topic I do not mean to minimize, but one which we are all-too-well aware of and to which many talented people are devoting their attention. I would like rather to call attention to the millions of fathers who, though they do not physically desert their families nevertheless, in effect, renege on their contribution to child rearing. They far outnumber the deserting fathers.

It is all too easy for us to see the mote in the other person's eye and not the beam in our own. I respectfully call attention here to the families of men in this very Congress, in our industries, in our universities and colleges. I call attention in fact to most fathers in this country. Their contribution to the rearing of children is minimal.

The trend of the times is in the direction of greater sharing of the child-rearing function by both parents (Bernard, Note 1).

The future must show the rebirth of understanding of the contributions of all caregivers to the growth and development of children. Although the father's role may necessitate redefinition, the power of the father again must be realized as it was in the 1800's (Alcott, 1851). More importantly the power of *all* caregivers must be realized.

Reference Notes

1 Bernard, J. *American Families — Trends and Pressures.* Prepared statement made to the Hearings before the subcommittee on children and youth of the committee on labor and public welfare, Washington, D.C., 1974.
2 Bronfenbrenner, U., and others. *Day care in context: An ecological perspective on research and public policy.* Washington, D.C.: Office of the Assistant Secretary for Planning and Evaluation, 1977. (ERIC Document Reproduction No. 157 637).
3 Gordon, I.J. *Parent involvement in compensatory education.* Champaign, Illinois: University of Illinois Press, 1970. (ERIC Reproduction Service No. ED 039 954).

4 Parke, R.D.; O'Leary, S.E. & West, S. *Mother-father-newborn interaction: Effects of maternal medication, labor and sex of infant.* Proceedings of the American Psychological Association, 1972.
5 Sawin, D.B. *Father's interactions with young infants: Current issues and future directions for research,* 1977. (ERIC Document Reproduction Service No. ED 154 925).
6 Stewart, A. *The father's impact on mother and child,* 1977. (ERIC Document Reproduction Service No. ED 136 954).
7 Yogman, M.W., and others. *Father-infant interaction,* 1976. (ERIC Reproduction Service No. ED 160 249).

References

Ainsworth, M.D. The development of infant-mother attachment. In B.M. Caldwell & H.N. Ricciuti (Eds.) *Review of child development research* (Vol. III), Chicago: University of Chicago Press, 1973.

Ainsworth, M.D. Patterns of attachment behavior shown by the infant in interaction with his mother. *Merrill-Palmer Quarterly,* 1964, *10,* 51-58.

Ainsworth, M.D., Bell, S.M., & Stayton, D.J. Infant-mother attachment and social development: Socialization as a product of reciprocal responsiveness to signals. In M.P.M. Richards (Ed.) *The integration of a child into a social world.* Cambridge, England: Cambridge University Press, 1974.

Alcott, W.A. *The young husband or duties or man in the marriage relation.* Boston: Charles D. Strong, 1851.

Baer, M. Women workers and home responsibilities. *International Labor Review,* 1954, *69,* 338-355.

Bell, R.Q. Stimulus control of parent or caretaker behavior by offspring. *Developmental Psychology,* 1971, *4,* 63-72.

Bell, R.Q. A reinterpretation of the direction of effects of studies or socialization. *Psychological Review,* 1968, *75,* 81-95.

Biller, H.B. The mother-child relationship and the father-absent boy's personality development. *Merrill-Palmer Quarterly,* 1971, *17,* 227-241.

Biller, H.B. *Father, child, and sex role: Paternal determinants of personality development.* Lexington, Massachusetts: D.C. Heath and Company, 1971.

Bowlby, J. *Attachment and Loss* (Vol. I). New York: Basic Books, 1969.

Bowlby, J. *Maternal care and mental health.* Geneva: World Health Organization, 1951.

Bowlby, J. The nature of the child's tie to his mother. *International Journal of Psychoanalysis,* 1958, *39,* 350-373.

Brazelton, T.B.; Koslowski, B.; and Main, M. The origin of reciprocity: The early mother-infant interaction. In M. Lewis and L. Rosenblum (Eds.) *The Effect of the Infant on Its Caregiver.* New York: John Wiley & Sons, 1974.

Bretherton, I., & Ainsworth, M.D. Responses of one-year-olds to a stranger in a strange situation. In M. Lewis & L.A. Rosenblum (Eds.), *The origins of fear.* New York: Wiley, 1974.

Bronfenbrenner, U. Toward an experimental ecology of human development. *American Psychologist,* 1977, *32,* 513-531.

Caldwell, B.M., Wright, C.M., Honig, A.S. & Tannenbaum, J. Infant day care and attachment. *American Journal of Orthopsychiatry,* 1970, *40*(7) 397-412.

Chess, S., & Thomas, A. Temperament in the normal infant. In J.C. Westman (ed.), *Individual differences in children.* New York: Wiley, 1973.

Clarke-Stewart, K.A. And daddy makes three: The father's impact on mother and young child. *Child Development,* 1978, *49,* 466-478.

Cohen, L.J. & Campos, J.J. Father, mother and stranger as elicitors of attachment behaviors in infancy. *Developmental Psychology,* 1974, *10,* 146-154.

Coser, R.L. (Ed.) *The family its structures and functions* (2nd edition). New York: St. Martin's Press, 1974.

deMause, L. *The history of childhood.* New York: Harper & Row Publishers, 1974.

Devore, I. Mother-infant reactions in free ranging baboons. In H. Rheingold, (Ed.) *Maternal behavior in mammals.* New York: John Wiley, 1963.

Doyle, A.B. Infant development in day care. *Developmental Psychology,* 1975, *11,* 655-656.

Fein, G.G. & Clarke-Stewart, A. *Day care in context.* New York: John Wiley & Sons, 1973.

Feldman, S.S., & Ingham, M.E. Attachment behavior: A validation study in two age groups. *Child Development,* 1975, *46,* 319-330.

Gearing, J. Facilitating the birth process and father-child bonding. *The Counseling Psychologist,* 1978, *7* (4), 53-56.

Goldfarb, W. The effects of early institutional care on adolescent personality. *Journal of Experimental Education,* 1943, *12,* 106-129.

Gollober, M. A comment on the need for father-infant postpartal interaction. *Journal of Obstetrical, Gynecological and Neonatal Nursing,* 1976, 6, 17-20.

Greenberg, M., & Morris, N. Engrossment: The newborn's impact upon the father. *American Jourrnal of Orthopsychiatry,* 1974, *44,* 520-531.

Harlow, H.F. The nature of love. *American Psychologist,* 1958, *13,* 673-685.

Harlow, H.F. & Harlow, M.K. Learning to love. *American Scientist,* 1966, *54,* 244-272.

Harlow, J.F. & Zimmermann, R.R. Affectional responses in the infant monkey. *Science,* 1959, *130*(33), 421-432.

Harper, L.V. The young as a source of stimuli controlling caretaking behavior. *Developmental Psychology,* 1971, *4,* 73-85.

Hines, J. Father . . . the forgotten man. *Nursing Forum,* 1971, *10,* 176-200.

Itani, J. Paternal care in the wild Japanese monkey, macacca fuscata. *Journal of Primates,* 1959, *2*(1), 61-93.

Josselyn, I.M. Cultural forces, motherliness and fatherliness. *American Journal of Orthopsychiatry,* 1956, *26,* 264-271.

Kagan, J. *Change and continuity in infancy.* New York: Wiley, 1971.

Kotelchuck, M. The infant's relationship to the father: Experimental evidence. In M.E. Lamb (Ed.) *The role of the father in child development.* New York: John Wiley & Sons, 1976.

Lamb, M.E. A defense of the concept of attachment. *Human Development,* 1974, *17,* 376-385.

Lamb, M.E. Fathers: Forgotten contributors to child development. *Human Development,* 1975, *18,* 245-266.

Lamb, M.E. Father-infant and mother-infant interaction in the first year of life. *Child Development,* 1977, *48,* 167-181.

Lamb, M.E. Interactions between two-year-olds and their mothers and fathers. *Psychological Reports,* 1976, *38,* 447-450.

Lamb, M.E. Twelve-month-olds and their parents: Interactions in a laboratory playroom. *Developmental Psychology,* 1976, *12,* 237-244.

Lamb, M.E. Interactions between eight-month-olds and their fathers and mothers. In M.E. Lamb (Ed.), *The role of the father in child development.* New York: Wiley, 1976.

Lamb, M.E. The role of the father: An overview. In M.E. Lamb (Ed.), *The role of the father in child development,* New York: Wiley, 1976.

Lamb, M.E. (Ed.) *The role of the father in child development.* New York: John Wiley & Sons, 1976.

Lamb, M.E. and Lamb, J.E. The nature and importance of the father-infant relationship. *The Family Coordinator,* 1976, 379-385.

Levine, J.A. *Who will raise the children? New options for fathers (and mothers).* Philadelphia: J.B. Lippincott Company, 1976.

Lewis, M., et al. Mothers and infants, girls and boys: Attachment behavior in the first two years of life. In F.J. Monks, W. Willard & J. de Wit, (Eds.) *Determinants of Behavior Development,* New York: Academic Press, 1972.

Lewis, R.A.; Freneau, P.J. & Roberts, C.L. Fathers and the postparental transition. *The Family Coordinator,* 1979, *28,* 514-520.

Lewis, M. & Rosemblum, L.A. (Eds.). *The effect of the infant on its caregiver.* New York: John Wiley & Sons, 1974.

Lewis, M. & Weinraub, M. Sex of parent × sex of child: Socio-emotional development. In R. Richart, R. Friedman, & R. Vande Wiele (Eds.), *Sex differences in behavior.* New York: Wiley, 1974.

Lynn, D.B. *The father: His role in child development.* Monterey, California: Brooks/Cole, 1976.

Mason, W. Social development of monkeys and apes. In I. Devore (Eds.) *Primate Behavior: Field studies of monkeys and apes.* New York: Holt Rinehart and Winston, 1965.

Mitchell, G.D. Paternalistic behavior in primates. *Psychological Bulletin,* 1969, *71,* 399-417.

Mitchell, G.D.; Redican, W.K.; & Gomber, J. Males can raise babies. *Psychology Today,* 1974, *7,* 63-67.

Nash, J. The father in contemporary cultural and current psychological literature. *Child Development,* 1965, *36,* 261-297.

Osofsky, J.D. & O'Connell, E.J. Parent-child interaction: Daughters' effects upon mothers and fathers' behaviors. *Developmental Psychology,* 1972, *7,* 157-168.

Parke, R.D. & O'Leary, S.E. Family intervention in the newborn period: Some findings, some observations, and some unresolved issues. In K.F. Riegel & J.A. Meacham (Eds.), *The developing individual in a changing world* (Vol. 2): *Social and environmental issues.* Chicago: Aldine, 1976.

Parke, R.D. & Sawin, D.B. The father's role in infancy: A re-evaluation. *The Family Coordinator,* 1976, *24,* 365-371.

Pedersen, F.A. & Robson, K.S. Father participation in infancy. *American Journal of Orthopsychiatry,* 1969, *39,* 466-472.

Rebelsky. F., & Hanks, C. Fathers verbal interaction with infants in the first three months of life. *Child development,* 1971, *42,* 63-68.

Redican, W.K. Adult male-infant interactions in non-human primates. In M.E. Lamb (Ed.), *The role of the father in child development.* new York: John Wiley & Sons, 1976.

Reiber, V.D. Is the nurturing role natural to fathers? *Maternal/Child Nursing,* 1976, *1,* 366-371.

Rendina, I. and Dickerscheid, J.D. Father involvement with first-born infants. *The Family Coordinator,* 1976, 373-378.

Resnick, J.L.; Resnick, M.B.; Packer, A.B.; and Wilson, J. Fathering classes: A psycho/educational model. *The Counseling Psychologist,* 1978, *7*(4), 56-60.

Rheingold, H.L. The social and socializing infant. In D.A. Goslin (Ed.), *Handbook of socialization theory and research.* Chicago: Rand McNally, 1968.

Sawin, D.B. & Parke, R.D. Fathers' affectionate stimulation and caregiving behaviors with new born infants. *The Family Coordinator,* 1979, *28* (4), 509-513.

Schaffer, H. & Emerson, P. The development of social attachments in infancy. *Monographs of the Society for Research in Child Development,* 1964, *29.*

Spitz, R.A. Hospitalism: An inquiry into the genesis of psychiatric conditions in early childhood. *Psychoanalytic Study of the Child,* 1945, *1,* 53-74.

Stern, D.N. Mother and infant at play: The dyadic interaction involving facial vocal, and gaze behaviors. In M. Lewis & L.A. Rosenblum (Eds.), *The effect of the infant on its caregiver.* New York: Wiley, 1974.

Thomas, A. Chess, S., & Birch, H.G. The origin of personality. *Scientific American,* 1970, *223,* 102-109.

West, M.M. & Konner, M.J. The role of the father: An anthropoligical perspective. In M.E. Lamb (Ed.), *The role of the father in child development.* New York: John Wiley & Sons, 1976.

Yarrow, L.J. & Pederson, F. Attachment: Its origins and course. *Young Children,* 1972, *24*(4) 302-312.

Yarrow, M.R.; Scott, P.; DeLeeuw, L., and Heinig, C. Child-rearing in families of working and nonworking mothers. *Sociometry,* 1962, *25,* 122-140.

Yarrow, M.R., Waxler, C.Z. & Scott, P.M. Child effects on adult behavior. *Developmental Psychology,* 1971, *5,* 300-311.

A Perspective on the Family and Juvenile Delinquency

Theron M. Covin, Ed.D.
Director, Child and Family Mental Health Experimental Project
P.O. Box 429 ABCH
Troy, Al. 36081

Abstract

Juveniles, ages 7–18, have become the most crime-prone group in the United States. The purpose of this paper was to explore the relationship between the family, the primary source of juvenile delinquency and juvenile delinquency. The presence of a criminal model, lax, strict and/or inconsistent discipline, lack of affection, rejection by parents, and the absence of parents were among the variables highly correlated with juvenile delinquency. Basic to the prevention of delinquency is the family environment where love and affection are felt by the child. The affectionate family can prevent juvenile delinquency.

183

A n alarming increase in crimes committed by children has occurred in the United States since World War II, especially in recent years. Federal Bureau of Investigation statistics show a 98% increase in arrests for violent crimes among children 17 years of age and younger between 1967 and 1976. The Ford Foundation's recent report (Strasburg, 1978) concludes that delinquency is far more widespread among children in the United States than most of us realize. The report reveals that juveniles age 7 to 18 years have become the nation's most crime-prone group. While children currently make up 20% of the total population in the United States, juveniles in this age group account for 43% of all arrests for serious crimes.

Causes of juvenile delinquency have been often reearched and discussed. Failure in school, low socioeconomic background, low IQ, poor family environment, and peer group influence are among the variables most often cited as "causes" of juvenile delinquency. Faulty vision has even been listed as a "cause" of juvenile delinquency (Thacher, 1978).

Nuermous data point to the family as the primary source of juvenile delinquency. For every juvenile delinquent, there is a delinquent home environment, for childre are not born delinquent. Rather, they are made that way by their families, usually by their parents.

Since the single most predictive indicator of juvenile delinquency is the child's family environment, various variables found in the family environment which are highly correlated with juvenile delinquency will be explored in this paper. A profile of the family least likely to produce children who are delinquent will also be given.

The Delinquent Family

Children who are delinquent generally come from a family environment where one or more of several conditions or phenomena are present.

Modeling

The first type of family setting which breeds delinquency is the family environment in which delinquent behavior is reinforced and maintained within the family by one or both adult caregivers. Bandura and

Walters (1959, 1963a, 1963b) and Walters (1966) viewed delinquent behavior as being an imitation of behavior seen displayed by other people who serve as models. Ullman and Leonard (1969) stated that parental figures in the home represent a source of reinforcement for delinquent behavior in children. Parents serve as models from which children learn their behavior. Walters (1966) stated that modeling principle: "Observation of aggressive social models, either in real life or in fantasy productions, increases the probability that the observer will behave in an aggressive manner if the model is rewarded or does not receive punishment for aggressive behavior," p. 60. Thus, one can content that the juvenile delinquent is only acting in a manner he has been taught through example. Shaw and McKay (1942) reported that most delinquents come from homes in which parents and siblings were delinquent. Glueck and Glueck (1950) found that 94 per cent of the delinquents in their study came from homes in which there were criminals. In a later study, Glueck and Glueck (1962) identified various kinds of sociopathic behavior such as alcoholism, brutality, and nonsupport as being present among fathers of delinquent males. Havighurst (1962) concluded that delinquents came from families where drunkeness and fighting were common, sexual promiscuity was visible, and where stealing was openly condoned. Peterson and Becker (1965) found that parents of juvenile delinquents reinforced the delinquent behavior in children. Parents of delinquents were likely to have police records of their own (Ahlstrom & Havighurst (1971), Conger (1973) and Cressy and Ward (1969). Lesser (1962) found that parental behavior which advised or supported aggressive behavior was positively correlated with delinquency. Bandura and Walters (1959, 1963c) concluded that parents of juvenile delinquents tended to condone aggressive behavior on part of the child while he was growing up and gave a considerable amount of encouragement and reward for aggressive behavior outside the home. Thus, the general conclusion is that families which model, reinforce, and maintained delinquent behavior within the family unit and encourages its generalization to settings outside the family, produce children who are delinquent.

Disciplinary Techniques

Parental disciplinary techniques have consistently been found to be highly correlated with juvenile delinquency. Delinquency can occur in families where discipline is too strict, too laxed, and/or inconsistent.

185

Kagan and Moss (1962) found that the amount of permissiveness shown by the parents toward the child during the first three years of life had lasting effects on the child. The more permissive the parents, the more aggressive the child. Other researchers such as Bach (1945), Pintler (1945), Yarrow (1948), Sears (1951), Hollenberg and Sperry (1951), Levin and Turgeon (1957), and Hartup and Himeno (1959) reported a similar trend. And, permissive homes breed delinquency. "Anything goes" seems to be the ideal. The parents have lost control of the children long ago. Discipline is minimal or non-existent. A sense of randomness prevails. Family members may go for weeks without engaging in an activity in which they all participate. Each family member does his own thing. Typically, parents in such a family are preoccupied with their own intrapersonal conflicts and have little time to devote to their children. The parents may even dislike the child and wish him to be taken away, therefore, is willing to ignore misbehavior and to even encourage behaviors for which the child may be removed from the home. Glueck and Glueck (1950) also found that juvenile delinquents came from homes where parental control is lax and a sense of permissiveness prevails.

On the other hand, restrictiveness on the part of the parents also leads to juvenile delinquency, (McCord, McCord, & Howard, 1961). In families where discipline is too strict, the child is usually given little freedom. Any signs of independence are instantly disciplined by the parents. Physically punitive methods of discipline are normally used, often to a severe degree. Bandura & Walters (1959) reported that most juvenile delinquents had fathers who used physically punitive methods of discipline.

While data show that permissiveness and restrictiveness both are highly correlated with delinquency among children, more evidence supports the theory that inconsistency in discipline, combined with physically punitive methods of control, is likely to breed juvenile delinquency. Glueck and Glueck (1950) found that delinquents came from homes where discipline was either lax or very erratic and where the father resorted to severe physical punishment on an inconsistent basis. Peterson & Becker (1965) concluded that in homes of juvenile delinquents, discipline tended to be either severe or lax, but most likely, to be an inconsistent alternative between the two and to involve physical punishment. Other researchers who agree include Powers & Witman (1951), Whelon (1954), McCord, McCord, & Zola (1959), Tait & Hodges (1962), Craig & Glick, (1964), and Havighurst (1971).

Broken Homes

There is some evidence that juvenile delinquents come from families in one or more of the parents are missing due to separation, death, divorce, etc. Ahlstrom & Havighurst (1971) and Wirt and Briggs (1959) indicated that broken homes are significantly associated with higher incidents of delinquent behavior. Ullman & Leonard (1969) concluded that broken homes result in inconsistent adequate figures in the child's life. The presence of many parental figures in the home increases the likelihood of non-interest or rejection by some, if not all, which leads to an inconsistency of reinforcement and a lack of the necessary models of socialized behavior. Hartley and Himeno (1959) found an increase in aggressive behavior in children following periods of social isolation.

Gregory (1965) found that delinquency tended to be higher among boys who had lost their fathers. Wilkins (1960) found a positive relationship between father absence in the home and the incidence of criminality. He suggested that the father is important for his role in developing the child's social controls. Bacon, Child, and Barry (1963) showed that crime is positively correlated with customs making for young boys having no father figures close at hand.

While the atmosphere created by a broken home can lead to deinquent behavior in children, Ahlstrom & Havighurst (1971) found the likelihood of juvenile delinquency to be far greater in non-broken homes characterized by mutual hostility, indifference or apathy, and a lack of cohesiveness than in broken homes characterized by cohesiveness and mutual affection and support.

Lack of Affection

Generally in families of delinquents there is no basic underpinning of affection for and acceptance of the child. In such families, usually the family members have been rejecting toward the child from quite early in life. Andrey (1960) found that delinquent boys tended to feel that their fathers had given them inadequate love. A consistent pattern of feeling rejected by the father was noted. Several researchers (Bandura & Walters, 1959). Glueck & Glueck, 1950; McCord, McCord, & Zola, 1959; and Powers & Witmer, 1951), found that fathers of delinquents were more likely than those of non-delinquents to be cruel, neglecting, and inclined to ridicule their children and less likely to be warm, affectionate, or passive. Glueck & Glueck (1950) stated that children in turn, were likely to have few close ties to their fathers and to consider them wholly unacceptable as models for conduct. Mothers of delinquents were more likely than those of non-delinquents to be rated as careless or inadequate in child supervision and as hostile or indifferent rather than as loving (McCord, McCord & Zola, 1959; Powers & Witmer, 1951; and Wattenburg, 1955). Lesser (1952) and Wittenborn (1966) found a very market relationship between parental rejection and aggressive behavior in children.

Combination of Variables

Environmental combinations of variables within the family unit are more likely to cause juvenile delinquency than one single variable. McCord and McCord (1958) found that the environmental combinations that was likely to lean to delinquency was inconsistent discipline, the presence of a criminal role model in the father, and the absence of maternal warmth or affection. Consistent discipline and love from one parent counterbalanced the father's criminal role model. Rejection (by the mother) is likely to reduce reinforcement of prosocial behavior and the presence of the criminal role model gives the information to the child that this is one alternative form of behavior which he is likely to follow. Bandura & Walters (1959) found that a combination of rejection, hostility, and the lack of socially approved guidelines as to what kind of behavior would receive parental reinforcement in the home, breeds juvenile delinquency. They also found that among juvenile delinquents, there tended to be a clear pattern of father rejection plus inconsistent discipline by both parents. Becker (1964) suggested that aggressive parents have aggressive children and these parents tend to use more physical punishment and less reasoning and praise. Bee (1975) concludes that disorganized family life, accompanied by erratic discipline, and rejection of the child leads to juvenile delinquency. Burt (1929) and Healy & Bronner (1926) found that permissiveness tends to result in even greater aggressiveness on part of the child of parents who are hostile themselves. Discipline by such parents tends to be a mixture of general laxity (especially on part of the mother) and instances of extremely high punitiveness (usually on part of the father). Restrictiveness may lead to higher aggression when combined with parental hostility (McCord, McCord, & Howward, 1961; Meyers, 1944; R. Sears, 1961; R. Sears, Maccoby, & Levin, 1957). However, restrictiveness in warm, loving parents leads to low aggression (Maccoby, 1961; Meyers, 1944; and R. Sears, 1961).

Summary

Variables which are likely to be found in the family environment from which the juvenile delinquent comes includes presence of a criminal role model, discipline which is too strict, too lax, and/or inconsistent, absence of one or both parents, lack of maternal warmth and/or affection from the father, and a combination of one or more of these.

Conclusion

The family, the primary source of juvenile delinquency, can serve to produce healthy nondelinquent children. Such a family, whether a broken home or not, seems to be one in which love is dominant and where acceptance, cohesiveness, and emotional support are present. Consistent discipline, combined with reasoning and a sense of fairness, is also present.

References

Ahlstrom, W.M. & Havighurst, R.T. *400 Losers.* CA: San Francisco Press, 1971.

Andry, R.G. *Delinquency and Parental Pathology.* Springfield, Ill.: Charles C. Thomas, 1960.

Bach, C.R. Young children's play fantasies. *Psychological Monographs,* 1945, 59, (2, Whole No. 272).

Bacon, M.K., Child, I.C., & Barry, H. A cross-cultural study of correlates of crime. *Journal of Abnormal Social Psychology,* 1963, 66, 291-300.

Bandura, A. & Walters, R.H. *Adolescent Aggression.* New York: Ronald, 1959.

Bandura, A. & Walters, R.H. Aggression. In *Child Psychology,* Part I. Chicago: National Society for the study of Education, 1963, pp. 364-415.(a)

Bandura, A. & Walters, R.H. *Social Learning & Personality Development.* New York: Holt, Rinehart & Winston, 1963.(b)

Bandura, A. & Walters, R.H. *The Social Learning of Deviant Behavior: Behavioristic Approach to Socialization.* New York: Holt, Rinehart, & Winston, 1963. (c)

Becker, W.C. Consequences of different kinds of parental discipline. In M.L. Hoffman & L.W. Hoffman (Eds). *Review of Child Development Research.* Vol. 1, New York: Russell Sage Foundation, 1964, pp. 169-208.

Bee, H. *The Developing Child.* New York: Harper & Row, 1975.

Burt, C. *The Young Delinquent.* New York: Appleton, 1929.

Conger, J.J. *Adolescence and Youth: Psychological Development in a Changing World.* New York: Harper & Row, 1973.

Craig, M. & glick, S. *A Manual of Procedures for Application of the Glueck Prediction Table.* New York: New York City Youth Board, 1964.

Creesey, D. & Ward, D.A. *Delinquency, Crime, and Social Process.* New York: Harper & Row, 1969.

Glueck, G.S. & Glueck, T. *Unraveling Juvenile Delinquency.* Cambridge, Mass.: Commonwealth Fund, 1950.

Glueck, G.S. & Glueck, T. *Family Environment and Delinquency.* Boston: Houghton, 1962.

Gregory, I. Interspective data following children's loss of a parent. *Archives of General Psychiatry,* 13, 99-109.

Hartup, W.W. & Himeno, Y. Social isolation vs. interaction with adults in relation to aggression in preschool children. *Journal of Abnormal Social Psychology,* 1959, 59, 17-22.

Havighurst, R.T. et al. *Growing Up in River City.* New York: Wiley, 1962.

Healy, W. & Bronner, A.F. *Delinquents and Criminals: Their Making and Unmaking.* New York: MacMillan, 1926.

Hollenberg, E. & Spery, M. Some antecedents of aggression and effects of frustration in doll play. *Personality.* 1951, 1, 32-43.

Lesser, G.S. Maternal attitudes and practices and the aggressive behavior of children. Unpublished doctoral dissertation, Yale University, 1952.

Levin, H. & Turgeon, V. The influence of the mother's pressures on children's doll-play aggression. *Journal of Abnormal Social Psychology,* 1957, 55, 304-305.

Macoby, E.E. The taking of adult roles in middle childhood. *Journal of Abnormal Social Psychology,* 1961, 63, 493-503.

McCord, J. & McCord, W. The effects of parental role models on criminality. *Journal of Social Issues,* 1958, 14, 66-75.

McCord, J., McCord, W., & Howard. Familial correlates of aggression in nondelinquent male children. *Journal of Abnormal Social Psychology,* 1961, 62, 79-93.

McCord, W., McCord, J. & Zola, I.K. *Origins of Crime.* New York: Columbia University Press, 1959.

Meyers, C.E. The effect of conflicting authority on the child. University of Iowa. *Studies in Child Welfare,* 1944, 20, 31-98.

Pintler, M.H. Doll play as a function of experimenter — child interaction and initial organization of materials. *Child Development,* 1945, 16, 145-166.

Powers, E. & Witmer, H. *Prevention of Delinquency: The Cambridge-Somerville Youth Study.* New York: Columbia University Press, 1951.

Quay, H.C. *Juvenile Delinquency: Reserach and Theory.* Princeton, N.J. Van Nostrand, 1965, 63-99.

Sears, P. Doll-play aggression in normal young children: Influences of sex, age, sibling status, father's absence. *Psychological Monographs,* 1951, 65, (Whole No. 323).

Sears, R., Maccoby, E.E., & Levin, H. *Patterns of Child Rearing.* Evanston, Ill.: Row, Peterson, 1957.

Sears, R. The relation of early socialization experiences to aggression in middle childhood. *Journal of Abnormal Social Psychology,* 1961, 63, 466-492.

Shaw, C.R. & McCay, H.D. *Juvenile Delinquency and Urban Areas.* Chicago: University of Chicago Press, 1942.

Strasburg, P.A. *Violent Delinquents.* New York: Ford Foundation, 1978.

Tait, D.D., Jr. & Hodges, E.F. *Delinquents, Their Families and the Community.* Springfield, Ill.: Thomas, 1962.

Thacher, M. "Flunking Flunking Flunking 20/20." *Human Behavior,* 1978, 7, 53-55.

Ullman, L.P. & Leonard, K. *A Psychological Approach to Abnormal Behavior.* New Jersey: Prentice-Hall, 1969.

Walters, K.H. Implications of laboratory studies on aggression for the control and regulation of violence. *Annual American Academy of Political Science,* 1966, 364, 60-72.

Wattenberg, W.W. *The Adolescent Years.* New York: Harcourt, Brace Jovanovich, 1955.

Whelon, R.W. An experiment in preventing delinquency. *Journal of Criminal Law, Criminology, and Political Science.* 1954, 45, 432-442.

Wilkins, L.T. *Delinquent Generations.* Home Office Research Unity, Research Report No. 3, London: Her Majesty's Stationary Office, 1960.

Wirt, R.D. & Briggs, P.F. Personality and environmental factors in the development of delinquency. *Psychological Monographs,* 1959, 73, 1-47.

Wittenborn, J.R. A study of adoptive children: III. Relationships between some aspects of environment for adoptive children. *Psychological Monographs,* 1956, 70, 3 (Whole No. 410).

Growing Up In An Alcoholic Family: The Effects On Child Development

Eldon M. Gade
University of North Dakota

Abstract

Parental abuse of alcohol has a documented detrimental effect on child development. This impact ranges from physical impairment to maladaptive psychological and educational behavior. Particularly, growing-up in an alcoholic family affects educational achievement, aspiration, self-concept, and social adjustment. Model programs for alcoholic family intervention, prevention, and treatment hold promise for reducing the effects of parental alcoholism on child development.

Introduction

The world of two children, both victims of parental alcoholism epitomize the effects of family alcoholism on child development (Cork, 1969).

First Jerome described his experience:

> Its always just the same. Dad goes to work, works and comes home drunk or else he brings the stuff home and gets drunk there. I wouldn't mind his drinking if he'd be quiet and leave us alone, but he always seems to want to pick a fight. If mom goes upstairs to get away, he starts in on us kids. (p. 3)

And Sally described her plight:

> I always feel sad, not just because my father drinks but because of the way he is . . . He's always getting mad and smashing things. Once when I was little, he came home late, mother hadn't kept his supper hot so he tipped up the table with everything on it. You can never forget those things . . . I hate him but sometimes I think Mom asks for it. She gets him going until he starts to drink. (p. 12-13)

There are at least 28 million children of alcoholic parents in the United States today (Allen & Hamilton, 1974). When these millions are added together with the millions of other children who have been occasionally abused or mistreated by intoxicated parents, or who are themselves abusers of alcohol, the casualties reach alarming statistics. Although the cost to public and private agencies for support of children ravaged by alcoholism has been placed at hundreds of millions of dollars each year, the cost in human suffering is incalculable.

Alcoholism: Inherited or Acquired?

In recent years, an interest in the prenatal effects of alcoholism has increased. The inferior physical condition of children of alcoholic parents has been recorded since antiquity, although the notion that alcohol damaged the parental germ plasm has been discounted. Most modern day research on the effects of alcohol on children prior to birth has focused upon studies of the poorer intrauterine environment of the fetus and the postnatal lack of adequate nurture and care by alcoholic parents. Several reports on "Fetal Alcohol Syndrome" (F.A.S.) conducted in the United States and England (Ferrier, Nicod & Ferrier, 1973; Hall & Orenstein, 1974; Jones & Smith, 1973; Jones, Smith, Ulleland & Streissguth, 1973) have indicated an increased rate of birth of maldeveloped or malformed infants of alcoholic mothers.

Altman (1976) has reported three case histories of ophthalmologic and systemic manifestations of the fetal alcohol syndrome. The three infants showed such abnormalities as delay in prenatal and postnatal growth, poor psychomotor performance, microcephaly, and limb and cardiovascular anomalies. The mother of two of the infants had a history of spontaneous abortions, possibly related to her chronic heavy alcohol consumption. The major eye defects were: smally eyes, telecanthus and divergent strabismus.

One effect of heavy drinking during pregnancy is the intoxication of the fetus since alcohol passes to the fetus in approximately the same concentration as the mother has in her blood (Waltman & Iniquez, 1972). Women about to give birth who were recently intoxicated for some period of time may suffer withdrawal symptoms and the fetus, of course, will also show symptoms of alcohol withdrawal and will require treatment just like the mother, even for treatment of delerium tremors (Nicholas, 1967). In a sense, then, these babies are born *drunk* and there may already be an established effect to the newborn child's nervous system.

The controversy over the causes of alcoholism is far from over, even though there is general agreement that alcoholism is linked to family factors.

For over 100 years, researchers have been seeking a scientific answer to the question: "Is alcoholism hereditary?" and some 30 years ago, Jellinek (1945) concluded that evidence didn't support a direct heritability theory of alcoholism. Rather, there seemed to be evidence that some people inherited a nonspecific tendency to develop personal problems which in some cases took the form of alcoholism.

At about the same time of Jellinek's findings, Roe's (1944) analyses of 36 children of alcoholic parents taken from their homes and reared in

195

foster homes had been reported and further supported the viewpoint that alcoholism was probably not inherited but instead, an effect of the home environment. However, more recently in the 1970's the nature-nurture issue has flared again. In a recent study by an American-Danish research team (Goodwin et al., 1973) the conclusion has been advanced that there is probably a genetic predisposition for the severest type of alcoholism. Goodwin (1971) produced figures to indicate that alcoholism rates among relatives were far higher than among the general population. Among people at large, alcoholism expectancy rates were estimated to be 3 to 5 percent among men and .1 to 1 percent among women. In contrast, alcoholism rates for sons of alcoholic parents may reach 25 to 50 percent and from 3 to 8 percent for daughters of alcoholics. One study reviewed by Goodwin noted that "periodic" and "compulsive" alcoholics — severest forms of the disease — had alcoholic children more frequently than did parents with less severe forms of alcoholism. The observation that home environments among the two groups were equally good or bad suggested that alcoholism may have a hereditary component.

In the American-Danish research study (Goodwin et al., 1973) 55 male adoptees (probands) who had at least one alcoholic biological parent, were separated from their parents during the first six weeks of life. They had been adopted by nonrelatives, and had no known subsequent contact with the natural parents. The adoptees were compared with 78 adopted males (controls) who met all the same criteria of the probands, except they had nonalcoholic natural aprents. The groups were matched in appropriate age at adoption and for adult age. All subjects were interviewed and studied by researchers who had no knowledge of the membership of the subjects in either group. Results of the classic study showed that: the probands had nearly four times the alcoholism rate of the controls; had twice as many drinkers in the "heavy drinkers" category; nearly 50% had received psychological treatment compared to 25% of the controls; and had a five times higher rate of psychiatric hospitalization. Finally, the study noted that probands were three times more likely to be divorced than the controls.

Further analysis of new data on a follow-up study by Goodwin (1973, 1974) suggested that severe alcoholism may cause genetic factors not present in milder cases. These severe and classical forms of alcoholism in part may have a genetic basis, whereas mere heavy drinking may have only psychological origins. As suspected, studies of the possible heretability of alcoholism have not gone unchallenged, but largely the criticisms (Tolar & Tamerin, 1973) have focused on inadequacies in the method of assessing the psychiatric illnesses of the adoptive parents and in classifying drinking behavior.

Current views of the nature versus nurture controversy over the etiology of alcoholism seems to leave room for both viewpoints and the answer to causation probably includes both genetic and environmental factors (Schuckit, 1973).

The Impact of Parental Alcoholism on Children's Development

While the relative impact of genetic and environmental factors is unsettled, there is, in contrast, general agreement that familial alcoholism has a disastrous effect upon child development. The children of alcoholics are not only at a considerable risk of suffering developmental problems, but of becoming alcoholics themselves.

Two studies were reviewed more extensively since they detailed the effects of parental alcoholism on behaviors of their children.

Cureton (1973) studied in depth the possible relationships between parental arrest records for drunkenness and their children's behavior problems in an average middle-sized city and its surrounding suburban area. The study data were available as a part of the nationwide Project TALENT testing program. Police files were used to determine arrest records of parents which were then matched with student data. A total of 1345 students in grades 8–12 were identified who had parents who had been arrested (996 fathers, 109 mothers, including 34 cases where both parents had been arrested for drunkenness). The number of students was 8 percent of the total student population of the community.

The most common adolescent behavior problem was school dropouts. For children from above average socio-economic homes, if either parent had an arrest record, 30 percent of the boys dropped out of school versus only 16 percent of the children with no parental arrest record. For girls, 19 percent dropped out who came from homes with arrested parents, versus 10 percent from homes with no drunkenness record. When children from lower socio-economic homes were compared, there was a 35 percent dropout rate for boys with parental arrest records compared with 23 percent for nonparental arrests; for girls, the rates were 27 percent against 22 percent. For boys, the dropout rates differed little between the arrests of father or mother; but for the girls, there was more effect if their mothers had been arrested. No noticeable pattern in racial difference in dropout rates were noticed for parental arrests. The next most common problem for students in this study concerned juvenile delinquency. The juvenile delinquency category excluded arrests for some traffic offenses. For above average socioeconomic homes the findings indicated that 15 percent of the boys of parents with drunkenness had police records, versus 10 percent of the nonarrested parents. Girls had a 3 percent record, versus 2 percent for nonarrested parents. In the below average socioeconomic category, it was found 21 percent of the boys had arrest records, versus 9 percent in the nonparental arrest group. For girls in this category, 3 percent had juvenile records, while 4 percent who had such records came from homes where parents had not been arrested for drunkenness.

School grades were also compared to parental arrest records. At the eighth and ninth grades, the boys achieved at the 45th percentile and girls at the 43rd percentile. At 10-12 grade levels, boys' grades were at the 48th percentile — while girls were at the 42nd percentile. The effect of school grades was most noticeable for girls if their mothers had been arrested. In 8-9th grades, the average was the 42nd percentile and in 10-12th grades, at the 35th percentile.

Aptitude and achievement test scores were grouped as a cluster from tests taken during the Project TALENT survey. Among these children whose parents had been arrested for drunkenness, their mean performance was below the average. Boys had a 38 percentile average in 8-9th grades and a 44th percentile in 10-12th grades, while girls averaged the 42nd percentile in 8-9th grades and the 41st percentile in grades 10-12. Again, as with school grades, girls were more affected in these scores if their mothers were arrested.

Attitudes toward school were obtained from a biographical questionnaire which was also part of the Project TALENT survey. The students were asked about paying attention in class, remembering teachers' instruction, getting assignments in one time, being criticized for sloppy work, enjoying school, applying themselves and other factors. Again, scores were below the mean for both boys and girls, around the 46th percentile. But, there was no noticeable relationship between mothers' arrests and the girls' or boys' attitudes toward school.

In summary, Cureton's (1973) study indicated that children in 9th grade and high school whose parents had arrest records for drunkenness showed more behavioral problems than other children in the same grades from the same community area. The differences were most noticeable in dropout rates and juvenile delinquency and less noticeable in school grades, test scores and school attitudes. There was some evidence that mother's arrests had more effect on their daughters than on their sons.

Zucker and Baron (1973) reported a study conducted in a community of around 15,000 people in one of the Middle Atlantic States. The focus was parental drinking behavior and the antisocial behavior of their adolescent sons. A total of 104 adolescent boys, then high school juniors and seniors, or dropouts were studied. The results indicated that parental use of alcohol was the most salient predictor of their son's own drinking behavior. Mothers' drinking patterns were more predictive than fathers' of their sons' behaviors, while the mother's heavy drinking behavior, anxiety, and uneasiness seemed to act as a suppressor.

Zucker and Barron also studied parental perceptions of their disciplinary practices. The fathers focused on the use of denial of privileges while the mothers saw themselves as using ridicule, denial of companionship, and open rejection of their son's. Mothers' perceptions frequently focused on rejection on the one hand while giving overprotection for their son on the other hand. The investigators also examined sons' perceptions of their parents' behavior. Mothers' emotional distance was related to sons' drinking. Increased problem drinking was also related to sons' perception of low paternal affection. The boys perceived their father as ineffective in building a strong father-son bond and as weak models of masculine identity. Perceptions of family climate included tension and open rebellion of parental control.

Zucker and Barron concluded that:

> The adolescent boys high intake and problem drinking, his antisocial behavior, and his rebelliousness in and resentment of the family maybe viewed as a set of behaviors and attitudes that allow him to separate from a family setting that has no future to it (both in terms of what the adolescent boy sees his father as having done, and also in terms of what the mother see themselves as having provided.) Put another way, there has been a failure of the affective environmental supports that provide for the development of solid positive identification with parental figures. Thus, by adolescence, the critical factor is the separation – escape, partly by way of alcohol abuse (p. 290-291).

Barron (1970) indicated that drinking and antisocial behavior of high school boys was associated with maternal deviant drinking. The battered baby syndrome was associated with alcoholism of the parents mostly by Callaghan and Fotheringham (1970). A systematic psychiatric examination of the parents of 50 hyperactive children showed increased prevalance rates of alcoholism (Cantwell, 1972).

Clinebell (1968) has noted that children of an alcoholic parent are frequently subject to shifts and reversals of parental roles, creating unpredictable and confusing behavior for the child. Another problem for the children occurred when the nonalcoholic parent because so obsessed by the spouse's drinking that there are few need-satisfying relations with the children.

Weir (1967, 1970) found that high school students with alcoholic parents had fewer peer relationships, and showed a greater trend toward maladjustment than their peers from nonalcoholic homes. Weir particularly found that high school students of alcoholic parents had higher absenteeism rates in school. Biographical analyses showed the young people with an alcohol problem in the family, had parents with less formal education and had more mothers who were employed than the nonalcoholic sample. The data also showed that students from the family alcohol problem group had a significantly larger percentage of fathers in the lower socioeconomic occupational groups. There were also smaller sized families among the students who had alcoholic parents.

Kammerer (1969, 1971), using the same school population as Weir, found that 9th and 10th grade girls who had a parent with an alcohol problem had significantly poorer scores on the *Minnesota Counseling Inventory* on family relationships, social relationships, emotional stability, conformity, mood, and leadership than girls of the same grade level whose parents had no alcohol problem.

She concluded (1969) that there would appear to be trends in general for the students from families with identifiable alcohol problems to experience more severely the adjustment problems of adolescence than do students from families without identifiable alcohol problems. The adjustment difference exists most dramatically for girls, and specifically, girls in the ninth and tenth grades. (p. xvi)

Fakhruddin (1967) found that identification at moments of intense affect caused the potentially alcoholic child to emulate the aggressiveness shown by his father during drunken outbursts.

Childhood maladaptive behaviors such as temper tantrums, fighting with peers and school troubles were found by Haberman (1966) to occur more frequently in the children of alcoholic patiets than with children of nonalcoholics. A study of 20 American skyjackers (Hubbard, 1970) indicated a remarkably uniform family characteristic of an oedipal conflict between a violent alcoholic father and a very religious mother. Bosma (1975) reported that children of alcoholic parents particularly manifest developmental problems in first grade and in early and late adolescence. Lowry and Lowry (1971) reported that parental alcoholism is frequently reported in cases of child battering.

Gade and Goodman (1975) reported the relationship of parental alcoholism to vocational interests. College age daughters of alcoholic parents have different vocational preferences than those from nonalcoholic family backgrounds. There was a tendency for these young women to have higher interests in the science and mechanical-outdoor areas. These vocational interests tended to be chosen by people who come from homes where neglecting, rejecting or casual child-rearing practices prevail. The study concluded that growing up with an alcoholic parent tended to have an impact on vocational interest patterns.

Miller (1976) reported, from a longitudinal study of multiproblem families, that 7 percent of children of alcoholic parents and only 2 percent of children of nonalcoholic parents labeled themselves as alcoholic. Children of alcoholics reported three times as many family problems. The children of alcoholic parents also reported more marriage failures, unemployment or work difficulties, and more difficulty supporting themselves and their families in later life. The results suggested that even when compared with parents of other multiproblem parents, alcoholic parents seemed to increase the amount of misery for their children.

Forty percent of juvenile delinquency was related to parental alcoholism, and alcohol was used by juveniles during fifty percent of the acts which led to commitment to the North Dakota State Industrial School. (North Dakota's Plan for Alcohol Abuse and Alcohol Prevention, Treatment and Rehabilitation Programs, 1975).

In France (Mainard, Berranger, and Caududal, 1971), a medical survey team, showed that parental alcoholism was mainly responsible for the brutal treatment that resulted in the hospitalization of 32 children.

In England, a study by Mik (1970) concluded that male identification was absent in boys of alcoholic fathers and that passive-aggressive traits dominated, possibly predisposing them to alcoholism.

201

An Examination of the Dynamics of an Alcoholic Family

Hecht (1973) discussed the role of the family as the basic unit of a child's education about controls, relationships, responsibility, and identification. In the home of an alcoholic, the children learned frequently that communication was in half-truths and there was a cover up of knowledge of hearing from parental drinking. Children learned to distrust parental talk and only trust their parents deed and actions. The children learned to live with broken promises, and double meanings. Boys and girls reported a tendency to negatively act out their own impulses following their parental models. In an alcoholic family the children rarely saw their parents and themselves working in partnership and the chance to enact rights, responsibility, and privileges of democratic family membership was lacking.

Hecht pointed out that healthy gender identification was also difficult for a boy or girl growing up in an alcoholic family. A boy often found his alcoholic father was passive or uninvolved as a family member or he was violent and impulsive in the father role. For a girl, an alcoholic mother often was a negative model of moodiness, guilt, and resentment.

Hecht also noted the inconsistencies and disorganization of an alcoholic family. All children need structure and time – binding activities to learn security. Boys and girls in an alcoholic family learned that parents are undependable and that rules and regulations are inconsistent. Affectional inconsistencies contributed to the desire to search and push for limits and boundaries of control. Insecurity, tension and anxiety among the children led to shame, social withdrawal, and psychosomatic disorder.

Hindman (1975) also discussed the family disorganization of the alcoholic. Frequently, both parents and children became social isolates because of the shame and insecurities of their home environment. Because of financial limitations, fighting, and internal strife the alcoholic family was socially isolated, seldom going out as a family unit. The children coped with parental alcoholism by acting out the problem through delinquency or by withdrawing into shyness, fantasy or even schizophrenia.

Fox (1972) pointed out that self awareness of the social stigma of parental alcoholism created a feeling of estrangement, isolation, and shame among the children in the family and there was reluctance to associate as a family in social outings. A poor self-concept among children of alcoholics is frequently noted and social isolation further intensified a feeling of low self worth and low self-esteem.

Jackson (1958) observed that among alcoholic fathers and their children the interaction often resembled a sibling rather than parental-child relationship. He further reported that the fathers seemed to be crying with their children for the mother's affection and attention.

One of the most intensive studies of the dynamics of an alcoholic family and its impact on children, ages 10-16 in the Toronto area. These "forgotten children" were the real victims of parental alcoholism and her interviews identified personality problems in almost all children. Half the sample had failed a grade in school. Many children reported difficulty in concentrating on school subjects because their drunken dad made them nervous and nightmares were frequently reported. Others stated that their goal of college was now in jeopardy because money saved for further schooling was being used up by costs of parental drinking. Some children lamented that future occupational ambitions were thwarted.

Cork reported that many of the children felt rejected by both their alcoholic and nonalcoholic parent. Although little deliberate rejection was felt the constant family quarreling, lack of parental recognition of the children's needs, and failure to give real love constituted a form of rejection amounting to neglect.

Social relationships also suffered with the children reporting peer isolation, lack of family togetherness and family turmoil. Further analyses of the sample by Crok showed that the majority lacked confidence, felt shamed, anxious, and afraid. Parental fighting and quarreling, and lack of love from parents were the principle complaints. The majority felt disgusted, angry, resentful and hurt by their parents drinking. They considered money problems, inconsistent parenting and loss of respect for their parents a major problem.

School Alcohol Education and Prevention Programs

A promising means of early intervention and prevention of alcohol abuse among the children of alcoholics or for the education of all children about alcohol abuse involves school programming.

Rouse et al. (1973) pointed out that school counseling and educational programs about alcohol abuse could provide intervention during children's formative years enabling them to develop more constructive means of coping with potential alcohol abuse.

203

Rouse et al. (1973) pointed out that school counseling and educational programs about alcohol abuse could provide intervention during children's formative years enabling them to develop more constructive means of coping with potential alcohol abuse.

The La Fe Youth Hostel program in Santa Fe, New Mexico employed counselors who visit public school stressing responsible decision-making and provided counseling services for students seeking more information or help with alcohol problems. School personnel identified young alcohol abusers or children of alcoholics and channeled them into the program. The facility also provided temporary residential care. (Hindman, 1976).

Weir (1970) stressed that an alcohol education program and counseling service can serve the dual function of direct help to young people in learning skills to cope with an alcoholic parent, at the same time help motivate alcoholic parents to seek treatment.

Weir (1967) designed an alcohol education and counseling program for high school students enrolled in a medium-sized parochial school. He was able to determine the effectiveness of the program by analyzing data between a group of students who had a parent with an alcohol problem, and other students enrolled in the school whose parents had no alcohol problem. The program developed by Weir (1967) was a brief program of alcohol education for an entire school based on an opportunity to develop a free choice toward the use of alcohol. The investigator considered alcohol education to be similar to the teaching of social issues. The total teaching program consisted of classroom instruction one hour per day, two hours per week on consecutive days, for three weeks, in regular high school classroom settings. Additionally, a volunteer counseling service was available for students who wanted to receive help concerning alcoholism. Twenty percent of the students from families with an alcohol problem received the counseling service, compared to only 5 percent from families without an alcohol problem. A total of 371 out of an enrollment of 420 high school students (grades 9-12) completed the alcohol education program, including all pre- and post-testing and other data. Weir concluded that the stress on awareness and self-understanding during the alcohol education program influenced positive attitude change toward alcohol use and alcoholism.

Direct Programs For Children of Alcoholics

The children of alcoholic parents are children at risk. This subject (Richards, 1976) has been poignantly brought forth in the use of titles such as: "The Forgotten Children," a "Hidden Tragedy," or a "Neglected Problem" (Cork, 1969; Bosma, 1972; Sloboda, 1974). Studies show that approximately one-half of alcoholics are themselves the children of alcoholics (Bosma, 1972; Sloboda, 1974). The case for primary alcohol prevention programs with the children of alcoholic parents seems well established, since the children themselves are a high risk group for developing alcoholism.

Other researchers have echoed the primary prevention theme. Chafetz et al. (1972) for example, noted that in order to prevent or minimize the progression of alcoholic problems, a profitable group to begin with were the children of alcoholic parents.

Total family intervention has become an important aspect of many alcohol treatment programs. Family treatment, according to Cork (1969) should not terminate when the alcoholic becomes abstinent because many problems still remain in the functioning and relationship of the family members. She observed that children in alcoholic families reported no improvement in family functioning when the drinking stopped unless there was continuing family therapy.

Alanon and Alateen

Involvement of the total family in alcoholism treatment has been promoted by the family systems approach. According to systems theory, the family is a collection of elements in interaction, each affecting the other but in different ways. Many authorities believe that early intervention and treatment programs for children of alcoholics should involve of the total family, along with special programs for the children.

Alanon and Alateen, outgrowths of the Alcoholics Anonymous philosophy, are attempts to help the whole family to live more effectively with the alcoholic. Alanon groups are comprised of non-alcoholic spouses whose wives or husbands have a drinking problem. Using group interaction and support, the groups try to increase self-understanding of their role in the on-going drinking behavior of their spouse, including the disruptive aspects of family life. Alateen, an organization for teenagers of alcoholic parents, is a primary resource in the support of young people.

While younger children often don't cognitively understand the dynamics of alcoholism in their family, they have had an emotional experience with it.

Adolescence is a period often of rebellion, independence and resentment toward the alcoholic parent. These negative feelings and attitudes can contribute toward sustaining alcoholism in the family. Alateen was designed to help these teenagers talk about and talk out these feelings of resentment in constructive ways. The purpose is to help the adolescent develop an understanding of his place in the alcoholic family and help develop means of reestablishing more healthy patterns of family interaction. In summary, Alateen is devoted to aiding the children of alcoholics to understand their parents' problems and to develop more effective ways to handle whatever social and emotional difficulties they themselves are encountering.

Richards (1976) has noted that although Alateen groups appear to be "highly successful," services may be underutilized, perhaps because the help appeared too late. The adolescent may have already established attitudes and values toward drinking, and already be an alcohol user. A second reason for Alateen's underuse included the recognition that many 13-18 year olds are already on the road to independency from their parents, and have already developed strong defense mechanisms about the effects of alcoholism. McElfresh (1970) has documented the defenses used by young people dropping out of an alcohol education program for teenagers. A dropout rate of 65 percent was recorded in the four week program and inlcuded the deniers, the minimizers (those who felt that as long as there was no abuse, alcoholism wasn't too bad) and the evaders, those who, although realizing a problem, chose to remain detached.

A new organization for preteenagers of alcoholic parents called Ala-tot has now developed with more than 25 chapters in various cities. The ala-tot programs reflect the special needs of younger children of alcoholic parents.

Another alcohol education program for young children is the KOLMAC Clinic in Silver Springs, Maryland (Richards, 1976). Data from the clinic indicated a need for an alcohol program for young children, since half of the women in the treatment were under 45 and half of the men were under 40. The majority of these parents had children under the age of 12.

The KOLMAC program for children ages 6-12 met with initial parental reservations because of guilt, desire to maintain denial of a problem, or a feeling of being incapable or bad parents. The purpose of the program was to learn from the child his level of knowledge of alcohol use and abuse, provide new education and a chance to express feelings, and a chance to determine if any childhood disturbances required further programs and treatment. The four hour-long sessions, spread over one month, were best categorized as "brief and focused play therapy."

Factual learning and a chance to experience release of affect in a controlled, focused activity group helps each child to expand his ego strength and add new coping mechanisms to his repertoire. The therapist techniques included use of identification, imparting of information, interpretation and reassurance. Through the use of such activities as child drawings, stories and wishes, pent up feelings of anger, guilt, fear and mistrust of parents and ambivalence toward the alcoholic role model could be expressed. Ambivalence toward the parental role model was considered a key issue to be identified, addressed and worked through, if future alcoholism was to be prevented.

Another emerging trend has been the treatment of the children of alcoholics alone, but preferably with parental consent. Sol (1967) a decade ago, exposed the misconception that children cannot be helped without parental involvement. He felt that 90 percent of the children with severe problems may go untreated if parental involvement is always a requirement.

Traditional treatment facilities for drug and alcohol problems have recently developed programs to include special services for younger clients. For example, in Duluth, Minnesota, the Young People's Residential Center has provided primary and long-term treatment in a therapeutic community setting for chemically-dependent persons, 14 to 25 years of age. Families were heavily involved in the program and admitted as co-patients. The program included instruction about the human body and helps them in exploring alternatives to maintaining physical health. Confidence building to deal with life stresses and the exploration of alternative lifestyles has been included in the program (Maloney, 1977).

Kalton et al. (1973) have described nontraditional treatment approaches for youthful substance abusers. At the Marin Open House in San Rafael, California, alcohol abusers ages 16-30 received help in free clinics, on an honor farm, and in sheltered workshops. An experimental curriculum on self-reliance was offered in a continuation high school. A Wilderness Project was also offered and some clients even participated in a training program which qualified them to become counselor aides.

Other Alcohol Abuse Program Modalities

Several existing projects are discussed in this section aimed at alcohol abuse prevention and included: community education, affective skills development, teacher training, and peer counseling.

Maloney, (1977) described a total community approach to carrying out an alcohol education delivery system for young people which had the advantage of involving many adults as well in the program. In Somerville, Massachusetts, a program of community organization and development received a community consensus on the goals of the alcohol education program and trained caregivers to identify early alcoholics and their families. The program trained teachers in the skills of responsible decision-making about alcohol use. The program also trained peer leaders to assist in classroom teaching, conduct rap groups in both the school and community and to provide outreach to youthful drinkers and to the children of families with alcoholism. The goal was a sequential school alcohol education curriculum for kindergarten through twelfth grade.

Alternative activities to the abuse of alcohol included vocational skill development, religious experiences, social involvement and physical activities in the Holland Patent, New York, school system program. A response to the problems of student drinking in a rural areas were met by utilizing school facilities for a variety of activities for both youth and adults. The program was designed to foster responsibility and create positive self-image and youth recreation, mini-courses, and adult activities ranging from macrame to dog obedience were offered, using volunteer instructors. Health education, Parent Effectiveness Training, and values clarification courses were also included. A favorable community response and wide participation have been reported. A favorable community response and wide participation have been reported, and no teenage drinking and driving deaths have occurred for a year, a contrast with earlier data (Maloney, 1977).

Dolan (1974) has described an example of a national level private sector-based program called Operation THRESHOLD, a responsible drinking education and community action program sponsored by the U.S. Jaycees. Some 18 different techniques and vehicles have been used to create awareness and understanding about alcohol abuse and alcoholism prevention. Participation with local schools has been encouraged.

Affective skills development for youth included the improvement of self-concept, appreciation of others' values and attitudes, decision-making skills, responsibility training, creativity, and preparation to cope with an ever-changing world, and, in Akron, Ohio, the YMCA developed a series of valuing activities for children ages 9-11 to influence decision-making and raise conscious concern about alcohol abuse. The project initially involved youths and group leaders of the Akron Gra-Y Clubs, and has now been expanded as a model for other YMCA groups around the country. (Maloney, 1977).

Curriculum development and teaching training programs were other responses to youth alcohol prevention. Lawrence and Sanders (1975) have reported that the Florida Alcohol Education Project which undertook an evaluation study of 41 existing curricula. The project has developed criteria for evaluating the usefulness and effectiveness of curriculum packages on alcohol education.

Maloney (1977) has written about the Intermediate School District #110 of Seattle, Washington where a 15 hour activities program per grade level on alcohol education has been developed. Each activity included a specified objective and the area the activity affected. All necessary resources and instructions, as well as evaluation materials, were included, along with suggestions on how the activity could be incorporated into different subject areas.

Peer counseling has enabled potential youth drug experimenters to rap with peers instead of being talked to by adults. Peer counselors were trained in techniques of active listening, decision-making, and values clarification in Dade County, Florida. This school system has developed project PRIDE to train 5,000 peer counselors who have helped 20,000 students identify, clarify and work out personal problems. Each secondary school has a "rap room" where peers can come to interact with each other in a nonauthoritative setting. Each school also has a resource specialist to help teachers to be more effective with youth and to help refer youths to community resource agencies that are appropriate. A parents' communications workshop was another component of the program. Evaluation has shown significant gains among participants in responsibility, leadership skills, positive self-concepts and better teacher-pupil communications. Boys' Harbor in New York City has developed another type of peer counseling alcohol program in which the school class itself selects its own peer counselors based on an agreed upon definition of leadership. Youth gangs have even been reached with their own personal growth training program (Maloney, 1977).

209

Summary

In summary, this paper has presented information about: the causative factors of alcoholism, the impact of parental alcoholism, the dynamics of an alcoholic family, and alcohol intervention, prevention, and educational programs. This paper has further documented the psychological, educational, sociological, and physical effects of family alcoholism. Innovative and alternative approaches to alcohol education and treatment programs hold promises for the reduction of the impact of family alcoholism on child development.

References

Allen and Hamilton, Inc. An assessment of the needs for children of alcoholic parents. Final Report. National Institute on Alcohol Abuse and Alcoholism. Washington, D.C.: U.S. Government Printing Office, 1974.

Altman, B. Fetal alcohol syndrome. Journal of Pediatric Ophthalmology, 1976, 13, (5), 255-258.

Barron, F. Family relationships, problem drinking and antisocial behavior amongst adolescent males. Unpublished Master's Thesis, Michigan State University, 1970.

Bosma, W.G. Children of alcoholics – a hidden tragedy. Maryland State Medical Journal, 1972, 21, (1), 34-36.

Callaghan, K.S., and Fotheringham, B.J. Practical management of the battered baby syndrome. Medical Journal of Australia, 1970, 1 (26), 1282-1284.

Cantwell, D.P. Psychiatric illness in the families of hyperactive children. Archives of General Psychiatry, 1972, 27 (3), 414-417.

Chafetz, M., Blane, H., and Hill, M. Children of alcoholics: observations in a child guidance clinic. In Susman, J. (Ed.), Drug Use and Social Policy. New York: AMS Press, 1972.

Clinebell, H.J. Understanding and counseling the alcoholic. New York: Abingdon Press, 1968.

Cork, M. The forgotten children: A study of children with alcoholic parents. Toronto: Addiction Research Foundation, 1969.

Cureton, L.W. Parents' police records for drunkenness and behavior problems of their children. In Chafetz, M. (Ed.), Research on Alcoholism: Clinical Problems and Special Populations. Proceedings of the First Annual Conference on Alcoholism. Washington, D.C.: U.S. Government Printing Office, 1973.

Dolan, J.S. Operation THRESHOLD. In Chafetz, M. (Ed.), Proceedings of the Fourth Annual Alcoholism Conference of the National Institute on Alcohol Abuse and Alcoholism: Research, Treatment, and Prevention. Washington, D.C.: Department of Health, Education and Welfare, 1974.

Fakhruddin, A.K. Identification of alcoholism. *Psychiatric Quarterly Supplement,* 1967, *41* (2), 307-310.

Ferrier, P., Nicod, I., and Ferrier, S. Fetal alcohol syndrome. *The Lancet,* 1973, *2,* 1496.

Fox, R. *The Effects of Alcoholism on Children.* New York: National Council on Alcoholism, 1972.

Gade, E.M. and Goodman, R.E. Vocational preferences of daughters of alcoholics. *The Vocational Guidance Quarterly,* 1975, *24* (1) 41-47.

Goodwin, D.W. Is alcoholism hereditary: A review and critique. *Archives of General Psychiatry,* 1971, *25* 545-549.

Goodwin, D.W. *Drinking Problems in Adopted and Nonadopted Sons of Alcoholics.* Report Submitted to the National Institute on Alcohol Abuse and Alcoholism, Washington, D.C.: January, 1974.

Goodwin, D.W., Schulsinger, F., Hermanson, L., Guze, S.B., and Winkour, G. Alcohol problems in adoptees raised apart from alcoholic biological parents. *Archives of General Psychiatry,* 1973, *28* 238-243.

Haverman, P.W. Childhood symptoms in children of alcoholics and comparison group parents. *Journal of Marriage and the Family,* 1966, *28,* 152-154.

Hall, B., and Orenstein, W. Noonan's phenotype in an offspring of an alcoholic mother. *The Lancet,* 1974, 680-681.

Hecht, M. Children of alcoholics as children at risk. *American Journal of Nursing,* 1973, *73* (10), 1764-1767.

Hindman, M. Children of alcoholic parents. *Alcohol Health and Research World.* 1975-1976. Winter, 2-6.

Hubbard, D.G. *Flights to fantasy among skyjackers. International Congress of Social Psychiatry,* 1970, 2, 253-255.

Jackson, M.J. *A follow-up study of the relationship between drinking behavior and participation in child care activities.* Unpublished master's thesis, University of Toronto, 1958.

Jellinek, E.M. Heredity of the alcoholic. *Quarterly Journal of Studies on Alcohol,* 1945, 6, 105-114.

Jones, K., and Smith, D. Recognition of the fetal alcohol syndrome in early infancy. *The Lancet,* 1973, *1,* 999-1001.

Jones, K., Smith, D., Ulleland, C., and Streissguth, A. Pattern of malformation in offspring of chronic alcoholic mothers. *The Lancet,* 1973, 1, 1267-1271.

Kalton, M., Dwarshuis, L., Gorodezky, M., and Dasber, A. *Innovative Approaches to Youth Services.* Madison, Wisconsin: Stash Press, 1973.

Kammerer, M.L. Adolescents from familiar with and without alcohol problems. *Quarterly Journal of Studies on Alcohol,* 1971, *32* (2), 364-372.

Kammerer, M.L. *Biographic, cognitive, demographic and personality differences between adolescents from families with identifiable alcohol problems and from families without identifiable alcohol problems.* Unpublished doctoral dissertation, University of North Dakota, 1969.

Lawrence, G. and Sanders, L. *Florida Alcohol Education Project.* University of Florida: Institute for the Development of Human Resources, 1974.

Lowry, T.P., and Lowry, A. Abortion as a preventive for abused children. *Psychiatric Opinion,* 1971, *8* (3), 19-25.

Mainard, R., Berranger, P., and Caududal, J.L. A frequent and serious consequence of parental alcoholism: the ill-treatment of children. *Revue de l' Alcoolisme,* 1971, *17* (1), 21-31.

Maloney, S.K. *Guide to Alcohol Programs for Youth,* Washington, D.C.: Department of Health, Education and Welfare, U.S. Government Printing Office, 1977.

McElfresh, O. Supportive groups for teenagers of the alcoholic parent. A preliminary report. *Medical Etiology and Clinical Research,* 1970, *3,* (1), 26-29.

Mik, G. Sons of alcoholic fathers. *British Journal of Addiction,* 1970, *65,* 305-315.

Miller, D. *Family Problems, social adaptation and sources of help for children of alcoholic and non-alcoholic parents.* San Francisco: Scientific Analysis Corporation, 1976.

Nichols, M. Acute alcohol withdrawal syndrome in a newborn. *American Journal of Diseases of Children,* 1967, *113,* 714-715.

North Dakota Department of Health. *North Dakota Plan for Alcohol Abuse and Alcoholism Prevention Treatment and Rehabilitation Programs.* Bismarck, North Dakota, 1975.

Richards, T.M. Alcohol education for young children of alcoholic parents. *Addictions,* 1976, *5* (4), 18-21.

Roe, A. The adult adjustment of children of alcoholic parents raised in foster homes. *Quarterly Journal of Studies on Alcohol,* 1944, *5,* 378-393.

Rouse, B.A., Waller, P.F., and Ewing, J.A. Adolescents' stress levels, coping activities and fathers' drinking behavior. *Proceedings, of the 81st Annual Convention of the American Psychological Association,* 1973, *8* 683-684.

Schuckit, M.A. Family history and half-sibling research and alcoholism. In Seitas, F. et al. (Eds.), Nature and Nurture in Alcoholism. *Annals of the New York Academy of Science,* 1973, *197,* 121-125.

Sloboda, S. Children of alcoholics: a neglected problem. *Hospital and Community Psychiatry,* 1974, *25* (9), 605-606.

Sol, G. *New Directions for School Psychologists in Big Cities.* Paper presented at the Annual Meeting of the Ontario Psychological Association, Toronto, 1967.

Tolar, A., and Tamerin, J.S. The question of a genetic basis for alcoholism: comment on the study by Goodwin et al. *Quarterly Journal of Studies on Alcohol,* 1973, *34,* 1341-1345.

Waltman, R., and Iniquez, E. Placental Transfer of Ethanol and Its Elimination at Term. *Obstetrics and Gynecology,* 1972, *40,* 180-185.

Weir, W.R. *A Program of Alcohol Education and Counseling for High School Students with and without a Family Alcohol Problem.* Unpublished doctoral dissertation, University of North Dakota, 1967.

Weir. W.R. Counseling youth whose parents are alcoholic: a means to an end as well as an end in itself. *Journal of Alcohol Education,* 1970, *16* (1), 13-19.

Zucker, R.A., and Barron, M.A. Parental behaviors associated with problem drinking and antisocial behavior among adolescents. In Chafetz, M. (Ed.) *Research on Alcoholism: Clinical Problems and Special Populations. Proceedings of the First Annual Alcoholism Conference of the National Institute on Alcohol Abuse and Alcoholism.* Washington, D.C.: U.S. Government Printing Office, 1973.

Management of
Behaviorally Disruptive and
Emotionally Disturbed Children:
A School Based Family Program

Larry E. Beutler, Ph.D.
M. Elena Oró-Beutler, M.A.
University of Arizona

The American education system is in the unique position of being the only institution that has contact with virtually every family in our society — the problematic, the high risk, the over achiever, the socialized, the leader — all pass under the scrutinizing eyes of school teachers and administrators. Hence, more than any other institution, including the church, the school system has the power to influence and change society. It is here that many of the negative influences of society and family might be interrupted or counteracted. Yet, schools have largely failed both in their efforts to pinpoint high risk children and in their efforts to dilute negative social influences.

The ability of a school system either to successfully intervene with or to anticipate the development of behavioral and emotional disturbances among children is frequently and severely limited without parent and family systems undergoing a mutually supportive change. As a consequence, when a child's behavior is deemed to be disruptive and unmanageable through school system alterations alone, they are usually referred to outside resources. Unfortunately, however, parents are frequently reluctant to accept referrals to agencies outside of the school system and even when it occurs, the acceptance of such a referral may perpetuate a family myth which maintains that "what happens at school is the school's problem and what happens at home is none of your business". Frequently, parents do not feel the degree of emotional investment in the educational program which is required in order to pursue recommendations made by the school if these entail activities outside of school and/or on someone's part other than the pupil involved. The maintenance of two distinct systems (family and school), each based upon its own reinforcement and control schedule, introduces additional confusion to the child's already disruptive behavior.

As a consequence of the foregoing concerns, in recent years schools have begun developing structured classes which are designed to facilitate parent involvement. Programs emphasizing behavioral technology (e.g., Becker, 1971), effective communications (e.g., Dinkmeyer & McKay, 1976), and self concept enhancement (Dreikurs, 1964), are examples of such efforts. In order to maximize the impact of parent classes, however, there is a need for integrated support services. In fact, the very introduction of parent classes may perpetuate the myth that schools are the primary determiners and hence, assume the primary responsibility for the child's misbehavior. The myth may best be laid to rest through the use of procedures which involve parents as an integral part of the educational system and which help them to assume more responsibility in the management of their child's educational program.

It becomes clear that many family problems cannot be effectively handled through the development of parent classes alone, especially as long as their focus is only on the child's behavior. In those cases where marriage problems are disruptive to education, there is ample need for initial marriage and group counseling in order to facilitate referral to outside agencies. Indeed, the school may have some responsibility for providing counseling services directly to parents in order to insure their taking advantage of referral sources when suggested.

Considering the foregoing problems, the current chapter is designed to describe initial plans and efforts to develop a family oriented, school-based program designed to create a coalition between parents, children, and school personnel for the effective alleviation of emotional and behavioral difficulties. Basic to our program is the training of one individual within each school, usually a school counselor, to implement and coordinate the various aspects of the program. The following pages will give an overview of the program as it is invisioned and will present what evidence is available on the utility of those aspects devoted to parent and counselor education. The program described is currently being developed and implemented in the Cypress-Fairbanks Independent School System near Houston, Texas.

Program Overview

The ultimate goal of this school-based family program, is not only to give students individualized help, but also to provide parental, family, and educational intervention for those persons who are significant in the child's life. The basic assumptions underlying this general goal are (1) that the child's problems are reflective of behaviors and attitudes among the family members themselves and (2) that since no problem exists in a vacuum, the responsibility for the child's education and behavior must rest squarely with the child and his family. We assume that the school should serve as a consultant to families in order to facilitate the educational process and to mitigate or alleviate interfering contingencies.

A designated school counselor assumes the responsibility of coordinating the development of a variety of parent education strategies, volunteer programs, and group counseling procedures. This designate or Home-School Coordinator, develops a cadre of school-based training and treatment modules which are loosely organized into three groups and from these a review committee selects the ones most appropriate to each case. The three broad groupings include programs involving target children themselves, parent training programs, and joint family interaction programs. When a child is assigned to one or more treatment modules from within any of the three groupings, appropriate resource training and treatment personnel are mobilized by the Home-School Coordinator.

Specifically, this coordinator is responsible for:

1. Establishing a student focused group counseling program,
2. Providing individual counseling for students,
3. Consulting with teachers on classroom management,
4. Establishing a behaviorally oriented child management class for parents,
5. Establishing a class in effective parenting and communication for parents,
6. Establishing self concept enhancement programs,
7. Establishing a counseling group for parents,
8. Coordinating parent volunteers for working within school systems, and
9. Training teachers both in group counseling methods and classroom management procedures.

The committee whose responsibility it is to tailor a program for each student, consists of a licensed psychologist, the Home-School Coordinator, the school principal or representative, and the student's teachers. As children manifest behavior problems, parents may be contacted and a series of meetings and evaluation conferences are initiated in order to establish performance contracts both with parents, the child, and the school officials. Such a procedure allows the implementation of behavioral strategies which are coordinated and consistent between both school and home environments, with parents serving as consultants as well as learners. By recruiting help from parents whose children have problems, we have hoped to allow these parents to gain a sensitivity of their own children's needs as well as to understand the principles of communication and learning which will facilitate the child's progress. Of particular concern in working with parents, is the need to preserve their sense of power, prestige, and status.

Training Home-School Coordinators

From the outset, it has been clear that a major need in the type of program proposed in the foregoing is to provide Home-School Coordinators both with the technology to implement various parent and family programs and to facilitate changes in their attitudes towards themselves, their professional roles, and their social world. We have found that a series of workshops is an effective vehicle for implementing such attitude change. These workshops are designed both to provide the coordinators with a basic technology for implementing the procedures listed and also to allow them to gain the experiential foundations which will sustain increased levels of flexibility and confidence in their new roles. The following describes the nature of the workshops which we have found useful and our initial assessment of their impact upon the attitudes and effectiveness of the designated Home-School Coordinators.

Workshop Organization and Content

A series of intensive workshops provide the basic nucleus for initial training of Home-School Coordinators. These workshops are supplemented by yearly booster sessions. We have found that four, two-day workshops are sufficient for initial training in role responsibilities and parent relationships. Subsequent and more brief workshops at the beginning of each year introduce new Home-School Coordinators to the responsibilities of their role and provide additional instruction in the implementation of the program. In our own efforts, the entire program has been designed for implementation in a step-by-step fashion. The first year has concentrated on the development of parent education groups, with subsequent years being devoted to the implementation of parent volunteer programs, parent counseling groups, and intensified work with individual skills and procedures to teachers so that classrooms might be managed most effectively and so that the various procedures implemented will be integrated into a total program.

We recommend that initial workshops occur across a two month period and be heavily devoted to experiential exercises as well as dydactic instruction. Instructional materials should include information on effective parent-child communications, family group work, behavior management of children, utilization of parents as volunteers and techniques of individual and group counseling. The workshops should be coordinated by a single individual but it is often useful to utilize the services of various additional workshop leaders which may provide the required expertise, materials, and direct instruction. We encourage all workshop leaders to emphasize an experiential approach to understanding the materials presented and also to provide the participants with practicum activities. We have found that many of the specific programs have already been developed and can be presented in such a way as to allow modular-implementation, by the counselor-coordinator. For example, systematic parent education classes have been described and are available with suitable accompanying materials. Reliance upon the programmed instructions presented by the adherents of behavioral parent training (e.g., Becker, 1971), and Systematic Training for Effective Parenting (Dinkmeyer & McKay, 1976), etc., facilitate the training process and enhance the effectiveness of the coordinators.

Results

Our evaluatiion of such workshops suggest that they are effective in changing personal attitudes and orientations. Through the course of such experiential workshop experiences, counselors become increasingly self actualized, responsive to their own feelings, spontaneous, and self accepting as measured by standardized tests. In our initial training sessions, 14 school counselors from both primary and secondary schools were selected for involvement. They were relatively experienced (mean = 10.4 years) and averaged about 35 years of age. They were evaluated during the first and last workshop sessions, the workshop consisting of four two-day seminars on parent-child communications, family group work, behavior management of children, and parent training classes. The specific instruments administered were the Personal Orientation Inventory (Schostrom, 1963), the FIRO-B (Schutz, 1963), and the Locus of Control Index (Rotter, 1966). The Personal Orientation Inventory (POI) was used to assess a number of dimensions relative to the person's sense of self awareness, flexibility, and general psychological adjustment. In contrast, the FIRO-B was used to assess the individual's interpersonal behavior, primarily those relating to their needs for inclusion, control, and affection. Finally, the Locus of Control Index represents an expression of the individual's perceived power over their environment. Conjointly, the three instruments were designed to assess a variety of interpersonal and personal skills which we thought may be relevant to their effective performance in the designated role as Home-School Coordinator.

An effort was made to obtain an appropriate untreated control group and in order to accomplish this task, the cooperation of counselors and psychological diagnosticians outside of the designated school district was solicited. Unfortunately, this control group turned out to be somewhat younger and less experienced than the experimental group. Moreover, initial evaluation on the measure of interpersonal adjustment suggested some clear differences in the groups which mitigated against this group representing a real control for the effectiveness of the training procedure. Given this initial lack of comparability between groups, changes in the treated group between pre and post tests became more significant.

Assessment of changes in performance which accompanied workshop attendance, suggested significant impact of our training procedure on several dimensions. Numerous variables showed significant change in the groups subjected to the workshop, whereas there were virtually no changes among the untreated group members. All but one of the eight variables which changed significantly from pre to post evaluation were in favor of the treated group. Specifically, during the course of the workshop we found reason to believe that counselors became increasingly present oriented, self reactive, flexible, and aware of their own needs and feelings. They also became more positive about themselves, more self accepting, and better able to establish intimate contact with other people.

The uniformly positive changes attest to the importance and power of the training program in affecting self actualizing potential. Although our findings can be only suggestive, both the empirical evidence and our subjective impressions lead us to believe that this type of workshop series is effective in initiating appropriate attitude changes on the part of school counselors and directing them towards greater effectiveness in their role of Home-School Coordinators. It is our experience that after training, coordinators become enthused about the program and are able to apply themselves enthusiastically. A separate question, however, revolves around whether or not such a program produces beneficial effects beyond those experienced by the counselors or Home-School Coordinators involved in the initial training sessions.

The following section will describe the implementation of three components of this program: (1) Parent training groups, (2) Parent volunteer programs, and (3) Coordination of family and school systems for classroom management.

Parent Training Groups

A major function of the Home-School Coordinators is to develop a cadre of parent education programs, variously emphasizing parent-child communications and other forms of parent management. An assumption underlying the effort to teach coordinators several methods of parent education, rather than a single one, is that not all parents are equally responsive to each type of program. Some parents may be resistant to a

221

program which emphasizes behavioral management, while others will find that such concentration upon discipline suits their own particular values.

As previously indicated, the procedures for implementing a variety of parenting programs have been sufficiently well developed and formalized as to allow clear demarcation of their emphases and a clear distinction of their procedures. A precise outline of what a parent education class consists of, within each modality, is not required within the current context, given the availability of such descriptions elsewhere (e.g., Becker, 1971; Dinkmeyer & McKay, 1976; Dreikurs, 1964). It is important to point out, however, that before implementing any such programs, coordinators must be thoroughly familiar with the material and be instructed in their implementation. Through our own efforts, we have become aware that regardless of the specific modality around which the parent education class is developed, there are certain uniform requirements for effective training.

For example, when the decision is made to initiate a parent group one must consider issues of informing the parents of the meeting place, dates, purpose, times, number of meetings, etc., and a meeting place which promotes an informal, friendly atmosphere is desirable. In our own case, we have found that meetings held within a counselor's home or after school hours facilitate this feeling of informality.

In order to meet the various needs of the school community, it is helpful if parents are given alternative meeting times from which to choose. The availability of the parents as well as the coordinator is considered and blocks of time for the meeting should be clearly specified and built into the school schedule. In order for parents to commit themselves to attend every meeting, they need to know the number of meetings entailed to complete the program and must have advance notice of any cancellations or changes. The particular number of sessions required for adequate training varies with the particular program chosen. However, a general estimate of approximately ten sessions is usually sufficient to accomplish many of the basic goals of the parent education training and facilitate the movement of the parents to a more individually tailored, subsequent training or treatment procedure if this becomes indicated.

In most schools, teachers are organized into teams, comprising similar grade level or academic subjects. In some cases, it is helpful if the counselor invites parents from one of the teams, thus providing a rationale for the invitation being given to some parents and not to others. In any case, our own experience suggests that a suitable group is composed of approximately 12 to 13 prospective members and that ultimate withdrawal or absenteeism will probably reduce the group to no less than ten participants.

Since the characteristics of each group are unique, it is important to emphasize the value of leader training in how to handle group process. Additionally, the various training manuals also provide helpful suggestions.

Some of our own particular hints include:

1. An alphabetical list of group members along with their addresses, telephone numbers, names and ages of children, with a copy to the school principal.

2. Consistent contact with each group member a day or two before the first meeting with follow up contacts when participants have missed a meeting. The initial contact should emphasize directions for the meeting place, time, and issues of commitment. When a parent volunteer program has been implemented, assistance from a volunteer who has been through the program is very useful.

3. Materials to be used at a given presentation should be organized and available beforehand. Handouts, posters, audio and video tapes, film strips, books, and magazines are all useful and help stir interest.

4. Sooner or later questions will be raised about the school district's philosophy and issues will become intense when they relate to specific children. A clear understanding of your school district's philosophy will come in handy.

5. It is frequently helpful for the facilitation of group cohesiveness to serve refreshments at the conclusion of each meeting. Much of the actual benefit of these groups seems to come from the soft and supportive atmosphere provided in this environment.

6. It is also helpful for the group leader or coordinator to remember that their job is not to solve personal or family problems during parent education classes. Hopefully, as the group members learn new skills they will be able to solve their own problems, but if not the group will then serve as a transition point for moving people to more intensive and individually tailored experiences.

7. Finally, we find that it is motivating for participants to receive a certificate of completion as a reward for their efforts.

Comparative Evaluation of the Training Programs

Although Home-School Coordinators were trained in three distinct methods of parent education, they ultimately evolved two basic, distinguishable approaches. In order to evaluate the comparative effectiveness of these approaches, coordinators were initially encouraged to implement that one which best suits their predilections and with which they were most comfortable. Over a two year period, 14 groups were initiated and 150 parents began the training with 100 completing the series. Most of the training was conducted by six counselors, three of whom initially selected a behaviorally oriented parent training module based upon Becker's book, *Parent and Teachers* (1971) and three elected a program which combined some principles from Parent Effectiveness Training and Dreikurs' (1964) concepts of misbehavior. The STEP (*Systematic Training for Effective Parenting*) represents this coalition and was developed by Dinkmeyer and McKay (1976).

The behaviorally oriented treatment program focused upon helping parents define objective, observable behavior and then modify the conditions which control that behavior in their children. It was emphasized that in order to influence someone's behavior, they must first be specific about the target of change and to keep an accurate record of its frequency. The use of token systems was described and homework was assigned to help the parents utilize this procedure. The manipulation of both social and non-social consequences was emphasized within the context of Becker's admonitions.

In contrast to the foregoing, the STEP program is based partially upon Dreikurs' four goals of misbehavior (Dreikurs, Grumwald, & Pepper, 1971; Dreikurs, Dreikurs, & Gray, 1968). These four goals include attention seeking, power seeking, revenge seeking, and withdrawal or assumed disability. Principles for changing behavior concentrate upon the development of meaningful and natural consequences, emphasizing communication and understanding of subconscious goals. The training emphasizes that parents learn the principle of problem ownership in confronting their relationships with the child. The direct communication of feelings is another focus through which these issues of ownership are transmitted.

In the course of training, dydactic instruction is facilitated through the use of posters, audio tapes, and other audio-visual material along with assignments for the transmittal of the effect into the home environment. In order to determine if the different treatment emphases produce different treatment effects, parents were followed through the course of their training. Psychological tests designed to reflect the experience of autonomy and control, interpersonal relationships, and subjective impressions of benefit, were used. Experience of subjective benefit was pursued from six months to a year after groups terminated in order to further assess the longevity of effect.

While the findings clearly indicate that both types of groups produce changes in the parents' sense of competency and self control, there were no major differences in the benefits obtained. Parents were uniformly pleased with the results and we were unable to clearly and distinctly isolate specific indicators or contraindicators for either treatment. Although there was some vague suggestion that those who are most benefited by the behavioral training differ somewhat from those who were benefitted from the STEP training, this was not sufficient to base strong conclusions upon. Nevertheless, the general suggestion was that parents who tend to value interpersonal control seem to experience more benefit from behaviorally oriented training programs whereas those who value emotional expression benefit more from the STEP program. The STEP training is more likely than behavioral training to produce increases in an individual's ability to express their emotions to others and also diminishes the intensity of neurotic wants for affection. Such a finding only raises the need for further pursuit of an effort to determine if certain people are better candidates for one treatment program than another.

Parent Volunteer Programs

A major aim of parent volunteer programs is to involve, otherwise defensive parents, in an active identification with the school system. The value of such a program is primarily to be had in the preservation of the parents' sense of integrity and status. Parents who place great emphasis upon status and who are threatened by their child's misbehavior, can sometimes be better approached if they feel that they are a part of the system rather than being oppressed by the educational system.

Though we find it ineffective to have parents deal with their own children, soliciting their help in working with handicapped children, poor learners, and record keeping duties (non-confidential material) does effectively incorporate them into the school management structure. Additionally, the provision of such volunteer labor takes many restraints off of other school personnel and allows them time to observe the parents in action and to provide guidelines and help which may then generalize to their relationships with their own children.

In the past, we have solicited parents to serve as "substitute" fathers or mothers for children from broken homes, tutors for underachievers, playground coordinators, activity planners, sources of transportation, and even lay counselors. They have consulted with other parents, assisted teachers in preparing classroom materials, and have often contributed much to the resolution of very difficult problems involving children other than their own. At times, we have found that some parents have been resistant to parent education classes when approached as "parents" but have been willing to involve themselves in such classes when it has been "to train" them in their role as volunteers. A major interest has been to treat parents as experts in their own rights, respecting their expertise, and soliciting their consultation in various areas of child management. Although their recommendations may not be followed, frequently the very solicitation of their opinion provides a stable bond between home and school which is then the basis for them overcoming many of their misgivings about the school's relationship to their own child.

Coordinating Family-School Systems in Classroom Management

Both parent training groups and parent volunteer programs come to bear in a coordinated effort to establish a consistent and systematic training-treatment program which employs both family and school systems. When parents have been trained, either through volunteer involvement or through formal classes, to apply consistent principles of behavior management or communication, the home-school coordinator, along with the classroom teacher can then develop a child-focused program which employs the same contingencies and reinforcements in the two diverse environments. Parents and teachers establish on-going dialogues in which both principles of behavioral control and principles of communication are emphasized, agreed upon, and implemented consistently. Such a program is designed primarily to diminish the degree of discrepancy between the rweward systems present in these two diverse environments and to provide increasing consistency for the child in his world of learning.

At times, daily telephone contacts are utilized to implement and maintain home and school consistency. At other times, a record sheet is sent home nightly with the studen and he or she may be rewarded at home for activities performed at school. Alternatively, there are times when the school may reward the child for activities performed at home. In virtually all cases, periodic meetings between the classroom teacher, the home-school coordinator, and the parents are necessitated in order to maximize the impact of the program and to maintain the degree of consistency needed to introduce stability to the child's environment. It is a frequent observation that both parents and teachers lose sight of the program's objectives and/or the contingencies are eroded or subtlely changed, unless consistent contact is emphasized and is built in to the system.

Conclusions

Reflecting upon our own experiences over the past few years, a program such as the foregoing has produced substantial effects in the case of many children uneffected by the usual and less integrated intervention efforts. Though most of our impressions rely upon subjective rather than objective data, we are convinced that a uniform effort to coordinate the activities of parents and school officials is needed before the social-education objective of the school will be realized. Though a potent force for social change, the lack of planned coordination among a variety of social systems has simply compounded the inconsistency present in modern day children 's environments. Multi-systems operating according to diverse rules has been exacerbated by the rapidly expanding technology and by rapidly changing moral systems in the American culture. Though much of the new behavioral technology has been included within school programs, it has not been adequately transmitted or utilized in family systems. Since there appears to be no ready end to the variety of social change and the ambiguities that it represents, more systematic and integrated efforts for cooperation must be made. These can only be made, however, if programs are designed which will maintain each family's sense of dignity, emphasize the responsibility of the family for each child, and will allow negotiations between the mutually respected systems of family and school to the determination of individually tailored programs for the variety of students which present behavioral and emotional difficulties.

References

Becker, W.C. *Parents and teachers.* Campaign, Illinois: Research Press, 1971.

Dinkmeyer, D., & McKay, G.D. *Systematic Training for Effective Parenting.* Circle Pines, Minn.: American Guidance Services, Inc., 1976.

Dreikurs, Rudolf, *Children: The challenge.* New York: Hawthorne Books, Inc., 1964.

Dreikurs, Rudolf, & Gray, Loren, *Logical consequences, a new approach to discipline.* New York: Hawthorne Books, Inc., 1968.

Dreikurs, Rudolph, Grumwald, Bernice, & Pepper, Floy C., *Maintaining sanity in the classroom.* New York: Harper & Row, 1971.

Rotter, J.B. Generalized expectancies for internal versus external control of reinforcement. *Psychological Monographs,* 1966, 80, Whole No. 609.

Shostrom, E.L. *Personal Orientation Inventory.* San Diego: Edits, 1963.

Shutz, W.C. *FIRO: A three dimensional theory of interpersonal behavior.* New York: Holt Rinehart & Winston, 1960.

Footnotes

[1]We wish to thank the counselors and administrators at Cypress-Fairbanks Independent School District for their sponsorship and assistance in this project.

Section III

The Community

A Nation's Interest

Richard S. Greene
Department of Special Education
Madera Unified School District
Thomas Jefferson High School
Madera, California 93204

Changing the Public School System

The public school system in itself is one of the most radical ideas in human history. Without question, it is the most potent agent for social change in our nation. Change is inescapable, but the decision on how to change the public school system, and what areas of public education are to change, rest with society.

The following recommendations are in order at this point:[1]

1. provide early childhood stimulation, education, and evaluation as part of the continuum of public education

2. conduct a study of histories of successful inner-city families who have learned to cope effectively with their environment

3. restructure education of teachers, administrators, and counselors, and retrain those now in the field

4. reexamine the present system of intelligence testing and classification
5. commit substantial additional funding for research and development in educational improvement for disadvantaged children and youth
6. thoroughly delineate what constitutes accountability and allocate sufficient funds to carry out the responsibility entailed, and hold the schools accountable for providing quality education for all children
7. involve parents, citizens, citizen groups, students and general and special educators in the total educational effort.

NARC Policy Statement

A policy statement made by the National Association for Retarded Children (NARC) in 1971 states that public education must be provided for all mentally retarded persons which include the severely and profoundly retarded. Many mentally retarded children are being denied education in the public schools because of their projected inability to contribute tangibly to society. Others are being denied education because the retarded person does not possess sufficient behavioral controls and/or self-care and verbal skills to make him amenable to traditional school curriculums, physical facilities, and competencies of teaching personnel.

The National Association for Retarded Children feels that the responsibility for developing appropriate educational techniques and/or modifying disruptive behavior in the classroom rests with the public school systems. Failure to adapt to classroom behavior or to learn at a prescribed level results from the use of inappropriate educational technologies.

Placement in the special classes should be based upon the child's special educational needs, regardless of diagnosis or the type of retardation. When special class placement is deemed appropriate by an interdisciplinary evaluation team, there should remain daily opportunity for the special class child to interact with regular class students in nonacademic situations and in academic areas where the special class student can compete on an equal basis. The National Association for Retarded Children feels that, whenever possible, the regarded child needs to be integrated into the mainstream of regular education.

According to the NARC, curriculums for the mentally retarded student should be designed with the intention of providing an individualized educational experience. Classroom activities and teaching materials should be relevant and geared toward practical aspects of daily living and effective integration in the community. There should be early emphasis on vocational skills which stress the effective use of leisure time through community, recreational, and social outlets.

Further provisions need to be made for an ongoing communication between educators and family members to insure that what is taught in the school curriculum has definite relevance to the daily activities of the home setting. Goal-setting needs to involve the family in the educational process for more complete follow-through in the home.

Special class placement of a child who appears to be mentally retarded may be appropriate when the following conditions exist:[2]

1. documented history of retarded overall functioning which is substantiated through qualified evaluation

2. constant impairment of adaptive behavior in child's home and community as well as in school culture and environment

3. no significant change in child's inferior performance and achievements after modification in school and home environment

4. significant continuing residual disability which cannot respond to environmental manipulation alone

5. interdisciplinary team's considered opinion that the curriculum in regular class will not maximize the child's potential for learning and achievements as effectively as a modified curriculum individually designed by a specially trained teacher for children with impairment of learning potential.

Lanterman Act

According to the Lanterman Mental Retardation Services Act,[3] some suggested guidelines in California to measure the adequacy of community services include the following:

Prevention — genetic counseling, preschool counseling to prevent cultural deprivation

Information and Referral — directory of services

Case Finding — family physician, medical facilities, day-care centers, mental health groups, public schools

Diagnosis and Evaluation — social evaluation, psychological evaluation

Care and Treatment — basic medical care, specialized treatment for dental defects, convulsive disorders, sensory defects, etc.

Family Counseling — planning for child care, management, training, accepting the retarded child, dealing with personal and emotional reactions

Home Training — public health, nursing, homemaker services, basic skills of self-care, self-control, communication and socialization

Nursery School Training — opportunities for parents and professionals to observe children

Special Education — EMR, TMR cooperative programs with Department of Rehabilitation, work training programs, adult education

Day Care — care of children for working mothers, promotion of self-care and social functioning

Short-Term Residential Care — temporary substitute homes, private schools, state hospitals, nursing homes

Long-Term Residential Care — state hospital, private residential schools and hospitals, foster home and family care, boarding homes, halfway homes

Vocational Services — state employment agencies and other manpower training and selective job placement, state vocational rehabilitation agency for counseling training and placement, sheltered workshop for transitional training and placement, extended employment and activity programs

Recreation — school recreation programs, public recreation department park activities, day and summer camp, social groups club, YMCA, YWCA, Boy Scouts and girl Scouts

Religious Training — Sunday school classes, church social, materials for home teaching

Legal Services — guardianship, legal counseling, adoption services

Statewide Supportive Services — licensing services, coordination among agencies, professional training research, planning, transportation; financial assistance through categorial aid programs.

Inner-City Educational Practices

There are some other concerns relating to the educational practices for the inner-city retarded children which are now resulting in some changing strategies across the nation:[4]
1. There is a lack of a definitive testing instrument which can adequately assess the intellectual potential of the mentally retarded.

2. Placement of the mentally retarded in special classes appears to be based on testing instruments which cannot measure the innate potential.

3. Placement of an inner-city child in special class is thought to lower the child's self-esteem, lower the expectations within the school system and within society.

4. Now there is some effort being made for placement of the retarded child in regular heterogenous classrooms and providing the child with supportive special educational services. From this it is anticipated that the child will achieve as well as or better than the mentally retarded in special classes.

5. It appears that little mobility exists for the educable mentally retarded to advance from special classrooms into the mainstream of education.

6. There is a lack of adequate curriculum approaches for the mentally retarded child which provides sequential development in sensory and perceptual training, motor skills, communications, language, vocational, social, and leisure-time activities.

7. There is a lack of systemically developed exemplary mediated teaching environment for the urban mentally retarded; also a lack of mediated learning activities clearly related to an educational technology network.

8. A need exists for the utilization of all resources that have a potential bearing on the education of the retarded.

9. There is a lack of parent-child centers concerned with the early childhood development of the retarded.

10. The negative attitudes of many school board members and administrators relating to an acceptable innovative and general program development for the mentally retarded results in an ineffective organized school structure.

11. There is concern with the educational system regarding the role of the education profession in relation to other agencies and disciplines involved in the comprehensive community approach to mental retardation.

12. There is inadequate delivery of health, nutrition, welfare, and other supportive services which could prevent much of the retardation now in existence.

13. Some education, health, and welfare facilities and services now available to families which could prevent mental retardation are not being effectively utilized.

14. A growing interest now exists in community involvement and com-

munity control of educational services to inner-city retarded children.

Some current estimates of the scope of the problem of mental retardation existing today across the United States are as follows:

1. There are almost six million persons, including preschool children, who require special education services.
2. Approximately 25 percent of all handicapped children are mentally retarded.
3. Approximately 46 percent of mentally retarded children now receive special education.
4. Approximately 26% of the personnel needed for special education are needed for the mentally retarded.
5. Approximately 47 percent of those needed for education of the mentally retarded and who were employed in 1967-1968 lacked proper certification.
6. Three-fourths of the nation's mentally retarded are to be found in isolated and impoverished urban and rural slums.

Some modest proposals in meeting an immediate pressing need for the development of an in-service training program are the following:[5]

1. It must occur largely in the teacher's classroom. To be of real value, the helper must see the real life physical and interpersonal conditions in which the teacher works.
2. It must emphasize the practical "how to" needs of new and inexperienced teachers.
3. It must be based on a mutual trust between teacher and trainer.
4. It must encourage the new and inexperienced teacher to look at himself as an experimenter, innovator, learner, and problem solver.

Some Major Problems

More major problems in the field of mental retardation exist and are becoming of national concern.[6]

Legala

There is a lack of a uniform legal code.

Commitment to an institution frequently results in assumption of global incompetence.

Laws frequently fail to distinguish between the mentally retarded and the mentally ill.

Institutionalization may void rights to handle money. Present guardianship fails to provide processes for parents to plan for personal care of the mental retardate. Has the mental retardate the right to decide whether he wants guardianship?

Criminal procedures seem to actually block recognition of mental retardation.

Social

Parents feel the choice is between home and institution. The right to suitable facilities is deemed necessary by the lack of diverse community facilities.

Does the individual who lives at home and wishes to live independently have the right to do so?

Society starts with the assumption that all mentally retarded persons are incompetent. Parents are guilty of this belief too.

Volunteer organizations and parents' groups have taken the child who is at home or in an institution into account and provides for their needs and assistance. Broadening concern is badly needed and could prove extremely effective.

Medical and treatment facilities are sometimes closed to the mentally retarded although their services would be appropriate.

Educational

Development of good programs and treatment plans are more important than evaluations.

Could the concept of education or training, including sensory motor training for more functional living, broaden our horizons beyond the three Rs?

Do we need adult education classes for the mentally retarded? We often do not teach the mentally retarded — we tell them.

Employment

The retardate is sometimes hired as temporary and therefore receives few or no benefits.

Unions make it difficult for an employer to hire the retarded. Workman's Compensation and Social Security also interfere.

235

Availability of jobs open to the retarded is limited.
Productivity is the sole standard of work success.
The mental retardate is often denied the title of Mr. or Mrs.
Employee attitudes toward the retardates' achievements are stereotypes.
Some employers insist upon excessive safety requirements for their mentally retarded employees.

Possible Courses of Action

Law

There should be a broad approach for an ongoing education for lawyers, legislators, school board members — all those responsible for making administration rules.
Comprehensive guardianship concepts need to be developed and implemented.

Social

Institute widespread programs to help families achieve a full understanding of the mentally retarded.
Develop a wide variety of community facilities for the mentally retarded which is suitable for each individual's needs and ability level.

Educational

All teachers should have some awareness and knowledge of exceptional children.
All teachers should be involved in a continuing education program to learn more about child development.
Educational programs to inform parents about the contents and methods of special education should be started.

Employment

The mentally retarded should receive the minimum wage or its equivalent.
An appropriate payment system should be used for work within an institution as well as for outside facilities.

Services of unions and insurance companies should be sought to make it easier for the mentally retarded to enter the world of work.

Meaningful activity programs after working hours should be developed.

Some Proposed Rights for Retarded People

Legal

Legal counsel should be available especially when commitment to an institution is being considered.

The mentally retarded should have the right to vote.

Social

The retarded should have the right to contribute to society – to pay taxes, give opinions, do things for others.

They should have the right to social acceptance.

They should have the right to satisfying living arrangements within or outside of the family.

They should have the right to make decisions even if this means making mistakes.

The retarded should have the right to reject any opportunities that may be offered.

Educational

The mentally retarded should have the right to choose their educational goals.

They should have teachers who believe the child's human rights come first.

They should be accepted at their own learning level.

They have the right to be taught to think for themselves.

Employment

The mentally retarded should be trained for available jobs.

They should have the right to change jobs or receive job training the same as workers in general.

They deserve the right to gain, seek, and hold employment to the best of their capabilities.

They should receive equal pay for equal work.

They have the right to earn an adequate living.

They have the right to the work of their own choosing.

Special Education Program Recommendations

In a conference on placement of children in special education programs for the mentally retarded, six recommendations were made?

Recommendation 1

Improve and restructure the current testing, placement, and evaluation process.

Action Taken

Develop tests appropriate to language and culture.

Adapt behavior guidelines.

Develop differential norms for various socioeconomic combinations.

Explore alternative to present testing programs on an experimental basis. Plan transitional programs for children moving from special education to regular classrooms.

Recommendation 2

Cease labeling the mentally retarded unless comprehensive assessment is made of abilities, physical health, and adaptive behavior.

Action: Minimal Interim Steps

Parental assessment of the children should be done.

There should be assessment of the child's functioning outside of school.

Evaluation of the child's interaction with peers should be made.

An assessment of the child's education abilities should include: evaluation of the child's strengths and weaknesses via

achievement testing
classroom observations
teacher interview.
Comprehensive assessment would include:
psychological measures
adaptive behaviors
social-cultural behavior
medical examiantions
educational achievements

Recommendation 3

Advocate educational justice and freedom for all children through recognition of each child as a unique individual.

Action Taken

In planning and implementing community partnerships, an effective role for students should be considered. Educators must identify and be identified with the dignity of human beings. They must devise ways to practice and demonstrate through effective action approaches to community involvement.

Recommendation 4

Sensitize teachers, administrators, school counselors, staff curriculum developers, and teacher-educators to the prevailing discrimination against children from social, cultural, and ethnic and economic backgrounds, different from the so-called norms.

Action Taken

Training programs for all teachers should seek to include the kinds of educational experience that will prepare them to serve the spectrum of children's needs.

In-service training programs need to be integrated early in the interdisciplinary training process.

There should be a reality-based curriculum with many different ways to provide for the needs of children.

Citizens can take part in the development of responsive school programs by serving as:

1. advocates
2. volunteers
3. advisers
4. consultants in curriculum developments and expanded program services
5. members of a monitoring and accountability system.

Recommendation 5

Use the existing legislation and the courts, if necessary, to achieve educational justice.

Action Taken

Implementation of existing legislation should be responsive to current needs of the local community.

Legal procedures should be created that will permit parents and/or children a judicial remedy and compensation for professional malfeasance.

Where comprehensive assessments were made, procedures for appeal of decisions for placement should be made and provided without cost to the appellant.

Recommendation 6

Support educational reform through federal, state, and local governmental and private funding.

Action Taken

Moneys must be made available to develop, implement, and evaluate various educational models for children with special needs. Examples are nongraded schools, learning centers, and resource rooms, staffed by methods and materials specialists and itinerant resource teachers.

Pacific Forum on Mental Retardation

The first Pacific Forum on Mental Retardation recommended that, for competitive employment of the mentally retarded, their most favorable characteristics be used as a criterion. These would include the following: an age range for either sex of eighteen to twenty-two years old; emotional stability; a high degree of social adjustment; and some previous training with emphasis on work habits, discipline, and punctuality.

IQ is not a decisive factor in differentiating success from failure. The total workshop provides a therapeutic environment and a program individualized as far as possible which should include:
1. opportunities for retardates to assume and act out adult roles
2. a staff understood by the retardates to be sympathetic, accepting, understanding, and nonpunitive although it makes reasonable demands and enforces general rules
3. counseling with parents which tends to be most effective when goals are fairly concrete and limited.

The Pacific Forum on Mental Retardation found these areas still need further investigation:
1. study of the self-concept of the retardate and the retardate's perception of social roles
2. study of the dynamics process and techniques of individualized group counseling with mental retardates
3. determination of behavioral components that constitute higher functioning for the retardates in a sheltered workshop.
4. development of differential teaching and training methods for various diagnostic and etiological categories of mental retardation.

In summary, the forum made the following recommendations:
1. Services given the adult retardate should be part of the total continuum of services to the retarded.
2. There is a need to develop earlier education programs to teach leisure-time skills and provide vocational opportunities at the adult level.
3. The adult must have the same training as the child in order to get along with other people.
4. Housing accommodations for the adult retardate should be explored.
5. Legal rights of the adult retarded should be explored.

In operating programs for the rehabilitation of the retarded three problems are posed according to Tsor-Yan Tsau of the Social Welfare Department in Hong Kong:[8]
1. How are we going to cope with the challenge of rehabilitating a retarded adult?
2. What is our responsibility to this segment of the population?

241

3. How realistic and adequate can such a rehabilitation program be in the face of the complex and keen competition of our society?

In the areas of providing relevant learning, massive reconstruction which will incorporate the following principles will be required:

1. The teacher from preschool to high school should be provided with a basic understanding of the central issues in impairment of adaptive behavior.

2. The abilities of special teachers and aides with different backgrounds of vocational experiences should be coordinated.

3. Research of many kinds is needed in unusual problems presented by clinical cases. Laboratory experiments, action research projects, and new approaches to learning documentation of parental reactions are a basis for providing counseling relief from stress or in planning community services and short-term and longitudinal coverage where medical intervention has occurred.

Some of the broader problems faced by special education are as follows:

1. Individualized planning should be done so that each child has access to the specialists' services needed to assist progress within the school.

2. Plan and implement a broad curriculum of work-based experiences jointly organized by the school and community. This has been pioneered successfully in some places for moderately to severely handicapped students and could be organized locally, using existing community organizations.

3. Provisions should be made for incorporation of handicapped students in the normal school curriculum and programs.[9]

A challenge respondent, Mrs. Marcela B. Garcia (Chief, Bureau of Public Schools, Manila, Philippines) states that in the area of relevant learning experiences in general, curriculum emphasis in on the prevocational type.[10] Only the academic subjects require curriculum adjustments, whereas the nonacademic subjects, such as music and art, require few curriculum adjustments.

Standards are set for each grade level, and these standards are considered goals. The mentally retarded child is helped to grow at his own pace under this type of curriculum; diagnostic and remedial phases are emphasized.

The development of appropriate language habits seems crucial to the retardate's progress, regardless of the level or stages of progress. In the language development areas, there is a need for explicit remedial training. For the child who is mildly retarded there now is a need for specific remedial programs in articulation, conceptual meaning, grammar and other areas.

Problems in Training Program Development

Special class programs, particularly EMR programs, should be immediately and intensively reevaluated with the following objectives in mind:[11]

1. to utilize the total resources of the school for the education of the EMR (This could result in fewer special classes and, in the long run, the elimination of almost all such classes as they are now structured.)

2. to plan more intensively with personnel outside the field of special education for the EMR in order that the total school resources may be utilized for the benefit of these children (work study programs, counseling)

3. To redirect teacher education programs to give special educational personnel, regular classroom teachers, and school administrators a broader perspective toward the education of the mentally retarded (teacher education programs need to emphasize the training of resource personnel to assist all school personnel with the educational problems of the retarded)

4. to reexamine manpower requirements in relation to program changes.

Recommendations for Communities

A community should:

1. support nursery schools to stimulate the social, cultural, and intellectual development of children

2. advocate early entry into the regular school system for children with particular handicaps but with cognitive abilities

3. recommend that severely retarded and multiple handicapped infants and children be kept at home and supported by domiciliary and day-care services

4. encourage experimentation to provide foster homes, hostels, residence and small village communities for the retarded

5. support sheltered workshops which have demonstrated that retarded

people can be usefully and productively employed (The next step is to encourage industry and local and provisional governments to set examples by employing the retarded adults.)

6. foster "normalization" of community programs for the retarded by developing new kinds of professional and subprofessional personnel as well as reorienting the existing professional disciplines.[12]

President's Committee on Mental Retardation

The President's Committee on Mental Retardation recommends the following changes in the future of residential services to the mentally retarded:

1. The mentally retarded should have the same constitutional rights and guarantees as every other American.

2. Good residential programs provide both long-term and short-term services.

3. The residential facilities should develop each individual's economic potential.

4. A residential facility coordinates its program with other regional and community mental retardation services for the development of a full range of comprehensive services.

5. Model residential environment should provide a warm, stimulating social setting, devoid of dehumanizing conditions.

6. Administration policies should recognize the importance of the interrelationships of parents, volunteers, staff, and residents.

The committee recommends additional areas which should be covered:13

1. intensive reevaluation of special education programs, particularly those dealing with the EMR, with the overall objectives of putting the full resources of the school to work for the retarded, enlarging teaching perspectives of special education personnel, and giving regular classroom teachers and school personnel better understanding of special education goals and methods.

2. the setting of performance standards for all levels of basic and supportive personnel with the maintenance of those standards being the responsibility of the staff

3. development of accreditation procedures for all facilities serving the needs of the retarded

4. setting up of in-training programs for all categories of staff who work with the retarded

5. broadening of national and international work study exchanges to include supportive staff so that everyone from the student to the professional, both basic and supportive personnel, has the opportunity of enriching the views and duties of the mentally retarded.

Proposal for Action: (Education and Training)

1. A set of curriculum guidelines should be prepared for every level of education of the mentally retarded. Curriculum guidelines would include stress on vocational and social preparation for work and life.
2. Individual committees, in communities should develop their own cirriculums to meet local conditions.
3. More materials on vocational and job-related subjects should be written in simple form for the retarded.
4. New concepts of vocational education that bring students out of the classroom into workday situations should be encouraged.
5. More work experience centers within living facilities should be encouraged.
6. Vocational education should play an important and a far more meaningful role in meeting the education and employment needs of the retarded.
7. Meaningful cooperative agreements must be developed in vocational education, vocational rehabilitation, public employment, and special education.

The Medical Profession

1. Rehabilitation Services Administration should encourage institutions with long-term rehabilitation programs to incorporate training in medical rehabilitation of the retarded into their curriculums.
2. The division of mental retardation of the Rehabilitation Services Administration should encourage university-affiliated training facilities to develop greater involvement in mental retardation programs by departments of physical medicine and rehabilitation.

Employment

1. Employers should be encouraged to review and scale down their educational requirements for jobs.

245

2. Tax relief should be considered for all handicapped workers, including the mentally retarded, to help ease the extra expense they face in carrying out their duties and daily routines of employment.
3. Sheltered workshops should be established in suburban industrial parks and regional shopping centers. Workshops can serve nearby industrial complexes by performing many routine tasks.

Independent and Sheltered Living

1. Living facilities for the mentally retarded should be established in the vicinities where they work. The facilities can include hostels, group homes, halfway houses, cooperative apartments, and community homes or farms.
2. Independent living facilities in institutions should be encouraged when possible. Facilities go hand in hand with the development of sheltered workshops won the premises.
3. Retarded persons in institutions with employment potential, as determined by rehabilitation counselors, should be given every possible service in order to help them attain jobs and independent living in the community.
4. Living facilities for the mentally retarded should provide for full recreational, medical, vocational, and social needs.

Promotion and Education

1. Labor unions should be encouraged to exempt low-echelon jobs from career ladders so that the mentally retarded might fill them.
2. State and local governments need to be encouraged to establish special hiring procedures for the mentally retarded, which are similar to those of the federal government.
3. Promotional efforts should be directed toward the top management to encourage written policy statements favoring jobs as a national focal point for the retarded; to middle management to encourage implementation of these policies; to rank-and-file workers to gain their acceptance of the retarded as a fellow worker.[14]

A decade of accomplishment has brought the following results:[15]
1. the beginning of national networks of mental retardation diagnosis and evaluation centers; launching of a network of mental retardation research, teaching and professional training centers, and the development of facilities and staff improvement programs
2. development by every state of a plan for mental retardation services

3. increased acceptance of the retarded as trainees in vocational rehabilitation programs and a rapid growth of employment opportunities for the trained retarded workers

4. major advances in the public awareness of the retarded and their needs.

Now concerted public and private measures at all levels can bring significant progress in overcoming mental retardation. Some of these areas are as follows:

1. development of more and better manpower recruitment and training programs for work with the retarded

2. development of more public and private partnership in mental retardation program services and research

3. better, more imaginative use of existing resources at all levels, broader realization and use of the resources that the retarded themselves represent

4. taking into account the special education training guidance and other needs of the mentally retarded in social and institutional planning for the future.

By using present knowledge and techniques from the biomedical and behavioral sciences, some of the following is now possible:[16]

1. to undo the harm done to thousands of children wrongly identified as retarded by faulty tests

2. to prevent the retardation that would occur because of social neglect and public disinterest in great segments of minority groups

3. to return one-third of the retarded now living in institutiions to community living and make them into useful citizens through training for productive employment

4. to reduce the occurrence of mental retardation by 50 percent before the end of the century.

To meet the demands of the President's Committee on Mental Retardation, society can do the following:[17]

1. Society can convene a concerned cross-section – both laymen and experts – as an interdisciplinary team which is responsive to the needs of the children and one which can provide unique visibility for these needs.

2. Society can define and communicate to government and to the public those areas of action where needed and recommended specific techniques for accomplishing change occur.

3. Society can provide a basis for realistic projections for the future.

4. Society can persuade organizations and individuals to work with

247

government bodies to update or change those laws or institutions which are found wanting.

5. Society can communicate our proposals to all levels of government and the private sector through a published report. The critical areas found to be most in want and need are in general:
(a) individuality
(b) learning
(c) health
(d) parents and families
(e) community and environment
(f) laws, rights, and responsibility
(g) child services institutions.

Trends and Projections

1. It is now estimated that over the next few years there will be about a 5 percent increase in the number of mentally retarded persons assisted by sheltered workshops.

2. There should be a modest number, approximately a five percent increase, of the number of mentally retarded persons employed in regular competitive industry.

3. There should be only a slight increase in the number of mentally retarded persons served by the vocational rehabilitation program.

4. There should be a fifteen percent increase in the number of mentally retarded students employed in school work programs.

5. There should be little if any change concerning the number of mentally retarded persons being trained in competitive industry.

In view of the trends and proejctions mentioned above, a comprehensive child development program needs to be planned. It would include:

1. family planning, information, and supplies

2. prenatal care for mothers — medical, nutritional, educational, and social

3. delivery of the infant and immediate postnatal care for motehr and child

4. education and counseling in child care

5. adequate food, dental and medical services, including medical treatment services for the remainder of the child's infant and preschool years

6. systematic cognitive stimulation for the infant and toddler to enable

the child to benefit from preschool and kindergarten programs

7. assurance through care, counseling, and education of an emotional climate conducive to operational personality development

8. exposure to social learning situations via group activities, and social interaction where these experiences are not provided by the home

9. day care, night care, and emergency care services where they are needed, which includes foster care and adoption

10. rehabilitation and special education.

Calendar Year of Employment Programs

1. 1938 – employment of handicapped workers in sheltered workshops.

2. 1938 – employment of handicapped workers in competitive employment.

3. 1956 – on-the-job training of clients sponsored by state vocational rehabilitation agencies.

4. 1964 – school work programs for mentally and physically handicapped students on an experimental basis – 1961; made a permanent part of the program.

5. 1966 – training sheltered workshop clients in industry.[18]

Developing the MR's Potential

The mentally retarded must be afforded every opportunity to develop their maximum potential. This can only be accomplished in a homelike environment where they are exposed to enriching experiences. The mentally retarded must become fully accepted and recognized as human beings. New ideas, meaningful goals, and significant programs must be based on current research and knowledge. Programs are needed to motivate and stimulate the retarded.

The staff should utilize every available skill and technique to enrich the retarded individual's social and mental development. The most suitable and desirable placement program for them is a family-like group in a small house unit where stress situations are minimized, dependency lessened, wholesome interpersonal relationships established, and interaction with adult and peer groups encouraged. Of necessity, the public needs to be reeducated along with communities and families in understanding and in fully accepting the mentally retarded. There is a continual need for institutional placement to care properly for those children who are unable to reside at home or to be cared for by community residential services. Improvement of programs can be brought about by smaller individualized living units, better supervision, a more concerned staff, more modern and positive attitudes in administrative structure and in-service training programs for aides and attendants, thus permitting more flexibility and less rigidity. Present-day rationale should deemphasize sheltering the mentally retarded from society, and instead assist the retarded in assuring their role in society. Major steps should be taken toward integrating them into the mainstream of society.[19]

Not enough attention is being given to the emotional and social problems created by the presence of the mentally retarded child in the family. The total load of rehabilitation work which could be coordinated at the federal level should be evenly distributed between state, federal, and private agencies.[20]

The mentally retarded need a state priority based on a cost benefit scheme: i.e., how a goal can be achieved at the lowest cost or how much benefit can be obtained when the cost is fixed. Goals must first be clearly established, and a classification of services musts be based upon the intended outcome — not on what has been currently done. The mentally retarded are in need of programs other than special education curriculums. These programs should build and encourage physical development, psycho-emotional stability, social stability, and legal services geared toward the protection of the rights and privileges of the mentally retarded.

Hamilton (1969) states that special education programs need to be geared toward the development of each child's maximum potential.[22] Family and genetic counseling need to be made available. Provisions need to be made for the establishment of day care centers and centers designed specifically for those in need of nursing care. Adequately equipped staff programs and well-equipped hostels with a limited number of residents need to be made available for temporary placement of mentally retarded children to provide short-term relief for family vacations, emergencies, or hospitalizations.

The individual state must reorganize its mentally retarded institutions, laws, and administration to direct, coordinate and improve mentally retarded treatment with a view toward eventual incorporation of the mentally retarded as functioning members of society.

An overall plan needs to be established which would oversee and coordinate all phases of mentally retarded activity from the initial diagnosis through treatment to final integration into society. Additional open and semiopen institutions for the mentally retarded child must be organized.[23]

A proposed family evaluation center, reevaluation and guidance services divisions should be developed and geared toward the family as a unit within the individual communities. Appropriate home-helping services can assist in alleviating residential placement and protection. Guidance of the individual MR child can be accomplished by the establishment of a citizens' advocacy services division. An additional proposal is a camping and community recreational services division that should encourage existing organizations to expand their programs for the MR. Now there is a definite need for a vocational services division encompassing administrative centers, residential services, and workshop centers. Transportation facilities need to be made available in order for the mentally retarded to utilize all services. The utilization of volunteer services in a constructive manner should be implemented; an intensive in-service training program for the staff should be developed; and a public information office should be made available.[24]

Future progress will require the development of epidemiologic research methods which would provide precise incidents and prevalent data. Adequate planning and substantial funding are required to enable services to keep pace with advancements in knowledge. Early and comprehensive diagnosis will include the ascertainment of the cause, degree, and type of mental retardation; an evaluation from somatic psychology and social, educational, and vocational viewpoints; determination of secondary handicaps; immediate and long-term planning; MR counseling and parental counseling. Present-day knowledge would be implemented to develop programs designed to significantly decrease the frequency of mental retardation and to facilitate additional etiologic identification, new and improved treatment methods, recommendations concerning child rearing practices and educational advances.[25]

Comprehensive diagnostic and remedial programs should broaden the scope of a clinic to include:[26]
1. a more complete evaluation of the child
2. the possibility of obtaining a clearer picture of the relationship between the physical and intellectual processes
3. the possibility of specific treatment feedback
4. clinic participation in broad multidisciplinary university training programs.

251

University centers concerned with developing a comprehensive approach to mental retardation and chronic diseases should consider the following basic questions:

1. How can the administration of a new multidisciplinary program be coordinated with presently operating university organizations?
2. How can the integration of disciplines be accomplished?
3. How much emphasis ought to be placed on training and how much on service?
4. How can specialized centers be most effectively utilized?
5. Can manpower needs be better satisfied by more specialists or better-trained generalists?
6. What kind of enforcement is needed to insure continuity of prescribed care by parents?

University centers will achieve their maximum potential if each of them will develop an MR program geared to meet the problems of its community.[27]

In addition to the state institutions' services, specific essential community services need to be prepared and provided:

1. diagnostic clinics to provide early and accurate diagnosis by a basic diagnostic team composed of a pediatrician, psychiatrist, social worker, public health nurse, and neurologist
2. parent consultation services
3. nursery school and recreational activities
4. classes for EMRs and TMRs
5. day-care centers
6. sheltered workshops, vocational training jobs recruitment and placement facilities to enable long-term planning for the MR.
7. community facilities to provide appropriate care and supervision for the MR subsequent to parent's death or disability.

The community program should be many-faceted to consider the differing degrees, etiologies, age groups, physical and emotional handicaps of the mentally retarded person. A wide variety of interdisciplinary services should be provided to utilize a large number of different professions.[28]

Plans for a comprehensive community program for mentally retarded adults include:[29]

1. community planning for all citizens and for all handicapped individuals
2. providing a continuum of unbroken services beginning in childhood
3. the interactions of both the professional who provides the services and by the mentally retarded's family who receives them

4. the research program's evaluation and preparation of professional workers

5. a coordinating mechanism which will make it possible for MR adults to obtain available services and for service agencies to coordinate their work in an effective manner.

Problems encountered in programs for EMR children include:

1. poorly trained or untrained teachers
2. poor financing
3. unimaginative state regulations
4. teacher reluctance to use paraprofessional personnel
5. poor social and family development.

Suggested methods of dealing with the problems are as follows: [30]

1. National standards of education and financing should be set.
2. Educational materials should be made relevant to everyday life.
3. An attempt should be made to identify the EMR earlier in life.
4. Special education teachers should be well trained.

It is felt that a global approach to the needs of the mentally retarded child, which will be based on the school-community agency concept and which would provide continuity of planning and programming, should be initiated and developed. Schools must meet and plan for the needs of each mentally retarded child. School personnel must make direct contact with parents or community agencies.[31]

The long-and short-term goals and objectives, together with the programs developed for the severely mentally retarded, should be based on a complete social and medical evaluation and history. Psychological evaluation activities relating to short-range objectives should build toward the long-range goals with emphasis on the daily living routines training program.

For the severely mentally retarded, the environment should be controlled and the programs should be structured so that sedentary and physical activity will alternate. Principles of consistency, persistency, and continuity are vital to a habit-development program. The progress of a severely mentally retarded individual in a group training program should be evaluated so that the parents can be informed about it; decisions about new programs and program emphasis and procedures can then be made.[32]

One alternative to large residential institutional care for the mentally retarded should be the creation of a community of small homes within an existing community. This would decrease the dehumanizing effects of the large residential institutions and lead to an increased functioning of the retarded. It is hoped that these homes would house residents of varying ages. The mentally retarded person should be carefully screened and prepared for this type of living.[33]

The actual design of the living community for mentally retarded persons should not be solely directed toward their protection, but should provide dynamic tension byw hich life in this community could offer opportunity for individual development. The mentally retarded are limited in their ability to express their experiences in a facility and are dependent upon how the use of the facility was demonstrated. These problems could be adequately solved by a multidisciplinary exchange of views in common language terms.[34]

Terminal placement for mentally retarded adults is in the sheltered workshop environment located within an industrial area, which generally employs thirty to forty individuals. The mentally retarded employees generally live in private homes, hostels, or residential facilities. The young mentally retarded are trained in sheltered workshops in general. They obtain their work skills in vocational centers from which they will go to regular competitive employment or to sheltered workshop employment.[35]

Some promising trends in the treatment of mental retardation seem to be appearing in the change of attitude toward the mentally retarded, residential care, planning and concern for the retarded adult, behavior modification programs, and manpower development.[36]

The program for mentally retarded adults must be developed with their total life history being taken into consideration. The period of early adulthood is a transition period in which occupational training needs to be emphasized. The mentally retarded individual's full adulthood can be accommodated in a sheltered workshop-type environment or in carefully supervised employment programs. It is the responsibility of the family and the community to see that the MR adult becomes a useful, productive, functioning member of society.[37]

Services involved in the management of families of the mentally retarded should include referral of cases, case evaluation, counseling, psychotherapy, training of guidance counselors for casework, direction supervision and control. Future management practices for the families of the retarded will be integrated with education for parenthood in general.[38]

The classroom teacher and the speech therapist can coordinate their daily lesson plans around similar activities. Specific activities can be emphasized each day — motor coordination, visual perception, laterality and body image, auditory discrimination, vocabulary building, and quantitative concepts. These programs should be concrete with much verbalization.[39]

The solutions to the mentally retarded individual's many complex problems will require a profound change in the structure of society. The mentally retarded have long been considered "surplus society" — that is, not an integrated part of society. Effective use of the total resources of institutions, together with effective institutional programs, greatly increase the potential of the MR for adaptability and full acceptance by society. The restructuring of the immediate family milieu, the rearrangement of societal institutions, and the manner in which these institutions are integrated aid in effecting changes in the values system of society. Programming for families of the mentally retarded or potential mentally retarded should now aim at providing a cultural milieu which will facilitate integration into the public culture.[40]

Programs such as Head Start are an attempt to prevent mild retardation which develops from economically and culturally impoverished homes. Retardates reaching an adult age need support, training, and help in finding meaningful productive employment in trade and service occupations. The oder retarded adult may find foster home, cottage, or partial institutional living preferable to full-time residential placement.[41]

Facilities for vocational evaluation and the training of the mentally retarded should provide space for observation of behavior and behavioral modifications which are physically adaptable to the changes in techniques that occur and which are able to compensate for intellectual defects of the retardate. Vocational evaluation includes observation of the retardate at work. This is followed by a determination of behavior which needs to be encouraged, and the elimination of behavior which is not vocationally adaptable and useful.[42]

The plea is now being made for an interdisciplinary approach to the problems of mental retardation with attendant parent care training and education. A cross-sectional exchange of views, with each member recognizing other members as making an indispensable contribution, is needed for an effective therapeutic team.[43]

The parents of the mentally retarded need and should be provided with an early diagnosis and an accurate assessment of the extent of the mental retardation handicap. The parents need to know what facilities are available for guidance and other help involving health visits to doctors. The institutionalized MR needs a warm homelike supportive atmosphere, rather than institutional or custodial care. The team of a nurse, educator, and social worker is needed, rather than the usual ward routine.[44]

The MR preschool child can best be heoped through early detection, diagnosis, and intervention. Public health services, understanding baby-sitters, and diagnostic centers could play significant roles for the mentally retarded and their families. The need is present for trained baby-sitters and preschools where a mentally retarded child can develop social skills. Behavior modification programs, day training centers of special classes in schools, speech training, and personnel-care classes are now needed.

For the mentally retarded adolescent, a prevocational training program needs to be made available as well as employment counseling and job placement. Structured socialization and recreational programs are necessary. The mentally retarded must have an opportunity to develop meaningful interpersonal relationships.

The mentally retarded adult needs sheltered workshops, while evening education programs are now needed for the less-retarded adult. The sheltered workshop situation is more desirable for the EMR. A factory-type atmosphere can be provided with some EMRs being placed in competitive employment. A continuum of services must be made available if the mentally retarded are to grow and develop to their maximum potential.[45]

Knowledge, research, and organization already in existence must be utilized to overcome the apathy prevelant in this country. No state has the right to feel smug about its accomplishments since *all* states can improve their programs. Most mentally retarded can be educated for gainful productive employment. There exists in the country today a woeful lack of training facilities.[46]

Society can at least double per capita expenditures in state institutions and reduce the size of these institutions. In addition, society can do the following:[47]

1. In each state, a board of impartial visitors to institutions, based upon knowledge of human welfare and demonstrated public service, should be appointed by the governor.
2. Within each state institution for the retarded, the staff of each department should have its own board of advisors. This board through regular

visits should have full knowledge of the institution's problems. Problems now hidden could be given the exposure necessary for proper solutions.
3. In each state, one university should be given the responsibility and resources to provide adequate training and counseling to all institutional personnel.
4. In each state, at least one institution for the retarded should become a center for compulsory periodic retraining of everyone employed by the state who works with the retarded. Each new employer should become a center for compulsory periodic retraining of everyone employed by the state who works with the retarded. Each new employer should have to spend a specified period of time in the training center.
5. A national qualified commission with authority should review state budgets for the care and treatment of the retarded, since many state facilities and programs are a disgrace to the nation and to the state which operates them.

These steps should be taken now as a beginning:[48]
1. No child should be kept in wards with adults. If no separate facilities exist, patient population should be rearranged.
2. Treatment programs stressing full educational and vocational training should be established. These programs should provide for individualized instruction.
3. Hospitals should explore all possibilities of using cottage homes, halfway houses, and other group setups — the philosophy being the less hospitalization the better.
4. Hospitals and society should abandon the notion that nothing can be done for mentally retarded children and set a goal of meaningful programs that really try to assist every child and give him and his family hope for the future.

Conclusion

The blatant neglect and ignorance shown by society with regard to the problem of mental retardation is disgraceful, to say the least. For a nation so rich in resources, compassion, and brainpower, it is truly startling that the mentally retarded have not achieved greater progress. For, after all, they too are human beings with feelings, emotions, desires and needs. They are not asking for pity or charity but, rather, for a chance to perform to the best of their ability and to lead as normal a life as they possibly can. Society thus far has not given them this opportunity and therefore must suffer the consequences: The mentally retarded today, for the most part, are a tax burden.

The stigma of being mentally retarded must be removed. The term "mental retardation" should be removed from the vocabulary of educators who insist upon labeling innocent children "MR" because of their inability to perform at grade level or because they score below normal on a standardized test. When this stigma is removed, it will represent a giant step forward for a minority that is still badly understood and inadequately served. It is time to educate the educators!

References

1. President's Committee on Mental Retardation, *The Six-Hour Retarded Child: A Report on a Conference on Problems of Education of Children in the Inner City* (Warrentown, Virginia: Airlie House, August 10-12, 1969), pp. 1-26.
2. Dr. Walter J. Cegelka et al., *Policy Statement on the Education of Mentally Retarded Children* (Arlington, Texas: National Association for Retarded Children, April 1971), pp. 1-16.
3. James M. Hall, *Lanterman Mental Retardation Services Act* (Sacramento, California: Human Relations Agency, 1971), pp. 11-13.
4. James E. Allan, Jr., *Education Problems of the Handicapped in the Inner City*, pp. 78-97 (from *Background Papers for the Conference on Problems of Education of Children in the Inner City*, August 10-12, 1969; Airlie House, Warrentown, Virginia).
5. James O. Miller, *An Educational Imperative and Its Fallout Implications*, pp. 20-43 (from *Background Papers for the Conference on Problems of Education of Children in the Inner City*, August 10-12, 1969; Airlie House, Warrentown, Virginia).
6. Pearl B. Diaria and Donald A. Pool, *Human Rights for the Mentally Retarded* (A report of a national conference held March 29-30, 1971, in Dallas, Texas), pp. 27-39.
7. President's Committee on Mental Retardation, *A Very Special Child – Conference on Placement of Children in Special Education Programs for the Mentally Retarded* (Lake Arrowhead, California, March 7-10, 1971), pp. 21-28.
8. Tsor-Yan-Tsau, challenge respondent to Dr. Akiliko Tahakaski, *Challenge to Programming: Serving the Adult Retarded* (from Mrs. Marianna Paige, ed., The First Pacific Forum on Mental Retardation, Washington, D.C.; September 28-October 1, 1971) pp. 39-45.

9. Marie D. Neale, Ph.D., *Challenges to Providing Relevant Learning Experiences to the Handicapped* (from Mrs. Marianna Paige, ed., The First Pacific Forum on Mental Retardation, Washington, D.C.; September 28-October 1, 1971) pp. 39-32.

10. Mrs. Marcela B. Garcia, challenge respondent to Marie D. Neale, Ph.D., *Challenges to Providing Relevant Learning Experiences to the handicapped* (from Mrs. Marianna Paige, ed., The First Pacific Forum on Mental Retardation, Washington, D.C.; September 28-October 1, 1971) pp. 33-36.

11. Darrel J. Mase "Problems in Training Program Development" (from Julus S. Cohen, *Manpower and Mental Retardation: An Exploration of the Issues;* Banff, Alberta, Canada; June 23-25, 1969), pp. 35-49.

12. Cyril Greenland, "Training Basic and Supportive Personnel" (from Julius S. Cohen, *Manpower and Mental Retardation: An Exploration of the Issues;* Banff, Alberta, Canada; June 23-25, 1969), pp. 51-75.

13. President's Committee on Mental Retardation, *MR 70- The Decisive Decade* (Washington, D.C.: Department of Health, Education, and Welfare, 1970), pp. 1-24.

14. President's Committee on Mental Retardation and President's Commitee on Employment of the Handicapped, *These Too Must Be Equal* (Washington, D.C.: Department of Health, Education and Welfare, 1969), pp. 6-18.

15. President's Committee on Mental Retardation, *MR 69 — Toward Progress: The Story of a Decade* (Washington, D.C.: Department of Health, Education and Welfare, 1969), pp. 4-8.

16. President's Committee on Mental Retardation, *MR 71 — Entering the Era of Human Ecology* (Washington, D.C.: Department of Health, Education and Welfare, 1972), p. 31.

17. Stephen Hess, "America's Children: The Road to Tomorrow," *Mental Retardation,* February 1971 (Washington, D.C.: American Association for Mental Deficiency), vol. 9, no. 1, pp. 66-67.

18. President's Committee on Mental Retardation, *Report to the President — Federal Programs for the Retarded, A Review and Evaluation* (Washington, D.C.: Government Printing Office June 1972), pp. 148, 216-218.

19. Wesley D. White, *Planning and Programming for the Retarded: Yesterday, Today and Tomorrow* (New York: National Association for Retarded Children, 1969).

20. Herbert Gross, "Aid in Rehabilitation of Handicapped Children and Youth in the Federal Republic of Germany," *Die Rehabilitation West Germay* 7(3): 136-146 (1968). (Washington, D.C.: Department of Health, Education and Welfare, *Mental Retardation Abstracts,* vol. 7, no. 4, October-December, 1970).

21. Wolf Wolfensberger, "An Attempt to Reconceptualize Functions of Services to the Mentally Retarded," *Journal of Mental Subnormality* 15(2):71-78 (1969), Omaha, Nebraska.

22. G.J.L. Hamilton "Philosophy Underlying a Service for the Mentally Retarded in Western Australia," *Australian Children Limited* 3(8):237-242 (1969).

23. Erne Maier, "What Must the Individual State Undertake in Order to Assist the Mentally Retarded?," *Lebensife* 8(3): 113-121 (1969).

24. Frank J. Menolascino, Robert L. Clark, and Wolf Wolfensberger, *The Initiation and Development of a Comprehensive, Countryside System of Services for the Mentally Retarded of Douglas County, Nebraska,* Greater Omaha Association for Retarded Children, vol. II, 1970, 111 pp. (Washington, D.C.: Department of Health, Education and Welfare, *Mental Retardation Abstracts,* vol. 8, no. 3, July-September, 1971).

25. George Tarjan, "Mental Retardation Implications for the Future," from Irving Philips, ed., *Prevention and Treatment of Mental Retardation* (New York: Basic Books, 1966), pp. 429-444.

26. Herbert Goldstein, "Special Education and the Director of a Mental Retardation Clinic," *New Frontiers in Mental Retardation* (Clinical Directors Mental Retardation Conference held June 5-7, 1966, at Asilomar, California), pp. 73-78.

27. Philip Calcagno and Robert Clayton, "University Affiliated Centers for Mental Retardation: The Georgetown Experience," *New Frontiers in Mental Retardation* (Clinical Directors Mental Retardation Conference held June 5-7, 1966, at Asilomar, California), pp. 111-115.

28. Harold D. Chope, "The Organization of Community Services for the Mentally Retarded," from Irving Philips, ed., *Prevention and Treatment of Mental Retardation* (New York: Basic Books, 1968), pp. 398-406.

29. Elias Katz, "The Mentally Retarded Adult in the Community," from Irving Philips, ed., *Prevention and Treatment of Mental Retardation* (New York: Basic Books, 1966), pp. 308-333. (*Mental Retardation Abstracts,* vol. 5, no. 4, October-December 1968).

30. "The Point is to Understand," (President's Committee on Mental Retardation, *Message 20,* July 1969.

31. Bernice G. Goodwin, Programming and the Metropolitan Public Schools, from R.C. Scheerburger, ed., *Mental Retardation: Selected Conference Papers* (Springfield, Illinois: Illinois Mental Health Department, 1969), pp. 179-184.

32. Charles P. Jubenville, "Programming for Severely Mentally Retarded," from R.C. Scheerenberger, ed., *Mental Retardation: Selected Conference Papers* (Springfield, Illinois: Illinois Mental Health Department, 1969), pp. 40-46.

33. Jean Vanier, "Homes for Retarded Adults," *Deficience Mentale/Mental Retardation* (Washington, D.C.: American Association on Mental Deficiency) 19(2): 2-5 (1969), in *Mental Retardation Abstracts,* vol. 8, no. 1, January-March, 1971.

33. Jean Vanier, "Homes for Retarded Adults," *Deficience Mentale/Mental Retardation* (Washington, D.C.: American Association on Mental Deficiency) 19(2): 2-5 (1969), in *Mental Retardation Abstracts,* vol. 8, no. 1, January-March, 1971.

34. Sauter A.M. DeWit, "Some Specific Aspects of Living Accommodations for the Severely Mentally Handicapped," from B.W. Richard, ed., *Proceedings of the First Congress of the International Association for the Scientific Study of Mental Deficiency,* Montpellier, France, September 12-20, 1967 (Surrey, England: Michael Jackson Publishing, 1968) pp. 496-497.

35. K. Grunewald, "Architectural Planning in Mental Retardation (Day Facilities)," from B.W. Richard, ed., *Proceedings of the First Congress of the International Association for the Scientific Study of Mental Deficiency,* Montpellier, France, September 12-20, 1967 (Surrey, England: Michael Jackson Publishing, 1968), pp. 701-702. (*Mental Retardation Abstracts,* vol. 7, no. 2, April-June 1970.)

36. Gunnar, Dybwad, "New Advances in the Field of Mental Retardation," *Australian Children Limited* 3(5): 136-148 (1968).

37. Edgar A. Doll, "Programs for the Adult Retarded," *Mental Retardation/MR* (Washington, D.C.: American Association on Mental Deficiency) 6(1): 19-21 (1968).

38. Wolf Wolfensberger and Richard A. Kurtz, eds., *Management of the Family of the Mentally Retarded* (Chicago, Ill.: Follett Educational Corporation, 1969).

39. L. Rubin and J. Fairley, "The Parallel Roles of the Teacher and the Speech Therapist in a School Situation for Mentally Defective Children," *Teaching and Training* 7(3): 67-74 (1969). (*Mental Retardation Abstracts,* vol. 7, no. 3, July-September, 1970.)

40. Bernard Farber, *Mental Retardation: Its Social Context and Social Consequences* (Boston, Massachusetts: Houghton Mifflin Co., 1968).

41. Hubert J. Grossman, "Implications for the Future," in Hubert J. Grossman, ed., *Mental Retardation* (symposium). (Chicago, Illinois: Pediatric Clinics of North America), 15(4): 1041 1046 (1968).

42. Densley H. Palmer, "Young Adult Training and Re-training Centers, in *Architectural Workshop: Conference Report of the Architectural Institute,* Portland, Oregon; October 16-17, 1967; pp. 32-38 (*Mental Retardation Abstracts,* vol. 6, no. 4 October-December, 1969).

43. V. Gorman and B.C. Ellis, "To Dispel Confusion," letter, *Nursing Mirror* 130(26): 37-38 (1970).

44. "Outlook for the Mentally Retarded," *Nursing Mirror* 130(25): 13 (1970), in *Mental Retardation Abstracts,* vol. 9, no. 1, January-March, 1972.

45. A. Stroller, "Creating the Life Style for the Intellectually Handicapped," from Australian Council for Rehabilitaiton of Disabled, *Handicapped Youth: Preparation for Life and Work* (National Rehabilitation Conference held at University of New South Wales, Sydney, Australia, May 26-30, 1969), pp. 108-114.

46. Edward M. Kennedy, "Does Anybody Care?" *Mental Retardation/MR* (Washington, D.C.: (American Association on Mental Deficiency) 7(2): 53-55 (1969), in *Mental Retardation Abstracts,* vol. 8, no. 2 April-June 1971.
47. Blatt Burton and Charles Mangel, "The Tragedy and Hope of Retarded Children," *Look Magazine,* October 31, 1967, pp. 97-104.
48. Sid Ross and William Kilpatrick, "Shame of the Nation: Snakepits for Mentally Ill Children," *Parade Magazine,* October 17, 1965, pp. 6-11.

Institutional Planning and Curriculum

R.S. Greene
*Department of Special Education
Madera Unified School District
Thomas Jefferson High School
Madera, California 93204*

Current Institutional Concepts

There is a need for new and improved residential facailities for the mentally retarded which should be constructed based on recommendations of the faculty and staff. Those working directly with mentally retarded patients have the best knowledge of their environmental needs and problem areas. Small, organized, structured group situations would provide adequate care and attention. The nurses would be able to assume the role of the mother-substitute. The mentally retarded should be given opportunities for emotional growth and development so that they may mature in a secure, stable, and adequate environment.[1]

Programs for the mentally retarded require several different types of facilities (residential) rather than the traditional multipurpose institution. The mentally retarded who do require hospital care need to reside in a simple setting which is designed and equipped to further their social and vocational rehabilitation. The main emphasis should be on creating and environment for individuals; each individual should have a room area and a pattern which promotes group living. This environment should be stimulating and adapted carefully to the needs of each group.[2]

Another important asset to the residential facilities for the mentally retarded is a carefully written policies-and-procedures m anual which will act as a guide to decision-making and the efficient management that benefits the entire hospital staff.

The residential care policy should be made by the governing body of the institution in conjunction with the recommendations of an advisory board. The advisory board will provide directions for action which will be modified by the administration staff to cover the retardates' daily needs. Procedures for carrying out the policies should be determined by the staff. The institutional policy manual should contain a brief history of the institution, its goals, and its objectives.[3]

Some of the roadblocks to enlighten residential care for the mentally retarded are to be found rooted in the mass cultural attitudes reflected in the traditional institutional care of the retarded. A major roadblock is medical institutions which are fashioned after the traditional psychiatric direction pattern, with its main focus being on pathology in diagnosis and consequently inattention to educational programming.[4]

The mentally retarded are human beings who need the same recognition, warmth, and sophisticated and professional care that all disabled individuals require. Administrators of residential institutions must structure the residential environment to provide basic care (shelter, nutritious foods, professional health services, and adequate clothing) determined not by scheduled money allotments, but by genuine need. Psychodynamics must be applied to the whole range of multiranged problems of the retarded.[5]

Traditional state institutions are moving away from their school or colony function and toward a hospital function which could and would provide intensive, specialized treatment and major training programs for therapeutic teams. The modern residential institution should assist the mentally retarded resident to attain maximum social, emotional, and intellectual maturation in order to enable the retardates to return to their own homes at the earliest possible time.[6]

Since hospitals for the mentally retarded can and should provide for educational training, shelter, special nursing care, control and/or preparation for future community care services, their nursing goals should direct themselves toward the following: helping mentally retarded persons live happy lives within the confines of a hospital setting; encouraging the full growth of independent thinking and problem-solving abilities; aiding in the development of good habits and attitudes, individual abilities, interests and aptitudes, favorable personality traits, work interests and proficiency, a code of ethics, a willingness to help others, powers of self-control, respect for the property of other persons, and the ability to accept responsibility. The actual hospital program should be realistically based on the belief that each mentally retarded person, regardless of the severity of his case, will yield to reconditioning.[7]

The nursing department of any institution for the mentally retarded should be responsible for the following:[8]

1. the development of a general nursing program which is coordinated with the total interdisciplinary care program of the institution
2. nursing services including the development of a nursing care plan for each resident which is to be based on an evaluation of the resident's needs
3. educational programs and research including a continuing education program for nursing staff training for care contact personnel and research for administration, supervisory and nursing care practices.

All services to the mentally retarded must be a part of a comprehensive child care program. The center and the operational emphasis must be at the community level; interagency programming must be coordinated. In developing a comprehensive community program, certain changes will have to occur: the elimination of program categorization of all government levels, reduction of funds at the university level, the limitation of funds to institutions which are a poor substitute for community services, large-scale programs for training subprofessionals, utilization of volunteers, involvement of families as a part of the treatment team, and the establishment of adequate interpersonal relationships.[9]

In order for a residential or institutional program to reach its full potential, it will be necessary for th institution to change from a mechanistic to a humanistic structure. A mechanistic organization is totally dependent upon input (employees, administrators); it is extremely difficult for a mechanistic organization to respond to change outside its environment. A humanistic organization is one that is fully integrated internally and externally and can adapt to political and social change.[10]

Despite the continuous progress within the institution and the success of new methods and programs in reducing the burden of the mentally retarded, the community still prefers the isolation of the retarded, the community still prefers the isolation of the retarded resident, rather than allowing him to use what he has learned in the community setting.

Boundaries between the institutions and the community still remain firm. The potential of a closed institution is that it can operate relatively free from community intervention. The closed institution can develop its own hierarchy of values to help the mentally retarded resident. The program of the institutions can be designed specifically for the mentally retarded resident, rather than for a society which is presently removed from the problem.[11]

The solution to the problem of where and how to care for the mentally retarded lies in differentiating between those mentally retarded residents who can achieve integration in the community and those who are so severely retarded that they will need long-term residential care.[12]

It is a fact that mentally retarded institutions represent a closed system incapable of self-renewal from within and unable to respond to the needs of society. A new direction is now needed – direct funding of families of retarded children so that the families may choose residential centers themselves.[13]

Institutional paternalism and isolation are two very real problems in hospitals and institutions for the mentally retarded. These institutions have been beset by inadequate facilities and staff which now make these problems impossible to solve. The trend of institutions for the mentally retarded is toward vegetation in both residents and staff. This trend, it would seem, can only be reserved by a major effort.[14]

To help a child fulfill personal needs and overcome a resistance to learning, and to preserve an organizational structure conducive to learning, the institutions must provide a therapeutic environment which integrates educational and treatment services. The educational and treatment services should move physically and philosophically closer to the local community.[15]

The goal of the reeducation of mentally retarded young people in the institutions is to have a social youth who recognizes norms acceptable to society. There now exists a need for the development of homes for the mentally retarded, coupled with special schooling and more internal industrial training possibilities. There is an existing need for homes with security and protection for the very difficult child lacking inner self-control.[16]

The creation of hostels or other residential facilities outside the institutions and the more effective preparation of the institutionalized resident prior to discharge are now needed if the transition from institutionalization to hospitalization is to be effective.[17]

Hostels should be designed to permit maximum individualization and self-dependence; they should be an essential link between the home and family. The problems of transfer from a hospital for the mentally retarded to a hostel is most acute, especially with adults, since hostels are usually designed for the older mentally retarded, and usually have a static population with only an occasional opening. There is a need for more hostels so those mentally retarded who qualify can receive maximum benefits.[18]

The profoundly mentally retarded now need a more structured rigidity in their programs, and they require an institutionally oriented program.[19]

Mentally retarded individuals should be considered for institutionalization only as a last resort — when the reasons are meaningful and significant. Problems in medical treatment, nursing care, behavior management or training must be severe enough to warrant residential placement.[20]

Most hospitals for the mentally retarded are in need of great changes. The most effective program requires that different types of mentally retarded persons be placed in different kinds of situations. The low-intelligence person should be accommodated in a home or hostel or special loding, while attending special schools or workshops. When the mentally retarded person has severe personality problems, this condition warrants treatment in a psychiatric hospital. When he has a severe disability, long-term institutional care should be considered.[21]

Trends and Concepts in Residential Care

The first consideration in the planning of an institution or residential facility is that people — human beings — are going to reside within the facility; the fact that the people are mentally retarded is a secondary consideration. The planning of this facility is held together by one thread, since the design and services are programmed for that particular facility.

The residential facility or institution for the mentally retarded has been the principal source of service to the mentally retarded. The modern concept taking place in the study of mental retardation is that the institution is but one of many sources of services to the retarded and that the institution at best suits the needs of only a very small percentage of the retarded. Many states within the United States are tending toward community and residential services for the retarded. The quality and the quantity of these community residential services are falling short of those offered by larger residential centers.

This does not mean that the community residential services should not be considered in the planning of a residential facility. To be a complete facility and to serve adequately all needs of the retarded, the community and residential facility should complement each other, and the services provided by each should be clearly defined so that there is no duplication or complication.

In the past, residential facilities have been supported by governments. Legislators have tended to favor opportunities (appropriations) for buildings, rather than for programs or personnel. The program itself in the planning stages becomes the ultimate goal; personnel and building must be considered early in the planning efforts.

Today, the traditional institutions will probably be reduced in population, and overcrowding will disappear as a result. Space standards will be raised together with new organizational patterns which will create smaller home-like units within large institutional facilities. Possibly, the principle of complete normalization and the principle of the small grouping will start to appear within the United States. An adaptation of the principle of normalization combining the necessary variations that will take place from one setting to another will make institutions human again.

It is the author's hope that this state of transition which institutions are now experiencing does not last for any length of time so as to damage the retarded or the retarded's future.

Some Basic Considerations in Planning

The effectiveness of the planning for services and facilities for the retarded individual is the ultimate test. In view of this, it will be necessary to examine the following recommendations before considering the philosophy and goals of the residential facility:

1. *Establishment of a realistic program to carry out the recommendations.* The program needs to be well conceived and thought out. A multidimensional approach that is realistic and practical, showing a deep and keen awareness of the community surrounding the facilities, is needed.

2. *Gaining and maintaining full support of community and professional leaders.* The facility needs support from the community professional leaders that is not only financial but moral as well. Professional leaders need to be on the board of advisors to act in an advisory capacity concerning the latest employment and vocational opportunities which exist in the community at the present time and which are anticipated for the future.

3. *Securing and maintaining financial support.* Full and adequate support for the institution over prolonged periods of time is necessary if the institution is to accomplish the results anticipated in the planning.

4. *Developing a professional staff necessary to provide quality services.*

Philosophy and Goals of Residential Facility

1. There should be residential care with emphasis upon diagnosis and therapy, and on an innovative educational curriculum with ample flexibility and adaptability.

2. There should be rehabilitation (both inpatient and outpatient) for the individual and his family. This should include vocational education and the social rehabilitation necessary to give the mentally retarded individual an independent life.

3. The research program should focus on an educational curriculum closely interrelated with that of the state department of education and with the public school program, together with the existing and anticipated positions in the community, surrounding communities, and state.

4. Emphasis should be placed upon the integration of services for the mentally retarded that will blend with those of the community and meet the community's needs in the future.

Facility or Residential Institutional Provisions

1. social and moral training

2. prevocational and vocational training and counseling; complete follow-up services

3. educational, vocational, prevocational and postvocational programs to give the mentally retarded child as many skills as possible within the limits of his ability so as to enable him to function as a fully independent individual

4. counseling and guidance, not only for residents but for families and all community agencies
5. programs tailored to the needs of each individual adult or child
6. day-care centers for service and training.

Consideration needs to be given to the following factors: (a) A homelike environment that blends in with that of the community, and which takes a realistic approach to community living. (b) The necessity of screening all potential admissions to the residential facility. Consideration should be given to the types of programs which might adequately suit the retarded child's situation. A tentative program needs to be set up that will take the individual through the first six months, with ample room for change. An education expert, a medical doctor, a psychologist, a counselor, and social worker need to be made available at this time.

Cooperative Educational-Vocational Placement

Prevocational needs should be considered at the time of admission. Public school admission with part-time residential placement needs to be thoroughly investigated as an alternative to full-time placement. Under this program, the residential retardate attends a public school while staying in the institution. It would resemble a program for adults who may work on the outside, but live within the institution.

The Institutional Program

Important considerations must be dealt with at the onset of planning an institutional program. Once the goals and statements are spelled out in writing, then the time has come to outline a complete program for the retardates who will reside within the institution.

These retarded persons would reside full time within the institution. The question of discharging a retarded person from an institution is a complex one which has many facets to it. While in an institution, the retarded person should be made to feel that he is contributing something of value to the world. The retarded individual who is institutionalized should not be denied stimulation from the outside. One of the many factors affecting the eventual discharge of the retardate is his ability to cope with conditions in the outside world.

The Open Space Concept

The "open space concept" involves the use of the complete facility by the retarded, whether it is an institution, a public school, a private school, etc. The concept involves complete exposure to the community, community life, and all of its resources. It implies full participation in community life while living in the institution, and greater freedom would be allowed. The amount of freedom is dependent upon the retardates' ability to cope adequately with the environment and incoming stimulation. This concept, as applied to special education for the mentally retarded, is the author's innovation.

Georgia Retardation Center

Let us start with a dimension of a program plan for the Georgia Retardation Center in Atlanta.

IQ Levels

Ambulatory Retardates

IQ 0-35: *Profoundly and severely retarded.* The profound and severely retarded require long-term residential care and constant attention as well as self-help skills.

IQ 35-50: *Moderately retarded.* The moderately retarded have some potential for return to the community, but on a limited and supervised basis. They are capable of simple vocational skills and self-help.

IQ 50-70: *Mildly retarded without referral for particular antisocial behavior.* The mildly retarded have good potential for rehabilitation. In the author's viewpoint, this type of retardate should not be placed in an institution. If necessary, however, this should be done only on a part-time basis in order to relieve a potential critical family situation. Perhaps, a day residential center within the residential facility itself needs to be considered for the retarded child in this category. Institutionalization in this case is definitely ill advised. Complete exposure to community life is the correct procedure.

A proposal has been made for a residential community vocational cooperative whereby the retarded individual may live at the residential facility, but still have the freedom of going out into the community for a

271

position under supervision of the facility, until such time as he is either able to return to his home or establish a residence of his own. It is the institution's responsibility to decide at what point the retardate is fully capable of establishing his own residence and maintaining it.

IQ 50-90: *Mildly retarded or with behavior disorder.* This retarded individual is usually placed outside the community because of overt antisocial behavior. He or she possibly will need additional vocational training and special education. He is an excellent candidate for vocation rehabilitation, but needs help in adjustment. A sheltered workshop situation might be an effective way of realizing this goal and of relieving his antisocial behavior. The residential vocational community cooperative principle might be further applied in this case and others like it.

IQ 40-70: *Moderately to mildly retarded.* This type of retardate is primarily within the residential facility for nursing home care. Physical rehabilitation may be a vital program component. The individual can be taught self-help skills as well as care for less able residents. A further but limited application of the sheltered workshop should be applied. He is a possible candidate for limited community exposure.

Nonambulatory Retardates

IQ 0-35: *Profoundly and severely mentally and physically handicapped.* This type of child is dependent upon nursing care. Some eelf-help skills can be taught. Emphasis is on communication. In the author's opinion, if these children are handicapped physically, but can transport themselves either with braces, wheelchairs, or any other means of transportation other than a stretcher, then they are good candidates for a sheltered workshop situation or even some limited exposure to the community. Don't isolate these children from the community if at all possible.

IQ 35-50: *Moderately retarded.* Nursing care should be provided with emphasis on as much self-help as the resident's potential will permit. Active participation in recreation and leisure programs should be encouraged. The same recommendations as were previously stated for the profoundly retarded should be included with the possible addition of some simple routine tasks assigned by the staff to aid in the upkeep of the institution for a higher self-esteem and individual dignity.

IQ 50-70: *Minimally retarded, but severely physically handicapped.* With this type of mental retardation, nursing care is needed in addition to academic educational programs, programs of self-help and occupational and physical therapy. The residential-community vocational cooperation program could be put into effect here in this situation and be projected to bring excellent returns. If necessary, a community workshop with sheltered needs like the halfway houses could be activated just before the retarded person is put out into the community environment where he must make all the necessary adjustments to community living.

Other Facilities Found at the Institution

The same services should be made available to other retardates besides those residents of the institution. These services need to be incorporated into the whole concept of residential care for the retarded. Training of those who are minimally or mildly retarded to help in these services will greatly enhance the residential total program and enhance the retarded individual's self-esteem.

Day or Night Hospital Care

This care refers to any individual who resides in the surrounding community and comes to the institution for training during the day while living at home. This day or night hospital care is mainly a demonstration for techniques development and manpower development.

Retarded in Community Services

There is a source of vocational training and manpower in service to the community never before tapped – "Retarded in Community Services." This is an excellent opportunity to use vocational training and techniques on the retarded individuals whose mental potential will permit it.

Foster Home Supervision

This is part of the institution's program whereby certain individuals who have formerly been under residential care and were sent out into the community need continued supervision for a period of time in a boarding house environment. It is felt by the institution that foster home supervision and placement should not be a direct function in the institution, but of the community and the state.

This supervision should be a definite service of the institution, due to the fact that the institution is best qualified to help in the adjustment process. The mentally retarded child must have a voice in the boarding house environment, and this should be accomplished before actual

273

placement. A conference needs to be held before placement so that all concerned may discuss their ideas and opinions; conferences should take place once every month to increase the effectiveness of the foster home supervisor.

Out-Patient Evaluation

Each resident before admission and referral from another institution should be completely reevaluated, and a program should be designed for the retarded individual's needs. This needs to be done before placement in a foster home (boarding house) situation. A general evaluation of the foster home is in order.

Cottages for Severely Retarded Ambulatory Individuals

In these cottages, there will be approximately 320 mentally retarded people with separate cottages for males and females. A maximum of four units comprise a building. These should remain autonomous except for the sharing of utilities. This is an excellent idea, and if carried to its ultimate conclusion would accomplish miracles. For the mildly retarded, hostel houses need to be established far enough away from the institution, but under the institution's supervision.

Facilities for Biological Research

The retarded individual who exhibits the potential ought to share in the use of the following equipment: animal housing, microscopy, chromatography, chemicals, computer rooms, library, janitorial services, protective devices, photography, and others. This equipment need not only be used for reseearch but also as a teaching device, both vocationally and academically.[22]

District Court Decision on Institutional Standards

A United States district court judge in an appendix to a decision in Alabama ordered that the following standards be adopted at state institutions for the mentally retarded. The judge called it "Minimum Constitutional Standards for Adequate Rehabilitation of the Mentally Retarded."

Some of the judge's decisions are as follows: The residents of the institutions should have a right to medical treatment and education and care which are suited to their needs, regardless of their degree of retardation. They should have a right to rehabilitation programs which will minimize the retardate's disabilities and maximize his abilities to cope with his environment. The institution shall recognize each resident, regardless of ability or status.

The district court ordered that no mentally retarded person shall be admitted if the institution cannot afford to initiate the rehabilitation program and services within the community. The residents of the institution should have the least restrictive conditions necessary to achieve rehabilitation.

For the purposes of standardized definitions of a borderline retarded as any person who is functioning one or two standard deviations below the mean on a standard intelligence test. Mildly retarded was defined as a person who is functioning two or three standard deviations below the mean on any standardized intelligence test.

The author would like to point out that all the state and district boards of education within the entire United States, as well as institutions, should standardize their definitions of the degrees of mental retardation. This in turn will cause the educational and vocational training of the mentally retarded to be more effective and will increase the sharing of innovations in curriculum and vocational training. The result would be a great step forward in the ongoing fight to combat mental retardation.

The court ordered the following minimum standards:

	Mild	Moderate	Severe/ Profound
Class Size	12	9	6
Length of school months	9-10	9-10	11-12
Minimum length of school days (hours)	6	6	6

Individualized Rehabilitation Plans

Before admission to the institution, each resident shall have a comprehensive social, psychological, educational, and medical diagnosis and evaluation by the appropriate specialists to determine if admission is warranted. Within fourteen days of admission, each of the residents shall have an evaluation made by a specialist for programming purposes. Each resident shall have an individualized plan formulated by the institution

275

with a description of the intermediate and long-range rehabilitation goals and a projected timetable for their attainments, including the criteria for discharge and a projected date of discharge.

As a part of the residential rehabilitation, each resident shall have an individual post-institutionalized plan. This is consistent with the author's view that such a plan represents an integral part of institutional life. It is only natural that there should be such a plan since there is a transitional period to adjust from an institutional environment to an independent community environment.

Institutional Records

The institutional records are to include:
1. identification data
2. resident's history
3. inventory of the resident's life skills
4. a copy of post-institutional plans and any modifications
5. a summary of the steps that have been taken to implement those plans
6. an analysis of the rehabilitation successes and failures with recommendations for any necessary modifications
7. a copy of the rehabilitation plans and any modifications
8. a summary of the resident's responses to his rehabilitation program which shall be scientifically documented
9. a monthly summary of the extent and nature of the residents' work activities
10. family visits and contacts
11. attendance and leaves from institution.

Humane Factors

Residents shall have the right to dignity, privacy, and humane care Although the person is in an institution, he is entitled to all the rights and privileges granted to the rest of the population. The opportunity for religious worship shall be made on a nondiscriminatory basis. Residents shall have the right to use the telephone, limited only by restrictions imposed by a qualified rehabilitation professional who will write an order explaining the purpose of the restrictions. Residents shall have the right to receive and send sealed mail.

Medical Program

No medication shall be given without the written consent of a physician. Residents shall not be given unnecessary or excessive medication. Medication in no way shall be used for preventive measures, for the convenience of the staff, as a substitute for a rehabilitation program, or in such quantities as to interfere with the residents' rehabilitation program.

Seclusion, defined as placement in a locked room, shall not be employed. Legitimate time-out procedures can be utilized under close and direct professional supervision as a technique in behavior shaping.

Electric shock devices shall be considered as a research technique for the purpose of attaining rehabilitation standards. Restraints shall not be employed as punishment and will only be applied if alternative techniques have failed and if these restraints impose the least possible restrictions consistent with their purposes. Corporal punishment shall not be employed.

Residents shall have the right not to be subject to experimental research or to any unusual treatment without their consent or the consent of next of kin after consultation with an independent specialist and legal counsel.

Institutional Maintenance

No resident of the institution shall be required to perform labor which involves operation and maintenance or work which the institution has contracted for. No resident shall be involved in the care, feeding, clothing, bathing, training, or supervision of other residents unless he has volunteered; has been specifically trained in the necessary skills; has the humane judgment required for this activity; is adequately supervised and is reimbursed in accordance with the minimum wage of the Fair Labor Standards Act.

Residents m a y be required to perform vocational training tasks provided the tasks are an integrated part of the residents' rehabilitation program, and are supervised by a staff member to oversee the rehabilitation aspect of the activity.

District Court Conclusions

The U.S. district court judge ordered that each resident be informed of the standards, assuming he is able to understand them. The superintendent of the institution shall be required to report in writing every six months to the next of kin the residents' progress in educational and vocational living skills and their medical conditions. The author believes that this is the procedure which every institution throughout the United States would be required to follow to protect all individuals concerned and the rights of the residential retardate.

The report will state any appropriate rehabilitation program which the retardatewas not able to participate in because of inadequate rehabilitation resources. Finally, each resident, when discharged to the community, shall have a program of transitional rehabilitation assistance.[23]

RESPITE CARE SERVICE — A NEW CONCEPT

Respite care is an appropriate service to families of the mentally retarded. In a variety of settings, for brief periods, it provides temporary care in or outside the home for the retardate.

Services Performed in the Home

Homemaker service. To bring qualified training persons into the home to supplement parental care and maintain family unity.

Nursing service. Trains members of families in retarded self-help training.

Services Performed outside the Home

Temporary-Care homes. Provides short-term emergency care for the retarded child or adult family emergencies or vacations.

Halfway houses. Provides a bridge between the state facilities and the community during the transition phase for residential retardates. From the author's point of view, this respite care service needs to be established within the institutions so that they fulfill their ultimate goal — total independence for the retardate.

Respite Home-Care Examples

Two respite home-care facilities, as primary models of this new concept in care for the retarded, are discussed on the next page.[24]

Wisconsin State Colony School. Short-term residential care has gradually become an integral part of care for the retarded at the Wisconsin State Colony School, located in   The short-term care can be instituted for the following reasons: (1) to provide care and treatment for those cases where admission may delay or eliminate the need for long-term residence requirements; (2) to provide through a development evaluation center, a diagnostic and evaluation service which the local community is unable to provide, but which is essential to the person's continued care and treatment in his home and community.

Clover Bottom Hospital and School, located in Tennessee, is a state facility initiated as a respite program, and the effect has been a dramatic reduction in the priority list wanting institutionalization. Some basic reasons for admission are the following: (1) behavioral modification and training for retardates; (2) interim placement before transfer to a foster home; (3) determination of effects of separation between family and the retarded.

A Concern for Community Problems

Communities all over the United States are facing the problem of fitting the mentally retarded person, adult or child, into the community life and the community environment. Parents and families of the retarded are constant being plagued by this problem. A possible solution is now at hand.

In Quincy, Massachusetts, for example, there is the South Shore Mental Health Center, which serves nine cities and towns with a total population of 250,000 persons. This community program uses the services of schools, courts, and church social agencies. Diagnostic services were requested from the mental health clinic which operates a program for the South Shore Associations for Retarded Children and for several years was attempting to develop a program for retarded preschoolers.

In the author's opinion, no one community, be it large or small, needs to try to organize a program for any one age level, if the state institution and the public schools are doing a complete and adequate job in fulfilling their requirements for the mentally retarded child. Full cooperation on all levels is guaranteed.

Although the first nursery school that was established by the mental health clinic was beneficial to the center, the parents, and the community in general, certain inherent difficulties eventually did arise, causing some community resistance.

The development of the preschool nursery program left one crucial concern which involved the smooth transition from nursery school to public school special class. A considerable amount of energy was invested in encouraging the development of public schools' special classes.

Consultants and specialists remain available in the health center during the entire educational experiences of the retarded to discuss issues or problems. Clinical services are integrated into the community workshop in South Shore through five team units developed within the clinics based on geographical areas. These teams handle all types of cases and offer exactly the same services as does the South Shore Center itself. A rather complete check is made and information gathered from all sources. When the child is old enough for nursery school or public school special education, it should be determined whether he should still be retained at the South Shore Center to learn additional skills such as toilet training. A number of sessions are held with the parents which may arrange from consideration of institutionalization to a request that the child be kept home for additional years in order to work on these basic social skills.

Occupational Training Center

A combination sheltered workshop, day care, and occupational training program was developed, and accepted children over six-teen years old. An occupational therapist was hired to serve as its director. During the early years, few if any youngsters were successful in obtaining employment outside the center. Later, it was agreed that the training center would focus on high-level retardates who could be trained successfully within a two-year period. It was further agreed that for those not eligible for occupational training, the center would develop a sheltered workshop.

Community Cooperative

Although this is excellent as far as it has gone, the need now is for a community cooperative, which is the author's term for those persons eligible for on-the-job training which should be provided for those skills who need permanent care.

In those cases where the training center sees in its follow-up that the retardate is unsuccessful on the job, then he is taken back to reassess his occupational situation and perhaps to move toward a slightly different job structure.

The next step is the development of a program to be collaborated on with the state school, which involves the reciprocal use of both staffs, utilizing the institution program and a consultation program. Long-range planning calls for all retardates who are being considered for institutionalization at the state school to go through the mental health services, whcih will act as a primary screening agent.[25]

Planning the Community Clinic

The question is just how much thought should be given to the planning of a community clinic for the retarded. The following opics should be considered:
1. types of clinical program
2. considering each retardate as an individual
3. traditional pediatrics, outpatients
4. traditional child guidance
5. single discipline guidance center's facilities directed by pediatricians, psychiatrists, psychologists, social workers, nurses, and educators
6. clinical types within the categories of infants, adolescents, and adults.

A program designed for newborn infants would have to include: (1) prevention of further organic damage; (2) health supervision for infants; (3) interpreting the child's conditions to the family; and (4) planning with the family for the child's care and assisting the family to get the necessary help.

With the teenage young adult and the adult come behavior and emotional disorders and difficulties. The cooperation of the state institution, the public schools, and the community are vital in planning a community clinic for the retarded. The sequences in establishing the various units of community ultimately be guided by community leadership decisions on what degrees of retardation and what age groups require attention first.

Some thought should probably be given to an extension of the community clinic into the community cooperative discussed earlier.[26]

Institutional Overcrowding

Another problem plaguing so many parents of the mentally retarded is that of overcrowding in institutions, residential facilities, community clinics, mental health programs, public schools, and special education classrooms. Many of these institutions have long waiting lists, and many children who need training are not receiving it since they are being forced to remain at home.

Home Training

The New Jersey Department of Institutions, being aware of this problem, decided to set up an experimental program called "Home Training" which would bring some of the program's services and techniques of the institutions to children in their own homes. In the author's opinion, there should be a spirit of cooperation between the institution or residential facility and the home, to integrate and make the programs and techniques work more effectively.

This type of program is to be supervised by the state department of education under the department of mental hygiene, as was done in the case of both New Jersey and Massachusetts. Although the home-training program is established primarily to help parents train their mentally retarded children so that they can remain at home, the teacher, who is the main source of techniques and programs, must be aware that some of the children's needs cannot be met outside an institution.

The Ideal Home Training Program

The ideal home training program would include the following four steps:
1. There will be home services for the mothers of the very young or of children who are not eligible to attend the centers or special school classes.
2. There will be a complete program for the purpose of maintaining community play centers.
3. The program will maintain special classes under the jurisdiction of a public agency.
4. The program will maintain a residential school.

In the author's opinion, the ideal home training program needs to make available consultants in all areas of concern to the retarded child. These educators, physicians, psychologists, and social workers should also be available to the parents for discussion or consultation on any problem that may arise. The parents need to feel free to select and consult with any of these specialists at any time.[27]

In Washington, D.C. a diagnostic and evaluation center under the Department of Public Health provides for a clinic. Included in its services on a selective basis are social caseworkers, short-term psychotherapy, home training, and referral to other community agencies. Services to aid in the home training program are worked out by child-development specialists who help the parents with their practical problems of daily living with a mentally retarded child.

Child Community Adjustment Cooperative

The community itself could profit from the utilization of the child-development specialists in the integration of these children into community life, so in the long run the adjustment to the communityw ould not be so difficult. This policy could be included in the home-training program and be called the "Child Community Adjustment Cooperatives." The children would be explained the ways of the community and the community would be explained the nature of retardation and the retarded child. The home-training programs handle a variety of cases and the advice is different in each case.

A Severely Retarded Boy
The mother of a two-year-old boy came to the clinic in an effort to avoid having to institutionalize her son. He seemed to have neurological seizures three to twelve times a day which made him lose contact with his environment.

In keeping with the diagnosis, the home-training program advised:
1. ways of handling the child
2. methods of feeding techniques, such as self-feeding at the beginning of each meal
3. a more convenient kind of seating arrangement
4. the use of food textures.

A Mongoloid Child
This boy had a relatively high social quotient which was adequate testimony to the mother's achievements in his training. The assistance of the home-training program was as follows:
1. providing support for the mother in her home-training efforts.

283

2. helping the mother to see the child's potential for further learning in specific terms

3. examining the child's eating habits, with the possibility of teaching the child to use his hands.

Institutional Home-Training Concept

This concept is based upon the cooperation that exists between the home and residential centers for the retarded. When the residential facility has had a retarded child for a while and when adequate progress has been made in the training of the child, the residential facility should then build the home-training program concept a step further by calling in the parents and showing them techniques and methods to improve the child's achievements. By enlarging the home-training concept into the institutional home training program, the way is then being cleared for an earlier discharge and a more independent retarded person.[28]

TOWARD BEING INDEPENDENT

Family Home Training Program

Home is a basic institution. It is primary and vital not only to our sense of security and well being, but as a foundation for our understanding and learning. These same basic learnings should take place within the home of each mentally retarded child, regardless of institutionalization or special day care centers.

The learning basics are as follows:

1. toilet training
2. dressing
3. cleanliness and manners
4. discipline
5. speech
6. play
7. group experience for the young retarded child.

Toilet Training

Toilet training is the very first step toward independence. It is a small but important step to the parents of a retarded child as well as the

parents of a normal child. Toilet training readiness may be indicated by the following:
1. Are there fairly long intervals between wetting?
2. Does he show signs of wanting to go to the toilet?
3. Can he get to the toilet by himself?
4. Does he care about learning?

Dressing

This step to independence will take longer to teach them toilet training. Generally, dressing is less satisfying to the mentally retarded child. Start when the child is very small and talk to him about different items of clothing. Later, the child will start playing with items of clothing; capitalize on this. To the mentally retarded child, learning comes in reverse order; that is, the child may learn to take off his clothing first, before learning to put it on. The following suggestions may help:
1. A mirror can be fun to the child when placed in front of him.
2. Give the child extra time to dress.
3. Don't insist on his dressing himself for every occasion.
4. Have the child pick up his own clothes.
5. Arrange shelves and hooks low enough for the child to reach.
6. Select clothes which are easy to put on and attractive.

Cleanliness and Manners

No one is completely qualified to tell when a child, especially a mentally retarded child, is ready to learn. This is a step toward independence. Simple assignments, such as washing hands, brushing teeth, and combing hair, do help. Start with one demand at a time, and make sure the child is ready and really cares. If he drools, teach him to keep his mouth closed, such as when he chews food. Remind him of this, and compliment him when he succeeds.

Discipline

Home is the place where everyone should feel he is an important part of the family. To discipline the mentally retarded child, let the child know exactly what is expected of him as a member of the family.

Disciplining the mentally retarded child means telling the child what he has done wrong and explaining to him what he should have done that would have been correct. If there are siblings, the punishment should be exactly the same for all. Punishment should be fair and consistent.

The goal of discipline is to teach the mentally retarded child to manage his own life. The child should have a say in everything which affects him directly. One should look for causes of misbehavior rather than constantly blaming the child for situations that may have caused his misbehavior.

Speech
Learning to talk is a milestone for any child, especially for the mentally retarded child. Some mentally retarded children will progress faster than others due to differences in the degree of retardation. Talk frequently to the child. Call objects by their correct names.

Play
Everyone expects children to play. A child who learns from play often shows great individuality in the play patterns he follows. At first, play is rough, especially with others. Since the mentally retarded child is inclined to play rough even at the junior and senior high school level, his play should be carefully supervised. However, punishment should be applied judiciously. If the child is punished too frequently he will be frustrated by feelings of anger and guilt, and will gradually withdraw from all group activity.

No one can tell anyone else exactly how to handle each situation that arises, since the situations vary when the child plays alone, when two brothers play, when a brother and sister play, or when a child plays with members of his peer group. A certain amount of friction and squabbling is to be expected and should be understood and handled with discretion.

Group Experiences
The following questions should be considered by parents whose children are engaged in group play and activities for the retarded:
1. Do you like the atmosphere; the feeling of the place?
2. Would you go there yourself?
3. How many children is each teacher responsible for? Does the teacher attend to her responsibility or ignore it?
4. Is the group small enough to insure calmness and order?
5. Is there enough space for each child to move freely?
6. Is the program well planned for the children?
7. Does the teacher permit a wide range of activities?

8. Does the teacher stop play when it is too rough or dangerous, or too unfriendly?

Some Suggested Toys and Equipment for Home or Group Play

Home Play

balls
keys on a chain
one or two soft cuddly animals
large balls
balloons
metal cars
bath toys (anything that floats).

For Outdoor Fun

sand and sandbox, accessories
things to climb on, such as a pile of logs, a rope ladder, or knotted rope
bog boxes to push or load
wheeled toys
wagons
barrels
sturdy gardening tools
tire to roll.

As the Child Grows

blocks
cars, trucks, trains
puzzles
housekeeping equipment
rubber horseshoes
musical instruments.

For Older Children

soap bubbles
paper, paint, an easel
clay
carpentry equipment
dough.

Residential-Home Training Family Cooperative: An Innovative Concept

The problems found in residential home care training and family training are in many ways alike. There needs to be a residential center where the parents of a retarded child can live with the child, observe the child's training, and learn the techniques employed. By being there, the parents will have avoided the inconvenience of the home training concept, thus shortening the child's guardianship by the residential center. The learning basics mentioned previously could be applied within the institutions.

There are problems in separating the retarded child from his parents, but these problems do not exist as frequently under the new concept of residential care centers. This new concept gives the child more security by providing a home atmosphere and doing away with the institutional environment. The transition period with adjustments is sharply reduced along with its many faceted problems.

Demonstration Classes within the Institution: A New Concept

These classes would be held within the institution and taught by the professional staff. The classes would give actual training techniques to the parents of the retarded child. The parents would observe the daily routine of the child for about one hour per day while he is in the classroom. The weekends would be left open for the parents and the child to work together. The institutional staff would be available in the event of problems.[29]

Through the social casework counselor, the parents can be helped to develop:

1. understanding of the degree of their child's handicap and what this will mean to his future
2. ability to understand their child's needs, assets, and difficulties
3. appreciation of the effect of the retarded child on family life
4. useful techniques such as enlightened understanding in order to help the handicapped child, the entire family, and the community
5. knowledge of resources relating to the retardation problem which are available to them.

The feeling of mutual support and understanding is enhanced under the institutional atmosphere which then makes it possible for the meetings (class demonstrations) to be: (1) treatment oriented, instead of solely supportive and informative; (2) helpful to parents considering their child's strengths and accomplishments as well as his limitations.

The leader or staff instructor can in turn provide: (1) intervention when discussion gets blocked or on an emotional level that only feeds self-pity; (2) help as parents become better informed of community resources which have programs for the retarded.

Although each meeting does not result in all goals being advanced, some are always achieved. The real treatment begins at the demonstration class meeting. This will give the staff some opportunity to learn and understand how husband and wife react to one another, to other parents within the group, to the social worker and others concerned for the child's welfare. It will let the staff see the parents' reaction to the retarded child and the community resources available.

Some institutions may recommend that parents attend certain staff meetings to join in the discussion concerning their child. As the parent talks and listens, he gains new ways of looking at his problems, feels less isolated, and gains emotional support.[31]

REFERENCES

1. V.A. Pounds, "Our Mental Subnormality Hospitals," *Nursing Mirror* (216 (8), pp. 34-35, 1968) from *Mental Retardation Abstracts,* vol. 6, no. 4, October-December 1969.
2. Gunnar Dybwad, "Changing Patterns of Residential Care for the Mentally Retarded: A Challenge to Architecture." From B.W. Richard, ed., Proceeding of the First Congress of the International Association for the Scientific Study of Mental Deficiency, held in Montpellier, France, Sept 12-20, 1967 (Surrey, England: Michael Jackson, Publisher, 1968), pp. 575-580 (*Mental Retardation Abstracts,* vol. 7 no. 2, April-June 1970).
3. American Hospital Association, *Developing Policies and Procedures for Long-Term Care Institutions,* Chicago, Ill., 1968. (*Mental Retardation Abstracts,* vol. 7, no. 4, October-December 1970).
4. Gunnar Dybwad, "Roadblocks to Renewal Care." From Frank J. Menolascino, ed., *Psychiatric Approaches to Mental Retardation,* (New York: Basic Books, 1970), pp. 552-574.
5. Howard W. Potter, "Human Values as Guides to the Administration of Residential Facilities for the Mentally Retarded." From Frank J. Menolascino, ed., *Psychiatric Approaches to Mental Retardation,* (New York: Basic Books, 1970), pp. 575-584. *Mental Retardation Abstracts,* vol. 9, no. 1, January-March 1972.

6. Donald M. Bramwell, "Changing Concepts of Residential Care." From Irving Philips, ed., *Prevention and Treatment of Mental Retardation* (New York: Basic Books, 1966), pp. 334-345.
7. Charles H. Hallas, *The Care and Training of the Mentally Subnormal*, 3rd ed. (Bristol, England: John Wright & Sons, 1967).
8. American Association on Mental Deficiency, "Guidelines for Nursing Standards in Residential Centers for the Mentally Retarded." Ad Hoc Committee Report, Subcommittee on Nursing, 1968 (*Mental Retardation Abstracts*, vol. 5, no. 4, October-December 1968.
9. John R. Marks, "The Future of the Institutions," *PCMR Message — Newsletter of the President's Committee on Mental Retardation*, February 1969, pp. 10-12.
10. Harry Stevens, "Multidimensional Problems of Administration in a Residential Setting." From W.J. Younie and I.I. Goldberg, eds., *Special Education Administration in the Residential Setting Proceedings*, (New York: Columbia University Teachers College, 1970), pp. 34-41.
11. Robert Dentler, "The Role of a Residential Facility in Modern Society. From W.J. Younie and I.I. Goldberg, eds., *Special Education Administration in the Residential Setting Proceedings* (New York: Columbia University Teachers College, 1970), pp. 1-10.
12. A. Shapiro, "Care of the Mentally Subnormal," *Lancet* (England) 2(7627) 957-958, 1969 (letter), (*Mental Retardation Abstracts*, vol. 8, no. 2, April-June 1971).
13. Donald J. Stedman, "A Recipe for Improving Residential Care: Add a Dash of Capitalism," *Mind over Matter* 14 (2) pp. 14-16, 1969.
14. H.C. Ginzburg, *Journal of Mental Subnormality*, Ch. 15, pt. 1 (28) 1-2, 1969 (editorial).
15. Ignacy I. Goldberg and William J. Younie "Education as a Function of the Residential Setting, *Mental Retardation MR* 71(1), pp. 12-14, 1969.
16. E. Miller, "The Re-education of Young People in Institutions and Its Future Development," *International Child Welfare Review* (May 1969), pp. 3-14 (*Mental Retardation Abstracts*, vol. 7, no. 3, July-September 1970).
17. J. Blake and D.A. Spencer "Care of the Mentally Subnormal," *Lancet* (England) 2(7630) pp. 1132-1133, 1969 (letter).
18. M.E. York-Moore, Paper no. 3, From Elizabeth Stephen, *Residential Care for the Mentally Retarded* (Oxford, England: Pergamon Press, 1970), pp. 25-34.
19. Elizabeth Stephen, ed., *Residential Care for the Mentally Retarded* (Oxford, England: Pergamon Press, 1970).
20. Peter Townsend, "Meeting the Needs of the Older Mongoloid Individual through Residential Care" (Madison, Wis.: *Wisconsin Association for Retarded Children: Mongoloid Conference Proceeding*, conference of the mongoloid individual, his family and his community, held April 10-11, 1968, in Milwaukee, Wis., 1969) pp. 35-38.

21. J.A. Whitehead, "Are Subnormality Hospitals an Anachronism," *Lancet* 1(7623), p. 740, 1969 (letter) (*Mental Retardation Abstracts,* vol. 8 no. 1, January-March 1971).

22. James A. Clements, M.D., *Planning a Residential Facility for the Mentally Retarded* (Georgia Retardation Center, 4770 Peachtree Road, Atlannta, Ga.).

23. Civil Action No. 3195-N, Jane P. Gordon, Clerk (in the United States District Court for the Middle District of Alabama, Northern Division, April 13, 1972, pp. 1-31.

24. Marianna Paige, *Respite Care for the Retarded — An Interval of Relief for Families* (Washington, D.C.: U.S. Government Printing Office), pp. 1-23.

25. Donald Ottenstein, M.D. and Saul Cooper, "A Community Mental Health Program for Mental Retardation — Community and Planning Aspects," *Journal of the American Academy of Child Psychiatry,* vol. 7, no. 3, July 1968, pp. 536-547.

26. Rudolph P. Hormuth, "Community Clinics for the Mentally Retarded Children," *Children,* September-October 1957, vol. 4, no. 5, pp. 49-54.

27. Cianci Vincentz, "Home Training for the Mentally Retarded Child," *Children,* May-June 1955, vol. 2, no. 3, pp. 26-31.

28. Laura L. Dittmann, "Home Training for Retarded Children," *Children,* May-June 1957, vol. 4, no. 3, pp. 43-48.

29. Mrs. Laura L. Dittmann, *The Mentally Retarded Child at Home* (Washington, D.C.: U.S. Department of Health, Education, and Welfare, Office of Child Development, Children's Bureau, 1971), pp. 1-96.

30. Helen L. Beck, "Counseling Parents of Retarded Children," *Children,* November-December 1959, vol. 6, no. 6, pp. 67-72.

31. Alice V. Anderson, "Orientating Parents to a Clinic for the Retarded Children," *Children,* September-October 1962, vol. 9, no. 5, pp. 97-102.

Institutions:
Curriculum Innovations

Richard S. Greene
Department of Special Education
Madera Unified School District
Thomas Jefferson High School
Madera, California 93204

We shall begin now a critical review of the kinds of programs and curriculums offered in a residential or an institutional setting.

Southern Wisconsin Colony and Training School

The child whose curriculum is now under consideration has been variously referred to as an imbecile, as moderately retarded, as a middle grader, or as trainable. According to the Wisconsin Colony and Training School, Union Grove, Wisconsin, this child will require care, supervision, and economic support for the rest of his natural life.

Development in certain areas is possible with this type of child. The areas of development are centered around the following skills and activities:

1. self-help skills
2. social skills
3. motor skills
4. academic skills
   (a) language development
   (b) number development
5. vocational skills
6. expressive activities.

The trainable child can benefit from learning skills in dressing, self-feeding, washing, and toilet training. This child can develop social skills such as learning to share, to get along with others, and to respect the property rights of others. He benefits from planned, well-organized programs that increase his motor skills.

The best expectation for the trainable, according to the Wisconsin Colony and Training School, is that they will never be more than marginally independent. With the trinable child's needs and abilities fixed in our minds, the following are some of the general objectives for the program:

(1) to teach the child to care for his everyday physical wants; to live with others, both children and adults; and (2) to develop the trainable child's capacity to the fullest so that he will be able to more adequately function in his limited environment.

The author wonders if that limited environment is ever stretched to see the outer boundaries or upper limits of the trainable child's capacity. Does anyone really know the full range, both upper and lower, of the trainable person's capacity? It might be very wise and innovative if some institutions for the trinable retarded would consider doing some testing (experimentation with the ranges of the limiting environment before setting goals and objectives).

The admissions criteria were divided into four areas of development and were considered as minimum standards for the trainable.

Physical. Ambulatory-trained to toilet habits; free from excessive drooling; some degree of coordination.

Mental. Mental age of 2.5; makes known wants and needs; I.Q. between 20 and 50.

Social. Able to respond to group situations in play and other activities.

Emotional. Able to react to a learning situation and stimuli.

Some of the criteria for exclusion from the program were the following:

1. unable to attend class
2. unable to adjust to group situations
3. unable to react to learning stimuli.

The following were some of the considerations for determining eligibility:

1. below 50 I.Q.
2. chronological age five to seventeen, with exceptions.

In the area of social competency, the following requirements were listed:

1. sufficient communications ability
2. responsiveness to adult direction
3. demonstrating some understanding and respecting the rights of others; accepting good rules.

From the author's point of view, the above criteria originally appeared as the objectives of the program. However, now these same standards appear in the program as criteria for admission. To the author this is contradictory and makes one wonder what are the ultimate goals and objectives for the trainable. When the trainable child is subject to exclusion, he is then under consideration for one or more of the following areas:

1. The Work Activity Training Center
2. The Work Placement Program (Industrial Therapy)
3. Placement
   (a) temporary discharge to work
   (b) temporary placement to work
   (c) temporary discharge to home placement
   (d) temporary discharge to a community resource — aid to disabled.

Residential Trainable Programs

The trainable programs are divided into three broad levels, with each of the three having its own set of goals and objectives.

Trainable I

Enrollment in this program is usually preceded by preschool attendance with the classes being made up of children whose ages range from five through nine. Their curriculum objective is to develop to some degree the art of self-help; the child may be better suited for the sheltered environment. Some skills to be learned in this curriculum are as follows:

Self-Help Skills	Work Skills
dressing	social skills
bathroom	communication skills
grooming	motor development
manners	gross motor activities
	fine motor activities

Expressive Activities
arts and crafts
music
dramatic plays

Trainable II

The trainable II program is based upon a sequence outlined from the Trainable I program which involved the very rudimentary and elementary concepts of living. Each of the trainable programs mature the trainable individuals and refine their basic life skills, making these individuals become more independent. The Trainable II program places emphasis on developing self-sufficiency, wholesome attitudes, and good peer relationships. The curricula for the Trainable II program includes the following:
social skills
communication skills
expressive activities
motor development
visual discrimination
manual skills (designed to aid the trainable in the use of household
    utensils and simple sewing)

Trainable III

The Trainable III program places heavy emphasis on the development of self-expression, social attitudes, and beginning vocational skills which are included in the curriculum. In the advanced classroom's experience, the trainable program places greater emphasis on work skills such as the use of lawn mowers and gardening tools.

A new area of the curriculum which is called "Quantitative Understanding" is explored in the advanced classroom experience. An example is simple numerical concepts. Under "Expressive Activities," the curricula stresses role-playing by the children of people with whom they are in daily contact. such as the attendant, the doctor, and the milkman. In addition, the activities include dramatization of simple well-known stories and fairy tales, as well as free expressive dramatic activities.

Preparation now has been made for the sheltered workshop concept to be integrated at this point in the curriculum. The trainable should be introduced into this concept, and community concepts should now have begun. If the institution or residential center is going to realize the lower and upper limits of the trainable mentally retarded, then it is the institution's obligation to press the trainable into the unknown, unexplored surroundings at the earliest possible moment, observing and taking careful notes for the future.

Work Orientation (Advanced Classroom and Integrated Experience)

According to the program, trainable individuals demonstrating a potential for some degree of economic usefulness either within the institution or at another residential setting, or demonstrating a potential for independent living, are enrolled in the work orientation program.

The curriculum in the work orientation program gives the opportunity for maximum development of habits, attitudes, and skills which are needed by a totally dependent individual. The trainable individual is introduced to experiences associated with gainful activities. Emphasis is placed on development of very basic work habits. Thus, the adult trainable are equipped to do meaningful tasks. The work orientation program could be described as a secondary program. In the author's opinion, the sheltered workshop cooperative concept, whereby the trainable obtains employment half the day, is a situation similar to the work the trainable would be doing in the sheltered workshop.

Work Orientation Shop

The vocational shop oeprates on broad areas of experiences such as woodworking, general plastics, and general leather.

Woodworking
finishing procedures
operation and safe practices of power equipment
preparation and application of wood, glue, lumber.

General Plastics
the use of hand tools
selection of plastics and related materials
acquaintance with plastics finish and surface
the plastics industry
plastic cement, uses and types
overlaying of plastic.

General Leather
leather, its sources and uses
selection of leather
proper use of hand tools; conditioners, dyes, and leather finishes.

Concurrent Work Experience

The concurrent work experience program is very similar to the sheltered workshop concept, with the main exception being that in the sheltered workshop cooperative the individual is receiving a minimal wage which builds his self-concept and worth.

According to the Wisconsin authorities, the Colony has a number of work areas throughout its operation which are needed to be placed in all institutions as a standard practice. Purposes of the program for the individual assigned to these areas are as follows: to provide new experiences; to provide an orientation to work; and to support classroom endeavors.

Some of the concurrent work experience tasks are of the following nature:

Food Service Job Training
prerinsing dishes
cleaning and scrubbing

Grounds Maintenance Job Training
lawn care

snow removal
Truckers' Helpers Job Training
paper truck
dump truck

Industrial Therapy Work Orientation

This program involves duties to be performed while living in a cottage:
general janitorial
room operation
food services
bakery, butcher, (boning, grinding)
kitchen
loading and unloading of trucks
soda-bar, waiting on tables, preparing, stocking
classroom, aiding teachers.

The residential trainable are exposed to a specialized curriculum in music, art, speech and hearing, and field trips. The field trips include those within the colony, such as to the barber shop, the beauty shop, and the electrical supply store.

Trips to commercial establishments in the city include drugstores, hardware stores, restaurants, drive-ins, and gas stations; trips to public service facilities in the city include the fire department and the police department; trips to medical facilities include doctors' and dentists' offices; trips to transportation and communication facilities include the bus depot, the airport, and the telephone company; trips to the city also include the social security office, banks, the courthouse, and recreational facilities such as the YMCA or YWCA.

Field trips can be taken whenever they relate best to the units being presented.[1]

Gracewood State School and Hospital

At Gracewood State School and Hospital in Gracewood, Georgia, the residents are housed in separate buildings called cottages, which house about sixty residents each. This condition should not be allowed because the principal of normalization could never be applied with such overcrowding. According to Dr. John Hamilton,[2] these overcrowded conditions are acknowledged despite the fact that some improvements have been made. The more severely retarded a resident is, the more time he spends within the cottage since it is thought that the environment there is beneficial to him. Contrary to this theory, the author believes taht the more time the retarded individual spends within an institutional environment, receiving little stimulation from the outside world, the more likely is his tendency to withdraw into himself. Outside stimulation from a variety of sources is of vast importance to any retarded individual.

The experimental site selected for the program was a unit containing five cottages in which more than 300 retarded females resided. Their ages, level of intelligence, and diagnostic distribution were representative of the institutional population. The five cottages were interconnected under one roof, each with a fenced-in outdoor play area. Included within the unit was a central kitchen and a large dining room. The unit was staffed by forty attendants, consultants, supporting staff, psychologists, cottage supervisors, resident training nurse, housekeeper, and maintenance staff.

One of the many basic problems with institutional living is that the residents are provided with minimal opportunities for new learning experiences, since their existing level of performance is said to be their optimal level of performance. Assumptions or understandings which are unfounded should not be allowed under any circumstances, in the author's opinion.

To help overcome the problem of overcrowding, two of the four cottages previously locked were made available. To enhance normal living conditions, room furniture and bedroom dividers were added to provide more privacy. Altering, modifying, and refining the environment were important to the experiment. According to Dr. Hamilton, a basic cause of improvement of residents' care lay in the charge of management, with more human treatment a fundamental requirements.

Controlling Behavior Problems

The procedure used in the experimental environment in dealing with behavior problems was one of specifying the behavior as clearly as possible, and then attempting to determine its reinforcing consequences. Only when these behavior problems were clearly specified was behavior modification programming used to alter the consequences. Most of the behavior problems of the retarded residents exhibited were disruptive in nature. The residents exhibiting behavior problems were grouped together in one cottage — Cottage II. The environment was conducive to the development and maintenance of residents showing undesirable bheavior because they were attention-seekers. After careful study of the retarded behavior, the author finds that firm but understanding discipline is the best rule to follow. If the retarded individual is corrected when the disruptive behavior occurs and has explained to him the correct behavior for the situation, then the pattern of the disruptive behavior is broken.

In this experiment, the punishment was confining the resident to an area for a period of thirty minutes immediately following the undesirable behavior. There was a row of chairs bolted to the floor, each chair having locked restraining belts and a bell-ringing timer. The child was strapped into the chair for a thirty-minute period and no one interacted with him during this period of confinement. A large number of behavior problems were controlled in this manner.

The author feels that the retarded resident should have been given an explanation of the correct or desirable behavior at the time he misbehaved. This would have been very effective because of the limited reasoning ability that some retarded individuals possess.

Dr. Hamilton is quick to point out that circumstances within the cottage environment needed to be consistent in the relatively restrictive environment of the cottage. Within the cottage environment numerous sources of variability and inconsistencies existed, such as uncontrolled behavior of cottage visitors and residents. The author feels that these should have been corrected before the experiment took place. This is a factor in the retardate's physical environment which cannot be overlooked. Altering and modifying of the environment should have consistently included behavior modifications. The sources, according to Dr. Hamilton, were uncontrolled behavior of cottage visitors, differences in understanding of the rules of the program, and uncontrolled behavior of the residents.

Developmental Skills

Toilet Training

In the experimental toilet training program, the initial attempt was made with ten profoundly retarded girls, who were moved to a separate section of Cottage I. Progress was rapid, and within two months accidents were occurring infrequently. The next experimental attempt was with twelve different profoundly retarded females with IQs below 20, who could not talk and who were totally dependent for care in feeding, bathing, and dressing. Concurrent with the toilet training program, the profoundly retarded girls were aided in self-dressing and feeding skills. All showed marked improvement within short periods of time and eventually mastered the necessary skills.

The procedure briefly was to follow a technique called "Command Training." According to Dr. Hamilton, the purpose was to give the resident instruction daily for seven days in following verbal commands, such as "sit down," "stand up," "go to the fountain," "go to the toilet." By the end of the seven-day period, the profoundly retarded girls had learned sixteen out of eighteen commands. They received commensurable and social rewards for their success.

The experimental toilet training program procedure took six phases. Each phase was eleven, nineteen, twenty-eight, and thirteen days; phase 6 was twenty-nine weeks, respectively. In each phase, the results clearly indicated success of toilet training increased rapidly for the first few days and remained at about 60 percent effective for all twelve girls. The author questions whether this type of toilet training procedure couldn't have been started earlier and achieved similar results.

Dr. Hamilton observed that the same twelve girls were moved to another section of the cottage under different personnel and the maintenance of toilet training proficiency continued without further programming. The reason for this success, according to Dr. Hamilton, was that in small groups more individual attention was possible and there was more flexibility in adjusting the program to the needs of the individual.

The author's view is that even profoundly or severely retarded individuals are capable of simple transfer of training. This transfer should be generalized to achieve this type of program.

Self-Dressing

Cecil Colwell, a consultant to Gracewood, developed a successful dressing program at Pinecrest State School in Louisiana. Colwell demonstrated a reinforcement shaping procedure that has become a standard. The retarded resident is reinforced for performing the last step in the dressing sequence and then successively larger sequence units are added in a reverse manner until the complete task is accomplished. The author questions the fact that these children are reinforced for dressing in reverse. Why not start the retarded resident correctly and allow him to learn the process in a correct manner?

The training was performed at three different cottages with different groups of girls in each. Again, rewards were given for correct responses.

Dr. Hamilton states that prior to the self-dressing program about 30 percent of the children's clothing items were put on correctly without assistance. After the first day of training using visual cues, dressing performance improved to an achievement level greater than 70 percent. Their proficiency was maintained and continued to improve over the next few weeks, resulting in an achievement level of greater than 95 percent.

The program was then discontinued, and the girls dressed in their regular living areas. Ratings were continually checked, and the average level of achievement was better than 90 percent. The author would thus conclude that the transfer of training and retention powers are present in the severely or profoundly retarded.

Self-Feeding

The reader should note the principle of generalization taking place here along with the transfer of training. What is being applied here is the principal of small group training.

The same twelve profoundly retarded residents who were in the toilet training program were used in the self-feeding program. As in the dressing program, the final step of the act was taught first with gradual increments until the sequences were complete. For example, a full spoon may be held to the child's lips at first until the child touches the spoon without help.

Dr. Hamilton reported that success in the self-feeding program was achieved whenever it was possible to provide unhurried, individualized training over an extended period of time. The resident of the toilet training program ate in a separate area and therefore acquired self-feeding skills within a few weeks.

Sheltered Workshop Program

Dr. Hamilton states that some characteristics of the institutionalized retarded are complacency, lethargy, inactivity, and dependency. To overcome these types of habits and attitudes in the mentally retarded, an experimental sheltered workshop program was instituted for most of the residents of Cottage IV. Some structured tasks were developed, and success was achieved in motivating the retarded individuals.

In collaboration with the local Dymo Tape Company the sheltered workshop started a program which consisted of the retarded individual screening scrap sections of tape, cutting out defects, etc. The other project included bow making, using both hand-operated and electrically operated machines. The profits were used for equipment for the cottage and recreational activities. The results indicated that there was high motivation which was prevalent through the cottage. The residents became more responsive to others and began to assist more in routine cottage activities. Many eventually were able to acquire and maintain regular job assignments in other areas of the institution.

Social Reinforcement Program

The Gracewood State School and Hospital observed that the institutionalized retarded adult's social attention factor may have been the most influential reinforcer in all behavior modification programs, in spite of the fact that with some profoundly retarded this was not so evident.

The author believes that the community cooperative would have a positive effect on the profoundly retarded resident who is now supported by research done at Gracewood. Dr. Hamilton states that the institutionalized retardates appear to be good candidates for social reinforcement techniques, as most of the institutionalized retardates have experienced social deprivation.

Pacific State Hospital Program

The Pacific State Hospital in Pomona, California, has a program called Hospital Improvement Project (HIP). This is a concept developed to provide an intensive rehabilitation program for severely and profoundly retarded children. When speaking of retarded children, this program is sometimes referred to as training rehabilitation. This is the same concept as that utilized in the education of the "normal child." There is a growing demand for this type of program in hospitals for the retarded. Recently, it was found that the profoundly or severely retarded can learn simple self-care habits and can benefit from regular activity.

The Children in HIP

A total of 118 children who resided in two wards, one for boys and one for girls, were selected for the HIP program. The children did represent the lowest functioning ambulatory children in the Pacific State Hospital. Their ages ranged from six to seventeen years. A total of 82 percent of the children had a measured IQ of below 30. (The author believes that the IQ score is a meaningless score and merits the least consideration in any type of innovative program. Observable behavior is the key factor, along with performance.) Their mental and social ages were under two years. A total of 75 percent of the children had been institutionalized for four years or more.

Very few of the children selected could care for their own personal needs: 90 percent of the children selected were not toilet trained; 20 percent needed to be fed. They needed aassistance for practically their entire dressing procedure. The majority had no intelligible speech: 42 percent were aggressive, and 30 percent were self-abusive.

Treatment Objectives for the Project

Some of the broad treatment objectives of the project were as follows:
1. application of the principle that children act according to what is expected of them
2. involvement of each patient is constructive, goal-directed activity
3. refinement of training techniques and procedures.
Some more specific goals of the project were the following:
1. achievement of the self-help basic skills
2. development of bodily coordination
3. exposure to new experience — increase in incoming stimuli
4. internalization of motivational forces
5. experiences with feelings of success and a sense of worth
6. basic socialization skills.

The Team Treatment Approach

The team that met and functioned to coordinate different rehabilitation approaches consisted of a physician, a social worker, a recreation therapist, a special education teacher, a psychologist, and the ward charges.

The author questions why a speech therapist, parents of the charges, and a curriculum specialist in the field of special educationw ere omitted from this team. Could the program have been improved and greater success achieved if these specialists and parents had also been included, especially if the key to the entire project's success was fluent communication?

The overall plan was to modify the day-to-day life experiences of the children, so as to maximize their capacity to learn and to modify the routine custodial care to that of teaching them to help themselves. Since this was the overall plan, the involvement of the parents should have played a key role in preparation for the eventual return of the retarded child to a foster home or sheltered workshop in the community. Greater success could then have been achieved.

Success of HIP

The success of the project seemed to occur in small increments, like a child who puts a puzzle together or uses his legs to pump himself on a swing.

The project itself took three years according to Pacific State Hospital authorities. Success can be viewed in varying degrees. In just about every area where training was attempted, success came in many varied forms. For example, having the children feed themselves, having them pick up and carry their own trays, clear tables, and dress themselves.

Removing the patients from the HIP indicated success of the project to the Pacific State Hospital authorities. A total of 30 of the original 118 children have been moved into higher functioning wards; 10 to school wards; and 18 into family care homes.

Looking at the HIP objectively, the author believes that its major success was still in training the retarded children to react within the institutionalized environment. No efforts or successes were achieved in training these children to react in an environment other than that of an institution. The range of abilities of these children or of any children, for that matter, has not been sufficiently tested unless one takes these children and places them in a strange environment and observes their reactions scientifically and objectively. It is a fallacy to hold these children back simply because of an IQ score or because of inappropriate behavior. Their behavior may be inappropriate because the children have never been exposed to another environment.

Extension of HIP

The second phase of the HIP is entitled "An Admission Release Program for the Severely Retarded," which includes a total treatment program for young children from the day of admission. The author believes that this project should be initiated prior to all other projects of a state hospital.

The goal of this second phase of the HIP is to return these children to their own homes or to place them in family care homes within eighteen to twenty-four months.

The four phases of the project are as follows:

1. Receiving — designed to meet the needs of the young newly admitted children;
2. Learning expansion and self-help skills — complete sequence of sensory-motor training, eating, dressing, and using the bathroom.
3. Learning to play — the use of common objects, group activities, and nursery school classes.
4. Preleave preparation — involved in hospital, school, and using community facilities. Parents or foster parents actively involved.

Basic Toys and Games

Basic toys were provided for a variety of activities for those children who, according to Pacific State Hospital authorities, were not ready for classroom activities. These toys provided a constructive outlet for the children, whether they were used for educational or recreational purposes.

Simple Toys

Musical toys such as pull toys, ducks that quacked, and toy xylophones may be used. These toys were used for the more severely retarded who would respond to little else.

Rhythm instruments provide a good way of giving the severely retarded freedom of expression.

At the most elementary level, bean bags were used for developing the child's grasping function.

Simple Games

Other basic games including "follow the leader," "tag," "musical chairs," games of imitation, and "freeze red light – green light" were taught.

Classroom Therapy

The purpose of the classroom therapy, according to Pacific State Hospital authorities, was to provide individual attention while learning. The author feels that the reason for individual attention is the same as that given for limited enrollments in special education classes in the public schools. This principle has not been an overwhelming success. Classroom therapy was first developed when a HIP activity therapist started that program in a ward. The therapy provides for the use of rehabilitation teaching techniques in a structured setting in the ward, characterized by consistent individualized instruction for each charge. The activity takes place in a setting similar to that of a nursery classroom, where educational toys are used. Hospital authorities claim that it is excellent preparation for the regular hospital school.

One of the basic principles of the program was that each child started at his own level, no matter how elementary. The author would question the validity of this principle. If it is carried to its ultimate conclusion, then how does one go about setting goals and objectives for the entire group?

Pacific State Hospital authorities claimed that the therapy sessions helped the children to increase their attention span by working under conditions of "delayed gratification."

Ward Organization – Grouping of Children

Institutionalized children from the two original wards were divided into groups of ten to twelve children. There was no specific basis for this division.

One argument was to divide the children on the basis of performance levels. Other wards thought that groups of children with mixed performance levels would be successful. Another thought was to establish groups that would help to develop some degree of group identity and cohesiveness. From a practical point of view, organization from a performance level proved most successful. Hospital authorities viewed that division on the basis of ability is advantageous. The person working with these children can gear techniques toward one type of patient. The chief argument was that the higher-functioning retardate in each group could serve as a model for the rest of his group. The fallacy of the argument was that in a practical classroom situation, this method did not prove successful.

The author has found from personal experience that once the children have been divided into groups for classroom therapy, they should then be further divided into subgroups which would consist of children of similar abilities. Each child would be given an individual assignment which would contribute toward the total group effort. The principle of small groups, if carried to its ultimate limits, would then prove successful.

Group Control – Some Simple Rules

According to Pacific State Hospital authorities, classroom therapy, if it is to be successful, must maintain absolute group control. Standard rules and procedures for the entire group must be adopted and enforced. Each child should be expected to adhere to the rules as much as he is able.

Rehabilitation Teaching Techniques

1. *Establishing a responsive group mood* – to arouse the child's feeling of acceptance and self-esteem during class sessions. The child should be aware that good behavior and good work is appreciated.
2. *Structure of teaching situations* – to gain child's attention. Give directions that are simple and concise.
3. *Verbal teaching guidance and reinforcement* – strive to develop concepts of understanding. Accomplish this by explaning, reminding, and identifying things throughout the classroom period.
4. *Nonverbal Teaching* – to enhance child's learning through the use of special guidance gestures where the hands or wrists of a child are manipulated. Hands of therapist should be placed directly over child's. Found very effective if verbal explanations are included.
5. *Motivation* – important to develop child's interest so that the child will want to achieve. This is accomplished through the use of rewards (crackers and pieces of candy). (The author questions whether this method is realistic.) The rewards as well as the verbal praise work together to show approval of a completed task.

Classroom Procedures — The Basic Structure

Classroom sessions were set up to provide a one-hour ward-structured activity five days a week. The author questions the introduction of the normalization concept at this point. Would it not have been better to take small groups of children into a public school classroom, possibly a kindergarten room, rather than a pseudo-educational environment, for this part of the HIP project? The undesirable behavior incidents would have been reduced in this environment.

It is to be noted that the highest group in each ward went one hour per day to a school program organized by the educational service department. This was essentially the same type of program, but was more advanced and included sensory motor training.

Class Routine or Curriculum

The first ten or fifteen minutes of an hour of "structured activity" was standardized and followed routinely by all the groups.

Flat salute. One child was asked to hold the flag. The others stood at attention and saluted while "The Star-Spangled Banner" and "America" were played. Children were reminded to look at the flag.

Use and purpose of treats. After the flag salute, the children were seated. Each child was given a treat, such as a cracker or candy. Treats were used to establish a responsive group atmosphere since the children were found to be under control and more attentive after eating.

Story record. A record of "Goldilocks and the Three Bears" was played. The group leader showed pictures of toy animals to help identify and associate word and picture.

Pull toy. Pull toy animal around the table directly in front of the child. This is done in the lower-level groups. While the toys are being pulled around in front of the children, the group leader explains and discusses a story related to the pull toy.

Quiet music — lights off. Music is played softly and lights are turned off in order to calm down a restless or noisy group.

Simple exercises. These exercises are performed within the confines of the classroom when children cannot go outdoors because of inclement weather.

Rehabilitation Lesson Begins

These lessons involved the therapist and the group leader both working individually with the children, primarily for the purpose of teaching each child how to play with educational toys. The author believes that basic elementary reading skills could be accomplished by having the child see the printed word which identifies the educational toy.

Associations and Recognition Concept

Spelling is taught primarily in the same manner as the elementary reading skills. For example, the word "one" is spelled out "o-n-e" and each child is given one block or one object to hold. Then the children are asked to say "one." In the author's opinion, these concepts and teaching would have enhanced the HIP greatly. Pacific State Hospital authorities are quick to point out that it is of vital importance to maintain consistency throughout the rehabilitation lessons so that the children progress in their learning of concepts.

Educational Toys

The educational toys used fall into three categories which are listed below:

ice cream carton	kitty-in-the-key
milk bottle	nuts and bolts
peg boards	keys
nested blocks	discrimination discs
nested cups	coordination boards
post office box	picnic baskets
string beads	snap beads

Parts-to-Whole Activities (Concept-Development Method)

There are three types of puzzles used: visual whole (three to six pieces); segmented parts (five to twenty-one pieces); and multiple-object segmented parts. In the first two types, the child should be able to visualize the whole from its parts. In the third type of puzzle, each

311

piece shows an entire object such as a boy, a dog, or a tree. When the puzzle is completed, it depicts a landscape scene showing all three objects.

Self-Help Activities

Montessori Board Skills. An example of the Montessori board would have two pieces of cloth fastened on opposite ends of one side of the board. The two pieces of cloth are separated in the center by a zipper which a child must learn to use in order to join the two pieces of cloth together. Another Montessori board might have a shoelace attached which a child must learn to tie into a bow.

Functional usage skills. This involves the practical theory learned on a Montessori board as applied to real dressing situations such as closing a zipper or tying a bow.

Appropriate arts and crafts. Arts and crafts activities, according to Pacific State Hospital authorities, fill a need for self-expression in the severely and profoundly retarded. The following activities are listed in order of their difficulty:

1. play with paper
2. handprints
3. plaster of Paris handprints
4. easel painting
5. finger painting
6. string painting
7. blot painting
8. pasting
9. crayon
10. balloon pictures
11. cutting
12. paper construction.

In the author's opinion, this is not a constructive activity because it does very little, if anything, to acquaint the child with community life or the natural environment in which the child lives. There are other activities which are beneficial to the community but which, at the same time, allow for self-expression. Such activities as woodworking and working with leather, for example, can be accomplished by the severely or profoundly retarded.

Sensory-Motor Training

Methods have been developed under the HIP for teaching the severely and profoundly retarded muscle control in their limbs. The

following is a list of activities used in the training methods:
1. "angles in the snow" (This is an activity designed to help a child discover his extremities and learn awareness of the position in space relative to his body.)
2. exercise mats and mattresses
3. exercising on mattresses – mattress walking
4. mattress rocking
5. jumping

Developing Other Sensory-Motor Skills

1. walking boards
2. stepping stones
3. crawling tunnel
4. Identification of body parts (Important sensory-motor training. Purpose of this type of activity is not so much the physical activity, but is to make the retarded child aware of the existence of body parts.)

General Physical Training

The exercise mats may be used in the following ways:

1. rolling
2. stomach rolls
3. rolling sit-up
4. sit-ups
5. bent knee sit-ups
6. scissors
7. feet left
8. toe touch.

Some different activities with which to experiment are the following:

1. wheel barrow walking
2., front somersaults
3. running
4. rocking boat
5. tumble tub
6. wheel toys – wagons

7. tricycles
8. roller skates.

According to the Pacific State Hospital, the following is the proper playground equipment to have under the HIP:

1. standard or tilt merry-go-round
2. tunnel
3. spring animals
4. standard swings
5. special standard slide
6. standard playground slide
7. simple climbers.

Swimming Pool Program

Under the Hospital Improvement Project at Pacific State Hospital, the swimming facilities incude a large circular wading pool (1½ feet deep with a fountain in the middle showering water into the pool), stndard "L"-shaped pool, sloping from 3 feet to 9 feet, a water slide, a diving board, and two ladders. Swimming aides helped in the program under the supervision of a therapist. No child was permitted to become dependent on the aides.

Equipment Used in the Training

1. standard U.S. Coast Guard-approved orange life jacket with shoulder straps
2. ski belts – fit around waist of child and buckle front
3. plastic kick boards
4. the shepherd's crook – to help children adjust to deep water.

Teaching Techniques

Toilet habits of the children should be under control. Technicians should put rubber pants on children who are not completely toilet-trained. There are two separate programs: the wading pool program and the swimming pool program. The purpose of the latter is to have the children get used to deeper water and also to learn the basic rules of water safety.

The basic swimming skills taught are as follows:

1. floating
2. kicking
3. arm movement
4. using arm and leg movements together
5. working in the deep end of the pool.

Integration into the Hospital Program

As previously pointed out, for any totally successful program in any state hospital, integration of the hospital program into the community environment is imperative in order to test the total effectiveness of the training within the institution. According to Pacific State Hospital, the integration of the HIP into other hospital programs represented the prerequisite for trips out into the community. The author believes that the HIP together with other hospital programs should now join forces to form a "Hospital-Community Cooperative," which would involve the total community.

One might say that this is advanced thinking, and that it takes time and planning. The answer to that is to start planning and thinking now. The severely and profoundly retarded must be exposed to all situations in the community environment in the future.

State-Community Cooperative

The Pacific State Hospital made use of the author's concept of a "State-Community Cooperative" by having the child receive stimuli from sources outside the surrounding community. This could take the form of overnight trips to various state buildings and points of interest. Possibly at the beginning, this concept can be achieved with the joint cooperation of other state hospitals or state facilities.

A list of activities might include the following:

1. train rides
2. the canteen
3. going to the show
4. special dance session — held at the Rehabilitation Center Clinical Program twice a week

5. Tuesday night dance (Volunteers offer their services for the Tuesday night dance; a teen-age rock and roll band from the community provide music.)
6. summer day camp (one day a week at one of the state parks).

The author suggests that prior to the camping experience a short film be shown introducing the state park to the children. Naturally, thhe child's understanding of the film would be limited. However, it is still a valuable learning experience for him.

Community Activities

Integration into community activities was the next step at Pacific State Hospital. Elderly men and women with limited incomes would act as guides for the children on trips. Station wagon trips could include the following:
local parks and playgrounds
drive-in restaurants
shopping trips
special sites – holiday excursions
drive-in movies
Knotts Berry Farm.
Integration with normal children was tried under this project. A fully integrated program is described, along with unique training techniques, in Forgotten Children (Leswing, 1972).
Bus trips would include visits to the zoo, the beach, day camps, and parks. For example, eight severely retarded girls from a day camp went to a park where they had the following activities: group nature hikes, singing, arts and crafts, "follow the leader," and "hot ptoato." The purpose of this park trip was to see how this type of patient would react to a camp environment and how the girls would benefit from and adapt to a new situation.
Pacific State Hospital's plan is very similar to that of the author's state and community cooperative concept, using the principles of normalization of small groups. Some parts of the Hospita Improvement Project follow the Montessouri method, while other aspects of the group are more advanced.[3]

Progress Evaluation

At this point in discussing institutional programs for the retarded, an evaluation needs to be made of the retarded individual's progress within the institution. The following topics should be considered: self-care, motor development, social maturity, language, personality characteristics, and occupational maturity.

Self-Care

Eating
likes to be fed
feeds self
finger feeds
feeds self with fork and spoon
drinks from glass unassisted
serves own plate
cuts own meat with knife.

Bathing
attempts to wash self in tub or shower
partially dries self, needs to be reminded
adjust shower or bath water temperature
bathes independently
dries self well.

Toilet Training
shows discomfort when wet or soiled
will sit on toilet unattended for short periods
will go to the toilet for bowel movement
seldom has accidents
stays dry at night.

Dressing
can dress and undress without assistance
selects correct clothes for climate or occasion
dresses self except for tying of shoes
is able to tie shoes after being show how to tie a bow knot
can put on different articles of clothing
can button, unbutton, zip, unzip
prepares self for bed.

Grooming
takes proper care of clothing (washing, hanging up items to dry)
keeps nails clean
makes attempt to brush hair
able to shine own shoes
frequent uses of deodorant.

Motor Development
turns head toward sound
rolls over
sits alone
crawls or creeps on all fours
rides tricycle
stands alone
walks alone
walks backward
unable to turn door knob to open door
winks eyes.

Social Maturity and Manners
smiles at familiar faces
notices other children, but still self-centered play
creates own games and activities with another child
will share toys and food
abides by rules set by group

Language
laughes
says single words
uses two words
speaks in short sentences
knows full name and sex
asks for things he wants
prints name
relates experiences
writes letters without help
reads adventure stories without help.

Personality Characteristics
has temper tantrum, if frustrated
picks on smaller boys and girls
appears insecure or frightened in many activities
is known as a loner, has few friends.

Occupational Maturity
can count three objects
can identify all money denominations
can make simple change with money
goes about job willingly and is eager to finish
can prepare simple meal
learns to use the telephone.

There are other classifications and other indications that the mentally retarded child can give which shows signs of a successful training program. Benshburg[4] is quick to point out that the evaluation of an individual is done regularly every six months. In the author's opinion, evaluations can and should be done every three months or even more frequently. Through consistent reevaluation of each individual resident, the program can become more effective with the help of the staff and the proper use of equipment.

References

1. John M. Garstecki, A Curriculum for the Residential Trainable Child (Union Grove, Wis.: Southern Wisconsin Colony and Training School, February 1970), pp. 1-73.
2. John Hamilton, Ph.D. *Environmental Control and Retardate Behavior,* Ch. 16, "Behavioral Intervention in Human Problems." (Gracewood, Ga.: Gracewood State School and Hospital, 1971), pp. 383-414.
3. Charles V. Keeran, Administrative Associate, Mental Retardation Program, Neuropsychiatric Institute, UCLA.
   Mary Bennett, Grants Consultant, Pacific State Hospital.
   Mary Trainor, Acting Project Administrator, Comepsnatory Education Project, Pacific State Hospital.
   Frances Grove, Retired Chief, Rehabilitation Services, Pacific State Hospital.

319

Linda J. Miller, Acting Program Assistant, Child Development Program, Pacific State Hospital.

H.I.P. Activity Manual: Directing Activities for Profoundly and Severely Retarded Children (Pomona, Ca.: Pacific State Hospital, January 1968), pp. 1-223. (The development of this manual was supported in part by the National Institute of Mental Health Grant MH-01825, *A Rehabilitative Program for the Profoundly Retarded;* and in part by Pacific State Hospital, Department of Mental Hygiene. State of California.)

4. Gerald J. Bensberg, "The Use of Evaluations in Planning the Training Program," Ch. 6, pp. 111-122. From Gerald J. Bensberg, ed., *Teaching the Mentally Retarded – A Handbook for Ward Personnel* (Atlanta, Ga.; Southern Regional Education Board, 1965).

Guidance, Counseling, and Curriculum Development

Richard S. Greene
Department of Special Education
Madera Unified School District
Thomas Jefferson High School
Madera, California 93024

One of the most common fallacies in the writing of a textbook on curriculum is the omitting of guidance and counseling as subject matter appropriate in the text. In order to have a total view of curriculum development, one must consider the guidance and counseling as part of the curriculum, especially when dealing with the mentally retarded child.

Psychotherapy is an advanced form of guidance and counseling. The typical school counselor is using psychotherapy on a somewhat modified scale with students every day. For the purpose of this textbook, the author shall use psychotherapy interchangeably with guidance and counseling and ignore the technical academic differences that do exist.

We shall now review the psychotherapeutic techniques used with some success on the mentally retarded child. Later, the author will describe some of his innovative techniques.

321

Nonverbal Techniques

With some mentally retarded students, the use of language is difficult, and the students therefore are relatively deficient in this area.

Play Therapy

It is common knowledge that play in a child's life is a natural phenomenon and an attractive activity. Through play, the child is able to express the conflicts, fears, and tensions which are inevitable in growing up. The child expresses these emotions without the necessity of language or communication. Play provides an escape or brief holiday from an uncomfortable situation which he encounters and which is becoming increasingly worse.

This type of therapy has far more advantages than that of unsupervised play. The therapist or counselor, within the broad limits of time, space, and safety, accepts without reservation the child and his methods of play.

The child is able to approach a closeness of contact which he may not be able to achieve in the threatening world of reality. The child can express himself and be understood by symbols (not by language), expressing hates, fears, terrors, and unacceptable desires.

Innovative Classroom Application

Play therapy can be performed within the confines of a kindergarten room or in a well-equipped gymnasium. This would require some extra equipment on the school's part, but nothing that would exceed the school's budget. If necessary, the junior or senior high mentally retarded students could be transported to an elementary school where this room would be available.

Within this atmosphere, the psychotherapist or guidance counselor could observe without restriction the child's fantasy world of play and through this method accumulate the necessary knowledge about the child so as to relieve the cause of illness rather than the symptoms alone. The child's play activities are observed within the classroom and accurate records are kept by the teacher for use in conferences with the guidance counselor. In severe cases, a trained psychotherapist could be brought in for consultation. The cause of conflicts, tensions, and hates would become more apparent so that a better course of counseling could be decided upon.

Artistic Media of Expression

The artist media of expression is most commonly used as an adjunct to psychotherapy with both retarded adults and children. The most common form of expression used is drawing. The advantages and opportunities to express feelings and ideas without verbalization are plentiful. It results in a tangible product which the child can claim as evidence of accomplishment.

Innovative Classroom Application

The classroom applications are varied. The special teacher can have the child do his drawings during a regular art period and then show the drawings to the counselor for evaluation. This is a unique way of counseling the child through art. The teacher and the counselor can work together to direct the child's future course without the counselor ever having to see the child. In some cases direct contact of the child with the counselor could result in a major problem.

VERBAL TECHNIQUES

Role Playing

Role playing or psychodrama is the spontaneous acting out of a problem with the aim of improving mental health. The problem is discussed before, but the plot and characters are developed freely. Role playing is very effective in providing the opportunity for testing and rehearsing new or alternative patterns of behavior in a sheltered and guided situation. Role playing provides for the expression of repressed feelings and infantile fantasies in a concrete form.

Innovative Classroom Application

This can be used effectively in a classroom, combining group psychotherapy within the classroom. The class itself can suggest new patterns of behavior or possible alternatives. The counselor and teacher can help guide and support through more direct counseling within the confines of the counselor's office. This provides a unique opportunity for the mentally retarded student in senior high school to test alternative methods of employment interviewing such as psychodrama in vocational guidance, career development, and other alternatives open. The retardate will gain a new and deeper understanding of himself — that is, a realistic self-appraisal.

Group Psychotherapy

Individual counseling is combined with group experience. The therapist plays a passive role, allowing the group to direct and solve the problems. The mentally retarded child who is afraid to close emotional contact can be absorbed into the group at a gradual pace, setting his own speed. Group therapy permits participation of ancillary personnel (cottage parents and nurses) in the planning and execution of therapeutic programs.

Innovative Classroom Application

Group psychotherapy lends itself to the classroom and can be combined in vocational guidance, psychodrama, artistic media, and most other forms of therapy. Teacher, counselor, and parents can participate with very little disruption in programming. All will gain a deeper understanding of the very nature of the problem.

Catharsis-Reflection and Clarification of Feelings

These techniques, which are intended to help the child to recognize and understand what he has just said and felt, are closely attuned to the child's frame of reference.

Innovative Classroom Application

This is a Rogerian nondirective form of counseling being done with the mentally retarded child, and can easily be carried out on an individual basis or possibly on a group basis. (More will be said about this technique a little later in the chapter.)

324

Other forms of psychotherapy frequently used in the classroom and unknown to most teachers are reassurance, support, advice, direct discussion, and orthodox psychoanalytic techniques such as free association, free talk, free play, and dream analysis and interpretations. These techniques have all been used in the classroom.[1]

Client-Centered Approach: Applicable Theory

The following points are characteristic of a Rogerian client-centered interview:
1. The therapist attempts to understand the reference to content feeling and to communicate the understanding.
2. He interprets what the client is saying.
3. He accepts what the client is saying.
4. He refines the client's point of view.
5. He answers questions and gives information.
6. He actively participates in the session.

Successful Classroom Application: Innovative Reasoning

The above six basic concepts formulate the basis of the author's recommendation to adopt the client-centered interview as one of the standard methods of counseling the mentally retarded child. This is especially true for the junior and senior high school mentally retarded student who needs understanding, some direction, and someone to talk with when frustration is apparent. The school counselor has the necessary training for this method and should be used not only in individual counseling, but in group counseling as well.

The author has tried the Rogerian method mentioned previously, adhering to the six basic principles, and found this method successful in most cases where the child had a problem which, with understanding and careful interpretation under the Rogerian approach, could be worked out successfully by the child.[2]

GROUP PSYCHOTHERAPY WITH CHILDREN

Activity Group Therapy: Applicable Theory

In this procedure, the children would be exposed to an environment that is accessible in every respect, where they would feel free to act out their natural impulses, hostilities, and fantasies. The furniture is made of planks, especially any that is designated for rough handling. The materials supplied are available in any school or similar environment. After one hour to an hour and one-half of activity, thirty to forty minutes are devoted to refreshment time. The therapist neither accepts nor rejects, approves nor disapproves of the child's behavior or play.

Successful Classroom Application: Innovative Reasoning

This type of therapy can be best done in a school yard with the counselor standing by. According to the procedures given in therapy instruction, the school equipment is all that is necessary, thus avoiding additional school expenses. An innovative process would be to gather these children in one group during a normal physical education period. The depth of understanding the counselor in a public school could receive from the individual observations of the children in an accessible environment would enhance greatly the guidance program now in effect. Catharsis, ego strengthening, and reality testing are operative in this type of group psychotherapy.

Transitional Group Therapy: Applicable Theory

This procedure is a combination of a group therapy and social group work. This method is designed for the mentally retarded student who is still not ready to participate in organized group life without close supervision, and conform to routines and limitations of planned group programs without a great deal of direction in social living. In this procedure there is definite organization and planned activity. The children are encouraged to elect their own president, vice-president, secretary, and treasurer. The therapist exerts leadership influence and helps the children carry out their plans.

Successful Classroom Application: Innovative Reasoning

Transitional group therapy would be invaluable in the senior high school setting for the mentally retarded. It would also be very useful at the junior high school level and possibly even at the fifth and sixth grade elementary school level. The mentally retarded child who would benefit most from this type of therapy would be the one who still has reservations or is psychologically unready to participate fully in activities of the total school program. This therapy is especially useful in obtaining cooperation in physical education (dressing, showering, etc.) and in elective situations. It is also useful for those who cannot adjust to unprotected activity, such as noon-time, postschool, and club functions.

Play-Group Therapy: Applicable Theory

In play-group therapy, the same principles and procedures employed for individual treatments are used, but with some modifications. Groups of three or four children, from four to five years old, are supplied with materials through which they can act out their fantasies, hostilities, and other problems that can be expressed through pretense, play, games, watercolor painting, etc.

There are many differences between play therapy and activity therapy. In activity therapy toys are more suitable for fantasies. The center of activity is a doll house with a number of rooms, appropriate furniture, male and female children, babies, animals, and toys. The rooms receiving the most attention in the doll house are the bedrooms and bathrooms. This method of therapy helps the children in acting out their fantasies and fears.

Successful Classroom Application: Innovative Reasoning

In public school practice, both in the classroom situation itself or in the counseling situation with appropriate materials, play therapy would add greatly to the counseling program. It would serve as a guide to the counseling program's direction and in achieving the desired effects. At the junior and senior high school level, the counselor would gain a deeper insight into the child's wishes, dreams, the root causes of his problems, and the child's ability to cope with his surroundings. Attitudes, feelings, and emotions would have an outlet for expression. A freer catharsis would result in a more adjusted mentally retarded individual.

Activity-Interview Group Therapy: Applicable Theory

This technique, which is somewhat similar to that previously described,

described, is employed with children of school age. The setting of the group is the same, except fewer provisions for creative and constructive activities are provided. In this technique the child is kept more at a play and conversational level. A doll house and appropriate materials are furnished. Children interact with one another. The children talk about problems, fantasies, preoccupations, strivings, hopes and desires.

Successful Classroom Application: Innovative Reasoning

From the author's viewpoint, this counseling technique would be especially useful at the elementary school level since the technique does permit the awakening of repressed thoughts and it increases ego strengths and the child's awareness. This is very important at this stage because if the mentally retarded child is given an effective guidance and counseling program in the elementary school, the junior and senior high guidance programs can be more effective and follow through on some of the insights and understandings gained in previous sessions.[3]

Directive Psychotherapy: Applicable Theory

The premise on which directive psychotherapy or counseling is based is as follows:
1. The therapist or counselor is a master educator who takes over where society, education, the family, and individual persons have failed.
2. Conditions for learning a new life-style should be established.
3. Someone must discover the problem, decide what steps should be taken to remedy it, and then see that appropriate action is undertaken.
4. In order to properly understand the issues, decisions must be made concerning the questions of when, where, how, and why.

Successful Classroom Application: Innovative Reasoning

Directive or eclectic counseling is the system now most widely used in the public schools' guidance and counseling programs across the nation. This technique incorporates the case histories, which include the identifying data, present problems, family history, and emotional and social background of the individuals. This type of counseling has proven to be successful only in some cases. The reassurance and supportive therapy given is sometimes rejected as false sympathy or patronization of the mentally retarded child – attitudes which the child interprets as ridicule. The inducing of insight, or restricting the mentally retarded child's reasoning ability, is interpreted by the author as a lack of faith in the child's ability, which is, of course, frustrating to the child's ego. An explanation of the problem needs to be given along with alternative solutions, but the mentally retarded child needs to find an independent solution for himself. This then becomes ego-strengthening and builds self-esteem.

Counselors must be made aware of the obvious fact that this type of guidance and counseling program is self-defeating because of its lack of flexibility and built-in rigidity of the directions.[4]

Psychodrama: Applicable Theory

There are a number of techniques by which psychodrama can be carried out. In this section the discussion of psychodrama will be limited to the techniques adaptable to the school counseling situations; that is, the techniques of self-presentation and of spontaneous improvisation.

Techniques of Self-Presentation: The simplest method of psychodrama occurs when the mentally retarded child starts the performance himself in the presence of the psychotherapist, and acts out a daily situation with crucial conflicts. The auxiliary egos are staff members who help patients get started through encouragement and instilling of confidence. The patient doesn't portray a situation partially but relives the situation completely with the help of his auxiliary ego who takes part in these concrete situations.

Techniques of Spontaneous Improvisations: This is a technique in which the patient does not enact events from his own life, but instead acts in fictitious roles. In this technique the auxiliary ego has two roles; one to get the patient started on a specific role; and two, to have the auxiliary ego be a participating actor in a role which is demanded by the situation.

Successful Classroom Application: Innovative Reasoning

Techniques of Self-Presentation: This technique is applicable in any counseling situation, either in the counselor's office or in the classroom. The auxiliary ego can be a teacher, vice-principal, or principal. It is ad-

329

visable to have the auxiliary ego be someone that the mentally retarded child trusts, such as the special education teacher. Many facets of interpersonal relationships can be evoked, as well as interaction and coping with environmental surroundings.

Techniques of Spontaneous Improvisations: Through this technique, the child learns to deal with environmental surroundings from divergent points of view — some plausable, others painful. Greater insight into reality can be gained in a mentally retarded child through this technique. The child gains a deeper insight into interpersonal relationships and their value and meanings. Concrete situations are brought to reality through many divergent views.

The mentally retarded child learns through concrete situations how environmental conditions are seen by others and how others cope with interpersonal relationships. The child perceives the entire picture through experience.[5]

Round-Table Psychotherapy: Innovative Applicable Theory

Round-table psychotherapy goals are to help people attain realistic perspectives regarding their problems, develop confidence in themselves, and perceive the attitudes of others in working out solutions to their problems. This therapy is based on the belief that a patient will gain better self-understanding by trying to understand and help others.

The therapy is set up in such a way that a panel of seven patients (mentally retarded students) discuss their problems in front of an audience of eighteen (the remainder of the class). The therapist is inactive. A prepanel discussion takes place with each student — for the purpose of encouraging him to discuss his problem freely.

Successful Classroom Application

One can plainly see how a learning situation which uniquely enough can involve the entire class has an obvious application for the mentally retarded child. The child has a depth of understanding which sometimes even adults lack; very often he is not given credit for this asset.

This type of counseling can take place within the classroom. The special education teacher would act as the therapist, and the counseling could be included in the curriculum as units on social living. Each mentally retarded child at different times would discuss a specific problem that confronts him.

Dynamic-Cultural Approach: Innovative Applicable Theory

Camilla Anderson is the founder of this technique relating to psychotherapy which is said to be similar to the methods of Sullivan, Horney, and Fromm.

The emphasis seems to be on helping the mentally retarded child to free himself from moral judgments and attitudes and to replace them with critical realistic appraisals. It is important to avoid the common complications of guilt and lack of pride. This therapy is based on the belief that the mentally retarded child needs to help free himself from such judgments in order to function. The counselor's job would be to aid the mentally retarded child in the process of getting acquainted with his own wants, feelings, capacities, and limitations, and then to evaluate ways to improve his functioning in practical terms.

Successful Classroom Application

This type of therapy gets down to the crux of the matter and clearly delineates the counselor's job. The mentally retarded child greatly needs an understanding of his function in society, the community, and the home. The child must become reality-oriented and learn to function independently.

Existential Analysis: Innovative Applicable Theory

From an existential point of view, the counselor would see the mentally retarded child in an environment of desperation, striving for his forgotten power-to-be. Man's plight is one of despairing for his spontaneous existence. Existential therapy emphasizes the importance of individual values and goals ad directs the mentally retarded child's attention toward understanding his personal world — the world of values.

A task assigned to the existential counselor is called "Logotherapy," the purpose of which is to reveal flaws in the mentally retarded child's world view (his system of values) and to help the child readjust to that view.

331

Successful Classroom Application

Successful application of this form of therapy would require a combining of the existential analysis and the dynamic cultural system which the author calls "An Existential Cultural Analysis." When combined, it would be a system of counseling that would exactly fit the mentally retarded child's needs.

General Semantics: Innovative Applicable Theory

In this approach semantics is applied to psychotherapy since it is believed that the mentally retarded child lacks a clear understanding of the use of words and their meanings. Vagueness in phrasing, defects in conceptualization, a lack of clarity in the use of symbols, an inability to define or think critically about values or life goals, or conceptualize needs and desires clearly — all of this is thought to cause frustrations and disappointments with whatever is achieved. As a result of poor language and poor clarity of thought, the mentally retarded child cannot identify properly his needs and desires.

The semanticist-therapist strives to improve communications of the mentally retarded child with the therapist and with others, and also to better the child's understanding of himself.

Successful Classroom Application

Some of the problems of the mentally retarded child are communication difficulties, poor command of language, and a failure to conceptualize or to think critically or realistically. The general semantics approach is a unique innovation in counseling techniques that could be used in almost any setting, such as the classroom, the counselor's office, or in an institution.

Assertion-Structured: Innovation Applicable Theory

E. Larkin Phillips based his theory on the idea that behavioral possibilities are selected by the perceiving-acting person to meet the situations which confront him. The behavior patterns of the mentally retarded child (or of any person) are understood in terms of the standards by which he chooses to live. Phillips called these behavior patterns "assertions."

According to this innovative counseling theory, the counselor would accept the idea that life for the mentally retarded child is a constant series of events concerned with the child's assertions — that is, winning (confirmation) or losing (nonconfirmation). When the mentally retarded child's assertions are met with nonconfirmation, the child and his environment are said to be in conflict.

Successful Classroom Application

From the author's viewpoint and experience, many assertions of the mentally retarded child are met with nonconfirmation because the assertions are not compatible with the environment. This problem is mainly due to communication language difficulties. The counselor's task is one of reality-orienting the child so that the assertions made will meet with confirmation instead of nonconfirmation. In order for this theory to be successfully applied to the child, it must be combined with other theories previously discussed.

Rational Psychotherapy: Innovative Applicable Theory

Rational psychotherapy is based on the theory that human emotion is caused and controlled by thinking positive. Positive emotions are elation and love; negative emotions are anger and depression. The theory contends that one may appreciably control one's feelings by controlling one's thoughts. The rational counselor would teach the mentally retarded child to understand how the child creates his own emotional reactions by what he is told and what he tells himself.

Successful Classroom Application

The rational counseling technique and the mentally retarded child's concept of self-esteem to coincide. The mentally retarded child has a low self-image (self-esteem) with thoughts which seem to have no definite base. The counselor should be aware of this therapy and should combine it into the full counseling program to obtain the maximum effectiveness.[6]

Richard S. Greene

PRINCIPLES OF CURRICULUM

Guidance and counseling is an integral part of the total curriculum. Within the curriculum, there are two major areas of thought and practice concerning "processes" in education. These areas are directly related to what should be taught (the value) and knowledge (how it shall be taught).

Curriculum has been defined a number of different ways. Some educators consider it as encompassing all of the life experiences of the students. Another point of view is that curriculum consists of all the activities engaged in by a student for which the school has responsibility. The author sees curriculum as being functional in value, vocational in orientation, and enriching to life experiences – as an adjunct to all the activities the student will engage in and is engaged in for the rest of his life.

The traditional definition of curriculum is that it is a systematic organization of subject matter in specific courses of study. There are two basic approaches to curriculum content and the scope of curriculum.

Subject-Matter Approach

In this approach to determine the curriculum content, emphasis is placed on minimum standards, specific subjects, methods and materials for each level of learning, and the required content and skills outlined in the curriculum. In this approach, the curriculum – not the teacher or the students – is viewed as the determining factor in what is to be learned.

The Experience Approach

Subject matter, materials, and methods are all dependent upon the individual situations and the students, and cannot be made to meet a standard. The needs and abilities of the student with the creativity of the teacher guide curriculum development and become the basis for curriculum content.

Curriculum content, from the author's point of view, needs to be developed with the following thoughts in mind:
1. creativity on the part of teacher and students
2. experiences, both of teacher and students
3. individual goals and objectives
4. curriculum goals and objectives

334

5. methods and equipment available for use
6. individual differences, curriculum activities
7. environmental conditions, at home, at school, and in the surrounding community
8. abilities of the teacher, students, and administration
9. background situations of all those concerned
10. future aspirations and realistic appraisals
11. flexibility, adaptability, innovations of curriculum on the part of the students, teachers, and administration.

Traditional Organization of Curriculum

Under this approach to organizing curriculum, the curriculum is based on standard subject matter, usually organized in order of difficulty.

Modern Organization: Problems and Experience

From this point of view, curriculum is seen in terms of its content as related to the problems of life in society.

A curriculum organized around this concept must be flexible, and the arrangement of learning experiences must be determined by the characteristics of the problems and the students' present level of understanding. Under this approach, the student would actually be guided through a curriculum created and organized to a large extent by his own needs and those of the other students.[7]

Curriculum Subjects

A typical sociovocational curriculum would contain the following:[8]
1. *Vocational English*
    letter writing
    job hunting
    completion of application forms
    completion of social security forms
    aptitude and standardized test taking
    use of dictionary and telephone directory
    oral expression
    use of communication services
2. Arithmetic
    banking

335

budgeting
buying
wages-payroll deductions
3. *Social studies*
military service orientation
governmental agency service
occuaption information
job requirements
survey of available jobs
citizenship responsibilities
4. *Science*
safety on the job
good health habits
5. *Vocational* (can be prework experience)
woodwork
metal painting
sewing
cooking
typing
child care
driver education (practical)
6. *Work experience*
role of the employer-employee
off-campus placement.

Montessori Curriculum

Genevieve Tarlton, Reddam headmistress of the Lilliput Schoolhouse in south Texas, has organized the curriculum of her school into fifteen learning categories which can serve as a model Montessori curriculum:[9]
1. *Care of self and environment*
2. Development of sensory skills
exploration of five senses
field trips
3. *Reading phonetics and sight recognition*
4. *Writing*
5. *Dictation* (spelling for first and second grades)

6. *English*
   pronunciation
   enunciation
   conservation
   vocational
7. *Foreign language*
8. *Drama*
   elocution
   role playing
9. *Music*
10. *Art*
    handwork
    freehand drawing
11. *Dancing*
    folk
    introduction to gymnastics
12. *Mathematics*
    introduction to geometry
13. *Science* (introduction)
    anatomy
    personal hygiene
    zoology
    ecology
14. *Social studies*
    geography
    newspaper
15. *Socialization*
    self and group, home and school
    lunch etiquette.

According to Montessori, the basic foundation of the learning program includes:

1. A Montessori-prepared environment
   sensorial learning
   daily living skills
2. Sequential perceptual motor training
3. Bodily activities with emphasis on
   coordination of body parts
   fluidity of movement

4. Development of social skills aimed at the development of
   positive self
   ability to relate to normal peers.
According to the Verdugo Montessori School (La Canada, Calif.), the
program helps the mentally retarded child develop:
respect for the rights of others
self-discipline
responsibility
cooperation
self-confidence.

Language-Art Curriculum

In a developmental communications program, far more than the
lack of a functioning vocabulary or delayed speech must be taken into
consideration in formulating plans for a language-art curriculum.

Some basic considerations in a language-art curriculum are as
follows:
The individual lives apart within himself
   does not respond to questions
   isolates himself with little if any activity.
The individual uses gestures and physical actions
   grabs or hits to get attention
   uses gestures, no words
   leads adults to what he wants
   plays alone.
The individual uses sounds to convey meaning
   produces simple sounds
   repeats sounds
   gurgles, coos, babbles
   plays near others or with one child.
The individual observes
   does not look when shown objects or pictures
   watches but does not appear to recall observations
   watches with interest objects, pictures, activities.
The individual listens
   responds to loud noises
   carries out one familiar instruction
   recalls some parts of story, record, or music.

The individual initiates actions, sounds, words
    repeats constantly
    repeats words on request.
The individual verbalizes spontaneously
    names people
    identifies objects
    says single words.
The individual converses, communicates with others
    writes, reads
    asks questions.

Expectations of the MR Child

Some expectations of the mentally retarded child, as listed by Baumgarter, are discussed below.[10] The author does not necessarily hold the same opinions due to the differences in the methods of formulating curriculum and theory and philosophy of mental retardation.

Arithmetic

Preliminary
how the difference between night and day, today and tomorrow
Primary
recognize distance, near and far
understand concepts few, many, more, less
Intermediate
use of calendar
tell time
measure with cup, yardstick, ruler
Junior High School
build own ideas needed for living in home, community
know value of coins, paper money; how to make change
Senior High School
use all functional arithmetic needed for living in home, community, and on job
know arithmetic used for transportation, taxes
know where to go for help

Physical Education

Preprimary

listen and follow directions
gain self-confidence in directed and creative movements

Primary

continue to grow in realistic concepts of self in directed and creative movements
use freedom of choice in activities where success can be achieved

Intermediate

learn to swim
participate in a balanced program
participate in organized games, folk dancing, group games, softball

Junior High School

participate in all organized gym activities on junior high level

Senior High School

understand personal limitations
understand and use abilities
evaluate abilities to use to best advantage and have well-balanced physical activites at home and at work.

Special Education Curriculum

Special education developmental curriculum must make progress for both chronological age and mental age abilities on all levels. Even when using this curriculum, there will still be academic differences among individuals that occur within any given group.
Primary Level Reading: Reading Readiness C.A. 6-10
M.A. 3-6½
1. Development of opportunities for children to speak naturally

A. Having telephone conversations
B. Dramatization in which simple parts are memorized

2. Developing visual auditory discrimination and memory
   A. Visual discrimination activities
      (1) Matching colors
      (2) Games involving the finding of likenesses and differences between objects
      (3) Matching pictures with words
   B. Auditory discrimination
      (1) Listening to records which have many common sounds
      (2) Blindfolding a child and having him identify classmate's voice
   C. Memory
      (1) Teach simple jingles and rhymes
3. Advanced reading readiness
   A. Prints name
   B. Understands street signs.

Intermediate Reading Level C.A. 10-12
6½-8

1. Emphasize word-attack skills
2. Teach sound blending with simple words; c-a-t, d-o-g
3. Increase practices in phonetic word-attack skills
4. Encourage independent word attack
5. Do not "overuse" phonetic drill.

Secondary Reading Level C.A. 12-18

1. Development of better reading habits through a wider use and selection of reading material
2. Increase reading range for information and pleasure
3. Increase the use of word-recognition skills
4. Increase silent reading speed.

According to Willey and Waite, spelling should not be introduced at the primary level, but on the intermediate level when the child has acquired a second-grade reading skill.

Primary Spelling Level C.A. 10-12
6½-8

1. Multiple teaching approach: visual methods, phonetic methods, visual-memory methods
2. In view of the above approach, a good method to use is to see, hear, say, then write and use the word.

Secondary Spelling Level C.A. 12-18
8-12

1. Learning words that will be necessary in letter writing
2. Learning words that will be necessary for vocations.

Primary Arithmetic Level C.A. 6-10
M.A. 3-6½

Grade expectancy — nursery to kindergarten.
The primary level experiences of arithmetic should include: time, money, temperature, weight, size, and fractions.

Intermediate Arithmetic Level C.A. 10-12
6½- 8

Grade expectancy: 1 to 3.
Intermediate arithmetic experiences should include:
1. Advanced counting, beyond 100 if possible.
2. Counting as the foundation of addition
3. Number facts — simple arithmetical operations
4. Subtraction — flash cards, number games
5. Counting by 2s, 5s, and 10s
6. Making change
7. Measuring pints and quarts
8. Writing numbers.

Secondary Arithmetic Level C.A. 12-18
M.A. 8-12

Grade expectancy: 2 to 6.

Some accomplishments under Willey and Waite's curriculum are as follows:
1. Add four digits and carry
2. Subtract four digits and borrow
3. Multiplication through nines, can multiply two-digit by two-digit number
4. Use simple fractions
5. Read thermometers
6. Tell time
7. Know money terms and values
8. Understand the services of a bank.

Willey and Waite feel that a good curriculum for the mentally retarded should maintain a careful balance between general education and the unit method to acquire basic skills and transfer them to the behavior areas. This author feels that a good curriculum for the mentally retarded is one which is functional, affords varying experiences, is academic, and vocational in orientation. It also should have a great amount of flexibility, creativity, and allow for innovations. A balance of the above-mentioned factors plus a very careful blend of good, unique teaching techniques will form the ideal special education curriculum.[11]

Occupational Curriculum

The mentally retarded child has a very limited academic future which the coordinators of the curriculum must be fully aware of. This condition must enter into the planning of the entire curriculum. Many writers discuss this point, but generally too briefly. The author intends to show how the occupational curriculum may be incorporated into units of study with some practical adaptations.

The following are examples of how the occupational curriculum may be adapted for use in the special education classroom in a social studies unit for different grade levels.[12]

Social Studies Unit — Division of Labor: Grades 5 and 6

Approach: Comparison of division of labor among different Indian tribes, Eskimo tribe, and a west African tribe. Resources would include films, filmstrips, transparencies, library research, and printed materials which class and teacher would go over.

343

Examples of questions to be used in developing concepts are as follows:
Who does what jobs?
What jobs are given to children?
What research should be done?
Does climate affect the job? If so, how?
What types of jobs are affected by climate?
Are there any kinds of work in these primitive societies which require cooperation?
What are the rewards and chances for leadership?
How do jobs of primitive men compare with the jobs of today?
Compare chances for advancement. Were there assembly lines in primitive tribes?

Social Studies Unit — Division of Labor: Grades 7 and 8

Approach: Study how federal, state, and local goverments have each developed a division of labor at all levels. Study work laws. Have people from the community who hold different positions come in and speak to the class. Outside speakers add greatly to the effectiveness of the unit on labor since they instill motivation and raise the interest level.
The following questions suggest how students can be stimulated:
To what extent has the division of work been divided in our different branches of government at all levels?
Why are there these differences?
How do they benefit us?
Which jobs are under civil service?
What is the purpose of civil service?

Social Studies Unit — Division of Labor: Grades 9 and 10

Approach: Visit a local manufacturing plant. The students should also visit city hall, the police department, the fire department, and the labor department. Discuss the visit back in the classroom. Films, filmstrips, and talks by visitors enrich the unit.
Some questions to stimulate the class are as follows:
What are the purposes of the division of labor in factories, offices, schools, and homes?
How do assembly lines differ in the manufacturing of radio and television sets, furniture, and cars?

344

How do skills differ in the requirements for each plant?

Social Studies Unit — Division of Labor: Grades 10-12

Approach: A banker, union leader, and business executive discuss each division of labor from their own point of view, followed by debates.
Questions on developing key concepts are as follows:
To what extent is the division of labor associated with free enterprise? With the National Labor Relations Board? With the Taft-Hartley Act? With strikes? What do they mean? What effect do they have?
What are the advantages and disadvantages of division of labor?
What is the effect of the division of labor on American society?
On unemployment?
The author has developed an occupational curriculum consisting of the following specialties:
Math — accountants, teachers, IBM computer operators
Science — doctors, U.S. health officers, scientists (all types)
History — lawyers, teachers
Geography — travel agents.
These occupations are first studied in class and, whenever possible, specialists in various fields give talks in class and answer the students' questions.

Program of Abilities, Inc.

An example of a unique prevocational program for the mentally retarded was started at Abilities, Inc. in Long Island, New York. The chief goal of the project was to determine the feasibility of employing the mentally retarded in a normal and competitive industrial program while they were still attending public secondary special classes.
Some of the other goals of the project were the following: Evaluating work potential — that is, skills and work adjustment as an aid in vocational counseling and planning; an intensive orientation and exposure to an actual competitive work situation.
Henry Viscardi is president and founder of this electronics firm, which competes successfully with local industry. This firm is now training and employing mentally retarded persons.

345

Setting and Subjects

A group of six female and nine male educable retarded students comprised the prevocational program in 1962 and 1963. These educable mentally retarded subjects spent three hours daily, 8 A.M. to 11 A.M. in the program and returned to their special classes every afternoon for academic learning.

Criteria for Acceptance

between sixteen and eighteen years of age
I.Q. between 60 and 80
no brain damage or physical handicap
no other special problems existing.

Academically their grade-level achievement ranged from the third- to the fifth-grade level in basic (tool) subjects.

Training Program

Three main points of emphasis in the actual training are the following:
basic orientation
job training
personal-social adjustment.

During the orientation period, the retardates were shown each department to familiarize with them the various plant operations. The retardates learned how to use basic electronic tools and how to set up and maintain a typical assembly plant work station. Work regulations were explained, including the use of time clocks and work breaks. Emphasis was placed on helping the retardates understand supervisory relationships and their role. Actual job training skills were planned from October to June. Retardates were trained in either industrial or commercial business skills. Their success was evaluated during the orientation period.

Nine retardates received training on industrial job skills which included soldering, mechanical and electrical assembly, and wiring of harness and cable assemblies.

Six retardates received commercial business training which included clerical skills, such as filing, collating, basic typing, and the use of adding and cash register machines. Banking operations taught included counting and sorting monies, collating and filing banking records, simple book-keeping and processing, and posting books on posting machines.

Impressions and Results

Results proved that the retardates' behavior indicated a total lack of preparation and readiness for the work situation. Results also indicated that their classroom academic curriculum or training was quite unrelated to the vocational environment. Academic achievement had been between a third- and fifth-grade level, but the majority of the retardates had great difficulty in transferring and applying these skills to a work-training situation.

The most unique result obtained in the prevocational training program was that a significantly large number of retardates gained the necessary skills and understanding of a competitive work situation to develop into productive workers.

Neuhaus believes that the experiences in this unique prevocational training program have implications for special education today. The prevocational program clearly points to the fact of the retardates' lack of preparation for the working world. Special education needs a more realistic orientation toward vocational goals, to know about the needs and demands of a working world.

In this author's opinion, academic subjects and the entire curriculum should have some practical application to a vocational future. For example, understanding deductions on a paycheck, reading work regulations, completing personnel forms, and using local transportation.[13]

An audiovisual experiment seeks now to improve training of the mentally retarded through a program of audiovisual slides designed to take account of special learning problems. Twenty-five mentally retarded individuals between the ages of eighteen and thirty with IQ scores of 60 to 80 were selected for the programs. Academic skills are from the third- to fifth-grade level achievement in the basic subjects. Entire work groups are well motivated and produce a normal competitive setting.

The retardates are placed in a department of Abilities, Inc., which best suit their skills. Each retardate is trained for at least four to fi ve job operations. He works alongside a worker who is normal mentally; the retardate is in no way isolated or protected from competitive demands. The supervisor initiates the conventional industrial training period with the retardates and continues the training period relationship until the

347

employee demonstrates an acceptable level of efficiency. It is at that time that the retardate becomes a part of the regular productive work force.

Retarded employees are presently working on job operations which include soldering, electrical and mechanical assembly, wire stripping, tinning, flagging, and laying and lacing of harness and capable accessories. On one of the job contracts, duties of the retardates were stacking laminations, packing and locking of rotor and stator assemblies and brush riggings, and impregnating the rotors and stators.

These and similar jobs are completed for IBM, Republic Aviation, McDonnell Aircraft, Bosch Arma, Ford Instrument, Western Electric, and Remington Rand.

Neuhaus plans to develop audiovisual programs relating to teaching the retarded basic knowledge about tool equipment and typical work or factory procedure and regulations. In this author's opinion, the curriculum of the mentally retarded in the light of these developments, as well as developments in modern technical and industrial society, needs to be oriented around the world of work and industry. This should begin in the elementary grades and continue through secondary school where, in the junior high school, actual work experience can be gained through industry.[14]

Madera School District Plan

The Madera (California) school district plan for a vocational education program which should be adopted to meet the needs of the mentally retarded student is as follows:

Objectives

1. Prepare each person for gainful employment upon completion of vocational instruction.
2. Provide students with career guidance and counseling to prepare for new occupations developed.
3. Provide each person with opportunities and incentives to enter advanced vocational training.
4. Develop a positive attitude toward the world of work by students, teachers, counselors, parents, and the community.
5. Provide career-related instruction in vocational areas.

1. *Vocational agriculture*
   agriculture production
   agriculture supplies and services
   agriculture mechanics
   ornamental horticulture
   agriculture resources
   forestry
2. *Distributive and office education*
   general office clerk
   stenographer
   clerk-typist
   general merchandising
3. *Home Economics*
   homemaking
   comprehensive homemaking
   food management production and services
   clothing and textiles
   fashion merchandising
4. *Industrial trades*
   auto mechanics
   electronics occupations
   millwork and cabinet

Work Experience

Work experience is an extension of the vocational education program and an integral part of the students' total education process. It prepares the mentally retarded student for full-time employment suitable to his abilities and interests, and enables him to work well with others.

Work Experience Education Programs

Exploratory work experience education is a program which provides the opportunities to sample systematically and observe a variety of working conditions.

General work experience education is a program which could provide mentally retarded students opportunities through supervised part-time employment with an overview of working conditions on a variety of jobs. These jobs need not be related to specific occupational goals of the students.

The purpose of vocational work experience would be to assist students in developing and refining those occupational competencies necessary to acquire employment.

Other goals would be to adjust to the employment environment, and to advance to the student occupational choice through a combination of related instruction and paid employment experiences at a work situation.

Cooperative Vocational Education

This is a program which the author believes would easily lend itself to suit the needs of the mentally retarded. It would be a cooperative agreement between the school and the prospective employer so that the mentally retarded student would receive vocational training in the classroom and practical, paid, on-the-job training at work.[15]

On-Campus Work Exploration Program

The most significant innovation in special education for the mentally retarded has been the combined school-work experience programs. Most of these programs involve the simultaneous participation of school and rehabilitation agency personnel. This program is designed to facilitate a successful transition from school to employment. The student usually spends part of the day or week in acquiring work experience and in learning specific job skills. A few programs have been organized so that the student spends full time for a period in on-the-job training and alternates this with a full period of school attendance.[16]

library	laundry
audio-visual section	garage
school offices	school grounds
mimeograph-duplication	custodial services
warehouse	storeroom
counselor's office	nurse's office
athletic section	cafeteria
student's store	

Off-campus training should be next. The mentally retarded students should be assigned to jobs consistent with their abilities and interests. The students should understand all the demands of the job before placement is made. After placement they should be helped to make periodic self-evaluations to supplement the evaluations of their work by the employers and the special education class teacher.

Special students (mentally retarded) should be taught:
1. to follow instructions in detail
2. to be at the right place at the right time
3. to complete assigned tasks without constant urging, guidance, and/or supervision
4. to evaluate work as it is done
5. to be trustworthy — keep hands off things which should not be handled
6. to profit from constructive criticism
7. to recognize when they need help so they may receive it
8. to take responsibility for their mistakes
9. to maintain good standards of conduct and personal appearance
10. to respect the dignity of work.

Girls need to understand the role of a wife and mother and learn how to perform necessary tasks including infant care. Boys need to understand the role of a husband and father and need manual training skills for home maintenance and repair. Also important are extended units of study which will include all facets of consumer education such as:
family budget
insurance
savings
social security
credit
clothing
taxes
supermarket
renting
major appliances and furniture
automobile and travel
knowledge of activities and services available within the community
knowledge of when and where to register to vote — the voting process.

Other Vocational Considerations
Level of vocational expectations

Is the MR realistic about his present and future employability?

Previous job training

What, if any, training opportunities did the MR have, and how did he progress?

Aptitudes and skills

Does the MR possess any ability which can be converted into wage-earning skills?

Work tolerance

Does the MR demonstrate sufficient attention, concentration, and sustained activity to render him potentially employable?

Work history

What kinds of tasks has the MR done which can be used to secure future employment?

Work habits and attitudes

What patterns of behavior and feeling has the MR demonstrated in job or work-life situations?

Economic status

How do the MR family's income and occupational level influence vocational planning?

Vocational expectations

How do the MR's family expectations of the MR influence planning for the MR child?

Social expectations

How do the MR's family expectations relative to sexual and other areas of social adjustment influence vocational programming for the MR?

Employment considerations: job-finding services

How disposed are employment agencies to serve the retarded? How does this fact influence the MR employable?

Job opportunity

How suitable are the vacancies for the retarded individual?

Employer's attitudes

How receptive is management toward hiring retarded workers?

Techniques in Improving Vocational Productive Capacities
Occupational preparation

Providing information dealing with world of work and work-related activities.
>Generalized work training — development of work personality through controlledwork experience.
>Job tryouts — brief periods of work experience in various types of occupations and work activities.
>Occupational training — acquainting the retardates with a specific type of work.
>Skill training — training in specialized skills.
>Employer preparation — acquainting the prospective employer with the assets and liabilities of a retardate.

Identification with work: models

Working in tandem with capable peers with whom the retardate can identify.
Field trips — visits to industrial or business firms in the community in which the retardate is to work.

Transitional work experience – establishing which working conditions, type of work,
and co-worker relationships can be varied and controlled for the purpose of training and assessment.

Suggested High School Curriculum

The following is an example of an EMR Program leading to graduation which could be developed in a high school:

9th Grade
English
general mathematics
general science
health
physical education
work study I (in school work
   experience)

10th Grade
English
general mathematics
state history
biology
physical education
work study II (in school work
   experience)

11th Grade
English
business arithemetic
American history
occupational education
work study III (out-of-school
   experience part-time)
senior science
physical education
one elective
Electives
basic foods 1,2,3
basic clothing 1,2,3
basic general shop
basic any unit shop
beginning typing
driver training
music or choir
band or orchestra
vocational agriculture

12th Grade
English
business arithmetic
home family relations (one
   semester)
sociology (one semester)
physics (one semester)
work study IV (full-time)
physical education
one elective
driver education (in coordination
with the Driver Education Program)

354

At each level – primary, intermediate, junior high, and senior high – the following life problems in our society should be taught and made an integral part of the curriculum. Program A and Program B could alternate between each succeeding year.

Program A
1. health education and sex education
2. homemaking and family living
3. understanding oneself and getting along with others
4. learning to earn a living including work study
5. citizenship.

Program B
1. learning safety rules
2. understanding the physical environment
3. aesthetic appreciation and enjoyment or nature
4. learning to travel and move about
5. use of leisure time.
    Academic skills included in the curriculum should include:
1. reading skills
2. oral written and listening skills
3. arithmetic skills
4. learning to use and manage money.

Learning Basic Skills

In the following suggested school subjects the student should be learning social, occupational, and self-care phabits and other basic skills in preparation for and in conjunction with his later education.
    Suggested curriculum emphasis is as follows:[18]

Young Elementary, ages 6-10

readiness	group membership	following directions
communications	dress	completing tasks
arithmetic	manners	manipulation
oral language	self care	(physical tasks)
development	health play	

355

intermediate, ages 10-13
quantitative concepts
qualitative concepts
practical science
family membership
physical development

Senior High, ages 15-18
consumer buying politics
practical law – driver education
insurance
community services
leisure time – physical education
adult social roles
work study
introduction into practical world of work
labor laws
job training placement

Junior High, ages 13-15
consumer buying awareness
practical law
news media
job description
budgeting
insurance
community orientation
social roles
vocational information
field trips to industry

Vocational Courses

Courses to be added to the school special education program which the author believes would benefit the mentally retarded in the world of work are as follows:

Industrial Education Curriculum – 10th Grade
drafting
general graphics
general crafts
advertising and display arts
printing
general electricity
general metalwork or machine shop
general woodwork
automotive mechanics

cabinet and millwork
cooking and baking
dry cleaning
electronics
radio and TV repair
refrigeration and air conditioning
tailoring
trowel trades
automotive body repair and re-finishing

Vocational Curriculum
aviation and power plant
general electricity I and II
general metalwork I and II
general woodwork I and II

Industrial Arts Curriculum — 11th Grade
drafting I and II
graphic arts I and II
general crafts I and II

11th Grade Vocational Curriculum
drafting
advertising arts and design
printing
industrial electricity
machine shop
automotive mechanics
automotive body repair and
  refinishing
cabinet and millwork
cooking and baking

cosmetology
Diesel engines
dry cleaning
electronics
radio and TV repair
refrigeration and air conditioning
tailoring
trowel trades
aviation power plant

12th Grade Industrial Arts Curriculum
drafting
general metalwork I, II, III

general electricity I, II, III
general woodwork I, II, III

12th Grade Vocational Curriculum
drafting
advertising arts and design
printing
industrial electricity
machine shop
automotive mechanics
automobile body repair and
  refinishing
cabinet and millwork
trowel trades

cooking and baking
cosmetology
Diesel engine
dry cleaning
electronics
radio and TV repair
refrigeration and air conditioning
tailoring
aviation power plants

Special Technical and Vocational Curriculum

Training Area	Specific Curriculum
Technical	basic technology
	construction technology (architecture)
	electronic technology
	mechanical technology
vocational	advertising arts and design
	automotive body repair and refinishing
	automotive mechanics
	cabinet and millwork
	cooking and baking
	cosmetology
	Diesel engine
	drafting
	dry cleaning and laundry
	electronics
	industrial electricity
	machine shop
	printing
	radio and TV repair

Diversified Cooperative Training

The author believes there should be community business and industrial establishents which are used as training agencies for a variety of occupations. There would be four hours of study in the high school and four hours of on-the-job training with regular beginning wages, supervised by the coordinator.

Cooperative Business Education

Cooperative business education is designed for on-the-job training in office occupations as a part of the regular special education program at the high school level.

Office Machines: Students in the office machine laboratory develop skills in the use of office machines such as adding and bookkeeping machines, adding-listing machines and rotary and key-driven calculating machines.

Clerical Office Practice: This course trains general office workers. It provides experience in the use of the typewriter for office work, job filing, record keeping, use of the telephone, switchboard operation, use of calculators, adding machines, typing stencils and masters, operation of duplicating machines, transcriptions, and other general office activities.

Comprehensive Vocational Program

This type of program deals with the full range of vocations and training that calls for a combined knowledge of mathematics and science which are involved in shop work as in carpentry and construction work.

Academic Subjects

General Vocabulary: This subject is for high-school-level students. Specific emphasis should include stress in word building, context clues, and word meanings. The course affords practice in the proper usage of new words.

Debate: This course includes the fundamentals of argumentation and discussion, as well as procedures in speech techniques, and research skills.

Creative Writing: This course gives the student practical experiences in various forms of writing and creativity.[19]

Occupations for the MR

The following occupations have been shown to be appropriate for the mentally retarded.[20] The author feels that the last two years of senior high school included in the curriculum for the mentally retarded should be special occupational preparatory classes.

assembler	golf course worker
ballroom furniture man	machine operator
beauty shop attendant	maid
bottling plant worker	messenger
bricklayer assistant	motel yardsman
cafeteria counter worker	moving van loader
carpet worker	orderly
cement worker	porter
cemetery worker	routeman

359

Richard S. Greene

check room attendant
child care worker
construction worker
cleaning woman
Department of Public Works
 Employee
dry wall sander
elevator operator
factory worker
laundress
dishwasher

shoe repairman
sales clerk
theater usher
waiter
waitress
warehouseman
seamstress
sewing machine operator
mender
marker

References

1. Halbert B. Robinson and Nancy M. Robinson, *The Mentally Retarded Child – A Psychological Approach* (New York: McGraw-Hill Book Co. 1965), pp. 479-506.
2. Nicholas Hobbs, "Client-Centered Psychotherapy." From James L. McCary and Daniel E. Sheer, eds., *Six Approaches to Psychotherapy* (New York: Dryden Press, 1955), pp. 11-61.
3. S.R. Slavson, "Group Psychotherapies." From James L. McCary and Daniel E. Sheer, eds., *Six Approaches to Psychotherapy* (New York: Dryden Press, 1955), pp. 129-178.
4. Federick Thorne, "Directive and Eclectic Personality Counseling." From James L. McCary and Daniel E. Sheer, eds., *Six Approaches to Psychotherapy* (New York: Dryden Press, 1955), pp. 234-286.
5. J.L. Moreno, "Psychodrama." From James L. McCary and Daniel E. Sheer, *Six Approaches to Psychotherapy* (New York: Dryden Press, 1955), pp. 288-340.
6. Robert A. Harper, *Psychoanalysis and Psychotherapy, Thirty-six Systems* (Englewood Cliffs, N.J.: Prentice-Hall, 1955), pp. 1-173.
7. William J. Maxwell, Robert J. Berstein, and Judith Berstein, *The Philosophy and History of Education* (New York: Monarch Press, 1963), pp. 109-114.
8. Richard Greene, *Forgotten Children: Techniques in Teaching the Mentally Retarded* (San Rafael, Cal.: Leswing Press, 1972), pp. 69-70.
9. Reginald C. Orem, ed., *Montessori Today* (New York: G.P. Putnam's Sons, 1971), pp. 67-69, 167-168, 183.
10. Bernice B. Baumgartner, *Guiding the Retarded Child: AN Approach to a Total Education Program* (New York: John Day Co., 1965), pp. 68-74, 112-114, 134, 136.

11. Roy DeVerl Willey and Kathleen Barnette Waite, *The Mentally Retarded Child, Identification, Acceptance and Curriculum* (Springfield, Ill.: Charles C. Thomas, 1964), pp. 73-191.

12. Max F. Baer and Edward C. Roeber, *Occupational Information: The Dynamics of Its Nature and Use* (Chicago, Ill.: Science Research Associates, 1964), pp. 474-482.

13. Edmund C. Neuhaus, "A Unique Pre-Vocational Program for Educable Retardates," *Mental Retardation,* August 1965, pp. 19-22. (Washington D.C.: American Association on Mental Deficiency).

14. Edmund C. Neuhaus, "Audiovisual Job Training for Mentally Retarded," *Rehabilitation Record,* March April 1964, pp. 32-37 (Washington D.C.: Vocational Rehabilitation Administration).

15. *MUSD Action,* Madera (California) Unified School District, November 14, 1972 pp. 1-2.

16. Rick Heber, ed., *Special Problems in Vocational Rehabilitation of the Mentally Retarded,* Madison Wis., November 3-7, 1963 (Washington, D.C.; U.S. Department of Health, Education, and Welfare), pp. 41, 56-60.

17. Jacques L. Cross, *Guidelines for the Administration of EMR Programs* (Columbus, O.: Ohio Department of Education, 1970), pp. 19-20, 32-33.

18. *Philosophy of Special Education for Mentally Retarded Minors* (Sacramento, Cal.: State Department of Education), p. V.

19. Joseph Hall, Registration and Educational Guidance Procedures, *Procedures Manual for Secondary School Personnel,* Curriculum Bulletin No. 1-G (Miami, Fla.: Dade County Public Schools, January 1962), pp. 41-73.

20. Paul V. Voelker, *A Curriculum Guide for Teachers of Mentally Retarded Pupils,* rev. ed. (Detroit, Mich.: Detroit Public Schools, Board of Education, 1964), pp. 108-124.

A Developmental Approach to the Mentally Handicapped Juvenile Offender: A Working Hypothesis

Byron R. Holmgren, Ed.D.
Coordinator of Special Education Programs
Troy State University

Abstract

Recent developments in the field of the mentally handicapped juvenile offender were reviewed. Several aspects of this social problem were discussed from a psychosocial developmental point of view. Critical developmental factors were examined which could influence the mentally handicapped youngster's decision to engage in delinquent behavior during the developmental period. An intervention model was proposed for dealing with the potential offender in the community. Suggestions were made relative to assisting the mentally handicapped youngster develop socialization skills, which have potential for enabling him to make a lifetime adjustment and become a contributing member of society.

One of the major interests manifested by special educational professionals during the 1970's was the concern for the mentally handicapped juvenile offender, hereafter referred to as the handicapped offender. A prolific assortment of literature has been generated through professional journals, monographs, institutes, workshops, symposiums, and research grants from governmental agencies. Much of the literature deals with such topics as criminal justice for the mentally handicapped offender, legal rights, rehabilitation, and special treatment programs for this population.

In contrast, a cursory review of the new texts on mental retardation reveals very little attention being given to the mentally handicapped offender, either from a theoretical or rehabilitative perspective. In view of the earlier literature on this topic, which attempted to equate mental retardation with criminal behavior, it is surprising that only a few writers have attempted to examine the handicapped offender in terms of developmental phenomena. The remainder of this chapter will discuss several developmental aspects of the handicapped offender, and suggest a hypothetical intervention model.

Child Development

Child development embraces essentially two broad maturational stages: the biological and the psychosocial. Human growth and development is an evolutionary process based upon a universally experienced sequence of biological, psychological, and social events.

Biological Development

The multiple factors contributing to human development are present at conception, and continue their influence throughout the span of life. As Robinson and Robinson (1976) have stated,

> This miracle of development follows a set of specifications and a timetable which are a joint product of the individual's unique biologic inheritance and the unique environment in which he lives. In view of the complexity of the process, it is clear that the possibilities of serious errors during the developmental period are almost infinite. (p. 51)

Excluding genetic aberations, hormonal problems, hereditary disease, metabolic error, or serious insult to the central nervous system, the mentally handicapped youngster develops very much like the normal child, albeit, at a slower rate. The reader who is interested in a penetrating examination of the developmental aspects of mental retardation should consult Cleland (1978).

Psycosocial Development

There are many psychological and social factors that contribute to the condition of mental retardation. Prominent among these factors are poor physical health, lack of cultural stimulation, and environmental deprivation. Approximately 75 percent of all mentally handicapped individuals fall into the cultural-familial etiological classification (Zigler, 1967). Sufficient evidence has accumulated during the past quarter century to support the notion that poverty, sociocultural deprivation, maternal deprivation, or a combination of these factors play a significant role in the perpetuation of the social ineffectiveness of mildly mentally handicapped individuals (Birch & Gussow, 1970; Ingalls, 1978; Zigler, 1970). For an extensive discussion of the devastating effects of poverty on human growth and development, the reader is referred to Hurley (1969).

The Retarded Offender

Recent literature seems to indicate that the mildly mentally handicapped juvenile offender is not noticeably different from the nonhandicapped in terms of delinquent behavior. However, a major distinction is made in view of the intellectual deficit and defective label attached to the offender (Cook & Solway, 1974; Miller, Zumoff & Stephens, 1974; Olczak & Stott, 1976).

Etiology and Classifications

Over the years there has been a gradual change in professional thinking regarding the causal relationship between mental retardation and criminal behavior. Santamour & West (1977) conclude that ". . . the disproportionate number of retarded offenders is a legal and administrative artifact, and not necessarily the result of a direct causal relationship between mental retardation and criminal behavior" (p. 5). The problem of labeling and classifying the handicapped offender is confounded by diagnostic classifications (Fitzhugh, 1973; Nassi & Abramowitz, 1976; Schwarz & Ruggieri, 1971; Steinbock, 1976) and epidemiological data (Olczak & Stott, 1976). Menolascino (1974) reports that since the time of Goddard's study in 1914, over 450 separate investigations on the intellectual aspects of handicapped offenders have been published, without providing conclusive evidence that intelligence plays a major role in delinquent or criminal behavior.

Characteristics

Since mental retardation is basically a cognitive deficit, researchers have given more emphasis to this aspect of development. The literature contains numerous studies dealing with the cognitive traits of the mentally handicapped and their learning processes. In contrast, very little research has been conducted with respect to affective characteristics (MacMillan, 1977).

Personality

Santamour & West (1977) have reviewed several studies which have attempted to delineate the personality traits of the handicapped offender. These traits appear to be similar to the characteristics exhibited by the general retarded population, and may be subsumed as follows: inadequate self perception, reduced tolerance for frustration, an inability to delay gratification, weak impulse control, and a lack of motivational drive. A depreciated self-concept appears to be one of the chief personality characteristics of the mentally handicapped person (Cobb, 1966; Rosen, 1975).

Delinquent Behavior

The handicapped offender becomes involved in criminal or illegal acts because he frequently misunderstands how to use institutions in society to attain desired goals in a legally sanctioned manner, and reacts to his own feelings of frustration without being able to fully evaluate the consequences of his own behavior. By definition, the handicapped offender is a socialization failure. The writer hypothesizes that the handicapped offender engages in illegal activity because he has not been adequately prepared, during the developmental period, to make appropriate value judgments with respect to life's choices. It has become evident that the intellectual level of the handicapped offender is not the primary etiology of his criminal behavior. Inadequate personality development and limited socialization skills play a significant part in the handicapped offender's decision to commit a crime (Sternlicht & Kasdan, 1976; Yochelson & Samenow, 1976).

Habilitation

Professionals in the field of mental retardation and corrections feels that the handicapped offender is in greater need of habilitation rather than rehabilitation, and, consequently, is a misfit in their system of services (Linkenhoker, 1978; Santamour & West, 1977). In view of correctional systems' failure to meet the habilitative needs of the mentally handicapped individual, the writer proposes a hypothetical construct as an intervention model for dealing with the potential offender who is mentally handicapped.

The writer takes the position that in order for society to adequately prepare a child for life adjustment, the three basic institutions (home, church, and school) must share a cooperative role in the socialization of the developing individual. Figure 1 illustrates the relationship between

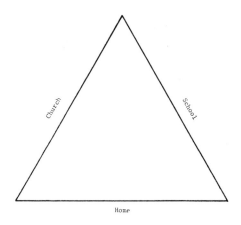

Figure 1. The institutional triangle.

the three institutions in providing knowledge, social skills, religious beliefs, and ethical principles for preparing the mentally handicapped child for life. The developmental period covered by this construct would be from age 0 to 21. The home and church would be responsible for assisting the child in acquiring socialization skills and religious and ethical principles during the first five years of life. From age 5 through age 21 public and/or private schools would join the home and church in helping the individual to realize these goals.

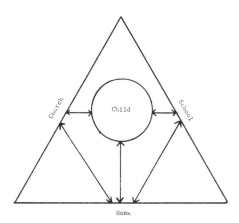

Figure 2. The interrelationship between the developing mentally handicapped child and the three significant social institutions.

Figure 2 illustrates the interaction principle that operates between these three institutions during the developmental period (age 0-21). The reader should observe that in the two constructs the home serves a foundation or base for promoting child and adolescent development. The other two institutions serve in complementary roles. It should also be noted that in Figure 2 the child is the focus of the interaction between the three supporting institutions. The basic premise here is that coordination, as well as cooperation between the three institutions, is required in order to provide a complete socialization process for the mentally handicapped child.

The Home

The family and home represent the basic social unit in our society. Parental emotions and attitudes play an important part in providing the kind of atmosphere that is conducive to child growth and development. Family structure, values, and religious belief exert a strong influence on child rearing practices. A common misconception about mentally handicapped individuals is that they are retarded in every dimension of their being. According to Jordan (1972):

> This oversimplification ignores the fact that retarded youngsters, like all young people, develop as a result of the way they are raised. Early training determines later effectiveness in retarded youngsters as well as in normal children. Only the more profoundly retarded child is an exception to this rule. (p. 111).

It has been demonstrated in the studies conducted by Skeels (1965) that adoptive children, whose biological mothers were mentally retarded, are achieving as adults at levels consistently higher than would have been predicted from the profiles of the biological parents. Clearly, the environmental impact provided by the adoptive parents made a difference. Child rearing practices, maternal attitudes, and family values help to mold the personality of mentally handicapped children in the same manner they do with normal children. In contrast, poor child rearing practices do contribute to delinquency (Robins, 1966).

The Church

The role of religion and the church in the parental acceptance of a mentally handicapped is well documented (Stubblefield, 1965). However, the role of the church goes beyond resolving what might be termed a theological crisis in families with mentally handicapped children. The role of the church must include counseling, religious education, and social work that will assist parishioners and members of the community in accepting the handicapped as a member of society. Perhaps the most important role of the church is to help the mentally handicapped youngster achieve a positive approach to his disability. In addition, the church must help in establishing values for the mentally

369

handicapped person and stimulate the faith and courage to live by these precepts.

Clergymen must interpret to other members of their congregation the needs of the mentally handicapped youngsters for attention, acceptance, affection, trust, respect, and love. The ministry of the church must assist mentally handicapped youth in achieving emotional stability and socially acceptable behavior. Finally, the church's ministry to mentally handicapped children and youth must be relevant to the general and specific problems created by the developmental disability.

The School

Special education services for the mentally handicapped should be able to provide many of the essential skills not addressed extensively by the home and church. Furthermore, special education should reinforce many of the values and socialization skills being taught in the home and church. It is the contention of this writer that if special education classes measure up to their unique conceptualization, then the curriculum and skills being taught should serve as a deterrent to the delinquent prone mentally handicapped youngster.

Teachers

Special education teachers are prepared to acquire a rather extensive repertoire of professional competencies that will enable them to deal with a variety of learning skills, situations, and behavioral problems in the special class. The special education teacher is prepared to serve as a committed professional educator, and should be knowledgeable regarding curriculum design and modification for exceptional children and youth. This same teacher is also prepared in behavioral management techniques and has acquired knowledge and skills for selecting a variety of appropriate learning resources for her students. Moreover, the special class teacher is prepared to provide a full educational menu in the cognitive, psychomotor and affective domains for meeting the formal educational needs of the mentally handicapped.

Curriculum Priorities

In the opinion of this writer, special education as a professional field has reached full maturity in this decade. As a result of this maturation, special education teachers are able to do more for exceptional children than at any previous period in our brief history. It is an exciting era for special education professionals. With the present level of our professional sophistication and our abundant resources, it is fitting that we briefly examine what we, as a profession, can do to reduce the number of handicapped offenders.

There are three curriculum areas in special education that need to be further developed and expanded for exceptional children and youth; they are: personality development, social learning, and prevocational preparation. These three curriculum areas appear especially pertinent to the potential handicapped offender.

Personality development. Cromwell (1967) has delineated five arbitrary levels of personality development applicable to the mentally handicapped. The five phases of this developmental pattern involves basic boundry discrimination, intact hedonic functioning, development of a conceptual motivational system, the development of effective interpersonal functioning, and the development of awareness of cultural expectations. The last three phases of Cromwell's developmental schema appear to have strong implications for personality development in the mentally handicapped during the adolescent period.

During the conceptual motivational phase of personality development, the mentally handicapped youngster becomes motivated to approach success and avoid failure. In the school setting the mentally handicapped youngster would be encouraged to make decisions that enable him to become more successful and reap a larger reward in the future. Emphasis would be placed upon attending to appropriate cues pertinent to the correctness of his performance. Personal accountability and responsibility would be stressed in this learning environment (Cromwell, 1967).

Cromwell (1967) defines interpersonal functioning as the ability of an individual to conceptualize the feelings, attitudes, and motives of another. "Whether correct or incorrect, the child with interpersonal functioning has a conception of what the other person is thinking and feeling" (p. 75). This level of social interaction is what White (1963) refers to as interpersonal competence. Developing interpersonal competence and effectiveness with mentally handicapped youngsters is a difficult and challenging task for the special education teacher. However, acquisition of interpersonal competence and affective learning must be built into every component of the curriculum if the school is to be effective in developing socialization skills with the mentally handicapped.

The development of cultural responsiveness is what Havighurst (1972) would refer to in his developmental task concept as developing a conscience, morality, a scale of values, and developing attitudes toward social groups and institutions. The delinquent behavior of the handicapped offender is indicative of his defective cultural development. The school, church, and home are in a favorable position to transmit cultural norms to the mentally handicapped youngster.

371

Social learning. A cursory review of any teaching methodology or curriculum guide for the mentally handicapped reveals the concern for developing social competence with this population. Goldstein (1969) has identified the essential characteristics of socio-occupational competence as the goals of the *Social Learning Curriculum (SLC)*. Social competence includes decisions and behaiviors concerned with self-management of personal affairs and establishing and maintaining a family and household. Occupational competence includes securing a job and responsible performance on the job. The ultimate goal of the *SLC* is to develop those knowledges and behaviors in the mentally handicapped that will facilitate their assimilation into our society at maturity. The classroom, the home and family, and the neighborhood are united in providing broad learning experiences for the mentally handicapped in this curriculum design.

The *SLC* as a curriculum construct represents the framework for developing a comprehensive instructional program for the mentally handicapped from grades K through 12. It is this and similar curriculum models that will enable mentally handicapped children and youth to acquire essential socialization skills for lifetime adjustment in a complex society.

Prevocational training. Today there is considerable emphasis being placed upon employment of the mentally handicapped. If special educators are insisting upon equal employment opportunities for this population, then they must adequately prepare their clients to compete for positions in the labor market. Employability, competence, and success on the job are inextricably linked to personality development, socialization skills, and practical prevocational training. Every aspect of career development for the mentally handicapped must be incorporated into the curriculum from early childhood through adolescent vocational training. Basic academic subjects such as reading, spelling, speech and language development, writing, and arithmetic must be carefully interfaced with the practical aspects of the prevocational curriculum from the first day that the mentally handicapped child is enrolled in a school setting. Much valuable time is misappropriated and ultimately lost during the early developmental period because the curriculum and school program have not been coordinated for the mentally handicapped. Several model prevocational curriculums for the mentally handicapped (Cormany, 1975; Goldstein, 1969; Greene, 1972; Smith, 1974) and programs (Colella, 1974; Freeland, 1969) have been developed during the past decade.

Summary

The preceeding sections have dealt with several developmental aspects of the handicapped offender. Several factors were examined which could influence the mentally handicapped youngster's decision to engage in delinquent behavior during the developmental period. An intervention model was proposed for dealing with the potential offender in the community. Suggestions were made relative to assisting the mentally handicapped youngster develop socialization skills, which have potential for enabling him to make a lifetime adjustment and become a contributing member of society.

The writer has indicated throughout this chapter that the process of human development occurs in a social matrix composed of people, institutions, cultural norms, interpersonal attitudes and behaviors. If the proposed working hypothesis and hypothetical constructs are worthy of consideration, they must be tested in the mentally handicapped youngster's cultural milieu.

References

Birch, H.G., & Gussow, J.D. *Disadvantaged children: Health, nutrition & school failure.* New York: Grune & Stratton, 1970.

Cleland, C.C. *Mental retardation: A developmental approach.* Englewood Cliffs NJ: Prentice-Hall, 1978.

Cobb, H.V. The attitude of the retarded person towards himself. Paper read at International League of Societies for the Mentally Handicapped 3rd International Congress, Paris, March, 1966.

Colella, H.V. Career development center: A modified high school for the handicapped. In S.J. Urban & T. Tsuji (Eds.), *The special needs of student in vocational education: selected readings.* New York: Arno Press, 1974.

Cook, T.H., & Solway, K.S. WISC subtest patterns of delinquent male retardates. *Psychological Reports,* 1974, *35,* 22.

Cormany, R.B. A careers unit for the junior high EMR student. *Education and Training of the Mentally Retarded,* 1975, *10,* 151-154.

Cromwell, R.L. Personality evaluation. In A.A. Baumeister (Ed.), *Mental Retardation: Appraisal, education, and rehabilitation.* Chicago: Aldine Publishing, 1967.

Fitzhugh, K.B. Some neuropsychological features of delinquent subjects. *Perceptual and Motor Skills,* 1973, *36,* 494.

Freeland, K.H. *High school work study program for the retarded.* Springfield IL: Charles C. Thomas, 1969.

Goldstein, H. Construction of a social learning curriculum. *Focus on Exceptional Children,* 1969, *1,* 1-10.

Greene, R. *Forgotten children: Techniques in teaching the mentally retarded.* San Rafael CA: Leswing Press, 1972.

Havighurst, R.J. *Developmental tasks and education* (3rd ed.). New York: David McKay, 1972.

Hurley, R. *Poverty and mental retardation: A causal relationship.* New York: Random House, 1969.

Ingalls, R.P. *Mental retardation: The changing outlook.* New York: John Wiley & Sons, 1978.

Jordan, T.E. *The mentally retarded* (3rd ed.). Columbus OH: Charles E. Merrill, 1972.

Linkenhoker, D. Juvenile delinquency and mental retardation. In L.E. Beutler & R. Greene (Eds.), *Special problems in child and adolescent behavior.* Westport CT: Technomic Publishing, 1978.

MacMillan, D.L. *Mental retardation in school and society.* Boston: Little, Brown & Co., 1977.

Menolascino, F.J. The mentally retarded offender. *Mental Retardation,* 1974, *12,* 7-11.

Miller, C.K., Zumoff, L., & Stephens, B. A comparison of reasoning skills and moral judgments in delinquent, retarded, and normal adolescent girls. *Journal of Psychology,* 1974, *86,* 261-268.

Nassi, A.J., & Abramowitz, S.I. From phrenology to psychosurgery and back again: Biological studies in criminality. *American Journal of Orthopsychiatry,* 1976, *46,* 591-607.

Olczak, P.V., & Stott, M.W.R. Family court placement of mentally retarded juvenile offenders and the use of intelligence testing: A reply to Sussman. *Criminal Justice and Behavior,* 1976, *3,* 23-28.

Robins, L.N. *Deviant children grown up: A sociological and psychiatric study of sociopathic personality.* Baltimore: Williams & Wilkins, 1966.

Robinson, N.M., & Robinson, H.B. *The Mentally retarded child* (2nd ed.). New York: McGraw-Hill, 1976.

Rosen, M. Independence for the mentally retarded. *Intellect,* 1975, *103,* 371-375.

Santamour, M., & West, B. *The mentally retarded offender and corrections* (National Institute of Law Enforcement and Criminal Justice). Washington DC: U.S. Government Printing Office, 1977.

Schwarz, B.E., & Ruggieri, B.A. *You can raise decent children.* New Rochelle NY: Arlington House, 1971.

Skeels, H.M. Effects of adoption on children from institutions. *Children,* 1965, *12,* 33-34.

Smith, R.M. (Ed.). *Clinical teaching: Methods of instruction for the retarded* (2nd ed.). New York: McGraw-Hill, 1974.

Steinbock, E.A. A definitional framework: Who is the retarded offender? In P.L. Browning (Ed.), *Rehabilitation and the retarded offender.* Springfield IL: Charles C. Thomas, 1976.

Sternlicht, M., & Kasdan, M.B. Criminal behavior in the mentally retarded: A psychoanalytic interpretation. *Transnational Mental Health Research Newsletter,* Spring 1976, *18,* pp. 2-4.

Stubblefield, H.W. Religion, parents and mental retardation. *Mental Retardation,* 1965, *3,* 8-11.

White, R.W. (Ed.). *The study of lives: Essays on personality in honor of Henry A. Murray.* New York: Atherton Press, 1963.

Yochelson, S., & Samenow, S.E. *The criminal personality* (Vol. 1). New York: Jason Aronson, 1976.

Zigler, E. Familial mental retardation: A continuing dilemma. *Science,* 1967, *155,* 292-298.

Zigler, E. Social class and the socialization process. *Review of Educational Research,* 1970, *40,* 87-110.

Selecting a Treatment Approach that Employs On-Line Staff as Behavior Change Agents*

Robert R. Smith

Abstract

Contemporary correctional administrators at the juvenile and adult levels of institutionalization are faced with the perplexing task of implementing effective behavior change strategies in correctional programs. This chapter provides a cursory review of the "medical" and "social learning" models of human intervention as well as examples of the concomitant staff training methods that have been developed within both such models.

Introduction

Contemporary correctional administrators have acknowledged the need to develop the interpersonal skills of correctional staff so taht the staff will support and aid whatever intervention strategy that is operative in the correctional setting. Because many such strategies are currently being used, it is often difficult to decide which one or combination to adopt. Currently, two major intervention strategies for juvenile or adult offender rehabilitation confront the administrator: the psychodynamic or "medical" model, by far the most prevalent, and the environmental or "social learning" model. In general, it appears that treatment procedures developed within the "medical" model lack an adequate research base, and such procedures also fail to encourage evaluation of their immediate or long-term effectiveness. In contrast, the "social learning" model has been developed within an extensive research framework (basic and applied) which stresses the importance of objective measurement of observable behavior and the importance of internal accountability and outcome effectiveness.

In this chapter, intervention strategies and concomitant staff training at two California institutions for delinquents and one Alabama institution for young adult offenders are briefly reviewed. Staff training procedures from the Alabama institution that were developed within the "social learning" model are more extensively presented and provide correctional administrators from both the juvenile and adult correctional settings with an example of how to develop such training.

General Comparison of the "Medical" and "Social Learning" Models

Most programs developed within the behavior change orientation in juvenile and adult corrections have been derived from psychodynamic or "medical" theories of personality. As Milan and McKee (1974) point out adherents of the "medical" model view deviant behavior as analogous to physical dysfunctioning. Antisocial behavior is interpreted as "symptomatic" of an underlying "mental illness" and the attempts to remediate the behavioral disturbance focus on restructuring basic personality constructs. Typically, these programs are not evaluated in terms of changes in the problem behavior itself, but in a less measurable change embodied in personality or attitude.

Such programs, in general, have naturally emphasized the role of line staff in rehabilitation and the knowledge and skills of either traditional psychotherapists (e.g. Fenton, 1961; Kassebaum, Ward and Wilner, 1971) or human relations experts (e.g. Frazier, 1972; Katrin, 1974). Line staff training in such programs has obviously stressed an understanding of the psychodynamic theories of personality or the importance of communication and facilitation.

In comparison to the "medical model" intervention strategies, adherents of the "social learning" model view deviant behavior as being learned. The principles underlying its acquisition and maintenance are viewed as being no different from those governing the acquisition and maintenance of any other behavior. Both deviant and non-deviant behavior are conceptualized as "normal," that is, the same basic laws and principles are assumed to underlie all forms of behavior. It is the environmental experiences of individuals which determine differing behavior patterns. Diagnosis in the social learning model requires precise specification of the problem behavior and the environmental conditions which control and maintain it. The objectives of treatment are to reduce the frequency of the problem behavior, to prevent the learning of additional undesired behavior, and to replace it with adaptive alternatives maintained by appropriate environmental contingencies (e.g. Bandura, 1969; Franks, 1969; Yates, 1970).

The social learning model, like the medical model, has also relied primarily on trained professional staff to implement behavior change programs. However, a large number of behavior modification projects have demonstrated the effective use of a wide variety of personnel as behavior change agents. For example, Ayllon and Wright (1972) and Craighead, Kazdin and Mahoney (1976) have revealed that behavior change paraprofessionals are being used in a number of settings including mental hospitals, public schools, group homes, and correctional settings. Smith, Milan, Wood and McKee (1976) also report on the successful use of correctional line staff as behavioral technicians. As reported by Smith et al. (1976), such staff are capable of (1) grasping the basic principles of the social learning approach to the understanding and remediation of human problems; (2) recognizing the role of objectivity, consistency, and reliability in the day-to-day operation of a behavior modification program; and (3) demonstrating the ability to integrate the theoretical orientation and requisite skills by conducting, under the supervision of a qualified professional, an actual behavior change project. A more complete description of this project will follow a cursory review of two projects in the juvenile correctional setting, one of which provides an extension of "medical model" procedures (i.e. Transactional Analysis or TA), the other, an extension of behavior modification procedures. The succeeding, more complete review of a training project involving line-staff as behavioral technicians not only provides sufficient information for a replication, the review adds credence to the value of generating objective measures in rehabilitation. Such measures, in time, need to be further extended to more critical juvenile and adult "free world" behaviors.

Selected Review of Transactional Analysis (TA) and Behavior Modification Application and Training in Juvenile Institutions

Transactional Analysis (TA) is a method of psychotherapy formulated by Berne (Frazier, 1972). Those who advocate TA as a method of intervention stress that the individual client is capable of being autonomous, that he makes his own decisions, and that he is responsible for them. The TA theory holds that decisions are reversible through the therapeutic contact between the patient and the therapist.

The formulation of TA revolves around the assumption that every individual has three ego-states – the Parent, the Adult, and the Child. The Parent is assumed to be derived from the individual's parents and has the potential of being critical, helping, or both. The Adult, on the other hand, observes reality, estimates probabilities, and uses facts to make decisions. The Child has its origin in early childhood experiences and may be adapting to the wishes of the internal Parent or acting on its own.

The TA therapist attempts to help the client to have a clearer understanding of his three ego-states. As described by Frazier (1972),

"The client learns to shut off his own internal destructive forces (the critical Parent), to gain a more accurate picture of himself as a person (the Adult), and to learn that he can be happy without harming himself and others (the Child) (p. 41)."

Frazier (1972) goes on to explain that

"(as) the individual (delinquent) develops an awareness,

spontaniety, and a capacity for intimacy, he no longer needs delinquent acts to maintain a lopsided equilibrium, and he is more likely to become a productive member of society (p. 41)."

During the spring of 1968, TA was experimentally introduced at the O.H. Close School for Boys in Stockton, California as the primary treatment model. Such an undertaking was part of a larger experiment, The Youth Center Project, in which behavior modification as an intervention strategy was simultaneously introduced in a nearby juvenile institution and was compared to the TA approach at Close. Staff of both schools were viewed as critical elements in treatment, so consequently, staff training programs were designed and conducted for all employees. The thrust here is on the Close School training regimen. Training at Close consisted of three-day therapy marathons that began with an introductory course in TA followed by a series of therapy sessions. Measures of training impact were based on the staff's perceptions of the marathons. There was a wide variety of responses to the training. One academic teacher believed that the marathon was a waste of time and another resented being forced into something over which he had no control. A social worker indicated that the marathon surpassed all of his expectations and that he would never again be the same. Jesness (1975) provides additional evaluation for the two general intervention strategies. Just prior to the implementation of both programs and two years later, both staffs were asked how they perceived the social climate of their institutions. Before implementation, both staffs viewed the social climate as similar. However, two years later, the TA staff were more convinced that Close School residents were being encouraged to be self-sufficient and independent and were receiving psychotherapeutic treatment that fostered insight and autonomy when compared with the behavior modification staff at Karl Holton.

However, as reported by Frazier (1972) and Jesness (1975), both Close and Holton releasees' recidivism rates were ten percent less than those of comparable releasees from other California juvenile institutions. As noted by Jesness (1975), perceptions of the institutions' social climates seemingly showed little or no relationship to successful adjustment outside such settings, but further research in this area was indicated before specific conclusions were drawn. At the very least, the Karl Holton model has provided procedures that seemingly can produce more reliable

381

measures of how observable phenomena (environmental changes) might contribute to successful postrelease adjustment. The Close School model is less capable of providing such measures.

More Complete Review of Line-Staff Behavior Modification Training

The early work of the Experimental Manpower Laboratory for Corrections (EMLC) located at Draper Correctional Center, Elmore, Alabama, consisted of investigating the use of behavior modification and contingency management techniques in the areas of remedial education and vocational skill training (Rehabilitation Research Foundation, 1968). To remedy such deficiencies, the focus of the EMLC was on providing immediate feedback and reinforcement in basic education and vocational training through the use of a programmed instruction (PI) (e.g. Clements and McKee, 1968; Milan and McKee, 1974).

Stemming from the EMLC's work in inmate training programs was an understanding of the key position held by correctional staff in any institutional treatment efforts. The EMLC's Correctional Officer Training Project conducted from May, 1970 to June, 1973, sought to assess the correctional staff's potential to serve as behavioral technicians. As indicated earlier, the behavioral technician is viewed as one who grasps the basic principles of the social learning model and possesses the requisite skills (e.g. objectivity, consistency, and reliability) necessary for the performance under professional supervision of the routine tasks required in the day-to-day operation of a systematic behavior modification program.

Selection of Line-Staff Trainees

A total of 40 correctional officers divided into three groups (15 in each of the first two groups and 10 in the third group) participated in the training program. A control group of 15 nontrained correctional officers was compared to the first two groups of 15 trainees and one control group of 10 nontrained officers was compared to the third group of trainees. Before the training project began, a brief interest questionnaire, to obtain a ranking of interest in training, was administered to the entire correctional officer population at Draper. Results of the questionnaire indicated that all Draper officers were interested in being trained and therefore provided a large sample from which to draw.

In selecting the officers for training, project staff considered the opportunities each officer had for interaction with inmates, obviously, since interaction was important to the application of the behavior modification techniques. Demographically, trainee and control officers ranged in age from 23 to 67 years, with a median age of 50 years. The reported education level ranged from the seventh grade to one year of college; the median grade reported to be completed was the eleventh. Tested education levels from Tests of Adult Basic Education indicated a mean grade level of 6.7 with a range of 3.2 to 10.9. Approximately 90 percent of the officers had lived the greater portion of their lives in Alabama, 65 percent of those in Elmore County (the location of Draper), and 35 percent in bordering counties, most of which, like Elmore County, are agrarian communities.

Training Procedure

For the training of the first two officer groups, the training staff employed a three-phase approach, preplanning, teaching, and review. The preplanning session was designed primarily as a brainstorming period during which strategies for presentations were discussed and a teaching format was formalized.

During the initial stages of the training of the first two groups, the teaching sessions were conducted on a seminar basis in order to stimulate discussion and were three hours long, three days a week. Each of the first two groups began with a problem-census so that the officers' special needs and job requirements could be considered along with planned subject-matter presentation. These sessions also gave the project staff an opportunity to note the trainees' concerns about institutional policies and the treatment of offenders. In turn, the officers were provided opportunities to discuss their own fixed behavior patterns and idealized notions about institution rules. The subsequent sessions presented behavior modification principles and techniques. The training curriculum covered the following subject matter: a historical review of corrections; identifying, defining, observing, recording, and graphing behavior; positive reinforcement and punishment; time-out; escape; avoidance; extinction and stimulus control; schedules of reinforcement; shaping, chaining and fading.

For the third group, self-instructional booklets (Rehabilitation Research Foundation, 1972) were used to present the subject matter; programmed booklets developed from the experiences with the first two groups. Officers were pretested on the material to be presented in each booklet and immediately upon completion were posttested on the same material. The officers completed two booklets per week in the classroom sessions and also attended a two-hour discussion session. Discussions centered on questions regarding the material and on recommendations for planned revisions of booklets.

For the first two groups of officers, practicum exercises were conducted after they completed the classroom portions of their training. Each of the first two groups of officers was subdivided into groups of five, each meeting with training staff in one-hour sessions three days a week. The practicum phase provided the officers an opportunity to practice behavioral management techniques in the institutional setting. Similar practicum exercises were planned for the third group of trainees, but, due to a turnover in the institution administration and a subsequent shift of institutional concerns, they were not begun.

Assessment of Training

A number of procedures were employed to assess the impact of training on the officers' performance. The most objective of the measures was an instrument (*Behavioral Observation Index*) designed to provide behavioral descriptions of officers' performance in the job situation. Another indicator of officers' performance was an inmate evaluation of the officers' ability to deal effectively with inmates. The officers' mastery of the principles and techniques of behavior modification was also evaluated – practicum exercises conducted by the first two groups of officers were evaluated for accuracy and consistency and the third group was tested before and after completion of the training booklets. A posttraining opinion questionnaire designed to elicit officers' impressions of the training was also administered.

The *Behavioral Observation Index* (BOI) developed by Witherspoon (1971) was used in the training project to obtain empirical data concerning the officers' behavior on the job. The original BOI included nine behavior indices which measured the effects of training on the officers' interactions with inmates. During the course of the training the BOI was modified to focus exclusively on officer/inmate interactions. Seventeen trained officers and fifteen controls were observed using the modified BOI that included the following items: (1) number of interactions with inmates, (2) percent personal interactions with inmates, (3) percent personal interactions with inmates initiated by the officer, (4) verbal contact score (content and tone of interactions), and (5) behavioral response score (percent positive reinforcement in interaction).

An *inmate evaluation* of the entire officer population at Draper was conducted before training was begun and after completion of each of the three training groups. A total of 56 randomly selected inmates evaluated the officers along four dimensions: (1) general caliber, (2) punitiveness, (3) concern with inmate welfare, and (4) fairness. The names of all officers were typed on index cards and the inmates ranked each of them from 1 (best) to 5 (worst).

The *practicum exercises* provided the opportunity to assess the ability of the first two groups of officers to apply the principles of the "social learning" approach in on-the-job situations. The specific behaviors dealt with in the practicum exercises were not necessarily important rehabilitation efforts, but were designed to be teaching devices for the officers in training. The officers were asked to select what they viewed to be "bothersome" inmate behaviors to target and consequate. Two members of the project staff visited each officer on the job in order to observe potential behaviors with which the officer might work. After the project staff and the officers agreed upon a behavior, the officers then collected baseline data. The data were discussed in small groups and the officers were encouraged to make suggestions for the correction of the problem. Each checkpoint in their practicum exercises — observing, graphing, correction (treatment), etc. — was correlated with the training material presented.

The *booklet tests* which were administered to the third group of officers before and after each programmed booklet consisted of multiple choice questions keyed to the content of each booklet. Two measures of performance were maintained for the group of officers who completed the booklets: (1) average score on pre- and posttests, and (2) the amount of time required to complete each booklet.

A *post-training questionnaire* was administered approximately four months following the training of the second group surveying both the first and second groups of officer trainees. The questinnaire was developed to provide information in two general areas: (1) training effectiveness and (2) correctional officers' reactions to the training. Officers were also asked to evaluate the training curriculum and to suggest institutional changes that would facilitate the training.

Results

Observations using the BOI indicated that more trained officers (38 percent) increased the frequency of their interaction with inmates than did non-trained officers (7 percent) $X2 = 4.43$, df $= 1$, p $< .05$) (Smith, Jenkins & Hart, 1973). In addition, more trained officers (76 percent) increased the frequency with which they used positive reinforcement in interactions with inmates than did non-trained officers (43 percent) $X2 = 3.68$, df $= 1$, p $< .05$). No significant differences were observed in the three remaining indices.

The *offender evaluation* suggested a trend for the trained officers to show greater changes (improvement) from pre- to posttraining evaluation as viewed by offenders than did the non-trained officers, although none of the differences were statistically significant. For instance, 10 of the 16 trained officers (63 percent) were seen by the offender group as increasing in their general caliber, i.e., in their overall effectiveness in dealing with the inmate population; 7 of the 14 non-trained officers (50 percent) increased in effectiveness. Twelve of the 16 trained officers (75 percent) were seen as decreasing in punitive behavior as comapred with only 8 of the 14 non-trained officers (57 percent). In interpersonal reactions with offenders, the offenders considered 11 of the 16 trained officers (69 percent) to be more concerned with the offenders' welfare; corresponding figures for the control group were 7 out of 14 (50 percent). It was only in the last category, fairness in dealing with offenders, that the controls showed a greater change than did the trained officers. Nine of the 14 controls (64 percent) gained as compared with 9 of the 16 trained officers (56 percent).

Twenty-six of the 30 original trainees from the first two groups of officers initiated *practicum exercises.* Six of these officers (23 percent) did not begin the treatment phases of their practicum. Reasons ranged from job changes to baseline indication of low occurrence of the behavior. Of the 20 officers who began treatment phases, 13 (65 percent) completed this phase, and nine ¡45 percent) returned to baseline conditions following treatment. One representative practicum exercise, which is described below, was designed to deal with a common institutional problem — encouraging offenders to report to work on time.

Statement of the problem. The officer in charge of the clothing room stated that a large number of men under his supervision were reporting to work late each day. He had previously made use of threats, disciplinary reports, and other aversive techniques, none of which had affected their behavior.

Method. The experimental design used was an A-B-A (reversal) — baseline, correction, and return to baseline. The officer recorded the frequency of tardiness for a 13-day baseline period. Correction consisted of explaining to the offenders that they should arrive to work on time, because their presence was necessary for an efficient work schedule. In addition, the officer announced that all men who had arrived on time would be released at the end of the eight-hour shift and that latecomers would have to report again for the evening shift (an additional two hours). Thus, the prompt offenders would be released earlier than they normally would, while latecomers would have to work an additional two-hour evening shift.

Results. Examination of Figure 1 reveals that the correction procedure initiated on day 14 was highly effective — the median number of men reporting on time increased to 85 percent, which the median test indicates is significantly higher than basline ($X2 = 12.85$, df $= p < .05$). In addition, the variability seen during the first half of the correction phase appears to have been eliminated during the second phase, and a fairly stable, high level of promptness appears to have emerged.

However, it was impossible at this stage to determine whether it was the officer's emphasis upon promptness and teamwork which resulted in the shift in performance, or if it was the contingency of earning the privilege of leaving on time with no further work assignment. During the third phase the officer returned to the work schedule in force during the first 13 days of the project — i.e., all men were required to be on time and work the entire eight-hour shift, plus an additional two hours in the evening. As is evident in Figure 1, the return of the baseline condition resulted in a general deterioration of promptness ($X2 = 8.37$, df $= 1$, $p < .05$).

Discussion. This project demonstrated that it was the correction procedure itself and the systematic application of the

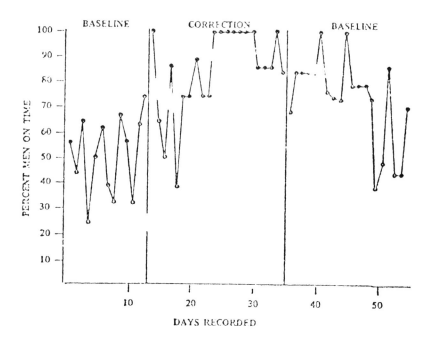

Figure 1. Percentage of Men Reporting to Work on Time
in the Institutional Clothing Room.

specified contingencies which gave the correctional officer the opportunity to become a change agent in the institution. The level of performance evident during baseline revealed the effect of his "best effort" prior to the applications of the methodology taught in the training project.

A second practicum exercise focused upon a similar problem in which the kitchen steward was concerned about men leaving the work area without permission.

Statement of the problem. Because of frequent unauthorized absences the kitchen steward was spending an inordinate amount of time searching for the missing workers. He wanted to avoid disciplinary action which would entail transferring the men to another job assignment, since they had completed the lengthy training regimen necessary for kitchen work.

Method. A reversal design was also employed in this exercise, beginning with a 10 day period of baseline data collection. The correction procedure was initiated on the eleventh day when the officer stated the importance of working a full eight hours. In addition, any man found absent from the work area without permission would be required to make up that time at the end of the shift.

Results. An examination of Figure 2 indicates that during the 10 days in which the correction procedure was in effect there was a significant decrease in the number of unauthorized absences ($X2 = 4.54$, $df = 1$, $p < .05$). Because the steward took annual leave during the return to baseline phase, only 5 days of data were collected. These data suggest that the 10 days of data might have had a lasting effect, since the difference between the latter two phases was not significant ($X2 = .60$, $df = 1$, $p > .05$).

Discussion. It appears that the correction procedure had immediate impact on the problem behavior. However, the number of observation days in the return-to-baseline phase was inadequate for an evaluation of long-term impact.

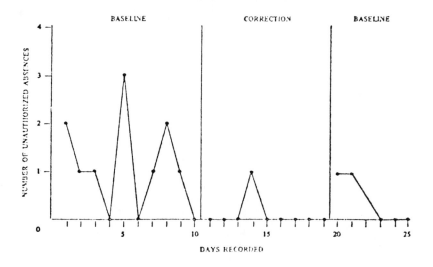

Figure 2. Number of Men Leaving the Kitchen Without Authorization During an Eight-Hour Work Shift.

In summary, the practicum exercises demonstrated that the officers were capable of employing the techniques and principles learned in training to the real-life job situation. The 13 officers who had completed the treatment phase of their individual projects reported satisfaction with the effects of their treatment regimens; in each case, the officer had produced a behavior change in the desired direction. In the projects of the 9 officers who had returned to baseline conditions, the effects of treatment were retained in 8 cases; in one case the effects were reversible.

All officers using the booklets increased their percentage of correct scores from pre- to posttraining. The range of scores was quite wide, ranging from 0 to 91 percent correct on the pretests and from 20 to 100 percent correct on the post-tests. The smallest average gain was 12 percent and the largest 80 percent, indicating that the officers' knowledge of behavior modification techniques and the history of corrections had increased. The average study time per booklet was about 34 minutes, with a range from 24 to 42 minutes.

Table 1 summarizes the *booklet test* data for the ten booklets used in the training. All officers increased from pre- to posttraining on all booklets. The range of scores is quite wide, ranging from 0 to 91 percent correct on the pretests and from 20 to 100 percent correct on the post-tests. The smallest average gain was 12 percent and the largest 80 percent, indicating that the officers' knowledge of behavior modification techniques and the history of corrections had increased. Also indicated in Table 1, the average study time per booklet was about 34 minutes, with a range from 24 to 42 minutes.

The *posttraining questionnaire* administered approximately four months after training indicated that the officer trainees responded favorably to the training situation and to their individual projects. In an overall evaluation of the training project, a significant majority of the officers (70 percent) responded that the most valuable aspect of training was learning new ways of dealing with offenders. Other responses included: learning techniques to use at home, gaining an understanding of why people behave as they do, and encouragement to continue what they have always done. Three officers reported having gained nothing from training.

Officers reported the need for some changes to be made within the institution, most of which would facilitate the use of behavioral techniques in the institution. Included among them were more time to work with offenders, more training, more authority for line staff, more administrative support, improved facilities, and more personnel. Four of the officers saw no need for change.

Summary

The behavior modification training at Draper was designed to test the feasibility of training correctional officers to become behavioral technicians. The training techniques included classroom instruction, discussion groups, practicum exercises, and programmed instructional booklets. The performance of 40 officer trainees was assessed before and after training and compared with 25 non-trained controls. The trained officers demonstrated knowledge of the basic principles of behavior modification as well as the ability to apply them in the institution. Trained officers were rated by project staff and offenders as engaging in more frequent and more positive interaction with offenders. The officers, themselves, described the training project as being beneficial to the performance of their duties.

General Discussion

While the "medical" model treatment program briefly reviewed in this chapter is far from an exhaustive list of all such programs, it is representative of the prevalent treatment efforts in corrections that employ on-line staff as therapeutic agents. Such programs have differing intervention techniques which require that correctional staff interact with

391

offenders in a number of ways – as a friend, a role model, or a therapist. Treatment may consist of large or small group counseling, informal discussions, or scheduled individual therapy sessions. However, when such programs are objectively evaluated, the similarities among them are more striking than are the differences. For the correctional administrator committed to improving the corrections process, the "medical" approach seldom offers any convincing evidence of its effectiveness. On the other hand, the behavioral or "social learning" model of human behavior not only presents an alternative conceptualization of the causes of criminal and delinquent behaviors, it provides a more effective vehicle for understanding, predicting, and modifying human behavior than has heretofore been available. It is anticipated that the successful correctional administrator of the future will be one who selects offender intervention strategy that allows for objective evaluation. The first few steps in developing such a strategy have been undertaken by the EMLC staff. The future of the social learning model approach in juvenile or adult offender treatment and staff training rests with implementation on a continuing systematic but more wide-scale basis and a thorough systematic evaluation of its impact with institutionalized and released offenders. The EMLC staff has provided the requisite guidelines and it certainly seems like there will be little to gain unless such implementation is undertaken, especially in light of this country's search for a more effective juvenile and adult offender treatment strategy.

References

Ayllon, T., and Wright, P. New roles for the paraprofessional. In S. Bijou and E. Ribes-Inesta (Eds.), *Behavior modification: Issues and extensions.* New York: Academic Press, 1972.

Bandura, A. *Principles of behavior modification.* New York: Holt, Rinehart & Winston, 1969.

Clements, C.B., and McKee, J.M. Programmed instruction for institutionalized offenders: Contingency management and performance contracts. *Psychological Reports,* 1968, 22, 957-964.

Craighead, W.E. Kazdin, A.E., and Mahoney, M.E. *Behavior modification: Principels, issues and applications.* Boston: Houghton Mifflin, 1976.

Fenton, N. *Group counseling: A preface to its use in correctional and welfare agencies.* Sacramento, Calif.: The Institute for the Study of Crime and Delinquency, 1961.

Franks, C.M. *Behavior therapy: Appraisal and status.* New York: McGraw-Hill, 1969.

Frazier, T.L. Transactional analysis training and treatment of staff in a correctional school. *Federal Probation,* 1972, 36, 41-46.

Jesness, C.F. The impact of behavior modification and transactional analysis on institution social climate. *Journal of Research in Crime and Delinquency, 1975, 12, 79-92.*

Kassebaum, G., Ward, D.A., and Wilner, D.M. *Prison treatment and parole survival: An empirical assessment.* New York: John Wiley & Sons, 1971.

Katrin, S.E. The effects on women inmates of facilitation training provided correctional officers. *Criminal Justice and Behavior,* 1974, 1, 5-12.

Milan, M.A., and McKee, J.M. Behavior modifcation: Principles and application in corrections. In D. Glaser (Ed.), *Handbook of Criminology.* Chicago: Rand McNally College Publishing, 1974, 745-776.

Rehabilitation Research Foundation, *Draper project final reports.* Elmore, Ala.: Author, 1968.

Rehabilitation Research Foundation, *Correctional officer training package in behavior modification.* Montgomery, Ala.: Author, 1972.

Smith, R.R., Jenkins, W.D., & Hart, I.A. *Correctional officer training in behavior modification: Final Report.* Montgomery, AL.: Rehabilitation Research Foundation, 1973.

Smith, R.R., Milan, M.A., Wood, L.F., and McKee, J.M. The correctional officer as a behavioral technician. *Criminal Justice and Behavior,* 1976, 3, 345-360.

Witherspoon, A.D. *A Behavioral Observation Index (BOI) designed to evaluate training of correctional officers in a prison setting.* Elmore, Ala.: Rehabilitation Research Founcation, 1971.

Yates, A.J. *Behavior therapy.* New York: John Wiley & Sons, 1970.

Notes

*The research reported in this chapter was supported by the U.S. Department of Labor, Manpower Administration, under Contract 21-01-73-38. Organizations undertaking such projects are encouraged to express their own judgment freely. Therefore, points of view or opinions stated in the chapter do not necessarily represent the official position or policy of the Department of Labor or other federal agencies mentioned herein.

Institutional Genocide:
An Attack on Black Children

Andrea D. Sullivan

The ex-convicts from English prisons built America through the elimination of the Indian, a revolutionary war, slavery and its system of trade, and a civil war. Concomitant phenomena focused upon Black codes, fugitive slave laws, KKK, vigilantes, lynch mobs, outlaws and family feuds (among hillbillies) particularly through the Southern Appalachia and the Southwest. These experiences were and are all considered to be legal, rational and sanctioned; or what authorities call "positive violence".

In subsequent decades America was confronted with the first urban criminal gangs arising in the "slums" of New York City. (Five Pts. & Bowery), and the merger of this element with the Mafia to perpetuate and expand organized crime. Presently, police violence, urban riots, political assassination, youth gangs, wife beating, medicaid and nursing home brutalities, and arguments in environment began centuries ago. We have been dependent upon violence; it is the action of respected people not just roughnecks and hoodlums. The 20th century has been symbolized by war, revolution and counter-revolution, and depression.

Our children and our street corner criminals act as mere reflections of that which is seen as effective expedient and legitimate behavior. Of course, the persons performing and the situations within which they perform determine whether or not the behavior is accepted and legitimate.

The rise in "illegitimate" behavior among people generally and juveniles specifically enables America or the components of the criminal justice process to justify its refusal to endure the burden of the job of human reparation; the devotion is to coercive control under the guise of "rehabilitation" and indeterminate sentence, and security.

One has only to receive the positive school of criminological thought to capture the essence of rehabilitation and indeterminate sentencing. It was Ceasare Lombroso who suggested that criminal types were distinguishable from non-criminals by observable physical anomalies of a degenerate or atavistic nature; needing severe social intervention of a therapeutic character. With an emphasis on Darwinism he proposed that the criminal was morally inferior and characterized by physical traits similar to apes, lower primates and "savage tribes". The innate criminality or pathological theories of delinquency ignore the possibility that deviance preserves the social stability while reinforcing the status of the ruling class. Abnormal aspects of deviant behavior and the criminal act rather than the criminal law is the major point of departure in the construction of etiological theory.

Contemporary programs which can be seen as having stemmed from the kind of framework developed by Lombroso, are the product of early enterprises of the "child savers"; upper middle class women who helped the create special judicial and correctional institutions for the labeling, processing and management of youth (Platt p. 3). Of the child savers, Anthony Platt says: "They brought attention to new categories of youthful misbehavior which had been hitherto unappreciated". Essentially, the movement reaffirmed ideal values and emphasized traditional institutions. Their ideas were a conglomerate of (1) the medical profession — emphasizing pathology, infection and treatment — (2) the tenets of social Darwinism — that man is intractable and the lower classes are innately morally defective and (3) the European criminologists who espoused biological origins of crime (Platt p. 18).

The court system, which was officially established in Illinois in 1899 through the assistance of the child savers, intervened in the youth's life to through the assistance of the child savers, intervened in the youth's life to save him from a bad environment. It denied the youth freedom without due process replacing it with a non-adversary system prohibiting counsel, the right of proper notice, and self-incrimination; approaching the youth in medical therapeutic terms.

The child savers were not particularly liberal or radical. They were concerned about the threat that urbanization, industrialization and immigration posed to their values. They promoted programs requiring longer terms of imprisonment, long hours of labor and militaristic discipline, and the inculcation of middle class values and lower class skills (Platt p. 176).

The approach of the child savers was community-oriented in that they enunciated a "cottage plan" each of which would house 40 youth and for the very young supervision was to be by women only. Education was another proponent to be under-scored – education by moral training, religion and labor. There were other postures such as young children being separated from adult offenders, due process not being required because reformatories are not for punishment, indeterminate sentencing, the careful choosing of guards, trying punishment when all else is exhausted, military drills to guard against idleness, education was not to go beyond an elementary one, and the predomination of industrial and agricultural training. (Platt p. 55).

The education program was deficient and elitist; as it is today, education is not for the masses. The instruction received did not provide for ambition, self-help or independence outside of one's present status and position in the system. Penal reformers exploited the rhetoric of the new education to give respectability to agricultural and industrial training in reformatories.

It is apparent that "education" was the primary vehicle through which the child savers felt that rehabilitation could become a reality. Obversely, I suggest that education or the lack of it and the system through which it is administered is a very critical aspect of the delinquency syndrome exhibited in inner cities.

The school system across the country do not take an active role in fulfilling its obligations as one of the institutions responsible in preventing marginality or alienation – major components of delinquency. Constantly being assessed by upper middle class values, methods of teaching for children born of this generation promote failure, lower the child's motivation to learn, aggravate difficulty in accepting authority and drain confidence thereby generating hostility and providing poor self-images. Without early learning and emotional problems being conquered, grade level promotions without individualized instruction mean cumulative failure. The loss of self-esteem is interpreted as a loss of concern or interest in material at which point the child is placed in special classes and excluded from extra-curricular activity. Rebellion, the flaunting of traditional standards and rejection of long range goals are defenses against exclusion.

The impact of industrialization upon migrant and immigrant cultures was/is overwhelming. Community disorganization, lack of education, and an economy that alienates the young, exacerbate temptions of illicit jobs. As was the case when other low income groups were residents of inner cities, delinquency was rampant. Black people being stifled by economic and racial segregation are not afforded the break from this cycle of poverty. The importance of mental rather than physical commissions and the high rate of unemployment mean confinement to cities with crowded schools and inferior services. The effect on black families and their communities is doubtless, pathetically and consciously genocide!

The more obvious institution which destroys the lives of young people and ravishes communities is the "criminal justice system". As with most if not all criminal justice statistics; an accurate amount of juveniles in jail is not available; the total amount of crime is said to be at least two times the amount recorded; the UCR conveniently places race within all data concerning arrest but neglects the same when reporting on discharge or dismissal, as well as trends of arrests for persons under 18.

However, the Department of Justice in 1970 conducted a National Jail Census in which 7,800 juveniles of which 66% were awaiting trial, were reported held in 4,037 American adult jails on a given day in 1970. The Children's Defense Fund visited 449 jails in 9 cities. The study documented the inadequacy of physical conditions finding that: 86% had no recreation, 89% had no educational facilities and 49% had no medical facilities. Of the 449, 38.1% said they did hold children regularly, 14.7% said they had children occasionally. A disproportionate member of the children (31.8%) were black, 4 out of 5 were male. The length of stay and the reasons they were there were often in violation of laws. Only 11% were held on serious charges or were threats to the community while 18% were status offenders (Children's Defense Fund, p. 4). A status offense is one that is applicable only to children — such as truancy, running away, consensual sex, sexual promiscuity, refusal to obey parents, obscene language, sleeping in the streets, wandering, frequenting places where liquor is sold and incorrigibility. This designation is different from delinquent, yet more often than not they are detained in jails while awaiting court hearings: Of 500,000 children recently estimated in pretrial detention for a given year, 1/3 are status offenders; 3 out of every 4 girls and 1 out of 3 boys. The alleged offenses are not compatible with the degree and type of confinement. They are more likely to be detailed than the serious delinquent (especially the females) and the younger they are the longer they'll be incarcerated.

Similarly in a study by Pawlak in 1972 in Michigan, it was observed that status offenders were more likely to be detained and held longer than the persons who had committed serious property or person offenses. The number of prior court contracts was more highly correlated with detention in jails than with the type of offense (Sarri p. 18).

The LEAA inmate study reported that "jail inmates are predominantly male, typically young, and generally poor and undereducated". Minority groups represented 44% of the total population. There is no reason to assume that the demographic variables for youth are any different with the exception that 75% of the females are held for status offenses.

Comprehensively, the National Council on Crime and Delinquency (1965) reported an estimate of 87,951 juveniles jailed during the year. Nationally, Illinois is a typical case in point: out of 160 jails, 142 held juveniles, but only 9 had separate accommodations; 5,580 are in county jails and 4,671 are in city jails; less than 50% provded medical care; 82% had less than 45 square feet of space per person (below the American Correctional Association standard of 75 square feet); 15% actively supervised inmates.

A 1972 study of the Institute of Government of the University of Georgia corroborates with the national picture. They surveyed six facilities from 1970-71 and sampled 1,086 youth. Analysis revealed that 54% were charged with victimless crimes or traffic offenses; 37% with property crimes; and 3% with crimes against the person. Thus, 61% could have been held in their own homes or local foster homes. Females, blacks and status offenders were overrepresented relative to the number of cases referred to court. Youth were referred more often during the school year and while maximum detention is 10-14 days, the average was 24.46 days, with an average range of 20.18 to 33.80 days.

Since 1959, standards for model juvenile court acts have all recommended retention of court jurisdiction over status offenders, but are against institutionalization. The FJDA provides for a juvenile to be detained "only in a juvenile facility or such a suitable place as the Attorney General may designate", in order to insure his appearance at trial or assure the safety of others. Whenever possible, the detention will be in a community-based facility located in or near his home. The detained juvenile is also not to be housed with adults or adjudicated delinquents. There are further provisions for daily care. The vague and non-specific language allows for obvious problems but that same language could have accompanying guidelines and interpretations to the benefit of juveniles since the bulk of them are not threats to the community.

Under the JJDPA the Federal Government provides millions of dollars to the state and local government for law enforcement programs and facilities for juveniles. As a condition to receive funds, the Congress requires: (1) that within two years of submission of their annual plans, status offenders be removed from juvenile detention or correctional facilities and placed in shelter facilities 42 U.S.C. Sec. 5633(2)(12); (1976 Supp.) and; (2) insure that juveniles who are adjudicated are not confined in any institution in which they have regular contact with adult persons 42 U.S.C. Sec. 5633 (2)(13). States are also required to establish an adequate system to see that requirements are met.

Both of these laws could be effective if the LEAA administered the program aggressively. However, LEAA has decided that compliance is the deinstitutionalization of 75% of status offenders. Secondly, LEAA guidelines do not prevent children from being placed in isolated areas of jails without regular attention. They have also permitted states to determine their own timetables as it relates to the separation requirement. The prohibition of verbal and visual contact with adults is not specifically delineated. Finally, states which are in non-compliance lose only the dollars allocated by the JJDPA which is only 1.5% of all government monies received by them; they may still get larger grants from LEAA under other programs that do not have a status offender stipulation (Children's Defense Fund p. 43).

Federal officials must be aware that 1/2 juvenile court judges have no undergraduate degree; 1/5 received no college education at all; 1/5 are not members of the bar (Commission p. 217), yet these persons are making judgments regarding incarceration in order to rehabilitate.

It has been estimated that the cost of all forms of federal, state and local rehabilitation amounts to less than five percent of the $5 billion spent annually on prison operations and construction. The U.S. spends less than $100 per inmate per year for recreation, religion, social work, medical care, psychotherapy, counseling, education, etc., for the more than two million men, women and children being processed and destroyed by the prison system (Chaneles p. 134). Yet successful rehabilitation of these persons will be determined by conformity to the values of the dominant class; "treatment" in prisons is designed to retain custody over the person requiring a positive change in behavior using negative stimuli.

The future of this country is slowly deteriorating. The highest rates of recidivism exist among those under 18; 26% (2,078,459) or all arrests are of children under 18; from 1960-1975, the arrests of children had gone from 485,007 per year to 1,184,105 or a 144% increase. Of all arrests of persons under 18 (about 2 million) 22% are black and of all arrests of persons over 18 (about 6 million) 26.4% are black. Finally, it is reported that 52.4% of arrestees for violent crimes are blacks under 18 and 26.6% of arrestees for property crimes are blacks under 18.

Of course, there are many questions of validity and reliability associated with arrest records and specifically with the arrests of low income persons. Notwithstanding these criticisms, children are still confronted with the "criminal justice process" at a very early age; before they have emotionally and spiritually developed, regardless of physical or mental attributes, many youth are given the ascription of "delinquent" or "deviant". By doing this, we are doing nothing more than "Blaming the Victim" as William Ryan so aptly suggests in his book of the same name.

Persons in law enforcement and research consistently identify a social problem such as "delinquency", study those persons affected byt he problem, decide how those people differ from the problem and create an agency to correct the differences in those people. By ignoring the real problems and the fact that some delinquent activity is such by social judgment, and "procedural definitions", the system fulfills its prophecies.

We must understand that this label of delinquent comes at a time when youth have already been alienated from the dominant culture and disrespected as though they have different goals, desires and motivations. It is suggested that they do not. Our society is one where imitation, materialism, and sensual phenomena are matters of great concern juxtaposed with independence, honesty and courage; the society is oppositional and contradictory yet demands conformity. All men are concerned about excitement, "manhood" and/or sexual prowess. However, the manifestations of those desires are differentiated depending upon the person's socio-political position in our society. Those that are "deviant" are such because of the label applied to actors in particular social settings and not because of some inherent human behavior. Persons who can afford the gambling casinos of the West Indies and the optimum in houses of prostitution of New York or Nevada or those who hold established positions of power need not enact their aggressions on the street corners or in the alleys of our communities. Thus, again, the identification of a problem, labeling and disenfranchisment focus on a more specific group with far-reaching and devastating consequences.

The powerlessness and relative deprivation which pervades our society — feelings of no control over one's destiny creates severe ego problems with proclivities toward aggressive action. The distinction of violent youth without qualification is another reliable determinant for abiding estrangement.

Critics have argued that the Juvenile Justice System has failed to achieve its stated goals. It has however certainly reached its more subtle ones of oppression and discrimination of youth that are under its jurisdiction.

Juvenile court officials are aware that the highest rates of recidivism exist among those under 18, that nearly 60% of all burglaries are committed by those under 18, that the majority of juveniles processed and detained are held because of an "offense" which would not be classified as such if committed by an adult, and that the behavior which is categorized as such an offense is vague and allows for judges to enforce subjective standards. If they are also aware of the trends in arrests of black youth, the consequences of such contact with the system, and the intent of both the Federal Juvenile Delinquency Act of 1974 and the Juvenile Justice Delinquency Prevention Act of 1974, then again, I submit that powerless children and communities are the objects of genocide.

References

Children's Defense Fund. *Children in Adult Jails.* Washington, D.C.: Washington Research Project, Inc., 1972.

Platt, Anthony. *The Child Savers.* Chicago: University of Chicago Press, 1969.

President's Commission on Law Enforcement and Administration of Justice. *The Challenge of Crime in a Free Society.* New York: Avon Books, 1968.

Sol Chaneles, "Prisons Can Be Rehabilitated — Now". *Psychology Today,* October 1976, pp. 129-134.

United States Department of Justice, Law Enforcement Assistance Administration. *Survey of Inmates of Local Jails.* Washington, D.C.: NCJISS, 1972.

Public Opinion About Legal Responsibility for Mentally Retarded Felons: Effects of Religiosity

Clarence E. Tygart
California State University, Fullerton

Abstract

Agreements with the following religious stances increased the propensity of a representative sample of California public opinion to endorse giving full legal responsibility to mentally retarded felons: 1) an after-life existence in which punishment is possible; 2) the mentally retarded have free-will; 3) unpunished earthly wrongs are punished in after-life; and 4) the after-life rewards unjust earthly sufferings. Respondents' political ideology did not alter the relationships among ideology did not alter the relationships among religiosity and legal responsibility for mentally retarded felons.

How should governmental agencies handle mentally retarded felons? For example, what type of court trial is appropriate for a mentally retarded individual accused of armed robbery? Should a mentally retarded individual suffer the death penalty in a capital crime?

Linkenhoker (1978) points out that laws are extremely vague regarding the concept of mental retardation for felons, both youth and adults. Some state laws fail to distinguish mental retardation from "moral defects" or mental illness. No state law in the United States has specific provisions which grant special diminished capacity status to mentally retarded offenders.

In some states, however, a lawyer is not precluded from making a diminished capacity defense from mental retardation. A mental retardation diminished capacity defense is rather common in California death penalty cases.

To what extent should the mentally retarded be held legally responsible for their crimes? Linkenhoker (1978:67) states: "The question is a critical but unresolved issue." The question is important both as needed immediate information for the criminal justice system and as its centrality for potential scientific knowledge.

Public opinion will be crucial in attempting to resolve the important issue of legal responsibility for mentally retarded felons. The public could influence legislators as they write laws. Also, judges are not isolated from public influences. Ultimately, criminal cases are decided by lay jurors who usually settle the question of the legal responsibility for the mentally retarded felon. The major burden of this paper is *how* and *why* do the public resolve the question of legal responsibility of mentally retarded felons. Responses from a representative sample of 800 adult residents of California in the year 1977 constitute the present data.

Data

Respondents were asked to assess legal responsibility for mentally retarded felons according to the degree of retardation and type of crime. First, however, respondents were asked at what chronological ages, assuming normal mental capacity, should individuals have complete legal responsibility for the following crimes: 1) murder with the possibility of the death penalty; 2) murder without the death penalty; 3) armed robbery; and 4) burglary. The respective mean ages listed by the respondents were: 1) 17.4; 2) 14.8; 3) 14.6; and 4) 13.9. Respondents preferred increased mental ages for legal responsibility with greater severity of possible penalty. Contemporary practices of less than adult sentences for youthful offenders would appear strikingly variant to California public opinion.

Chronological age of the mentally retarded felons affected respondents' opinions. Respondents were given situations where the felons were of the chronological ages of fifteen and thirty-five. For the chronological ages of fifteen and thirty-five, felons were presented as having mental capacities of ages four and eight for each of the four previously mentioned crimes.

Table 1 shows the various percentages which define mentally retarded felons as legally responsible for each of the sixteen situations. With the exception of death penalty homocide, a majority hold legally responsible the age thirty-five felons even with mental ages of four and eight years. These respondents seem to believe that the mentally retarded do benefit from having obtained advanced chronological ages.

Table 1. Respondents Ascribing Legal Responsibility to Mentally Retarded Felons: Chronological Age of Felons, Degree of Retardation and Type of Felony.

	Percent Endorsing Legal Responsibility	
	Felons aged 15 yrs.	Felons aged 35 yrs.
Offenses	Mental age 8 yrs.	Mental age 8 yrs.
Murder with death penalty possible	9%	26%
Murder without death penalty possible	44%	69%
Armed robbery	48%	81%
Burglary	59%	88%
	Felons aged 15 yrs.	Felons aged 35 yrs.
	Mental age 4 yrs.	Mental age 4 yrs.
Murder with death penalty possible	3%	13%
Murder without death penalty possible	21%	52%
Armed robbery	27%	58%
Burglary	29%	61%

Again, with the exception of death penalty homocide, those with mental ages of eight years are held legally responsible when chronologically fifteen years old.

Religiosity

The data discussed show that *how* the public resolves the question of legal responsibility of mentally retarded felons hinges upon: 1) the type of crime; 2) chronological age of the felon; and 3) degree of mental retardation. Thus, the public shows considerable variance concerning *how* mentally retarded felons are held legally responsible. The next concern of this paper is *why* the variance in the public assessing of legal responsibility of mentally retarded felons.

For at least two decades, research has demonstrated the effects of religiosity for individuals' stances on socio-political issues (Tygart, 1971). Generally, lesser religiosity is associated with increased liberal or leftist positions on topical socio-political issues. Greater religiosity tends to increase conservatism. Also, increased religiosity may decrease interest and involvements in socio-political issues.

Central to the liberal-conservative argument is the different assumption concerning the possibilities for deliberate, progressive social change. The "liberals" or "leftist" position is traditionally optimistic concerning such possibilities, while the "conservative" or "rightist" position is less optimistic. In liberal ideology much of the cause for crime is societal conditions. Human weaknesses or individual inadequacies are the more important causation for crime in the conservative perspective. In the apparent case of crime among the mentally retarded, the locus of the cause of crime seems necessarily individual rather than societal. This is not, of course, suggesting that mental retardation is "deserved" or avoidable; nor does conservative or liberal ideology advocate a lack of compassion for the mentally retarded.

Why, therefore, should religiosity make a difference among the public assessing legal responsibility for mentally retarded felons? Apparently, less possibility exists for liberal-conservative arguments concerning causation. Different conceptions about after-life invite an expectation that religiosity might differentiate the public's views concerning legal responsibility for mentally retarded felons.

Beliefs concerning after-life — rewards and punishment and soul enhancement — are especially relevant for the issue of legal responsibility for mentally retarded felons. In traditional theology, a prerequisite for the soul is the individual's free will, free choice, and free behavior. Also, behavior from an individual's freely chosen alternative is a fundamental postulate for an individual's legal responsibility for criminal behavior.

The religious position which allows individuals the possibilities of after-life reward, at least somewhat, necessitate possibilities of legal punishment for felons. Also, such individuals incur the potential for after-life punishment. To some extent the religious free will position trades after-life existence for earthly legal responsibility. Conversely, not having legal responsibility, perhaps, decreases the plausibility of after-life existence.

The traditional religious free-will positions define ultimate symmetry between individuals' actions and rewards-punishment. Should legal punishment not result from earthly punishable conduct, after-life punishment possibilities are increased. Religious penitence and/or forgiveness might somewhat suffice for the absence of legal punishment. Undeserved earthly suffering could enhance the status of the after-life soul. Being unjustly punished for crimes and suffering for righteous causes are examples of possible soul enhancements.

The independent variables of the present study are beliefs concerning: 1) an after-life existence in which punishment is possible; 2) the mentally retarded being defined as having "free will"; 3) individuals being punished in after-life for unpunished earthly crimes; and 4) individuals being rewarded in after-life for unjust earthly suffering or punishment. Affirmative stances are anticipated as increasing the propensity of respondents to give legal responsibility to mentally retarded felons.

Respondents' general political ideology will serve as an alternative explanation for respondents' views on the legal responsibility of mentally retarded felons. As previously discussed, research has shown that traditional religiosity is associated with more conservative stances for issues other than mentally retarded felons. Political liberalism-conservatism will be used as a control variable to ascertain if the anticipated effects of religiosity are reduced and/or eliminated.

Results and Discussion

While 82% of these respondents believed in an after-life, only 59%

409

thought that some would be punished in an after-life. Seventy-one percent (71%) agreed that the "behavior of the mentally retarded are basically free-will choices on the part of the mentally retarded person." Some respondents seem reluctant to take the free-will position to the point of possibility of after-life punishment. A minority of 37% took the position that individuals are punished in after-life for unpunished earthly crimes. An even smaller minority of 34% felt that individuals would be rewarded in after-life for unjust earthly suffering or punishment.

Table 2 shows the strengths of the associations of respondents' agreeing with each of the four beliefs of the independent variables and giving legal responsibility to the mentally retarded felons. All of the bivariate measures of association are strong, with a Pearsonian r of .58 as the weakest association. The view that individuals are punished in after-life for unpunished earthly crimes was the strongest bivariate predictor of respondents giving legal responsibility to mentally retarded felons.

To what extent do each of the four independent variables, per se, explain the variance of the dependent variable? Table 2 also shows the multivariate partial correlations of the four independent variables and the dependent variable.

As was the case in bivariate analysis, the belief in after-life punishment for unpunished earthly crimes was the largest contributor to the explained variance. As the mean R^2 of .64 indicates, the combined multivariate effects of the four independent variables explains 64% of the varaince among respondents giving legal responsibility to mentally retarded felons for the sixteen situations.

The independent variables displayed considerable amounts of interrelationships. The interrelationships ranged from r's of .56 to .78, with a mean of .63. Since the independent variables were highly interrelated, much of the variance in multivariate analysis was not an independent contribution from just one of the independent variables. Instead, much of the explained variance in multivariate analysis were effects from the independent variables generally. Respondents who agreed with the position that individuals are punished in after-life for unpunished earthly crimes usually endorsed the three other statements of the other independent variables.

As previously discussed, political ideology constituted the control variable or alternative explanation. Political ideology was measured by respondents' self-eclassifications and positions on five topical issues. Respondents were asked which best described their general political

Table 2. (continued)

Religious Stance	Offense	Chronological Age 35 yrs. Mental Age 8 yrs. Correlations	
		Bi-variate	**Multi-variate**
After-life punishment for unpunished earthly wrongs	Murder with possibility of death penalty	.79	.41
	Murder without possibility of death penalty	.80	.37
	Armed robbery	.79	.37
	Burglary	.76	.33
		R = .83	
	Mental Age 4 yrs.		
	Murder with possibility of death penalty	.79	.40
	Murder without possibility of death penalty	.82	.44
	Armed robbery	.81	.45
	Burglary	.81	.38
		R = .85	
	Chronological Age 15 yrs. Mental Age 8 yrs.		
	Murder with possibility of death penalty	.77	.38
	Murder without possibility of death penalty	.78	.36
	Armed robbery	.74	.31
	Burglary	.75	.29
		R = .82	
	Mental Age 4 yrs.		
	Murder with possibility of death penalty	.81	.38
	Murder without possibility of death penalty	.78	.39
	Armed robbery	.78	.43
	Burglary	.79	.41
		R = .84	

continued . . .

Table 2. (continued)

Religious Stance	Chronological Age 35 yrs. mental Age 8 yrs. Offense	Correlations Bi-variate	Multi-variate
Free will for the mentally retarded	Murder with possibility of death penalty	.79	.33
	Murder without possibility of death penalty	.68	.34
	Armed robbery	.69	.31
	Burglary	.70	.32
		R = .84	
	Mental Age 4 yrs.		
	Murder with possibility of death penalty	.60	.31
	Murder without possibility of death penalty	.72	.35
	Armed robbery	.77	.35
	Burglary	.73	.32
		R = .82	
	Chronological Age 15 yrs. Mental Age 8 yrs.		
	Murder with possibility of death penalty	.78	.30
	Murder without possibility of death penalty	.80	.32
	Armed robbery	.76	.35
	Burglary	.75	.31
		R = .81	
	Mental Age 4 yrs.		
	Murder with possibility of death penalty	.72	.29
	Murder without possibility of death penalty	.74	.34
	Armed robbery	.78	.33
	Burglary	.76	.35
		R = .82	

continued . . .

Table 2. (continued)

Religious Stance	Chronological Age 35 yrs. Mental Age 8 yrs. Offense	Correlations Bi-variate	Multi-variate
After-life punishment for unpunished earthly wrongs	Murder with possibility of death penalty	.79	.41
	Murder without possibility of death penalty	.80	.37
	Armed robbery	.79	.37
	Burglary	.76	.33
		R = .83	
	Mental Age 4 yrs.		
	Murder with possibility of death penalty	.79	.40
	Murder without possibility of death penalty	.82	.44
	Armed robbery	.81	.45
	Burglary	.81	.38
		R = .85	
	Chronological Age 15 yrs. Mental Age 8 yrs.		
	Murder with possibility of death penalty	.77	.38
	Murder without possibility of death penalty	.78	.36
	Armed robbery	.74	.31
	Burglary	.75	.29
		R = .82	
	Mental Age 4 yrs.		
	Murder with possibility of death penalty	.81	.38
	Murder without possibility of death penalty	.78	.39
	Armed robbery	.78	.43
	Burglary	.79	.41
		R = .84	

continued . . .

Table 2. (concluded)

	Chronological Age 35 yrs. Mental Age 8 yrs.	Corrrelations	
Religious Stance	**Offense**	Bi-variate	Multi-variate
Soul enhancement for unjust earthly suffering	Murder with possibility of death penalty	.78	.46
	Murder without possibility of death penalty	.77	.41
	Armed robbery	.79	.42
	Burglary	.58	.36
		R = .83	
	Mental Age 4 yrs.		
	Murder with possibility of death penalty	.80	.44
	Murder without possibility of death penalty	.68	.31
	Armed robbery	.68	.30
	Burglary	.64	.28
		R = .77	
	Chronological Age 15 yrs. Mental Age 8 yrs.		
	Murder with possibility of death penalty	.70	.29
	Murder without possibility of death penalty	.68	.31
Armed robbery	.68	.30	
Burglary	.64	.28	
		R = .77	
	Mental Age 4 yrs.		
	Murder with possibility of death penalty	.75	.34
	Murder without possibility of death penalty	.71	.35
	Armed robbery	.63	.27
	Burglary	.62	.29
		R = .76	

views: 1) liberal; 2) somewhat liberal; 3) moderate; 4) somewhat conservative; or 5) conservative. The following were coded as conservative responses: 1) endorsement of the death penalty; 2) opposition to the proposed "equal rights for women" constitutional amendment; 3) favoring reduced government spending for welfare; 4) opposition to mandatory busing 5) opposition to the Panama Canal treaty.

Respondents' self-placements on the liberalism-conservatism continuum and stances on the five topical issues were very interrelated. The relationships ranged from 4's of .54 to .77, with a mean of .68. When the five topical issues were computed as independent variables and respondents' self-classifications were treated as the dependent variable, an R^2 magnitude of .82 was obtained. Only 2% of the respondents who endorsed conservative positions on all five issues classified themselves as "liberal" or "somewhat liberal," and only 4% as middle of the road."

Is propensity to give legal responsibility to mentally retarded felons attributable to respondents' general political conservatism rather than to aspect of religious beliefs? If this alternative explanation is correct, the effects of religious beliefs for the dependent variable should be greatly reduced when political ideology and stance are entered in the multivariate analysis.

At the bivariate level, all the six items measuring political ideology were related to legal responsibility for mentally retarded felons. These bivariate relationships ranged from r's of .44 to .65, with a mean of .54. However, when placed in multivariate analysis along with the religiosity measures, none of the political items made a statistically significant contribution to explain the variance for the dependent variable items. Politically conservative stances, per se, did not increase the propensity of respondents to give legal responsibility to mentally retarded felons.

Probably the most noteworthy failure of the political items to make independent contributions is the death penalty area. Conceptually, favoring capital punishment for "normal" felons suggests a possible affinity for greater willingness for capital punishment for mentally retarded felons. Nettler's (1959) classic study shows a positive relationship between the free-will position and endorsement of the death penalty for "normal" felons. This present research suggests that the free-will position, along with other consistent religious beliefs, increases the probability of endorsing the death penalty for both "normal" and "mentally retarded" felons. However, these data suggest that approval of capital punishment for "normal" felons is neither an independent or an intervening variable in explaining willingness to give legal responsibility to mentally retarded felons in capital crimes. Endorsement of the death penalty for "normals" without the congruent religious belief stances does not increase the willingness of respondents to approve legal responsibility for mentally retarded felons in capital crimes.

Conclusion

The present research has conceptualized certain beliefs concerning the possibility of individuals making choice decisions as religious stances. Human behavior which results from individuals' choices allows the applicability of God's judgments. Rewards, punishment, and soul enhancements are aspects of God's judgments. However, the free-will versus determination argument is broader than religion. The various resolutions of this eternal argument have important implications besides religion.

The free-will versus determinism issue is a prominent concern which is at least as universal as Western philosophical tradition. The assumption of a legal system is that crimes are committed by individuals making free-will choices. Punishment is proper and mandatory when criminal choices are made. Being subject to punishment, the individuals gain the legal procedural rights to their society. Most important, from the perspective of the proponents of free-will, the free-will individual acquires the dignity of freedom. In a religious sense, the ultimate reward of this acquisition is the possibility of eternal life.

References

Boslow, H. and Kandel, A., "Psychiatric aspects of dangerous behavior." *American Journal of Psychiatry,* 1965, 222 (6), 646-656.

Dennis, F., *The mentally retarded public offender and the law,* Tallahassee: Florida Press, 1966.

Linkenhoker, D., "Juvenile delinquency and mental retardation." in L. Beutler and R. Greene (eds.), *Special problems in child and adolescent behavior,* Westport: Technomic Publishing Co., 1978, 67-73.

Nettler, G., "Cruelty, dignity and determinism," *American Sociological Review,* 1959, 24 (August), 375-384.

Nettler, G., *Understanding crime*, New York: McGraw-Hill, 1968.
Tygart, C.E., "Religiosity and university students' anti-Vietnam war attitudes," *Sociological Analysis*, 1971, 32 (Summer), 120-129.
Westwell, A.E., "The defective delinquent," *American Journal of Mental Deficiency*, 1951, 56, 283-289.

Theory and Practice
of Cognitive-Behavioral Treatments with
Delinquents*

Verda L. Little
Virginia Commonwealth University

and

Philip Ç. Kendall
University of Minnesota

Juvenile delinquency remains a major problem in this society in spite of efforts to reduce its incidence. According to Shah (1975), one out of nine young persons is likely to be referred to a juvenile court for involvement in a delinquent act committed before the age of 18. Even higher rates of delinquency are reported in some surveys, and the effect of the repeat offender on delinquency rates has been demonstrated (Wolfgang, Figlio, & Sellin, 1972).

*Portions of this paper were adapted from V.L. Little and P.C. Kendall, Cognitive-behavioral interventions with delinquents: Problem solving, role-taking, and self control. In P.C. Kendall and S.D. Hollon (Eds.), *Cognitive behavioral interventions: Theory, research and procedures.* New York: Academic Press, 1979.

In general, efforts of rehabilitation of delinquents have shown highly variable results, and the heterogeneity of the population remains a stumbling block to successful treatment. The numerous theories of delinquency (see Solomon, 1978) and classification systems (e.g., Quay and Parsons, Note 1; Warren, 1971) have failed to provide the basis for treatment programs that reliably produce desired treatment effects. Given this state of affairs, it seems logical to consider that more fruitful interventions with this problematic population may be the treatment of specific problems that are common among those young people who are labeled "delinquent."

The cognitive-behavioral position focuses upon both cognitive and behavioral excesses and deficits (Kendall & Hollon, 1979). In relation to delinquency, the areas of problem solving, role-taking, and self control appear to be major concerns. This chapter will consider the evidence for deficiencies in social cognition among delinquents, discuss the relationship of such deficiencies to behavior, and report data which suggest the application of cognitive-behavioral interventions for this population.

Problem Solving

The type of problem solving that is of concern to us in this chapter has to do with effective coping in social situations — *interpersonal problem solving*. Unlike the human problem solving literature that deals with *im*personal tasks (e.g., Simon & Newell, 1971), *inter*personal problem solving is less a function of intellectual ability (Allen, Chinsky, Larcen, Lochman, & Selinger, 1976) and deals with solving problems that involve people.

Evidence of the importance of an interpersonal problem solving ability in successful coping with life comes from studies of both normal and non-normal populations, and Jahoda (1953; 1958) has suggested that the capacity to problem solve in life situations is one criterion for defining positive mental health. Indeed, both longitudinal (Offer, 1969) and cross-sectional (Coelho, Hamburg, & Murphey, 1963) studies have documented the ability of normal adolescents to solve a wide variety of everyday problems. The latter authors found that normal college freshmen "were typically active in exploring problem-solving opportunities and used them in a way that reinforced their self-image as effective doers, working toward valued goals" (p. 442).

Correspondingly, the presence of interpersonal problem-solving deficits in non-normal groups has been reported in the literature. These findings are supported further by the fact that different research approaches have produced similar outcomes. For example, Freedman (Note 2) developed a set of interpersonal problem situations typically faced by high school-aged males, and she administered the set to a group of average high school students, a group of outstanding "superstar" high school students, and a third group of residents of state training schools for delinquents. The results indicated that the delinquent group was significantly poorer in providing effective solutions to the problem situations than either of the two other groups. These findings support the notion that legally-defined problematic behavior in adolescence (i.e., delinquency) is, in part, related to inadequate interpersonal problem solving skills.

One of the most extensive projects attempting to link interpersonal problem solving deficiencies to non-normal behavior is that of Spivack, Platt, Shure and their associates at the Hahnemann Medical College and Hospital in Philadelphia. These investigators have defined and measured a series of interpersonal cognitive problem solving (ICPS) skills which they have shown to be related to social adjustment at various ages (Spivack, Platt, & Shure, 1976). Those skills found necessary for successful coping in social situations include: sensitivity to interpersonal problems, tendency to link cause and effect spontaneously (causal thinking), readiness to view possible consequences of actions (consequential thinking), ability to generate solutions (alternative thinking), ability to conceptualize step-by-step means for reaching specific goals (means-ends thinking), and the ability to view situations from the perspective of other involved individuals (perspective taking).

These skills are thought to develop at different ages, and whether they are demonstrated by a particular child in an interpersonal situation appears to relate to two factors: (a) the child may have a cognitive deficit and has failed to learn the skills, or (b) the situation may arouse emotions that prevent the child from using typical social sensitivities and/or prevent the child from freely exploring the options. According to Spivack et al. (1976), the role of the helping agent may be to improve the child's skills and/or reduce the emotional components that are interfering.

Much of the research conducted by the Hahnemann group has involved young children with an emphasis on primary prevention as well as remediation of interpersonal problem solving deficits (Shure & Spivack,

1978). A few studies, however, have focused on adolescents. The populations that have been investigated include emotionally disturbed adolescent boys who were characterized as "impulsive" (Spivack & Levine, Note 3), male and female adolescent patients at a private psychiatric hospital (Platt, Spivack, Altman, Altman, & Peizer, 1974), and incarcerated heroin addicts aged 19 to 21 (Platt, Scura, & Hannon, 1973). In each case, when a non-normal group was compared with a matched group of normals, those adolescents who were having adjustment problems were found to be deficient in three of the interpersonal cognitive problem solving skills: means-ends thinking, alternative thinking, and perspective taking. The methods of measurement were:

1. Means-ends thinking. Each subject was given the beginning and end of a series of stories, each of which simulated a real-life problem to be solved, and was asked to fill in the middle indicating how the character arrived at the stated outcome. Scoring considered the individual steps to reach the goal (means), awareness of possible obstacles, and awareness of the passage of time. Norms for various groups are available with the test manual (Platt & Spivack, Note 4).

2. Alternative thinking. The subjects were asked to think of all the things a person could do to solve a series of four interpersonal problems. Scores were based upon the number of discrete and relevant solutions generated for each problem (Spivack et al., 1976).

3. Perspective taking. Each subject was asked to make up a story about the picture on each of four Thematic Apperception Test (TAT) cards. Upon completion of the stories, the subjects again viewed each card and retold the story from the point of view of each of the characters. Scoring was based on the subject's ability to coordinate the stories and to take into account the internal state of each character (Spivack et al., 1976).

In contrast with these three areas of deficiency, two other ICPS tests failed to differentiate between the normal and non-normal adolescents: measures of causal thinking and sensitivity to interpersonal problems. The test of consequential thinking discriminated between groups in only one of the studies (Spivack & Levine, Note 3).

The notion that maladjusted adolescents are poor problem solvers in social situations thus has some experimental as well as face validity. Unfortunately, the measures of specific problem solving skills used by the Hahnemann group have focused only minimally upon delinquents per se. Additional research in this area would be most valuable.

422

Treatment of ICPS Skills Deficits

Although a comprehensive training program for adolescents and adults with problem solving deficits has been described (Platt, Spivack, & Swift, Note 5), there has yet to be reported an experimental analysis of its effectiveness. The proposed program of the Hahnemann group focuses on the *process* of solving problems rather than the content of problems, and the practice of skills is emphasized. Detailed scripts for use by a group leader are presented as well as basic materials for group exercises. Home-work assignments are also provided for the students, who are given their own workbooks (Platt & Spivack, Note 6).

Although the program itself has not yet been evaluated, the authors do rely heavily on research from three areas. First are the research findings of the Hahnemann group, both those which were described above and the results of other studies with children and adults. The second source of material is a set of training exercises developed by Siegel and Spivack (Note 7) to treat chronic schizophrenics, a program which was based partially on D'Zurilla and Goldfried's (1971) five-stage approach to problem solving. The techniques described by Siegel and Spivack deal with finding new facts, making decisions, and presenting one's point of view.

The third body of knowledge used to develop the training program is the general psychological literature, from which a variety of specific tasks and techniques have been adapted. Modeling and group discussion which were used in the successful treatment of institutionalized delinquents (Sarason, 1968; Sarason & Ganzer, 1969; 1973) are given emphasis throughout. Similar use is made of Meichenbaum and Cameron's (1973) technique of training patients to talk to themselves and McFall's (McFall & Marston, 1970; McFall & Lillesand, 1971) behavioral rehearsal techniques. Also incorporated in the program are Spohn and Wolk's (1963) discussion task which improved the social participation of schizophrenics, modifications of the Matching Familiar Figures (MFF) task (Kagan, Rosman, Day, Albert, & Phillips, 1964), Draughton's (1973) technique of duplicating facial expressions, and Morton's (1955) use of the TAT.

The first half of the training program teaches a sequenced series of prerequisite skills thought to be necessary for the individual to learn the specific problem solving skills contained in the second half of the program. Given the explicitness of the instructions and the materials provided, the application of this program to a delinquent population should not be very difficult and would likely prove to be quite informative. A useful first step would be the assessment of problem solving skills to determine the extent of the specific deficits, as well as to provide a baseline for subsequent posttesting. Random assignment of delinquents with problem solving deficits to treatment and control groups offers a simple research design, with analyses of variance used to determine differences between treatment and control groups in regard to posttreatment skills, behavioral adjustment, and/or recidivism to assess the utility of the program for the population studied. The viability of the problem solving aspect of cognitive-behavioral interventions with delinquents remains an important question for future research to answer. Nonetheless, the Hahnemann problem solving program appears soundly based and ready for testing. Other approaches to problem solving treatment are also promising, and some research with delinquents has been reported.

D'Zurilla and Goldfried (1971) posit that the goals of problem solving and behavior modifcation are the same and that training in problem solving may be viewed as one of several behavior modification techniques for facilitating effective behavior. The five stages of problem solving outlined by D'Zurilla and Goldfried include (1) general orientation or "set," (2) problem definition and formulation, (3) generation of alternatives, (4) decision making, and (5) verification. The third stage, generation of alternatives, is similar to the "alternative thinking" skill of the Hahnemann group. The fourth stage, decision making, may encompass "means-ends thinking," since one might logically assume that decisions would be based on a comparison of step-by-step plans for reaching certain goals. "Consequential thinking" may also be involved.

A test of the D'Zurilla and Goldfried (1971) model of problem solving in combination with the communication models of Piaget (1972) and Gordon (1970) was conducted with mother-adolescent dyads (Robin, Kent, O'Leary, Foster, & Prinz, 1977). Treatment included a review of problem solving, discussion and role playing of specific conflicts, self-monitoring of negative communication patterns and teaching of effective communication skills, social reinforcement, and therapist feedback about performance and discussion of the use of the skills at home. After five 1-hour sessions, mother-adolescent dyads demonstrated highly significant increases in problem solving behavior while a waiting list group showed little change. Unfortunately, self-report measures completed by mothers and adolescents indicated that treatment effects did not carry over to the home environment.

Treatment outcome research specifically utilizing the D'Zurilla and Goldfried (1971) model of problem solving with delinquents has not yet been reported, but a study is currently underway at a state learning center for male delinquents (Bowman, Note 8). In addition to teaching problem solving as a process, Bowman's approach also includes relaxation training and verbal self-instructions. Treatment subjects will be compared with an attention control group who spend an equal amount of time with an adult who "active listens" while they talk about their problems. Although its emphasis is on problem solving, the Bowman (Note 8) study will speak to the efficacy of a combination of cognitive-behavioral interventions with delinquents.

A more actively researched problem solving model of intervention with delinquents involves a behaviorally oriented short-term treatment of families (Alexander & Parsons, 1973; Parsons & Alexander, 1973). Although the teaching of problem solving was not the specified objective, the treatment procedures fit the conceptualization of problem solving training. For example, the therapists "actively modeled, prompted, and reinforced in all family members; (a) clear communication of substance as well as feelings; and (b) clear presentation of 'demands' and alternative solutions; all leading to (c) negotiation, with each family member receiving some privilege for each responsibility assumed, to the point of compromise" (Alexander & Parsons, 1973, p. 221). In a later report of follow-up to their two treatment studies (Klein, Alexander, & Parsons, 1977), the problem-solving focus of treatment is more clearly stated: "The ultimate goal of the therapeutic process then becomes one of training the family in effective problem solving techniques in order for the family unit to more adaptively meet the developmental changes occurring as children reach adolescence . . ." (p. 471). This short-term therapy was found to be superior to client-centered therapy, a psychodynamic family program, and a no-treatment control group. A 6-18 month follow-up indicated a significant reduction in recidivism for the delinquents in the training groups.

By focusing the treatment on the family unit instead of the individual delinquent, Alexander and Parsons hoped to reduce the incidence of delinquency among the siblings in the family as well as the recidivism of the original delinquents. A 2½-3½-year follow-up indicated that they had done just that (Klein et al., 1977). The problem-solving intervention resulted in sibling court involvement one-third to one-half below that of the comparison groups, as well as a continued significantly lower rate of recidivism for the original problem adolescents. These results are particularly encouraging in view of the demonstrated long-range impact of treatment on the targeted delinquent and the apparent contribution to primary prevention of delinquency.

Within the framework of "behavioral contracting," Stuart and associates (Stuart, 1971; Stuart & Lott, 1972; Stuart, Tripodi, Jayaratne, & Camburn, 1976) have trained over 200 families of predelinquents and delinquents. While their results are generally promising, one of their conclusions was that factors other than contracts themselves, such as the facilitation of communication or the process of negotiation, may be the real determinants of treatment outcome (Stuart & Lott, 1972). In the latest study (Stuart et al., 1976), the researchers suggested that contracting be conducted as part of a "more comprehensive intervention package that includes techniques aimed at modifying communication patterns within the family, academic skill-building at school, and improving peer experiences for the adolescent . . ." (p. 260). Another study of contingency contracting (Weathers & Liberman, 1975) failed to produce any systematic effects in six families of delinquents. Interestingly, this program included communication skills training and videotape feedback as well as contingency contracting. The authors suggested that contracting be viewed as a "supplementary aid" in a broader range of interventions with delinquents and stated, "In working with families that are decimated by divorce, crime, drug abuse, and woefully inadequate communciation and negotiation skills, the introduction of a contingency contract is worth about as much as the paper it's printed on" (Weathers & Liberman, 1975, p. 365).

Positive results were obtained in a study with predelinquent adolescents and their parents which focused on the negotiation process (Kifer, Lewis, Green, & Phillips, 1974). The negotiation process was analyzed into component behaviors: complete communication, which involved stating one's position and requesting the other person to respond; identification of issues, which referred to statements that explicitly identified the point of conflict; and suggestion of options, which appears to be equivalent to D'Zurilla and Goldfried's (1971) "generation of alternatives" and the Hahnemann group's "alternative thinking." Subjects received instructions, practice, and feedback about hypothetical conflict situations. Unfortunately, only three parent-child pairs were trained and no control group was used. A multiple baseline design across pairs and careful measurements, however, provided internal validity. The results indicated an increase in the three component behaviors of the negotiation process as well as in the per cent of agreements reached. Home observations revealed that the increases were maintained in the natural environment, and eight of nine situations which were discussed by adolescent-parent pairs after training resulted in agreements. Thus it appears that teaching the process of problem solving can produce desirable transfer of training to the home environment. The method of obtaining follow-up data may be critical here, as Robin et al.'s (1977) self-reports from subjects failed to indicate generalization to the home of what appeared to be a highly successful training program. While one cannot deny that generalization may *not* have occurred in the Robin et al. study, these variable results suggest that researchers should consider possible critical differences between the self-reports of subjects, especially adolescents and their parents, and observations by trained observers. Unfortunately, Kifer et al. (1974) did not report effects on further court contacts by their subjects.

The work of Sarason and associates noted earlier (Sarason, 1968; Sarason & Ganzer, 1969; 1973) involved institutionalized delinquents, and although the focus was on the differential effects of modeling and group discussion as treatment methods, an examination of these successful treatment programs suggests that the critical variable in the training may have been the teaching of problem solving skills. The sessions were presented to the boys as "learning opportunities designed to enhance their ability to cope with situations that, for them, are problem areas" (Sarason, 1968, p. 262). Both the modeling and discussion treatment groups showed positive change in attitudes and behavior greater than a no-treatment group. In a second study (Sarason & Ganzer, 1973), boys "were given examples of desirable and undesirable ways of coping with social, vocational, and educational situations" (p. 443). This type of training appears to provide practice in "alternative thinking" and possibly "consequential thinking." At any rate, both the modeling and structured discussion approaches had greater concurrent and long-term positive effects than a no-treatment control group, with the treatment effects not significantly differing between the two treatment groups. While we are highlighting the problem solving aspects of the treatments, it should be noted that the treatment program in both of these studies included practice in role-taking, another area of deficiency found in non-normal adolescents (discussed below), but no effort was made to assess the effects of role-taking training per se.

Scopetta (1972) provided a training procedure that included the playing of problem-solving skits by paraprofessional members of an institutional staff, role-playing of the situations by subjects who observed the skits, and group discussion. Delinquents who participated in this training showed significant reduction in anti-social behavior when compared with a problem-solving discussion-only group. Again, this treatment may have facilitated role-taking skills, but measures of role-taking were not included as dependent variables. Disappointing results were obtained when a similar training procedure was implemented with delinquents living in a group home (Thelen, Fry, Dollinger, & Paul, 1976). A major difference between the two studies was the use of a videotaped actor by Thelen et al. instead of live models as in the Scopetta (1972) procedure. Subjects in the Thelen et al. program role-played the model's part after observing the videotape of the actor in various problematic interpersonal situations, viewed the original videotape again, and then role-played the situation for a second time. Behavior ratings of training subjects improved significantly from baseline during the period of training when group home situations were portrayed, but gains were not maintained when the training shifted to school situations or at the time of follow-up. Control subjects who observed lecture tapes emphasizing social skills showed no changes.

Conclusions

There is evidence that successful coping with one's environment requires a set of interpersonal problem solving skills. Furthermore, adolescents who exhibit deficits in such skills are much more likely to appear in non-normal groups, such as delinquent, than in normal groups. Three specific cognitive deficits have been found: means-ends thinking, alternative thinking, and perspective taking. In regard to delinquents specifically, there is evidence that they are poor problem solvers in interpersonal situations. A number of promising treatment programs to remediate problem solving deficits have been devised, but their application to delinquents has been limited. Results of the treatment efforts reviewed herein, however, suggest that this congitive-behavioral approach to treating delinquents may be quite valuable. When families are available, teaching problem solving skills to the entire family unit appears to offer the greatest payoff in terms of recidivism and prevention of sibling delinquency. However, even when only the individual delinquent youth is available, problem solving treatment offers a promising approach. As has been noted previously, further research certainly is indicated.

Role-taking

Piaget (1926) has described the young child as an unwitting prisoner of his own egocentric view of the world. Thus embedded in his own point of view, the child is unable to "decenter" — that is, to shift his attention from a single aspect of an object or an event to simultaneously process a number of important aspects. When one centers upon a given aspect of the perceptual field to the exclusion of other aspects, distortion occurs. This distortion can be partially corrected when focus is shifted from one part of the perceptual field to another, but mature thought occurs only when the individual is able to simultaneously decenter — that is, to consider a wide number of aspects of a situation at the same time.

In the interpersonal sphere, the young child operates from his own individual perspective and remains ignorant of and unconcerned about differing perspectives of other people. This limited perspective is reflected in his communications, which typically fail to take into account the informational needs of the other person and hence have the flavor of a monologue. During the process of normal development, the child becomes aware that ther are other points of view, and his communications increasingly reflect the awareness of the perspective or role of the other. In addition, self control develops as the child learns to relate his behavior to the needs of others. The development of role-taking ability thus releases the child from the prison of his own point of view and permits him to interact successfully in the social sphere. Although Piaget (1962a, 1962b) called attention to the operation of the concepts of egocentrism and decentering in interpersonal behavior, the major thrust in that direction in both theory and research has come from other theorists and investigators.

In a relatively early work, Mead (1934) proposed that the ability to adopt alternative perspectives in regard to one's self is the very essence of social intelligence. He used the term "empathy" to refer to the capacity to "take the role of the other," and he suggested that practice at role-taking leads to social sensitivity and the emergence of the self-concept and self control. Mead's concept of the "self" consists of the self as

429

subject, or the "I," and the self as object, or the "me." The "me" is considered to be a representation of the "role of the other," that is, group values that are assimilated as one's own and which control the impulsive, spontaneous aspect of the self. In taking into account the possible reaction of another person to one's action, a person is then taking the role of the other and, as such, becomes aware of another aspect of himself.

Taking his theory largely from Piaget, Flavell (Flavell, 1963; 1974; Flavell, Botkin, Fry, Wright, & Jarvis, 1968) devised methods for assessing role-taking ability that have been used extensively in research. In the method most frequently used, the child is asked to tell a story from a series of seven cards. Three of the cards are then removed, thus drastically altering the story, and the subject is asked to tell the story from the point of view of a person who has just entered the room and has seen only the four cards. The subject's problem is to suppress his previous perspective, derived from seeing all seven pictures, and to look at the four pictures naively.

Feffer (1967; 1970) holds that the cognitive representation of the role of the other in the self-organization is a prerequisite of effective social interaction. For example, a pervasive isolation between the roles of giving and taking within self-organization leads to a very real conservation problem. The problem is how to give without diminishing one's self, or how to stop from taking too much. Feffer suggests that a mature cognitive structuring of the situation would represent the giving-taking relationship by "a network of schemas within self-organization in terms of which all possible variations of role and reciprocal can be generated and coordinated with one another" (Feffer, 1970, p. 209). Within such a structure, giving would result in another aspect of the self simultaneously receiving; while in getting, another aspect of the self sacrifices. Interpersonal events thus are construed by Feffer as being comprised of interacting participants who occupy such roles and reciprocals as giving-taking, asking-answering, and dominating-submitting.

To investigate this formulation, Feffer (1959; Feffer and Suchotliff, 1966) devised a measure of self-organization called the Role-Taking Task (RTT). This is a projective task using TAT cards in which the subject's role-taking ability is assessed from his skill in refocusing on his initial stories from the perspective of the other actors in the story.

Following the cognitive-developmental tradition of Piaget, Chandler (1973; Note 9) examined egocentrism using a hybrid of the techniques of Flavell et al. (1968) and Feffer (1959; Feffer & Suchotliff, 1966). In

Chandler's task, the subject is presented with a sequence of cartoons depicting interpersonal episodes and is asked to tell the story from the point of view of a central character and then from the viewpoint of a late-arriving onlooker. Role-taking ability is determined from the extent to which privileged information known to the subject is inappropriately ascribed to the bystander. This task differs from Feffer's in that different perspectives are insured, and it simplifies the procedure of Flavell by including the bystander in the cartoons instead of having another person come into the room.

In addition to the instruments described above, a variety of other measures have been utilized to assess role-taking and "empathy" in children and have produced variable findings. Some researchers have attempted to differentiate "cognitive" and "affective" elements of role-taking. For example, Rotenberg (1974) defined cognitive role-taking as the ability to predict the responses of another person in actual everyday situations, without being involved with the other person's feelings. The cognitive task was a guessing game in which each subject was asked standard questions about how his partner would respond in a number of social interactions. Affective role-taking was defined as "the behavioral disposition to relieve the distress of others" (Rotenberg, 1974, p. 180). The measure of affective role-taking disposition was the extent to which the subject reduced noxious noise to a partner, who was purportedly attached by earphones to an "awakening machine." Juvenile delinquents were found to be no different from nondelinquent agemates on cognitive role-taking, but they were significantly poorer than nondelinquents on affective role-taking. These results suggest that discrimination between affective and cognitive components of role-taking may be useful, especially in regard to delinquents. The relation of Rotenberg's (1974) measures to the more widely researched instruments described above is unknown, however, and the precise definition of role-taking remains an issue among researchers.

Attempts to arrive at greater specificity of the construct generally have resulted in the conclusion that role-taking is multi-dimensional in nature and that role-taking tasks can be ordered in a developmental hierarchy (Urberg & Docherty, 1976). Extended investigations into "levels" of role-taking, including some longitudinal studies, also support the hierarchical nature of role-taking (Selman, 1971a; 1971b; 1976; Selman & Byrne, 1974; Selman, Jaquette, & Lavin, 1977).

In general, there is some evidence to indicate that role-taking is

431

composed of a number of component skills and that differences among measures have contributed to the variable research results reported. When adolescents are of concern, it seems reasonable to utilize an instrument such as Chandler's (1973; Note 9), which appears to assess higher-level role-taking skills (Urberg & Docherty, 1976; Kurdek, 1977; Borke, 1972). Alternatively, the work of Rotenberg (1974) suggests that it may be useful to utilize separate measures of affective and cognitive role-taking in research with delinquents.

Role-taking: Normal Development

Research results indicate that role-taking ability is, in part, a function of age. Findings are reasonably consistent in this regard, although there are some disagreements about the particular age at which specific dimensions of role-taking appear. Flavell et al. (1968) indicate that the preschool schild has not yet achieved the first step — an awareness that perspective exists. By the time he enters school, however, he is likely to have some understanding of perspective variation. Research with Feffer's (1959) RTT has revealed the following developmental pattern: at about age 6 there is a discontinuity between versions of the story — uncorrected decentering; between 7 or 8, a fluctuating form of coordination between perspectives is seen; and a synthesis of the different perspectives begins to become clearly evident at about 9 years of age (Feffer & Gourevitch, 1960). In a study designed to explore the lower limits of role-taking behavior (Urberg & Docherty, 1976), findings suggest that some dimensions of role-taking occur earlier than 6 years old. Nevertheless, there is general agreement that profound changes in role-taking occur during the period of middle childhood, and by early and middle adolescence the individual's perspective-taking has developed to the point that the person can take the role of a third-person observer of himself and others in interaction, taking into account the feelings, thoughts, and intentions of all involved (Shantz, 1975).

According to Piaget (1928), acquisition of role-taking skills or decentering is a maturational process which occurs as a result of active involvement with the environment and subsequent readjustments of cognitive structures. A necessary condition is held to be social exchanges, and Piaget emphasized the role of peers in this developmental process. "Discussion among equals" is a liberating force that enables a child to step outside of his own perspective, become aware of contradictory points of view, and finally to re-establish equilibrium through resolution of competing views. Games with rules, verbal exchanges, and group actions all contribute to the demise of egocentrism. Flavell (1963) emphasized the influence of reinforcements, especially negative ones, from interactions with peers in the development of role-taking ability. Maccoby (1959) proposed that a child learns role-taking by practicing covertly the actions observed in adults with whom he interacts and who control the resources he needs. Such covert role-playing, according to Maccoby, is a way of learning "not only adult-like social actions directed toward others, but of learning reactions toward the self" (p. 252). Kerckhoff (1969) discusses a similar phenomenon using the term "identification," which he holds is basically "a special case of role-taking-role-playing." Although Bandura (1969; 1971; 1976) does not address role-taking ability per se, his theoretical point of view and empirical findings in modeling studies support the acquisition of such ability through a social learning process. According to Bandura (1977), most competencies are acquired and perfected by exposure to instructive example and reinforced practice. This line of thinking leads to the conclusion that role-taking ability, like other skills of living, is a learned phenomenon which occurs through interactions with the environment.

Role-taking Deficits in Non-normal Groups

Effects of role-taking deficiencies are apparent when normal and non-normal groups of children are compared. Chandler (Chandler, Greenspan, & Barenboim, 1974; Chandler, Note 9) found marked developmental delays in role-taking ability among institutionalized emotionally disturbed children as compared with adusted peers. Similar findings of the Hahnemann group (Platt et al., 1974) were noted earlier in our section on problem solving. Selman et al. (1977) reported that a clinic sample performed significantly lower than their public school peers on tasks assessing reasoning about interpersonal relations and the resolution of interpersonal problems, although there were no differences between groups on tasks of logico-physical reasoning. In addition, these authors reported that preliminary analyses of a two-year follow-up indicated that the results were replicated.

Another area of abnormality in which role-taking ability has been examined is that of mental retardation. In a series of studies using Feffer's RTT, Affleck (1975a, 1975b, 1976) found a direct association between role-taking ability and the interpersonal competencies of retarded children. In the latter study, retarded subjects who were higher in role-taking ability than their retarded peers were found to be more likely to use tactics that took into account the needs of the other person rather than simply making a request for the person to do something. It is important to note that in some studies, role-taking ability does show a moderate correlation with intelligence. Yet when IQ is held constant or partialed out, role-taking deficits continue to discriminate between normal and non-normal children.

The deviant behavior and thinking of delinquents and psychopaths also have been attributed to role-taking deficiencies (Gough, 1948; Sarbin, 1954). Gough proposed that the psychopathic personality is pathologically deficient in role-playing ability, suggesting that such an assumption accommodates the already-known facts about psychopathy. The notion that role-taking places a number of constraints on behavior was strongly stated:

> This role-taking ability provides a technique for self-understanding and self-control. Learned prohibitions . . . may be observed by "telling one's self" not to behave in a certain way . . . Role-playing, or putting one's self in another's position, enables a person to predict the other's behavior. Finally, role-playing ability makes one sensitive in advance to the reactions of others; such prescience may then deter or modify the unexpressed action. (Gough, 1948, p. 363)

In order to test his assumptions about role-taking deficiencies in psychopaths, Gough (1957) developed a socialization scale which is a part of the self-report, paper-and-pencil California Psychological Inventory. Gough (1960) reported a number of validation studies with this scale, which has been found to discriminate between delinquent and non-delinquent youths (see Megargee, 1972). More recently, Kendall, Deardorff, and Finch (1977) reported that the socialization scale not only successfully differentiated delinquents from non-delinquents, but also discriminated first offenders from repeat offenders. Delinquents have been found also to score lower on a similar self-report empathy scale than non-delinquents (Hogan, 1969; 1975). The relationship of these scales to the more behavioral measures of role-taking described above, however, has not yet been examined.

Evidence that delinquents exhibit role-taking deficits on a behavioral task comes from studies which utilized the assessment technique of Chandler (1973; Note 9). This procedure requires the subject to set aside his own perspective and report only information that a late-arriving bystander could know about a situation. Chandler (1973) found significant differences between 45 chronically delinquent boys and 45 non-delinquent boys living in the same community, and he reported role-taking deficits in a "substantial proportion" of delinquents he tested. Little (Note 10) administered Chandler's measure to 37 female delinquents in a state learning center and found role-taking deficits in 73 per cent of the residents. The evidence appears consistent — role-taking deficiencies are common among delinquents as well as among other non-normal groups of children. The question that arises next is: How can role-taking deficits be remediated and what behavioral effects can be anticipated from such remediation?

Role-taking: Remediating the Deficits

As noted earlier, many interpersonal problem solving programs (e.g., Platt et al., Note 5; Sarason, 1968; Sarason & Ganzer, 1969; 1973) make deliberate use of role playing as a training procedure, but role-taking ability per se has not been specifically examined as a dependent variable in these programs. A recent exception is research with the problem solving training program of Elardo and associates (Elardo & Cooper, 1977), which has been tested with elementary school children up to ages 9 and 10. Not only was role-taking and social competence shown to be positively correlated (Elardo, Caldwell, & Webb, Note 11), but children in an experimental group who were taught problem solving and role-taking in their regular classrooms gained in role-taking ability, problem solving skills, and classroom adjustment (Elardo & Caldwell, Note 12). Flavell's (1968) measure was used to assess role-taking skills before and after treatment.

In a recently reported study with hyperactive children (Douglas, Parry, Marton, & Garson, 1976), a multi-faceted cognitive training program geared toward self control included teaching problem solving strategies, modeling, and training in self-verbalizations. Contingency management techniques were used when a child was especially unmanageable. A number of the self-verbalizations used for playing games or cooperating on a task with a peer seem to represent some direct teaching of role-taking ability. For example, the trainer modeled thoughts such as, "I guess Tom wants to win as much as I do. He'll be unhappy if he loses too many times" (Douglas et al., 1976, p. 395). One of the dependent measures on which change occurred was the MFF (Kagan et al., 1964), a widely-used measure of cognitive impulsivity. Rather large improvements were found after training on both the latency and error scores from the MFF, and these changes held up well at a three-month follow-up. It is important to note that children in the Douglas et al. (1976) program did not show improved classroom behavior as rated by their teachers and that role-taking per se was not assessed.

Although Allen et al. (1976) reported some positive results from their problem solving training of elementary school children, they recommended greater use of role playing and behavioral rehearsal in order to enhance implementation of the problem solving strategies that were taught. Role-taking skills were not measured. While children's problem solving skills increased significantly after training, behavior as assessed by teacher and peer ratings did not improve.

As was true for interpersonal problem solving, reports of the efficacy of role-taking training with delinquents have been minimal. The research findings that have been reported, however, are promising. In a simple but innovative treatment project, Chandler (1973) assigned 45 chronically delinquent boys between the ages of 11 and 13 to one of three groups. Fifteen subjects were randomly placed in an experimental treatment group which met one-half day a week for 10 weeks to write, perform, and view videotapes of skits about boys their age. Another group of 15 spent the same amount of time producing animated cartoons and documentary-style films about their neighborhood on 8-millimeter color film. The third group served as an assessment control. All subjects resided in the community rather than in an institution, although all were considered by court officials to be serious and chronic delinquents, and all had committed one or more crimes which would have been felonies if committed by an adult.

There were significant improvements in role-taking ability in the experimental group that received role-taking training as compared to the other two groups (Chandler, 1973). In addition, an 18-month follow-up of court contacts showed that the experimental training group committed about half as many known delinquencies as they had during the 18 months before training, a significantly greater improvement than for either of the other two groups. A later study with emotionally disturbed children in an institution (Chandler et al., 1974) produced significant improvement in role-taking ability following similar remedial training, although attempts to assess effects on behavior produced only mixed findings.

Recent research by Little (Note 10) partially replicated and extended the work of Chandler (1973). Little randomly assigned 18 institutionalized female delinquents aged 13 through 16 (matched on the basis of role-taking deficits) to treatment and attention control groups which met twice a week for three weeks. The treatment groups improvised skits about the kinds of people they might encounter in everyday living, both adults and peers. Each skit had a part for every girl in a group of 5 or 6 girls. After the subjects selected the parts they wanted to play, the skits were performed and videotaped. The group then watched the videotape and each girl reported what it was like to play the role she had enacted. The procedure was repeated until every girl had played every part, and a new skit was then devised and played as before. The attention control group spent an equal amount of time in creating a videotaped documentary about the institution in which the girls resided.

Role-taking errors were found to decrease significantly from pre to post-testing for both treatment and control groups with the treatment group showing a greater decrease, but not significantly so. The institution's token economy failed to reveal any meaningful pattern of point totals. MFF scores failed to dscriminate between groups, and there was no systematic relationship between MFF and role-taking scores for 30 subjects for whom data were complete.

The fact that both treatment and control subjects improved significantly in role-taking ability over the course of the study suggests the possibility that factors in the cooperative effort to make a videotaped documentary or a period of residence in the institution facilitated the acquisition of role-taking skills. Chandler's (1973) assessment-only and attention control groups were not significantly different following the training period, and there is research support for the hypothesis that a living situation with opportunity for frequent peer interaction facilitates the acquisition of role-taking skills (Nahir & Yussen, 1977; Hollos & Cowan, 1973). In the Little (Note 10) study, an insufficient number of subjects were available to form an assessment-only group which might have clarified this issue for delinquents in an institutional setting. Follow-up in terms of court contacts after discharge is still in progress.

Conclusions

The extension of Piaget's theory and research to the development of cognitive processes as they operate in interpersonal situations has proved to be a fruitful approach to understanding social adjustment in children and adolescents. Furthermore, it seems clear that deficiencies in role-taking typically appear in non-normal groups of youngsters — emotionally disturbed, retarded, and delinquent.

There is evidence that role-taking ability can be taught to both children and adolescents within a problem-solving package or more simply in a program which provides opportunities for practice, modeling, and feedback, all of which appear to operate in the normal acquisition of role-taking skills. Delinquents have been successfully treated by both approaches, and one researcher (Chandler 1973) who implemented fairly short-term role-taking training demonstrated reduction in court contacts over an 18-month period following treatment as well as an immediate reduction in role-taking deficits. There is also some evidence that institutional living may facilitate the acquisition of this social cognition skill, and further research to explore this possibility as well as the efficacy of training for deficient delinquents is highly recommended.

Self Control

Society demands an increasing amount of "self control" as the child develops, and by the time of adolescence, serious consequences often follow from a failure to measure up to these demands. For purposes of this discussion, self control is viewed as the individual's governing of his own behavior to attain certain ends. In a cognitive-behavioral framework, this governing requires both the cognitive skills necessary to generate and evaluate alternatives (which may be considered a legislative function) and the behavioral capacity to inhibit acting on the discarded alternatives and to instead engage in the selected option (an executive function) (Kendall & Wilcox, Note 13).

Our position states that a child/adolescent will exhibit self-controlled behavior to the extent that he possesses a response repertoire that contains the necessary cognitive and behavioral skills and is motivated to use them in a particular situation. It is to the question of response repertoire that this discussion is largely directed, although the

438

importance of motivation to use self-controlling responses is not minimized. The point is simply that if the response is lacking, motivation is a moot question. Thus remediation of deficits must precede motivational issues, although the use of incentive motivations should be incorporated in the training of the self-control procedures.

Self-control: Normal Development

The newborn infant arrives on the scene with minimal control over himself and his existence. The pattern of motor development unfolds in an orderly sequence, however, and both maturation and learning contribute to the development of motor control (McCandless, 1961). It is in the second year of life that language begins to have an impact on behavior, and as is true for motor control, maturation and learning both are involved in the acquisition of *language* as a controlling mechanism.

According to Mussen (1963), the verbal instructions of adults have no observable effect on motor behavior of infants only a few months of age. By the time a child is 1 or 2 years old, however, an adult's instructions produce orienting and investigatory responses in the child. And by the time a child is 3 or 4, verbal instructions can release the action the child is already set to perform or can initiate some new action. Such instructions, however, cannot yet inhibit an action once started or shift the child from one action to another. The 3- or 4-year old child normally can follow rather complicated instructions given by an adult, and it is at this age that he begins to regulate his own behavior on the basis of verbal self-instructions. As speech continues to develop, it comes to serve more of a regulatory function for the child. Between the ages of 4½ and 5½ the child's self-verbalizations shift from overt to covert, or primarily internal, speech.

The relation of language to behavioral control has been of concern to psychologists for a number of years. Writing in 1924, Allport stated that human beings developed spoken language to control and direct their own behavior and to control the nonsocial environment as well as for social control. An early experimental study (Waring, 1927) demonstrated the greater power of verbal cues than nonverbal cues over the motor behavior of children. Waring reported that language approval (spoken word) had an immediate effect and was superior to non-language approval (nod and smile) in improving learning. She interpreted these findings as supporting her hypothesis of a strong linear relationship between early language habits and early habits of "conduct control."

Development of speech as a regulator of behavior has been extensively examined by Russian psychologists, and much of this work is reported in detail by Luria (1961). The apparatus typically used in these studies consists of a rubber bulb and a panel of sound and light stimuli that can be variably presented or patterned. The child's squeezes of the rubber bulb are recorded by an electrically-driven event recorder to produce a written record of behavior. Results of research with this apparatus indicate that early control of behavior occurs through competing motor responses and exteroceptive feedback. While speech initially serves an impellant (action producing) function, this function of speech recedes and the leading role passes to the inhibiting functions. In the final stage of the development of speech as a controlling mechanism, ". . . the external developed forms of speech become reduced, and the decisive influence is now exerted by that higher form of internal speech which constitutes an essential component both of thought and volitional action . . ." (Luria, 1961, p. 95).

In his theory of cognitive development, Piaget (1926) proposed a distinction between egocentric, or internal, speech and socialized speech. In egocentric speech there is no attempt by the child to adapt his talk to the needs of the listener, whereas in socialized speech there is a clear intention to communicate. Piaget held that egocentric speech disappeared as the child approached 7 years of age and his egocentrism declined. Vygotsky (1962) disagreed with Piaget's view of the fate of egocentric speech and stated that such speech simply "goes underground," or turns into inner speech, rather than disappearing. In an adult, according to Vygotsky, inner speech represents a person's "thinking for himself," and this process serves the same function for the adult that egocentric speech has for the child. Vygotsky hypothesized that inner speech develops and becomes established at about the beginning of school age and that this occurrence is what produces the quick drop in egocentric speech observed at that stage. This view is consistent with that of Luria (1961) and other Russian investigators. In general, Russian research indicates that behavior that is learned with the use of language is acquired quickly, generalizes widely, and is highly stable. In stating the case for the importance of language, Mussen (1963) wrote, "Children over 5 years of age function and control their behavior primarily by means of verbal mediation; that is, by means of what American psychologists call mediated generalization or verbal mediation" (p. 46).

Research with a task similar to Luria's (Birch, Note 14) and with American children revealed an age-related developmental sequence of verbal inhibition of motor behavior similar to that found in Russian children. When told "press" to a green light and "don't press" to a red light, all children 5½ to 6½ years old reached the 90 per cent criterion of success. In contrast, only 75 per cent of 4½- to 5½-year-olds and 37.5 per cent of 3½- to 4½-year-olds achieved criterion. The influence of learning on this apparently maturational phenomenon was examined by Bem (1967), who demonstrated that previously deficient 3-year-olds could be trained to make the required number of lever presses to match the number of light signals presented. The procedure used involved a sequence of verbal training, verbal fading, motor training, verbal-motor training, and verbal-motor fading. Bem suggested that some analogue of fading may be the "real world mechanism" by which speech becomes internal and verbal self control is acquired.

The interaction between verbal and nonverbal behavior was examined within an operant framework by Lovaas (1961), who showed that aggressive nonverbal behavior could be increased by reinforcement of aggressive verbal behavior. Lovaas (1964) also demonstrated that verbal operants such as "fast" or "slow" can control both the rate of their own occurrence as well as latency, rate, and choice of manual responding. In discussing the development of verbal control of motor behavior, Lovaas suggested such contributing factors as: the imitation of parents' verbalizations; the reinforcement for acting congruently with one's statements; and the self-reinforcement from behaving according to one's plan or previous verbalization.

In an extensive review of theories and their report of four studies of private speech, Kohlberg, Yaeger, and Hjertholm (1968) provided support for the cognitive developmental approach shared by Piaget and Vygotsky and lend credence to Vygotsky's hypothesis of what happens to speech — it becomes private. In the Kohlberg et al. (1968) studies, private speech was found to be common among 4- to 6-year-olds and to gradually decline thereafter. On the basis of theory and the findings of their studies, these authors hypothesized a hierarchy of private speech representing 7 different developmental levels. Only one of their categories constitutes self-guiding comments, and this category is placed at Level 5 in the sequence of development of private speech. The two later levels are held to be "inaudible mutterings" and "silent inner speech."

One study specifically addressed the relative efficacy of the differential modes of delivery of verbalizations in governing nonverbal behavior (Meichenbaum & Goodman, 1969a). These researchers used a finger-tapping task with kindergarten and first grade children, and the findings indicated the expected developmental sequence. Kindergarten children's motor performance in response to cues "faster" or "slower" was similar to that of first grade children when self-verbalizations were aloud, but whispered cues using only lip movements had little control over performance of kindergarten children. By contrast, the first grade children performed better when the cues were covert rather than overt. On the basis of these results, the authors suggested that younger children should be encouraged to self-verbalize out loud and then gradually fade the cues to implicit or "silent" speech.

In summary, there is considerable evidence that self control develops largely as a function of a child's development of language mechansims and that such development follows an established, age-related sequence. Next we turn to a discussion of the characteristics of children who have failed to develop self control and to some results of efforts at teaching private self-guiding speech to remediate self-control deficits.

Self Control: Remediation of Deficits in Self-Verbalization

Children's self-verbalizations and their role in the control of behavior have been examined in relation to the characteristic response styles of children's cognitive behavior or conceptual tempo. For example, the cognitive tempo dimension of reflection-impulsivity indicates the child's consistent tendency to reflect over alternative response possibilities before giving an answer rather to respond impulsively. Unlike the area of role-taking in which assessment instruments abound, verbal self control research has made major use of a single instrument — the MFF (Kagan et al., 1964). This test requires subjects to select the exact match for a stimulus figure from among a selection of six similar figures, and latency to first response and errors are noted. Research with the MFF has shown that reflection-impulsivity is an important dimension of cognitive development related behavioral concomitants (see Messer, 1976; see Finch & Kendall, 1979). For example, impulsivity has been shown to be related to certain educational deficits and clinical syndromes. More impulsives are found among children diagnosed as hyperactive, brain damaged, epileptic, and mentally retarded. Impulsives do less well in school and are poorer readers. The reflective child is better able to sustain attention, is less aggressive, and makes more advanced moral judgments.

Meichenbaum and Goodman (1969b) designed a study specifically to explore the relationship between conceptual tempo and the verbal control of behavior. Results indicated that the self-verbalizations of impulsive children of kindergarten age were less directive of actions than those of reflectives. While reflectives responded to the semantic aspects of their self-instructions by tapping several times to each utterance, the impulsive children used self-instructions in a motoric manner — that is, they tapped each time they uttered a word. This finding is reminiscent of Luria's discussion of the impellant power of words, a force which only later gives way to an inhibiting function when the meaning of words becomes over-riding. Impoulsives in the Meichembaum and Goodman (1969b) study also responded to "don't push" with motor responses more frequently than did the reflectives. In addition, impulsive children showed significantly less verbal control of motor behavior under the covert condition of self-instruction (lip movements only) than did the reflective children, whereas overt self-instructions produced no difference in frequency of errors. The authors suggested that socialization factors play a vital role in the acquisition of "speech-for-self," a suggestion which takes on added importance regarding delinquents.

Several researchers have successfully altered the cognitive style of impulsivity by teaching children to use self-directed verbal commands (e.g., Douglas et al., 1976; Finch, Wilkinson, Nelson, & Montgomery, 1975; Palkes, Stewart, & Kahana, 1968; Kendall & Finch, 1976; 1978; Kendall & Wilcox, Note 15; Miechenbaum & Goodman, 1971). The procedure follows essentially the developmental sequence outlined by Luria (1961). The child is instructed to pay attention to a model who talks aloud while performing a task, then whispers the instructions, and then repeats the task while thinking the self-guiding words. The child then follows the same sequence of self-talk, thus practicing the verbal self-instruction (see Kendall, 1977).

An impulsive cognitive style also has been altered by modeling (Debus, 1970; Ridberg, Parke, & Hetherington, 1971; Yando & Kagan, 1968; Denney, 1972) without the structured practice of self-instructions. In one of the studies reported by Meichenbaum and Goodman (1971), a

443

comparison of modeling with a combination of modeling and training in self-instruction showed that both conditions resulted in a significant increase in latencies to respond but that only the self instructional training resulted also in a decrease in errors on the MFF.

Many of the studies teaching self-verbalizations have involved the use of impersonal material as training tasks rather than interpersonal situations. Even so, some carryover of reduction in impulsivity in social settings such as classroom behavior has been noted (Kendall & Finch, 1976; Kendall & Wilcox, Note 15). Such generalization is not always the case, however, and Meichembaum and Asarnow (1979) have reviewed this research with an emphasis on metacognitive development. In the previously-mentioned Douglas et al. (1976) cognitive treatment of hyperactive children, improvement in classroom behavior did *not* occur even though a wide range of tasks and games were used in training. Treatment effects did generalize to reading, and a three-month follow-up indicated that reading improvement was maintained as well as increases in latency and reduction in errors on the MFF.

On the basis of her research with aggressive boys, Camp (1977) postulated that maintaining response inhibition in both impersonal and interpersonal tasks may depend on an effective linguistic control system. According to Camp, difficulty in inhibiting aggressive behavior "could involve a weak or inconsistent response to covert commands as well as a high threshold for activating self-regulating verbalizations" (p. 152). Camp's treatment study (Camp, Blom, Hebert, & Van Doorninck, 1977), in which young aggressive boys were taught to "think aloud," found improvement on several measures and supports the notion that self-guiding covert speech is important to self control in children and that self-verbalizations can be taught directly. Furthermore, such skill acquisition appears to affect behavior.

The evidence in regard to adolescents generally and to delinquents particularly is less clear. One recent study (Williams & Akamatsu, 1978) utilizing the Meichenbaum & Goodman (1971) self-guidance procedure with delinquents produced only mixed results. The children's form of the MFF was used as training material, and the adult form was a dependent measure. Both a self-instructional training group and an attention-control group which practiced MFF items with the instructions to go slowly and carefully performed better than an assessment-control group following training. Only the self-instruction group showed generalization of training effects to the WISC-R picture arrangement subtest, and the three groups did not differ on a delay of gratification measure. One of the possible explanations for their finding of equal effectiveness of training on the MFF that is suggested by Williams and Akamatsu (1978) is exposure to "basic problem solving skills," although this would not explain why only the self-instruction training group effects generalized to another task. As noted earlier, verbal self-instruction is contained in some problem-solving programs (e.g., Bowman, Note 8) with delinquents, but the teaching of self-guiding speech as the major focus of treatment has been only minimally explored.

The successful self-control treatment of an aggressive 16-year-old (McCullough, Huntsinger, & Nay, 1977) apparently included training in verbal mediation, although systematic instruction in self-verbalizations as used in the treatment of children was not implemented. In an attempt to apply the McCullough et al. (1977) self-control treatment to delinquents, Huntsinger (Note 16) trained 12- to 16-year-old male residents of a state learning center. During four individual sessions over the period of one month, self-control treatment subjects learned to recognize both internal and external cues that accompanied their anger and were then taught to interrupt their behavioral sequence using thought stopping, muscle relaxation, and breath control. Role playing and video-tape feedback were used to teach these new ways of handling anger. Following this short-term training, no differences were found between self-control treatment subjects, a discussion-only group, and a nontreated control group on the dependent measures, which included aggressive behavior as reflected in the institution's token economy. It can be seen that this self-control treatment is reminiscent of some of the problem solving programs described earlier except that it focuses narrowly on the handling of anger. It is difficult to completely understand the negative results of this study, although the lack of a specific focus on self-instructional training and/or the brevity of the training may have been significant factors. One should also consider the possible unreliability of the institution's token economy, since the Little (Note 10) study in a similar institution found no meaningful pattern of differential point totals from the token economy. The matter of reliable dependent measures of behavior in institutions appears to be unresolved (e.g., Chandler et al., 1974), although some success in obtaining reliable staff ratings of delinquents' behavior with a rating scale has been reported (e.g., Sarason & Ganzer, 1973).

445

Conclusions

The critical function of language in self control has been considered, as has its sequential, age-related development. The treatment of impulsive children by self-instructional methods that closely approximate the normal process of development appears to offer an efficacious approach to remediation of at least some self control deficits.

Although research with an adolescent population is minimal, successful treatment of adults with the same procedure (Meichenbaum & Cameron, 1973) suggests that adolescents may similarly benefit. From observation of the behavior of delinquents, one is led to speculate that for many of these youngsters, words serve more of an impellant function than an inhibitory function as described by Luria (1961). Such a speculation, of course, remains to be substantiated by research. Self-instructional training with adolescents may require the use of tasks with a higher interest level than those used with younger children, presentation to the subjects of an acceptable rationale for the training, or similar special adjustments in the training procedures which have been shown to be efficacious with younger children. in the Williams and Akamatsu (1978) study, delinquents were told that the training was to help them do better in school. The use of an expectancy scale indicated that the training groups did not differ in the degree to which they felt the training might be effective. All in all, exploration of speech as a source of self regulation for delinquents appears warranted on the basis of the theory and data presented herein. Implementation of the self-instructional treatment described is within reason in terms of time, energy, and cost, and the payoff may be well worth the effort.

Final Comments

The cognitive-behavioral approach to the treatment of delinquents appears to offer a promising adjunct to behavioral programs and perhaps an efficacious alternative to traditional methods of working with this problematic population. It is important to note, however, that this approach is recommended for the treatment of certain delinquents, not delinquency. One should not assume that all youngsters who are categorized as "delinquent" are deficient in the cognitive skills discussed. For example, 27 per cent of the girls tested in a state learning center did *not* show role-taking deficits (Little, Note 10). This mitigates against the tendency to simplistically equate social egocentrism with delinquency. It may be, as Chandler (1973) noted, that role-taking deficits are more a measure of social ineptitude than of an antisocial orientation, since social egocentrism characterizes a broad spectrum of persons who have failed to make a successful adjustment to life. The consistent finding that congitive deficits *do* occur in a large proportion of those labeled "delinquent," however, suggests that remedial programs should be implemented.

It should be apparent that the cognitive-behavioral approach described herein emphasizes the commonalities between delinquents and other non-normal groups of adolescents. According to this line of thinking, the difficulties of many delinquents may stem from developmental deficits, and the treatment of choice may be an intervention that has its foundations in the normal developmental process. Further research will determine to what extent these hypotheses are supportable. At any rate, the theory and data herein may encourage the perception of delinquents as a manageable population, in the sense that their developmental deficits can be remediated, rather than as a deviant, antisocial group for whom punishment is required.

Though the focus of this chapter has been on remediation of deficits, one should not overlook the potential of these training programs for primary prevention of problems in social adjustment. Indeed, even at the preschool level, youngsters trained in ICPS skills were found to make better school adjustments than their agemates who were not trained (Shune & Spivack, 1978). It is possible also that role-taking training in the 5th and 6th grades, when role-taking ability normally is mature, could prevent serious behavioral problems at home, in school, and with the law. Likewise, verbal self-instructional programs in the first grade, when covert self-guiding speech is present in normal children, might serve to decrease the behavior problems of children who otherwise may become labeled impulsive, hyperactive, aggressive, or delinquent. At any rate, it is highly recommended that research be conducted to determine further the possible effects of intervention before interpersonal difficulties become acute.

A question that emerges from the preceding review and discussion is: What is the best cognitive-behavioral treatment for delinquents? Obviously, the answer at this point can be no more than suggestive, and it is also obvious that the treatments are not independent. The comprehensive, research-based problem solving training program of the

447

Hahnemann group has not been tested with delinquents, but other problem solving approaches that have been implemented have shown positive results. The more narrow focus on one problem solving component, role-taking, also produced positive changes in behavior of delinquents, although efforts at replication were not successful. The one study in which verbal self-instruction was taught to delinquents produced variable results, but findings with other populations, both children and adults, suggest the technique is a viable one.

Certainly, further investigation of the efficacy of these cognitive-behavioral interventions with delinquents is indicated before widespread implementation is undertaken. The present evidence suggests, however, that whether one addresses the social inadequacies of delinquents at the level of interpersonal problem solving, role-taking, or verbal self control, remediation of cognitive deficits may be indicated for a large proportion of this otherwise heterogeneous population.

Reference Notes

1. Quay, H.C., & Parsons, L.B. *The differential behavioral classification of the juvenile offender.* Laboratory report, Temple University, Philadelphia, Pa., 1971.

2. Freedman, B.J. *An analysis of social-behavioral skill deficits in delinquent and non-delinquent adolescent boys.* Unpublished manuscript, University of Wisconsin, 1974.

3. Spivack, G., & Levine, M. *Self-regulation in acting-out and normal adolescents* (Rep. M-4531). Washington, D.C.: National Institute of Health, 1963.

4. Platt, J.J., & Spivack, G. *Manual for the means-ends problem-solving procedure (MEPS).* Philadelphia: Hahnemann Medical College and Hospital, Department of Mental Health Sciences, 1975.

5. Platt, J.J., Spivack, G., & Swift, M.S. *Interpersonal problem-solving group therapy.* Philadelphia: Hahnemann Medical College and Hospital, Department of Mental Health Sciences, 1975.

6. Platt, J.J., & Spivack, G. *Workbook for training in interpersonal problem-solving thinking.* Philadelphia: Hahnemann Medical College and Hospital, Department of Mental Health Sciences, 1976.

7. Siegel, J.M., & Spivack, G. *Problem-solving therapy: The description of a new program for chronic schizophrenic patients.* Philadelphia: Hahnemann Medical College and Hospital, Department of Mental Health Sciences, 1973.

8. Bowman, P.C. *A cognitive-behavioral treatment program for impulsive youthful offenders.* Unpublished manuscript, Virginia Commonwealth University, 1978.

9. Chandler, M.J. *Egocentrism and childhood psychology: The development and application of measurement techniques.* Paper presented at the meeting of the Society for Research in Child Development, Minneapolis, April 1971.
10. Little, V.L. *Developmental role-taking deficits in institutionalized juvenile delinquents.* Paper presented at the meeting of the Southeastern Psychological Association, Atlanta, March 1978.
11. Elardo, P.T., Caldwell, B.M., & Webb, R. *An examination of the relationship between role-taking and social competence.* Paper presented at the Southeastern Conference on Human Development, Nashville, Tennessee, April 1976.
12. Elardo, P.T., & Caldwell, B.M. *The effects of an experimental social development program on children in the middle childhood period.* Unpublished manuscript, University of Arkansas at Little Rock, 1976.
13. Kendall, P.C., & Wilcox, L.E. *Self-control in children: The development of a rating scale.* Manuscript submitted for publication, 1978.
14. Birch, D. *Some effects of the verbal system on the nonverbal behavior of preschool children.* Paper presented at the meeting of the Society for Research in Child Development, 1967.
15. Kendall, P.C., & Wilcox, L.E. *A cognitive-behavioral treatment for impulsivity: Concrete versus conceptual labeling with nonself-controlled problem children.* Manuscript submitted for publication, 1978.
16. Huntsinger, G.M. *Teaching self-control of verbal and physical aggression to juvenile delinquents.* Unpublished manuscript, Virginia Commonwealth University, 1976.

References

Affleck, G.G. Role-taking ability and interpersonal conflict resolution among retarded young adults. *American Journal of Mental Deficiency,* 1975, *80,* 233-236. (a)

Affleck, G.G. Role-taking ability and the interpersonal competencies of retarded children. *American Journal of Mental Deficiency,* 1975, *80,* 312-316. (b)

Affleck, G.G. Role-taking ability and the interpersonal tactics of retarded children. *American Journal of Mental Deficiency,* 1976, *80,* 667-670.

Alexander, J.F., & Parsons, B.V. Short-term behavioral intervention with delinquent families: Impact on family process and recidivism. *Journal of Abnormal Psychology,* 1973, *81,* 219-225.

Allen, G.J., Chinsky, J.M., Larcen, S.W. Lochman, J.E., & Selinger, H.V. *Community psychology and the schools.* New York: John Wiley & Sons, 1976.

Allport, F.H. *Social psychology.* New York: Houghton Mifflin, 1924.

Bandura, A. Social-learning theory of identificatory processes. In D. Goslin (Ed.), *Handbook of socialization theory and research.* Chicago: Rand McNally, 1969.

Bandura, A. Psychotherapy based upon modeling principles. In A.E. Bergin & S.L. Garfield (Eds.), *Handbook of psychotherapy and behavior change.* New York: Wiley, 1971.

Bandura, A. Effecting change through participant modeling. In J.D. Krumboltz & C.E. Thoresen (Eds.), *Counseling methods.* New York: Holt, Rinehart, & Winston, 1976.

Bandura, A. *Social learning theory.* Englewood Cliffs, N.J.: Prentice-Hall, 1977.

Bem, S.L. Verbal self-control: The establishment of effective self-instruction. *Journal of Experimental Psychology,* 1967, *74,* 485-491.

Borke, H. Chandler and Greenspan's "ersatz egocentrism": A rejoinder. *Developmental Psychology,* 1972, *7,* 107-109.

Camp, B.W. Verbal mediation in young aggressive boys. *Journal of Abnormal Psychology,* 1977, *86,* 145-153.

Camp, B.W., Blom, G.E., Hebert, F., & Van Doorninck, W.J. "Think aloud": A program for developing self-control in young aggressive boys. *Journal of Abnormal Child Psychology,* 1977, *5,* 157-169.

Chandler, M.J. Egocentrism and antisocial behavior: The assessment and training of social perspective-taking skills. *Developmental Psychology,* 1973, *9,* 326-332.

Chandler, M.J., Greenspan, S., & Barenboim, C. Assessment and training of role-taking and referential communication skills in institutionalized emotionally disturbed children. *Developmental Psychology,* 1974, *10,* 546-553.

Coelho, G.V., Hamburg, D.A., & Murphey, E.G. Coping strategies in a new learning environment. *Archives of General Psychiatry,* 1963, *9,* 433-443.

Debus, R.L. Effects of brief observation of model behavior on conceptual tempo of impulsive children. *Developmental Psychology,* 1970, *2,* 22-32.

Denney, D.R. Modeling effects upon conceptual style and cognitive tempo. *Child Development,* 1972, *43,* 105-119.

Douglas, V.I., Parry, P., Marton, P., & Garson, C. Assessment of a cognitive training program for hyperactive children. *Journal of Abnormal Child Psychology,* 1976, *4,* 389-410.

Draughton, M. Duplication of facial expression: Conditions affecting task and possible clinical usefulness. *Journal of Personality,* 1973, *41,* 140-150.

D'Zurilla, T.J., & Goldfried, M.R. Problem-solving and behavior modification. *Journal of Abnormal Psychology,* 1971, *78,* 107-126.

Elardo, P.T., & Cooper, M. *Project AWARE: A handbook for teachers.* Menlo Park, Calif.: Addison-Wesley, 1977.

Feffer, M.H. The cognitive implications of role-taking behavior. *Journal of Personality,* 1959, *27,* 152-168.

Feffer, M. Symptom expression as a form of primitive decentering. *Psychological Review,* 1967, *74,* 16-28.

Feffer, M. A developmental analysis of interpersonal behavior. *Psychological Review,* 1970, *77,* 197-214.

Feffer, M., & Gourevitch, V. Cognitive aspects of role-taking in children. *Journal of Personality,* 1960, *28,* 383-396.

Feffer, M., & Suchotliff, L. Decentering implications of social interaction. *Journal of Personality and Social Psychology,* 1966, *4,* 415-422.

Finch, A.J., Jr., & Kendall, P.C. Impulsive behavior: From research to treatment. In A.J. Finch, Jr., & P.C. Kendall (Eds.), *Clinical treatment and research in child psychopathology.* Hollingswood, N.Y.: Spectrum Publications, 1979.

Finch, A.J., Jr., Wilkinson, M.D., Nelson, W.M., III, & Montgomery, L.E. Modification of an impulsive cognitive tempo in emotionally disturbed boys. *Journal of Abnormal Child Psychology,* 1975, *3,* 47-51.

Flavell, J.H. *The developmental psychology of Jean Piaget.* New York: Van Nostrand Reinhold Co., 1963.

Flavell, J.H. The development of inferences about others. In T. Mischel (Ed.), *Understanding other persons.* Oxford, England: Blackwell Basil, 1974.

Flavell, J.H., Botkin, P.T., Fry, C.L., Wright, J.W., & Jarvis, P.E. *The development of role-taking and communication skills in children.* New York: Wiley, 1968.

Gordon, T. *Parent effectiveness training.* New York: Wyden, 1970.

Gough, H.G. A sociological theory of psychopathy. *American Journal of Sociology,* 1948, *53,* 359-366.

Gough, H.G. *Manual for the California psychological inventory.* Palo Alto, Calif.: Consulting Psychologists Press, 1957.

Gough, H.G. Theory and measurement of socialization. *Journal of Consulting Psychology,* 1960, *24,* 23-30.

Hogan, R. Development of an empathy scale. *Journal of Consulting and Clinical Psychology,* 1969, *33,* 307-316.

Hogan, R. Empathy: A conceptual and psychometric analysis. *The Counseling Psychologist,* 1975, *5,* 14-18.

Hollos, M., & Cowan, P.A. Social isolation and cognitive development: Logical operations and role-taking abilities in three Norwegian social settings. *Child Development,* 1973, *44,* 630-641.

Jahoda, M. The meaning of psychological health. *Social Casework,* 1953, *34,* 349-354.

Jahoda, M. *Current concepts of positive mental health.* New York: Basic Books, 1958.

Kagan, J., Rosman, B.L., Day, D., Albert, J., & Phillips, W. Information processing in the child: Significance of analytic and reflective attitudes. *Psychological Monographs,* 1964, *78* (1, Whole No. 578).

451

Kendall, P.C. On the efficacious use of verbal self-instructional procedures with children. *Cognitive Therapy and Research,* 1977, *1,* 331-341.

Kendall, P.C., Deardorff, P.A., & Finch, A.J., Jr. Empathy and socialization in first and repeat juvenile offenders and normals. *Journal of Abnormal Child Psychology,* 1977, *5,* 93-97.

Kendall, P.C., & Finch, A.J., Jr. A cognitive-behavioral treatment of impulse control: A case study. *Journal of Consulting and Clinical Psychology,* 1976, *44,* 852-857.

Kendall, P.C., & Finch, A.J., Jr. A cognitive-behavioral treatment for impulsivity: A group comparison study. *Journal of Consulting and Clinical Psychology,* 1978, *46,* 110-118.

Kendall, P.C., & Hollon, S.D. (Eds.). *Cognitive-behavioral interventions: Theory, research, and procedures.* New York: Academic Press, 1979.

Kerckhoff, A. Early antecedents of role taking and role playing ability. *Merrill-Palmer Quarterly,* 1969, *15,* 229-247.

Kifer, R.E., Lewis, M.A., Green, D.R., & Phillips, E.L. Training predelinquent youths and their parents to negotiate conflict situations. *Journal of Applied Behavior Analysis,* 1974, *7,* 357-364.

Klein, N.C., Alexander, J.F., & Parsons, B.V. Impact of family systems intervention on recidivism and sibling delinquency: A model of primary prevention and program evaluation. *Journal of Consulting and Clinical Psychology,* 1977, *45,* 469-474.

Kohlberg, L., Yaeger, J., & Hjertholm, E. Private speech: Four studies and a review of theories. *Child Development,* 1968, *39,* 691-736.

Kurdek, L.A. Structural components and intellectual and behavioral correlates of cognitive perspective taking in first through fourth grade children (Doctoral dissertation, University of Illinois at Chicago Circle, 1976). *Dissertation Abstracts International,* 1977, *37,* 3581B. (University of Microfilms No. 77-541).

Lovaas, O.I. Interaction between verbal and nonverbal behavior. *Child Development,* 1961, *32,* 329-336.

Lovaas, O.I. Cue properties of words: The control of operant responding by rate and content of verbal operants. *Child Development,* 1964, *35,* 245-256.

Luria, A.R. *The role of speech in the regulation of normal and abnormal behavior.* New York: Liveright, 1961.

Maccoby, E.E. Role-taking in childhood and its consequences for social learning. *Child Development,* 1959, *30,* 239-252.

McCandless, B.R. *Children and adolescents — behavior and development.* New York: Holt, Rinehart, & Winston, 1961.

McCullough, J.P., Huntsinger, G.M., & Nay, W.R. Self-control treatment of aggression in a 16-year-old male. *Journal of Consulting and Clinical Psychology,* 1977, *45,* 322-331.

McFall, R.M., & Lillesand, D.B. Behavior rehearsal with modeling and coaching in assertion training. *Journal of Abnormal Psychology,* 1971, *77* 313-323.

McFall, R.M., & Marston, A.R. An experimental investigation of behavior rehearsal in assertive training. *Journal of Abnormal Psychology,* 1970, *76,* 295-303.

Mead, G.H. *Mind, self, and society.* Chicago: University of Chicago Press, 1934.

Megargee, E.I. *The California Psychological Inventory handbook.* San Francisco: Jossey-Bass, 1972.

Meichenbaum, D., & Asarnow, J. Cognitive behavior modification and metacognitive development: Implications for the classroom. In P.C. Kendall & S.D. Hollon (Eds.), *Cognitive-behavioral interventions: Theory, research, and procedures.* New York: Academic Press, 1979.

Meichenbaum, D., & Cameron, R. Training schizophrenics to talk to themselves: A means of developing attentional controls. *Behavior Therapy,* 1973, *4,* 515-534.

Meichenbaum, D., & Goodman, J. The developmental control of operant motor responding by verbal operants. *Journal of Experimental Child Psychology,* 1969, *7,* 553-565. (a)

Meichenbaum, D., & Goodman, J. Reflection-impulsivity and verbal control of motor behavior. *Child Development,* 1969, *40,* 785-797. (b)

Meichenbaum, D., & Goodman, J. Training impulsive children to talk to themselves: A means of developing self-control. *Journal of Abnormal Psychology,* 1971, *77,* 115-126.

Messer, S.B. Reflection-impulsivity: A review. *Psychological Bulletin,* 1976, *83,* 1026-1051.

Morton, R.B. An experiment in brief psychotherapy. *Psychological Monographs,* 1955, *69* (Whole No. 386).

Mussen, P.H. *The psychological development of the child.* Englewood Cliffs, N.J.: Prentice-Hall, 1963.

Nahir, H.T., & Yussen, S.R. The performance of kibbutz- and city-reared Israeli children on two role-taking tasks. *Developmental Psychology,* 1977, *13,* 450-455.

Offer, D. *The psychological world of the teen-ager.* New York: Basic Books, 1969.

Palkes, H., Stewart, M., & Kahana, B. Porteus maze performance of hyperactive boys after training in self-directed verbal commands. *Child Development,* 1968, *39,* 817-826.

Parsons, B.V., & Alexander, J.F. Short-term family intervention: A therapy outcome study. *Journal of Consulting and Clinical Psychology,* 1973, *41,* 195-201.

453

Piaget, G.W. Training patients to communicate. In A.A. Lazarus (Ed.), *Clinical behavior therapy.* New York: Brunner/Mazel, 1972.

Piaget, J. *The language and thought of the child.* New York: Harcourt, Brace, 1926.

Piaget, J. *Judgment and reasoning in the child.* New York: Harcourt, Brace, 1928.

Piaget, J. *The moral judgment of the child.* New York: Collier Books, 1962.(a)

Piaget, J. Plays, dreams and imitiation in children. New York: Norton, 1962.(b)

Platt, J.J., Scura, W., & Hannon, J.R. Problem-solving thinking of youthful incarcerated heroin addicts. *Journal of Community Psychology,* 1973, *1,* 278-281.

Platt, J.J., Spivack, G., Altman, N., Altman, D., & Peizer, S.B. Adolescent problem-solving thinking. *Journal of Consulting and Clinical Psychology,* 1974, *42,* 787-793.

Ridberg, E.H., Parke, R.D., & Hetherington, M. Modification of impulsive and reflective cognitive styles through observation of film-mediated models. *Developmental Psychology,* 1971, *5,* 369-377.

Robin, A.L., Kent, R., O'Leary, K.D., Foster, S., & Prinz, R. An approach to teaching parents and adolescents problem-solving communication skills: A preliminary report. *Behavior Therapy,* 1977, *8,* 639-643.

Rotenberg, M. Conceptual and methodological notes in affective and cognitive role taking (sympathy and empathy): An illustrative experiment with delinquent and non-delinquent boys. *Journal of Genetic Psychology,* 1974, *125,* 177-185.

Sarason, E.G. Verbal learning, modeling, and juvenile delinquency. *American Psychologist,* 1968, *23,* 254-266.

Sarason, I.G., & Ganzer, V.J. Social influence techniques in clinical and community psychology. In C.D. Spielberger (Ed.), *Current topics in clinical and community psychology* (Vol. 1). New York: Academic Press, 1969.

Sarason, E.G., & Ganzer, V.J. Modeling and group discussion in the rehabilitation of juvenile delinquents. *Journal of Counseling Psychology,* 1973, *20,* 442-449.

Sarbin, T.R. Role theory. In G. Lindzey (Ed.), *Handbook of social psychology* (Vol. 1). Cambridge, Mass.: Addison-Wesley, 1954.

Scopetta, M.A. A comparison of modeling approaches to the rehabilitation of institutionalized male adolescent offenders implemented by paraprofessionals (Doctoral dissertation, University of Miami, 1972). *Dissertation Abstracts International,* 1972, *33,* 2822B. (University Microfilms No. 72-31, 901)

Selman, R.L. The relation of role-taking to the development of moral judgment in children. *Child Development,* 1971, *42,* 79-91. (a)

Selman, R.L. Taking another's perspective: Role-taking development in early childhood. *Child Development,* 1971, *42,* 1721-1734. (b)

Selman, R.L. Toward a structural analysis of developing interpersonal relations concepts: Research with normal and disturbed preadolescent boys. In A. Pick (Ed.), *X Annual Minnesota Symposium on Child Psychology.* Minneapolis: University of Minnesota Press, 1976.

Selman, R.L., & Byrne, D.F. A structural developmental analysis of levels of role-taking in middle childhood. *Child Development,* 1974, *45,* 803-806.

Selman, R.L., Jaquette, D., & Lavin, D.R. Interpersonal awareness in children: Toward an integration of developmental and clinical child psychology. *American Journal of Orthopsychiatry,* 1977, *47,* 264-274.

Shah, S. Juvenile delinquency: A national perspective. In J.L. Khanna (Ed.), *New treatment approaches to juvenile delinquency.* Springfield, Ill.: Charles C. Thomas, 1975.

Shantz, C.U. The development of social cognition. In E.M. Hetherington (Ed.), *Review of child development research* (Vol. 5). Chicago: University of Chicago Press, 1975.

Shure, M.B. & Spivack, G. *Problem-solving techniques in childrearing.* San Francisco: Jossey-Bass, 1978.

Simon, H.A., & Newell, A. Human problem-solving: The state of the theory in 1970. *American Psychologist,* 1971, *26,* 145-159.

Solomon, H.M. The dynamics of delinquent behavior. In P.F. Cromwell, Jr., G.G. Kellinger, R.C. Sarri, & H.M. Solomon. *Introduction to juvenile delinquency.* St. Paul, Minn.: West Publishing Co., 1978.

Spivack, G., Platt, J.J., & Shure, M.B. *The problem-solving approach to adjustment.* San Francisco: Jossey-Bass, 1976.

Spohn, H.E., & Wolk, W. *Effect of group problem-solving experience upon social withdrawal in chronic schizophrenics. Journal of Abnormal and Social Psychology,* 1963, *66,* 187-190.

Stuart, R.B. Behavioral contracting within families of delinquents. *Journal of Behavior Therapy and Experimental Psychiatry,* 1971, *2,* 1-11.

Stuart, R.B., & Lott, L.A., Jr. Behavioral contracting with delinquents: A cautionary note. *Journal of Behavior Therapy and Experimental Psychiatry,* 1972, *3,* 161-169.

Stuart, R.B., Tripodi, T., Jayaratne, S., & Camburn, D. An experiment in social engineering in serving the families of predelinquents. *Journal of Abnormal Child Psychology,* 1976, *4,* 243-261.

Thelen, M.H., Fry, R.A., Dollinger, S.J., & Paul, S.C. Use of videotaped models to improve the interpersonal adjustment of delinquents. *Journal of Consulting and Clinical Psychology,* 1976, *44,* 492.

Urberg, K.A., & Docherty, E.M. Development of role-taking skills in young children. *Developmental Psychology,* 1976, *12,* 198-203.

Vygotsky, L.S. *Thought and language.* Cambridge, Mass.: M.I.T. Press, 1962.

Waring, E.B. *The relation between early language habits and early habits of conduct control.* New York: Teachers College, Columbia University, 1927.

Warren, M.Q. Classification of offenders as an aid to efficient management and effective treatment. *Journal of Criminal Law, Criminology and Police Science,* 1971, *62,* 239-258.

Weathers, L., & Liberman, R.D. Contingency contracting with families of delinquent adolescents. *Behavior Therapy,* 1975, *6,* 356-366.

Williams, D.Y., & Akamatsu, T.J. Cognitive self-guidance training with juvenile delinquents: Applicability and generalization. *Cognitive Therapy and Research,* 1978, *2,* 285-288.

Wolfgang, M.E., Figlio, R.M., & Sellin, T. *Delinquency in a birth cohort.* Chicago: University of Chicago Press, 1972.

Yando, R.M., & Kagan, J. The effect of teacher tempo on the child. *Child Development,* 1968, *39,* 27-34.

Training Correctional Staff and Inmates in Interpersonal Relationship Skills

Ray E. Hosford
University of California
Santa Barbara

and

C. Scott Moss
Federal Correctional Institution
Lompoc, California

This chapter discusses two experimental counseling and interpersonal relationship training programs which were developed, implemented and evaluated within federal correctional institutions. The subjects in one study were correctional staff who volunteered for the training while those in a second group were inmates who volunteered to participate in a peer-counseling program.

Importance of In-service Training

One need only to consider the rate of recidivism to understand the need for improving both the concept and programs of correctional rehabilitation. For example, as late as 1967, the State of California was reporting an 85% recidivism rate of felons incarcerated in state facilities at that time (California Prisoners, 1967). Although more recent data indicates that federal institutional recidivism rates are much lower — 30-35% (Task Force Report, Note 1) — the number of individuals for whom incarceration failed to prove to be a deterrant to future crime is still very significant. Costs to society in terms of subsequent monies needed for law enforcement, incarceration and recidivism are staggering not to mention the psychological trauma and material costs which future victims of crime have to pay. More basically, however, these data suggest that incarceration in itself may have little effect in reducing subsequent criminal behavior. Indeed, Menninger (1969) contends that incarceration serves more to promote subsequent criminal behavior than to reduce it. Although the American prisons have had as their objective since 1870 — to interrupt an individual's criminal behavior pattern long enough to effect rehabilitation (cf. Commission on Attica, 1972) — and although many programs have been tried to promote rehabilitation, e.g., probation, parole, education, vocational training and changes in administrative policies (cf. Hosford & Moss, 1975; Sutherland & Cressey, 1970), recidivism rates continue to climb.

Whether prisons are to continue to exist as convenient "garbage cans" into which society casts its misfits or whether they are to serve as society's rehabilitation agents for criminal behavior is a question which former Federal Correctional Institution, Lompoc warden, Frank Kenton, says must be answered if we are to determine ways to reduce the soaring crime rate in America (Kenton, 1975). Southerland and Cressey (1970) however, point out that our prisons cannot become rehabilitative agents of society as long as their staffs are trained to be and act as guards rather than agents of change. Out of necessity, officers are provided training in methods of control but little or no instruction in how criminal behavior is acquired, maintained and modified. Nor are they given training in interpersonal relationship and counseling skills that may be crucial in changing attitudes and subsequent behavior of incarcerated persons. Some research evidence exists (cf. Tyler & Brown, 1967; Bednar, et al., 1970; Phillips, 1968; Hosford & Moss, 1975; Hosford, George, Moss &

Urban, 1978) which indicates that systematic in-service training programs can be effective in improving the rehabilitation skills of staff toward helping inmates channel their personal, social, academic, and vocational skills in more positive directions.

F.C.I.-Lompoc Program

At the Federal Correctional Institution at Lompoc, California, we have been evaluating the effects of several staff and inmate training programs to determine their efficacy in promoting the knowledge and skills presumed necessary for promoting rehabilitation outcomes. One such program investigated the effectiveness of live vs. videotaped in-service training programs on the subsequent behavior of correctional staff who volunteered for the training. Specifically, the study sought to assess the efficacy of these two modalities for promoting the following five specific outcomes: 1) basic knowledge and skills necessary in counseling and relating effectively with inmates, 2) verbal and non-verbal reinforcement interviewing techniques, 3) process steps involved in conducting a counseling session, 4) attending skills, and 5) reduction in overt anxiety behaviors emitted during counseling interviews.

Subjects and design. The participants in this particular in-service training program were 17 prison staff case managers and correctional counselors (officers selected to work as institutional counselors) who volunteered to take a six-day training program in techniques of behavioral counseling. Nine subjects were randomly assigned to receive "live" training sessions and eight to wait-control procedures. The latter group was subsequently provided the training vicariously via videotapes made of the live training conducted three months earlier.

The training sessions utilized a behavioral counselor training program developed by Hosford and de Visser and produced by the American Personnel and Guidance Association (Hosford & de Visser, 1974). This program consists of a step-by-step training manual and eight 16 mm color films which demonstrate the various process steps and intervention strategies used in this approach to counseling. At the beginning of the live training sessions, each subject was randomly assigned to one of three triads for purposes of practicing in the afternoon the various skills discussed and demonstrated during the morning sessions. Each member of the triad took turns rehearsing the roles of a counselor, inmate, and observer. Specific step-by-step instructions for each role were

459

provided in the training manual (Hosford & de Visser, 1974). For example, the observer's task was to rate the counselor's performance on each target skill using a rating scale included in the manual. Each triad's practice session was videotaped and the tapes were evaluated by the training staff. Prior to the practice session the following day, each participate was provided feedback relative to his/her performance on the target skills specified for that practice period. As part of this feedback, each participant was told which skills he/she had demonstrated competently and which ones should receive additional practice. The practice sessions were addressed to developing skills in 1) relating more effectively, 2) listening and helping inmates define their problems in terms of specific behaviors they needed to increase or decrease in order to solve their problems, and in 3) using reinforcement and other basic counseling skills during the simulated counseling sessions. The training sessions followed closely the step-by-step format utilized in the Hosford — de Visser training manual, i.e., reading and discussion of the topics and/or skills being studied, viewing a film specifically made to model those behaviors, practicing the skills demonstrated, with participants receiving both peer and staff feedback of their performance of those target skills.

Evaluation

To determine whether the participants did indeed improve their knowledge and skills in counseling inmates, each participant and control subject were administered a paper and pencil knowledge test and randomly assigned to counsel one of four inmates who had volunteered to assist in the training. Videotapes made of the "counseling" sessions were subsequently evaluated by two judges who were otherwise not associated with the study. Using the four counselor rating scales included in the Hosford — de Visser training manual (Hosford & de Visser, 1974), each judge independently rated all 17 tapes in random order to avoid serial effects. Interjudge reliability coefficients for the four rating scales used ranged from .90 to .98. To compare the ratings of the participants to those of the control group, a multivariate analysis of variance (MANOVA) was computed to determine whether an overall difference existed between the two groups. The computer program developed by Joreskog, van Thillo and Gruvoeus (1971) was used resulting in a X^2 of 38.36 which, for five degrees of freedom, is significant at the .001 level. Subsequently, t-ratios were then computed to determine the extent to which these two groups differed on the five criterion measures which the training sought to promote. As predicted, those staff members receiving training demonstrated significantly a) more knowledge about specific counseling theory and practice, t (16) = 10.29, p < .001, b) more steps involved in the behavioral counseling process, t (16) = 3.82, p < .002, c) more verbal reinforcements during their counseling, t (16) = 2.17, p < .04, and d) better overall counseling skills, t (16) = 2.21, p < .04. The two groups did not differ, however, in terms of the judges' ratings of frequency of overt anxiety behaviors, e.g., fidgeting, demonstrated during the experimental counseling sessions. This latter outcome was used as a "control" variable in that the training was specifically designed to promote the first four competencies and did not include instruction on ways to reduce overt anxiety behaviors.

Three months following the initial training sessions, the 8 control subjects were provided the training by means of videotape. Ten one-hour tapes were edited from those videotapes made of the earlier training. Material taped during the live training sessions that was not related to the four outcomes being promoted, e.g., discussions of personal problems having little or no relevance to the skills or knowledge objectives for that session, were edited from the tapes. The participants viewing the training on videotape practiced the skills modeled on the tapes in randomly assigned triads as was done in the live training program. At the completion of the training sessions, each subject was again randomly assigned to counsel one of the four volunteer inmates. These sessions were videotaped and evaluated using the same rating scales as were used in the earlier live training program. When comparing the counseling competencies of those who received the videotape training with those who participated in the live sessions, *the two training methods were equally effective in promoting the desired knowledge and skills* in all but the demonstration of the number of steps involved in the behavioral counseling process. Those in the live training group demonstrated a significantly greater number of behavioral counseling process steps than did those in the videotape training group. Although data were available for pre-post comparisons in that the videotape group served first as a no-treatment control group in the earlier study, additional analyses using this same data would, in effect, violate independence of the data needed for satisfying the assumptions needed for making any statements of inference. Comparison of means, however, shows that after videotape training, staff members consistently demonstrated better counseling skills than before training. (See Table 1).

Table 1. Means for Pre and Post Tests of Videotape Training Group.

Target Behavior	$\overline{M}$ Prior to Training	$\overline{\overline{M}}$ After Training
1. No Behavioral Counseling Process Steps Used	9	11
2. Frequency of Reinforcement	8	12
3. Overall Counseling Skills as rated by the Hosford-de Visser Scale	18	24
4. Counseling Knowledge Test	41	74

The importance of the study lies not so much in the fact that those receiving training performed better counseling and interviewing skills than did those staff members not receiving training. Such outcomes are indeed crucial for demonstrating the validity of in-service training programs. However, the fact that the training was almost equally effective when presented vicariously on videotape as when provided live should be particularly important to correctional institutions and other agencies which have large numbers of staff to retrain and little resources available to do so. It may be possible for correctional training officers to use a variety of step-by-step training programs presented on videotape by professionals who otherwise would be too costly in terms of providing numerous in-service live training sessions. Also important about the present study is that the effectiveness of the in-service training program was assessed not by the usual measures of evaluation — participant ratings of how much they liked the training — but relative to what the participant could *do* better after the training. Thus subject competencies rather than subject attitudes were the primary assessments used in determining the program's effectiveness. The highly significant results obtained strongly suggest that staff behavior did change as a result of participating in the training. Of course, follow-up and reinforcement for continual demonstration of these newly gained skills would be needed if a permanent change in behavior were to be expected.

Inmate Training

In addition to staff training, we have recently explored the possibilities of training inmates themselves in peer-counseling techniques. Because of the severe shortage of professional mental health personnel in corrections and because staff members serving as correctional counselors often must serve much of their working time in custodial rather than counseling functions, mental health programs have begun to explore the use of peer counseling as a means of helping larger numbers of inmates learn ways of solving their personal problems. Peer counseling programs have been shown to be highly effective, particularly with individuals who might otherwise not seek counseling (Varenhorst, Note 2). Kerish (1977), for example, found that inmates who themselves completed a 100-hour training program in the fundamentals of transactional analysis and in group counseling techniques received significantly higher job performance and living unit behavior staff ratings than did a matched group (matched in terms of length of time incarcerated in the institution) who did not participate in the peer counseling programs. In addition, inmates participating in the program reported significantly more positive self concepts than did the controls.

The present study was designed to explore the effectiveness of the videotaped counselor training mentioned above in training inmates to serve as peer counselors for their fellow offenders. Although the aforementioned videotape program had been used successfully in helping staff persons acquire more effective counseling and interpersonal relationship skills, it was not known whether such training would prove effective with inmates. The material which the 10-hours of videotapes covered was addressed primarily to counseling skills and knowledge *per se* rather than to counseling techniques that staff could use with inmates. Thus, while the sessions did not generally show staff as counselors and inmates always as clients, the models demonstrating specific skills were staff and/or professional psychologists not employed at the institution. Having had inmates or same age persons as the models on the videotapes might have aided identification and subsequent imitative learning. Basically the videotapes by means of lecture and demonstration covered six topics. The first dealt with ways to help individuals define their problems in behavioral terms; that is, to state their problems in terms of what they were *doing* or *not doing* that they wanted to change. Secondly, the training showed the importance of and ways in which a counselor can help others learn to consider the advantages and disadvantages of a variety of possible alternatives *before* engaging in a course of action to solve a problem. Helping "clients" set up meaningful and attainable goals was next, followed by ways in which

463

individuals can do some self-observations of their own behavior to gain a "quantifiable awareness" of their problem. Following the presentations of these skills, the tapes demonstrated several basic kinds of counseling techniques such as systematic reinforcement and vicarious modeling. The sixth topic dealt with ways that those helping others could evaluate the effects of their counseling interventions to determine whether or not these procedures were helping those seeking assistance.

Subjects

The original study began with 15 inmates at the McNeil Penitentiary who volunteered to participate in the peer-counseling training program. Of these, four were paroled before the training was completed, a fifth was transferred to another facility and a sixth escaped from the institution. Thus, the actual study for which data are available consisted of nine inmates who actually completed the training.

The training sessions were conducted in the same way as those used earlier in staff training, i.e., the subjects viewed the tapes, asked questions relative to what they observed, practiced the same skills in triads, and were videotaped roleplaying the roles of client, observer and counselor. The inmates' performances on the videotapes were — as for staff — rated each day at the close of training and each participant was given written feedback of his performance relative to ratings received on the evaluation scales adopted from the Hosford — de Visser training program (Hosford & de Visser, 1974).

Analysis

Each inmate subject counseled a randomly assigned inmate "client" both prior to participating in the training and upon completion of the program. In both cases, videotapes were made of these counseling sessions to determine whether participation in the training resulted in better counselor performance. The "clients" used in these evaluations were volunteer inmates who presented each trainee with a particular problem and some relevant background information to that situation. The "problems" and background data, e.g., past criminal record, education attainment, family situation were all contrived and provided the inmate "clients" prior to their session with the trainee counselors. The "clients" underwent a short training program designed to train them to ask specific questions and to demonstrate several verbal and nonverbal behaviors indicative of being noncooperative. Examples of problem questions expressed by the inmate "clients" included 1) How do I get my wife to wait for me?, 2) Can you help me with my problem of being afraid to return to my family after being gone for nine years?, and 3) I'm getting hassled by the officers about my poor attitude and lack of production in industries.

Each inmate trainee was assured that he was not being evaluated individually (which was true) but that the data were being accumulated to evaluate the training program as a whole. No information was provided (nor was it requested) about any participant to the institution staff. Each inmate trainee, however, was told that he could mention it to his unit team if he so desired.

The videotapes made of each subject's pre and post-test counseling session were coded, randomized and rated by an advanced doctoral student in counseling psychology at the University of California, Santa Barbara. The evaluator had no knowledge of the study *per se* or whether a particular tape represented a pre or post assessment. Rating scales provided in the Hosford — de Visser training program (Hosford & de Visser, 1974) were used for this purpose.

Findings. In comparison to skills demonstrated on videotape prior to participating in the peer counseling training program, the nine inmates after training demonstrated significantly more verbal and nonverbal reinforcements contingent upon the inmate "client" stating some constructive action he could take to solve his problem or emitting an affective statement relative to his problem situation, $t (8) = 3.41$, $p < .005$. They also demonstrated significantly more knowledge on a knowledge test about counseling after training than before, $t (8) = 7.5$, $p < .001$, and significantly better interpersonal relationship skills, $t (8) = 3.45$, $p < .005$. That is, their ability to establish rapport with a client and to help him describe his problem in terms of specific behaviors was judged significantly better on tapes coded to rate after training than on those made prior to training.

Significance to the Field

These findings are particularly significant for corrections in that the training program required little in terms of personnel and other resources. Too, had the videotapes used in the training presented inmates as the model counselors rather than the correctional staff or professional psychologists, perhaps the results would have been even more impressive. Further, because few staff persons can effectively "wear the two hats" of counselor and guard, few inmates will engage in any significant self disclosure for fear of subsequent staff or fellow inmate reprisals. Although professional psychologists and psychiatrists are not viewed by inmates as guards per se, they are institutional staff. Then too, the ratio of professionally trained mental health personnel to inmates is extremely small, which makes all but crisis counseling impossible in terms of available time. Thus, utilizing inmates for helping other inmates may represent a tremendous source of untapped manpower not to mention the possibility of peers being perceived by inmates as more trustworthy than are staff — particularly those who must serve as guards in addition to counselors. For many inmates, self disclosing to staff is viewed as "copping out" to the system and can serve to alienate them from other inmates. Perhaps by using selected peer inmates who have been trained in interpersonal relationship skills and in basic decision making strategies, inmates may participate more fully in the rehabilitation process.

Summary

These two studies are representative of the kinds of mental health training programs being instigated from time to time within the Federal Prison System. Several other programs have been carried out which have utilized the same training format and materials adopted from the Hosford-de Visser training manual. In addition, the mental health staff at F.C.I.—Lompoc, have developed programs in training staff in group counseling techniques (Hosford, Moss & Louscher, Note 3).

Reference Notes

1. Task Force Report: General Accounting Office Audit of Bureau of Prisons' Programs. Washington, D.C., U.S. Bureau of Prisons, 1972 (unpublished manuscript).
2. Varenhorst, Barbara. Modifying behavior through peer counseling training and career decision-making. Paper presented at the Ninth Annual Southern California Conference on Behavior Modification, Los Angeles, Oct. 15, 1977.

3. Moss, C. Scott, Hosford, R.E., & Louscher, P. Kent. Outcomes of group counseling training on correctional staff behavior. Unpublished manuscript, F.C.I., Lompoc, Lompoc, California, 1978.

References

Bednar, R.L. Zelerhart, P.F., Greathouse, L., & Weinberg, S. Operant condition-ing principles in the treatment of learning and behavior problems with delinquent boys. *Journal of Counseling Psychology*, 1970, *17*, 492-497.

California Prisoners. Sacramento: California Department of Corrections, 1967.

Commission on Attica. *The official reports of the New York special commission on Attica.* New York: Bantam Books, 1972.

Hosford, R.E., & de Visser, L.J.M. *Behavioral counseling: an introduction.* Wash-ington, D.C.: APGA Press, 1974.

Hosford, R.E., George, G.O., Moss, C.S., & Urban, V.E. The effects of behavioral counseling training on correctional staff. *Teaching of Psychology*, 1975, *2*, 124-127.

Hosford, R.E., & Moss, C.S. *The crumbling walls: The treatment and counseling of prisoners.* Urbana, Ill.: University of Illinois Press, 1975.

Joreskog, K.G., van Thillo, M., & Gruvoeus, G.T. *ACOVSM: A general computer program for analysis of covariance structures including generalized MANOVA.* Princeton, New Jersey: Educational Testing Service, 1971.

Kenton, F.F. Prisons: Rehabilitative or custodial institutions. In R.E. Hosford & C.S. Moss (Eds.) *The crumbling walls: The treatment and counseling of prisoners.* Urbana, Ill.: University of Illinois Press, 1975.

Kerish, B.R. The effect of peer counseling in a correctional setting. Unpublished doctoral dissertation. University of California, Santa Barbara, 1977.

Menninger, K. *The crime of punishment.* New York: Viking Press, 1969.

Phillips, E.L. Achievement place: Token reinforcement procedures in a home-style rehabilitation setting for "pre-delinquent" boys. *Journal of Applied Behavioral Analysis*, 1968, *1*, 213-223.

Sutherland. E.H., & Cressey, D.R. *Criminology.* New York: Lippincott, 1970.

Tyler, V.O., Jr., & Brown, G.P. The use of swift brief isolation as a group control device for institutional delinquents. *Behavior Research and Therapy*, 1967, *5*, 1-9.